THE LITURGY DOCUMENTS
A PARISH RESOURCE

VOLUME TWO

THE LITURGY DOCUMENTS
A PARISH RESOURCE

Volume Two

LITURGY
TRAINING
PUBLICATIONS

Editor: David A. Lysik
Production editor: Bryan M. Cones, with assistance
   from Marie McLaughlin and Theresa Pincich
Cover designer: Barb Rohm
Production artist: Mark Hollopeter
Indexer: Mary Laur

Cover art: *The Prevalence Ritual: Baptism* by Romare Bearden (1964, photomechanical reproductions, synthetic polymer and pencil on paper board, 9⅛ by 12 inches), Hirshhorn Museum and Sculpture Garden, Smithsonian Institution, Gift of Joseph H. Hirshhorn, 1966. Photo by Lee Stalsworth. © Romare Bearden Foundation/Licensed by VAGA, New York, NY.

The Prevalence of Ritual: Baptism was chosen for the cover of *The Liturgy Documents, Volume Two,* because it expresses visually what the texts collected in this volume seek to promote: a deep understanding of the integral importance of ritual in Christian life. In this way, it contributes to the fundamentally educational purpose of this volume.

THE LITURGY DOCUMENTS: A PARISH RESOURCE, VOLUME TWO © 1999 Archdiocese of Chicago: Liturgy Training Publications, 1800 North Hermitage Avenue, Chicago IL 60622-1101; 1-800-933-1800; orders@ltp.org; fax 1-800-933-7094. All rights reserved.

ISBN 1-56854-245-3
LDOC2

CONTENTS

ABBREVIATIONS

AAS   *Acta Apostolicae Sedis,* (1909–)

AG   Vatican Council II, decree *Ad gentes divinitus* (on the church's missionary activity) (December 7, 1965)

BB   *Book of Blessings*

BCL   Bishops' Committee on the Liturgy, NCCB

c.; cc.   canon; canons

CB   *Ceremonial of Bishops* (1989)

CCC   *Catechism of the Catholic Church* (1992)

CCCB   Canadian Conference of Catholic Bishops

CCEC   Code of Canons of the Eastern Churches *(Codex canonum ecclesiarum orientalium)* (1990)

CCL   *Corpus christianorum, Series Latina* (Turnhout, 1953–)

CD   Vatican Council II, decree *Christus dominus* (on the pastoral office of bishops in the church) (October 28, 1965)

CDF   Congregation for the Doctrine of the Faith

CDW   Congregation for Divine Worship

CEILT   NCCB, *Criteria for the Evaluation of Inclusive Language Translations of Scriptural Texts Proposed for Liturgical Use* (1990)

CIC   Code of Canon Law *(Codex iuris canonici)*

1917 CIC   1917 Code of Canon Law *(Codex iuris canonici)*

CP   Consilium, instruction *Comme le prévoit* (on the translation of liturgical texts for celebrations with a congregation) (January 25, 1969)

CR   Congregation of Rites

CSEL   *Corpus scriptorum ecclesiasticorum latinorum* (Vienna, 1866–)

CT   John Paul II, apostolic exhortation *Catechesi tradendae* (October 16, 1979)

DD   John Paul II, apostolic letter *Dies domini* (on keeping the Lord's day holy) (May 31, 1998)

DE   Pontifical Council for Promoting Christian Unity, *Directory for the Application of Principles and Norms on Ecumenism* (1993)

DedCh   *Dedication of a Church and an Altar* (1978, rev. 1989)

DMC   CDW, *Directory for Masses with Children* (1973)

DV   Vatican Council II, dogmatic constitution *Dei verbum* (on divine revelation) (November 18, 1965)

EACW   BCL, *Environment and Art in Catholic Worship* (1978)

EM   CR, instruction *Eucharisticum mysterium* (on the worship of the eucharist) (May 25, 1967)

FYH   NCCB, Bishops' Committee on Priestly Life and Ministry, *Fulfilled in Your Hearing: The Homily in the Sunday Assembly* (1982)

GIapp   Appendix to the *General Instruction of the Roman Missal* for the Dioceses of the United States (rev. 1985)

GILOH   CDW, *General Instruction of the Liturgy of the Hours* (1971)

GIRM   CDW, *General Instruction of the Roman Missal* (1975)

GMEF   BCL, *God's Mercy Endures Forever: Guidelines on the Presentation of Jews and Judaism in Catholic Preaching* (1988)

GNLY	*General Norms for the Liturgical Year and the Calendar* (1969)	**PCS**	*Pastoral Care of the Sick: Rites of Anointing and Viaticum* (1983)
GS	Vatican Council II, pastoral constitution *Gaudium et spes*, (on the church in the modern world) (December 7, 1965)	**PG**	J.P. Migne, *Patrologiae cursus completus: Series Graeca.*
GSPD	NCCB, *Guidelines for the Celebration of the Sacraments with Persons with Disabilities* (1995)	**PGR**	NCCB, Secretariat for the Liturgy and Secretariat for Black Catholics, *Plenty Good Room: The Spirit and Truth of African American Catholic Worship* (1990)
HLS	NCCB, *This Holy and Living Sacrifice: Directory for the Celebration and Reception of Communion under Both Kinds* (1984)	**PL**	J.P. Migne, *Patrologiae cursus completus: Series Latina*
		PO	Vatican Council II, decree *Presbyterorum ordinis* (on the life and ministry of priests) (December 7, 1965)
IRL	Congregation for Divine Worship and the Discipline of the Sacraments, *Inculturation and the Roman Liturgy: Fourth Instruction for the Right Application of the Conciliar Constitution on the Liturgy, nn. 37–40* (1994)	**PS**	CDW, circular letter *Paschale solemnitatis* (on preparing and celebrating the paschal feasts) (January 16, 1988)
		RBaptC	*Rite of Baptism for Children*
		RCIA	*Rite of Christian Initiation of Adults*
IST	BCL, *In Spirit and Truth: Black Catholic Reflections on the Order of Mass* (1987)	**RConf**	*Rite of Confirmation*
		RM	John Paul II, encyclical *Redemptoris missio* (on the permanent validity of the church's missionary mandate) (December 7, 1990)
LG	Vatican Council II, dogmatic constitution *Lumen gentium* (on the church) (November 21, 1964)		
LM	*Lectionary for Mass,* second *editio typica* (1981)	**RMarr**	*Rite of Marriage*
		RomM	*The Roman Missal*
LMT	BCL, *Liturgical Music Today* (1982)	**RPen**	*Rite of Penance*
MCW	BCL, *Music in Catholic Worship* (1972, 1983)	**SC**	Vatican Council II, constitution *Sacrosanctum concilium* (on the sacred liturgy) (December 4, 1963)
n.; nn.	number; numbers		
NCCB	National Conference of Catholic Bishops	**SCC**	CCCB, *To Speak as a Christian Community: Pastoral Message on Inclusive Language* (1989)
OCF	*Order of Christian Funerals.*		
OE	Vatican Council II, decree *Orientalium ecclesiarum* (on the Catholic Eastern churches) (November 21, 1965)	**SCh**	*Sources chrétiennes* (Paris, 1941–)
		UR	Vatican Council II, decree *Unitatis redintegratio* (on ecumenism) (November 21, 1964)
OT	Vatican Council II, decree *Optatam totius* (on the training of priests) (October 28, 1965)	**VQA**	John Paul II, apostolic letter *Vicesimus quintus annus*
par.	parallel passages in the synoptic gospels	**WWHSH**	*What We Have Seen and Heard: A Pastoral Letter on Evangelization from the Black Bishops of the United States* (1984)

GENERAL INTRODUCTION
Frederick R. McManus

The diverse documents on the liturgy in this collection cover the period from 1969 to 1998. Whether they come from Roman congregations or commissions, or national conferences of bishops, they share one characteristic: They are of high quality in themselves, well thought out, and conducive to sound Christian worship. Some are significant parts of church law, chiefly the introductory sections of the Roman liturgical books; others are ancillary but very valuable in one way or another. Whether normative or merely guiding in what they propose, all the documents in this collection offer a reasoned exposition of sound doctrinal, liturgical and pastoral principles. To put it differently, they respond very well to the debater's adage, "Authority is the weakest argument."

This is not to denigrate the church authorities from whom the documents come, but rather to recognize that, in the great tradition of church law, even the most juridical of rules must be rooted in *reason*. Unhappily, the twentieth-century codes of canons lack this explicit dimension, offering bare injunctions without much rationale. Liturgical pronouncements follow a better tradition: Each decree of the Second Vatican Council, every apostolic or papal constitution, and the documents of the present collection follow first this admirable pattern of reasoned explanation, offering rules only after laying a reasoned doctrinal foundation. It would be hard to equal, for example, the doctrinal breadth of the 1971 *General Instruction of the Liturgy of the Hours*, or the profound message of the 1998 apostolic letter of John Paul II, "On Keeping the Lord's Day Holy."

The immense value of the several treatments of ecumenism and liturgy in this volume, as well as those concerning culture and liturgy, is obvious enough. Equally important are national documents (those of the U.S. National Conference of Catholic Bishops and the Canadian Conference of Catholic Bishops), both in themselves and also as demonstrations of regional collegiality and subsidiarity in pastoral and liturgical arenas. One splendid instance is the NCCB's 1990 *Criteria for the Evaluation of Inclusive Language Translations of Scriptural Texts*, which treats an issue of continuing importance and in which the U.S. episcopal conference was at one with both academics and pastoral ministers.

This reference to language takes us back to the earliest document in the collection, the Roman instruction of 1969 "On the Translation of Liturgical Texts for Celebrations with a Congregation." This was and is an authentic reflection of Vatican II's thrust toward "noble simplicity" in the liturgy, and is a guide to faithful but free translations of Latin texts. Because the Roman liturgy is a melange of rites and words from many centuries and places, one of the most welcome assertions in the document is that liturgical translation is only a school or discipline for the necessary development of newly composed texts for a living, lively worship.

This instruction displays several other elements to be kept in mind as the rest of the documents in this volume are studied and appraised. First, like other aspects of the inculturation of faith and practice, rigidity is no more appropriate in language than in music and the arts. The 1969 document evolved over several years in light of the experience of the major joint commissions on translation—chiefly those of the French-, German-, Italian- and English-language groups. The process of drafting the document respected the common language and literary tradition of each group. Pope Paul VI himself played a major role in the final form of the instruction, even though it is not a papal document or a "law" but rather a source of invaluable guidance. Its real worth lies in the objective value of its injunctions, which are completely opposed to slavish or verbatim translation. Instead, they support openness, the importance of sense and meaning in texts for liturgy, and suitability in the sung and spoken language of contemporary liturgy.

One reason for the broad and sound insights of the 1969 instruction on liturgical language is that it was composed on the heels of Vatican II. The great council's spirit was at a high point as the church began the gradual reform of the Roman liturgy, a reform that took more than two decades to complete (the *Book of Blessings* and *Dedication of a Church and an Altar* did not appear until 1989). The reform also opened the way to regional adaptation. The 1994 instruction *Inculturation and the Roman Liturgy,* for example, eloquently expresses an excellent theory of the process of inculturation; it is also a regression to a narrower canonical mode, forgetting Vatican II's willingness to accept deeper adaptations from outside Roman traditions and the explicit openness of Vatican II to a non-Roman liturgical rite or "use."

This is not to canonize or absolutize the 1969 instruction, for all its wisdom and prescience. Today, after 30 years of still-broader experience, even it needs to be supplemented by a critical concern for inclusive, non-discriminatory language in contemporary worship and by an even greater emphasis on the spoken rather than written words of the liturgy—while totally welcoming new, original liturgical texts suited to the Christian tradition of the twenty-first century.

Each of the documents in this collection deserves this kind of reflection on its meaning in text and context—especially on the rationale that is offered for its directives. And, like the Western liturgical reform itself, each document must be seen as a starting point for progressively more open expressions of Christian faith and devotion.

APOSTOLIC LETTER *DIES DOMINI*

ON KEEPING
THE LORD'S DAY HOLY

JOHN PAUL II
1998

OVERVIEW OF *DIES DOMINI:* ON KEEPING THE LORD'S DAY HOLY

Barry Glendinning

In May of 1998, on the solemnity of Pentecost, Pope John Paul II issued an apostolic letter of singular importance. From the first words of the text, it is known as *Dies domini* (The Lord's Day).

Future generations will recognize *Dies domini* as a landmark document in the history of the church. Building on the finest insights of the Second Vatican Council, it turns the page on the way we understand the resurrection, Sunday and our assembly for eucharist.

Dies domini should be on the curriculum of every Catholic college and seminary. It should be studied by every catechist and by everyone who presides at liturgy. And it should become the common domain of all the people of God.

What follows is a brief commentary on the master themes of the apostolic letter. One may hope that it will whet the appetite for a full-fledged study of the text. The numbers in parentheses refer to the paragraph numbering of the official text.

THE RESURRECTION

The first striking feature of *Dies domini* is its unalterable focus on the resurrection of the Lord. From beginning to end, the text is filled with references to the risen Lord, the day of the resurrection, and Sunday as the weekly Easter.

Pope John Paul's focus on the resurrection is so insistent and so strong that he can have only one purpose in mind: to re-establish the resurrection as the radical center of our faith, our celebrations, and our Christian lives.

The pope calls us back to our historical roots when he says, "The resurrection of Jesus is the fundamental event upon which Christian faith rests . . . [It is] the true fulcrum of history, to which the mystery of the world's origin and its final destiny leads" (#2). Indeed, "the event of Easter [is the] true source of the world's salvation" (#19).

Turning the Page

With this insistence on the primacy of the resurrection, *Dies domini* reverses a theological trend that began in the Middle Ages and continued until the Second Vatican Council: an almost total concentration on the passion and death of Christ. Of course, this focus coloured not only our theology but our celebrations and the whole of our Christian lives as well.

The Second Vatican Council began the restoration. It spoke once again the language of the paschal mystery: "He [Christ the Lord] achieved his task of redeeming humanity and giving perfect glory to God principally by the paschal mystery of his blessed passion, resurrection from the dead, and glorious ascension, whereby 'dying he destroyed our death and, rising, he restored our life'" (*Constitution on the Sacred Liturgy*, 5).

Here the work of redemption is held together in the mystery of Christ's passage through death to life. In similar fashion *Dies domini* speaks of "the universal redemption accomplished by Christ in his death and resurrection" (#59). And, as a passage through death to life, the resurrection—Christ's victory over sin and death—is the focus of the church's faith and life. It was Jesus himself who said, "I am the resurrection and the life" (John 11:25) and it was likewise he who said, "I came that they may have life, and have it abundantly" (John 10:10).

One can scarcely exaggerate the importance of this return to the resurrection as the radical center of our Christian faith. With effective catechesis and preaching, all of us will once again know and proclaim that we are an Easter people and that Alleluia is our song.

SUNDAY

The second striking feature of *Dies domini* is its presentation of Sunday—called the Lord's Day since apostolic times—as the day of the resurrection, the victory day of the risen Christ: "For the Christian, Sunday is above all an Easter celebration, wholly illumined by the glory of the risen Christ" (#8). Put simply, Sunday is the weekly Easter of the church and of the world: "It is *Easter* which returns week by week, celebrating Christ's victory over sin and death" (#1).

The pope draws upon the early writings of the church to underline the significance of the Lord's Day. He refers to Pseudo-Eusebius of Alexandria, who calls it "the lord of days," and he quotes Saint Jerome, who says that "Sunday is the day of the resurrection, it is the day of Christians, it is our day" (#2).

Moreover, lest we should think that Sunday is merely a fond remembrance of a past event, *Dies domini* points out that Sunday *makes present* the day of the resurrection: ". . . Sunday is the weekly Easter, recalling and making present the day upon which Christ rose from the dead" (#75).

All of this means that Sunday is a festive day of joy. Quoting the *Constitution on the Sacred Liturgy*, Pope John Paul calls Sunday "the fundamental feast day" of the church (#2). "It is the festival of the 'new creation'" (#8), and from the beginning "Christians celebrated the weekly day of the risen Lord primarily as a day of joy" (#55). "Rightly, then, the psalmist's cry is applied to Sunday: 'This is the day which the Lord has made: let us rejoice and be glad in it'" (#1).

Turning the Page

Thanks to Pius XII and then the Second Vatican Council, the solemnity of Easter once again stands out as the preeminent annual festival of the church.

Dies domini now draws our full attention to a fact of enormous importance for our Christian lives: every Sunday is the day of the resurrection made present in the world; every Sunday is Easter, the day of festive joy.

For a long time we have not clearly connected Sunday and the resurrection. Most of us would have described Sunday as a holy day or a day when we "go to Mass"—and a rather somber day as well.

Dies domini changes all that. It opens up a whole new vision of who we are and what we are about. It tells us that authentic Christian life is celebration and that its hallmark is resurrection joy.

The third striking feature of *Dies domini* is its treatment of the eucharistic assembly. Its teaching can best be described under two headings.

1. The Presence of the Risen Lord

As we have seen before, Sunday, the weekly Easter, recalls and makes present the day on which Christ rose from the dead (#75). Thus, when we come together as church on the Lord's Day, the risen Christ is present in our midst: "As the day of resurrection, Sunday is not only the remembrance of a past event: It is a celebration of the living presence of the risen Lord in the midst of his own people" (#31).

This remarkable presence is our special cause for joy. We "relive with particular intensity the experience of the apostles on the evening of Easter when the risen Lord appeared to them as they were gathered together" (#33). In this same regard, the pope quotes Paul VI, who said, "It is Christ crucified and glorified who comes among his disciples to lead them all together into the newness of his resurrection. This is the climax, here below, of the covenant of love between God and his people: the sign and source of Christian joy, a stage on the way to the eternal feast" (#58).

Moreover, the risen Lord calls us together: Pope John Paul extols "the Sunday gathering of the entire community, obedient to the voice of the risen Lord who calls the faithful together to give them the light of his word and the nourishment of his Body as the perennial sacramental wellspring of redemption" (#81).

2. The Eucharistic Assembly

Dies domini forges a strong bond between the eucharistic assembly and the church. In fact, the church is this assembly: The Sunday assembly expresses fully "the very identity of the Church, the *ekklesia,* the assembly called together by the risen Lord" (#31). Thus: "Each community, gathering all its members for the 'breaking of the bread,' becomes the place where the mystery of the church is concretely made present" (#34).

Turning the Page

Our common impression has been that Christ becomes truly present in the eucharistic assembly only at the time of the consecration. The *Constitution on the Sacred Liturgy* (#7) corrected this view, and the *General Instruction of the Roman Missal* reads as follows: "Christ is really present to the assembly gathered in his name; he is present in the person of the minister, in his own word, and indeed substantially and permanently under the eucharistic elements" (#7).

Pope John Paul II reminds us that the eucharistic assembly is God's undertaking and that none other than the risen Lord gathers us together. This insight changes the whole complexion of the Sunday assembly, moving it from obligation to an invitation to joy.

UNITY: THE GOAL OF THE ASSEMBLY

God's plan of salvation unfolds in the eucharistic assembly: It is "to reunite the scattered children of God" (#31). Hence the Sunday assembly must be seen as "the privileged place of unity . . . the setting for the celebration of the *sacramentum unitatis* [sacrament of unity] which profoundly marks the church as a people gathered 'by' and 'in' the unity of the Father, of the Son and of the Holy Spirit" (#36).

THE RISEN LORD SPEAKS WITH US

Within the eucharistic assembly, the risen Lord initiates a living dialogue with the people of God: ". . . *the liturgical proclamation of the word of God* [is] *a dialogue between God and his people*" (#41). "It is Christ who speaks, present as he is in his word 'when the sacred scripture is read in the church'" (#39).

HE GATHERS US AT THE EASTER BANQUET

The Lord's words, which speak of the "wonders of salvation" (#41), lead us forward to "the Easter banquet, in which Christ himself becomes our nourishment" (#44). Here the eucharist becomes "the great 'thanksgiving'" (#42). Here we make our response to God, "a response which Christ has already made for us with his 'Amen' and which echoes in us through the Holy Spirit" (#41). And here we share communion of life in Christ: "Sharing in the Lord's supper is always communion with Christ, who offers himself for us in sacrifice to the Father" (#44).

Thus, "to share in 'the Lord's Supper' is to anticipate the eschatological feast of the 'marriage of the Lamb'" (#38). In the Easter banquet we "receive a foretaste of the joy of the new heavens and the new earth" (#37).

HE CHARGES US TO LIVE IN SOLIDARITY

Important covenant obligations flow from our encounter with the Lord. Pope John Paul reminds us that ". . . communion with Christ is deeply tied to communion with our brothers and sisters" (#44). "[T]he eucharist is the place where fraternity becomes practical solidarity, where the last are first in the minds and attention of the brethren, where Christ himself—through the generous gifts from the rich to the very poor—may somehow prolong in time the miracle of the multiplication of the loaves" (#71).

Turning the Page

Many of us have been unaware of the place the eucharistic assembly holds in God's plan of salvation. We have sometimes overlooked the wonders of the assembly, perhaps in part because this is an age in which "religion is a matter between me and God."

Dies domini echoes the tradition of the church when it reminds us that "[t]hose who have received the grace of baptism are not saved as individuals alone, but as members of the mystical body, having become part of the people of God" (#31).

CONCLUSION

Dies domini enriches our lives with a magistral teaching on the risen Christ. The Lord's resurrection is the radical center of our faith. Every Sunday is the day of the resurrection made present in our midst. And the Lord's assembly, set on the Lord's Day, gathers the world into the Easter banquet of the risen Christ, there to share communion of life with him in God. In the order of salvation, the eucharistic assembly is "an epiphany of the church" (#34) and the wellspring that renews the world (#81).

OUTLINE

APOSTOLIC LETTER *DIES DOMINI*

ON KEEPING THE LORD'S DAY HOLY

INTRODUCTION

MY ESTEEMED BROTHERS IN THE EPISCOPATE AND THE PRIESTHOOD,
DEAR BROTHERS AND SISTERS!

1.   The Lord's Day—as Sunday was called from apostolic times[1]—has always been accorded special attention in the history of the church because of its close connection with the very core of the Christian mystery. In fact, in the weekly reckoning of time Sunday recalls the day of Christ's resurrection. It is *Easter* which returns week by week, celebrating Christ's victory over sin and death, the fulfillment in him of the first creation and the dawn of "the new creation" (cf. 2 Corinthians 5:17). It is the day which recalls in grateful adoration the world's first day and looks forward in active hope to "the last day," when Christ will come in glory (cf. Acts 1:11; 1 Thessalonians 4:13–17) and all things will be made new (cf. Revelation 21:5).

Rightly, then, the psalmist's cry is applied to Sunday: "This day which the Lord has made: Let us rejoice and be glad in it" (Psalm 118:24). This invitation to joy, which the Easter liturgy makes its own, reflects the astonishment which came over the women who, having seen the crucifixion of Christ, found the tomb empty when they went there "very early on the first day after the Sabbath" (Mark 16:2). It is an invitation to relive in some way the experience of the two disciples of Emmaus, who felt their hearts "burn within them" as the Risen One walked with them on the road, explaining the scriptures and revealing himself in "the breaking of the bread" (cf. Luke 24:32, 35). And it echoes the joy—at first uncertain and then overwhelming—which the apostles experienced on the evening of that same day, when they were visited by the risen Jesus and received the gift of his peace and of his Spirit (cf. John 20:19–23).

2.   The resurrection of Jesus is the fundamental event upon which Christian faith rests (cf. 1 Corinthians 15:14). It is an astonishing reality, fully grasped in the light of faith, yet historically attested to by those who were privileged to see the Risen Lord. It is a wondrous event which is not only absolutely unique in human history, but which lies *at the very heart of the mystery of time*. In fact, "all time belongs to [Christ] and all the ages," as the evocative liturgy of the Easter Vigil recalls in preparing the paschal candle. Therefore, in commemorating the day of Christ's resurrection not just once a year but every Sunday,

the church seeks to indicate to every generation the true fulcrum of history, to which the mystery of the world's origin and its final destiny leads.

It is right, therefore, to claim, in the words of a fourth century homily, that "the Lord's Day" is "the lord of days."[2] Those who have received the grace of faith in the Risen Lord cannot fail to grasp the significance of this day of the week with the same deep emotion which led Saint Jerome to say: "Sunday is the day of the resurrection, it is the day of Christians, it is our day."[3] For Christians, Sunday is "the fundamental feast day,"[4] established not only to mark the succession of time but to reveal time's deeper meaning.

3.   The fundamental importance of Sunday has been recognized through two thousand years of history and was emphatically restated by the Second Vatican Council: "Every seven days, the Church celebrates the Easter mystery. This is a tradition going back to the Apostles, taking its origin from the actual day of Christ's Resurrection—a day thus appropriately designated 'the Lord's Day.'"[5] Paul VI emphasized this importance once more when he approved the new General Roman Calendar and the Universal Norms which regulate the ordering of the liturgical year.[6] The coming of the third millennium, which calls believers to reflect upon the course of history in the light of Christ, also invites them to rediscover with new intensity the meaning of Sunday: its mystery, its celebration, its significance for Christian and human life.

I note with pleasure that in the years since the Council this important theme has prompted not only many interventions by you, dear brother bishops, as teachers of the faith, but also different pastoral strategies which—with the support of your clergy—you have developed either individually or jointly. On the threshold of the Great Jubilee of the Year 2000, it has been my wish to offer you this Apostolic Letter in order to support your pastoral efforts in this vital area. But at the same time I wish to turn to all of you, Christ's faithful, as though I were spiritually present in all the communities in which you gather with your pastors each Sunday to celebrate the eucharist and the Lord's Day. Many of the insights and intuitions which prompt this Apostolic Letter have grown from my episcopal service in Krakow and, since the time when I assumed the ministry of Bishop of Rome and Successor of Peter, in the visits to the Roman parishes which I have made regularly on the Sundays of the different seasons of the liturgical year. I see this letter as continuing the lively exchange which I am always happy to have with the faithful, as I reflect with you on the meaning of Sunday and underline the reasons for living Sunday as truly the Lord's Day, also in the changing circumstances of our own times.

4.   Until quite recently, it was easier in traditionally Christian countries to keep Sunday holy because it was an almost universal practice and because, even in the organization of civil society, Sunday rest was considered a fixed part of the work schedule. Today, however, even in those countries which give legal sanction to the festive character of Sunday, changes in socioeconomic conditions have often led to profound modifications of social behavior and hence of the character of Sunday. The custom of the weekend has become more widespread,

a weekly period of respite, spent perhaps far from home and often involving participation in cultural, political or sporting activities which are usually held on free days. This social and cultural phenomenon is by no means without its positive aspects if, while respecting true values, it can contribute to people's development and to the advancement of the life of society as a whole. All of this responds not only to the need for rest, but also to the need for celebration which is inherent in our humanity. Unfortunately, when Sunday loses its fundamental meaning and becomes merely part of a weekend, it can happen that people stay locked within a horizon so limited that they can no longer see "the heavens."[7] Hence, though ready to celebrate, they are really incapable of doing so.

The disciples of Christ, however, are asked to avoid any confusion between the celebration of Sunday, which should truly be a way of keeping the Lord's Day holy, and the weekend, understood as a time of simple rest and relaxation. This will require a genuine spiritual maturity, which will enable Christians to "be what they are," in full accordance with the gift of faith, always ready to give an account of the hope which is in them (cf. 1 Peter 3:15). In this way, they will be led to a deeper understanding of Sunday, with the result that, even in difficult situations, they will be able to live it in complete docility to the Holy Spirit.

5.   From this perspective, the situation appears somewhat mixed. On the one hand, there is the example of some young churches, which shows how fervently Sunday can be celebrated, whether in urban areas or in widely scattered villages. By contrast, in other parts of the world, because of the sociological pressures already noted, and perhaps because the motivation of faith is weak, the percentage of those attending the Sunday liturgy is strikingly low. In the minds of many of the faithful, not only the sense of the centrality of the eucharist, but even the sense of the duty to give thanks to the Lord and to pray to him with others in the community of the church seems to be diminishing.

It is also true that both in mission countries and in countries evangelized long ago the lack of priests is such that the celebration of the Sunday eucharist cannot always be guaranteed in every community.

6.   Given this array of new situations and the questions which they prompt, it seems more necessary than ever *to recover the deep doctrinal foundations* underlying the church's precept, so that the abiding value of Sunday in the Christian life will be clear to all the faithful. In doing this, we follow in the footsteps of the age-old tradition of the church, powerfully restated by the Second Vatican Council in its teaching that on Sunday "Christian believers should come together, in order to commemorate the suffering, resurrection and glory of the Lord Jesus, by hearing God's word and sharing the eucharist, and to give thanks to God who has given them new birth to a living hope through the resurrection of Jesus Christ from the dead" (cf. 1 Peter 1:3).[8]

7.   The duty to keep Sunday holy, especially by sharing in the eucharist and by relaxing in a spirit of Christian joy and fraternity, is easily understood if we consider the many different aspects of this day upon which the present letter will focus our attention.

Sunday is a day that is at the very heart of the Christian life. From the beginning of my pontificate, I have not ceased to repeat: "Do not be afraid! Open, open wide the doors to Christ!"[9] In the same way, today I would strongly urge everyone to rediscover Sunday: *Do not be afraid to give your time to Christ!* Yes, let us open our time to Christ, that he may cast light upon it and give it direction. He is the One who knows the secret of time and the secret of eternity, and he gives us "his day" as an ever new gift of his love. The rediscovery of this day is a grace which we must implore, not only so that we may live the demands of faith to the full, but also so that we may respond concretely to the deepest human yearnings. Time given to Christ is never time lost, but is rather time gained, so that our relationships and indeed our whole life may become more profoundly human.

CHAPTER I
DIES DOMINI
THE CELEBRATION OF THE CREATOR'S WORK

"THROUGH HIM ALL THINGS WERE MADE" JOHN 1:3

8.   For the Christian, Sunday is above all an Easter celebration, wholly illumined by the glory of the Risen Christ. It is the festival of the "new creation." Yet, when understood in depth, this aspect is inseparable from what the first pages of scripture tell us of the plan of God in the creation of the world. It is true that the Word was made flesh in "the fullness of time" (Galatians 4:4); but it is also true that, in virtue of the mystery of his identity as the eternal Son of the Father, he is the origin and end of the universe. As John writes in the prologue of his gospel: "Through him all things were made, and without him was made nothing that was made" (1:3). Paul too stresses this in writing to the Colossians: "In him all things were created, in heaven and on earth, visible and invisible. . . . All things were created through him and for him" (1:16). This active presence of the Son in the creative work of God is revealed fully in the paschal mystery, in which Christ, rising as "the first fruits of those who had fallen asleep" (1 Corinthians 15:20), established the new creation and began the process which he himself will bring to completion when he returns in glory to "deliver the kingdom to God the Father . . . so that God may be everything to everyone" (1 Corinthians 15:24, 28).

Already at the dawn of creation, therefore, the plan of God implied Christ's "cosmic mission." This *Christocentric perspective,* embracing the whole arc of time, filled God's well-pleased gaze when, ceasing from all his work, he "blessed the seventh day and made it holy" (Genesis 2:3). According to the priestly writer of the first biblical creation story, then was born the "Sabbath," so characteristic of the first covenant, which in some ways foretells the sacred day of the new and final covenant. The theme of God's rest (cf. Genesis 2:2) and the rest which he offered to the people of the Exodus when they entered the Promised Land (cf. Exodus 33:14; Deuteronomy 3:20; 12:9; Joshua 21:44; Psalm 95:11) is re-read in the New Testament in the light of the definitive Sabbath rest (Hebrews 4:9) into which Christ himself has entered by his resurrection. The People of God are called to enter into this same rest by persevering in Christ's example of filial obedience (cf. Hebrews 4:3–16). In order to grasp fully the meaning of Sunday, therefore, we must re-read the great story of creation and deepen our understanding of the theology of the Sabbath.

"IN THE BEGINNING, GOD CREATED THE HEAVENS AND THE EARTH" GENESIS 1:1

9.   The poetic style of the Genesis story conveys well the awe which people feel before the immensity of creation and the resulting sense of adoration of the One who brought all things into being from nothing. It is a story of intense religious significance, a hymn to the creator of the universe, pointing to him as the only Lord in the face of recurring temptations to divinize the world itself. At the same time, it is a hymn to the goodness of creation, all fashioned by the mighty and merciful hand of God.

"God saw that it was good" (Genesis 1:10, 12, etc.). Punctuating the story as it does, this refrain *sheds a positive light upon every element of the universe* and reveals the secret for a proper understanding of it and for its eventual regeneration: The world is good insofar as it remains tied to its origin and, after being disfigured by sin, it is again made good when, with the help of grace, it returns to the One who made it. It is clear that this process directly concerns not inanimate objects and animals but human beings, who have been endowed with the incomparable gift and risk of freedom. Immediately after the creation stories, the Bible highlights the dramatic contrast between the grandeur of humanity, created in the image and likeness of God, and the fall of humanity, which unleashes on the world the darkness of sin and death (cf. Genesis 3).

10.   Coming as it does from the hand of God, the cosmos bears the imprint of his goodness. It is a beautiful world, rightly moving us to admiration and delight, but also calling for cultivation and development. At the "completion" of God's work, the world is ready for human activity. "On the seventh day God finished his work which he had done, and he rested on the seventh day from all his work which he had done" (Genesis 2:2). With this anthropomorphic image of God's "work," the Bible not only gives us a glimpse of the mysterious relationship between the Creator and the created world, but also casts light upon the task of human beings in relation to the cosmos. The "work" of God is in some ways an example for men and women, called not only to inhabit the cosmos, but also to "build" it and thus become God's "co-workers." As I wrote in my encyclical *Laborem Exercens*, the first chapters of Genesis constitute in a sense the first "gospel of work."[10] This is a truth which the Second Vatican Council also stressed: "Created in God's image, men and women were commissioned to subdue the earth and all it contains, to rule the world in justice and holiness, and, recognizing God as the creator of all things, to refer themselves and the totality of things to God so that with everything subject to God, the divine name would be glorified in all the earth."[11]

The exhilarating advance of science, technology and culture in their various forms—an ever more rapid and today even overwhelming development— is the historical consequence of the mission by which God entrusts to man and woman the task and responsibility of filling the earth and subduing it by means of their work, in the observance of God's Law.

SHABBAT: THE CREATOR'S JOYFUL REST

11.   If the first page of the Book of Genesis presents God's "work" as an example for men and women, the same is true of God's "rest": "On the seventh day God finished his work which he had done" (Genesis 2:2). Here too we find an anthropomorphism charged with a wealth of meaning.

It would be banal to interpret God's "rest" as a kind of divine "inactivity." By its nature, the creative act which founds the world is unceasing and God is always at work, as Jesus himself declares in speaking of the Sabbath precept: "My Father is working still, and I am working" (John 5:17). The divine rest of the seventh day does not allude to an inactive God, but emphasizes the fullness of what has been accomplished. It speaks, as it were, of God's lingering before the "very good" work (Genesis 1:31) which his hand has wrought in order to cast upon it *a gaze full of joyous delight.* This is a contemplative gaze which does not look to new accomplishments but enjoys the beauty of what has already been achieved. It is a gaze which God casts upon all things, but in a special way upon human beings, the crown of creation. It is a gaze which already discloses something of the nuptial shape of the relationship which God wants to establish with the creature made in his own image, by calling that creature to enter a pact of love. This is what God will gradually accomplish in offering salvation to all humanity through the saving covenant made with Israel and fulfilled in Christ. It will be the Word incarnate, through the eschatological gift of the Holy Spirit and the configuration of the church as his body and bride, who will extend to all humanity the offer of mercy and the call of the Father's love.

12.   In the Creator's plan, there is both a distinction and a close link between the order of creation and the order of salvation. This is emphasized in the Old Testament, when it links the *shabbat* commandment not only with God's mysterious "rest" after the days of creation (cf. Exodus 20:8–11), but also with the salvation which he offers to Israel *in the liberation from the slavery of Egypt* (cf. Deuteronomy 5:12–15). The God who rests on the seventh day, rejoicing in his creation, is the same God who reveals his glory in liberating his children from Pharaoh's oppression. Adopting an image dear to the prophets, one could say that in both cases *God reveals himself as the bridegroom before the bride* (cf. Hosea 2:16–24; Jeremiah 2:2; Isaiah 54:4–8).

As certain elements of the same Jewish tradition suggest,[12] to reach the heart of the *shabbat,* of God's "rest," we need to recognize in both the Old and the New Testament the nuptial intensity that marks the relationship between God and his people. Hosea, for instance, puts it thus in this marvelous passage:

> I will make for you a covenant on that day with the beasts of the field, the birds of the air, and the creeping things of the ground; and I will abolish the bow, the sword, and war from the land; and I will make you lie down in safety. And I will betroth you to me for ever; I will betroth you to me in

righteousness and in justice, in steadfast love and in mercy. I will betroth you to me in faithfulness; and you shall know the Lord. (2:18–20)

13.   The Sabbath precept, which in the first covenant prepares for the Sunday of the new and eternal covenant, is therefore rooted in the depths of God's plan. This is why, unlike many other precepts, it is set not within the context of strictly cultic stipulations but within the Decalogue, the "ten words" that represent the very pillars of the moral life inscribed on the human heart. In setting this commandment within the context of the basic structure of ethics, Israel and then the church declare that they consider it not just a matter of community religious discipline but *a defining and indelible expression of our relationship with God*, announced and expounded by biblical revelation. This is the perspective within which Christians need to rediscover this precept today. Although the precept may merge naturally with the human need for rest, it is faith alone which gives access to its deeper meaning and ensures that it will not become banal and trivialized.

14.   In the first place, therefore, Sunday is the day of rest because it is the day blessed by God and made holy by him, set apart from the other days to be, among all of them, "the Lord's Day."

In order to grasp fully what the first of the biblical creation accounts means by keeping the Sabbath holy, we need to consider the whole story, which shows clearly that every reality, without exception, must be referred back to God. Time and space belong to him. He is not the God of one day alone, but the God of all the days of humanity.

Therefore, if God sanctifies the seventh day with a special blessing and makes it his day *par excellence*, this must be understood within the deep dynamic of the dialogue of the covenant, indeed the dialogue of marriage. This is the dialogue of love which knows no interruption, yet is never monotonous. In fact, it employs the different registers of love, from the ordinary and indirect to those more intense, which the words of scripture and the witness of so many mystics do not hesitate to describe in imagery drawn from the experience of married love.

15.   All human life, and therefore all human time, must become praise of the Creator and thanksgiving to him. But our relationship with God also *demands times of explicit prayer*, in which the relationship becomes an intense dialogue, involving every dimension of the person. The Lord's Day is the day of this relationship par excellence when men and women raise their song to God and become the voice of all creation.

This is precisely why it is also *the day of rest*. Speaking vividly as it does of renewal and detachment, the interruption of the often oppressive rhythm of work expresses the dependence of human beings and the cosmos upon God. *Everything belongs to God!* The Lord's Day returns again and again to declare this principle within the weekly reckoning of time. The Sabbath has therefore been interpreted evocatively as a determining element in the kind of sacred architecture of time which marks biblical revelation.[13] It recalls that *the universe and history belong to God;* and without a constant awareness of that truth, men and women cannot serve in the world as co-workers of the Creator.

TO "KEEP HOLY" BY "REMEMBERING"

16.   The commandment of the Decalogue by which God decrees the Sabbath observance is formulated in the Book of Exodus in a distinctive way: "Remember the Sabbath day in order to keep it holy" (20:8). And the inspired text goes on to give the reason for this, recalling as it does the work of God: "For in six days the Lord made heaven and earth, the sea, and all that is in them, and rested on the seventh day; therefore the Lord blessed the Sabbath day and made it holy" (v. 11). Before decreeing that something be *done,* the commandment urges that something be *remembered.* It is a call to awaken remembrance of the grand and fundamental work of God which is creation, a remembrance which must inspire our entire religious life and then fill the day on which men and women are called to *rest.* Rest therefore acquires a sacred value: The faithful are called to rest not only *as* God rested, but to rest in the Lord, bringing the entire creation to him, in praise and thanksgiving, intimate as a child and friendly as a spouse.

17.   The connection between Sabbath rest and the theme of remembering God's wonders is found also in the Book of Deuteronomy (5:12–15), where the precept is grounded less in the work of creation than in the work of liberation accomplished by God in the Exodus: "You shall remember that you were a slave in the land of Egypt, and the LORD your God brought you out from there with mighty hand and outstretched arm; therefore the LORD your God commanded you to keep the Sabbath day" (Deuteronomy 5:15).

This formulation complements the one we have already seen; and taken together, the two reveal the meaning of the Lord's Day within a single theological vision that fuses creation and salvation. Therefore, the main point of the precept is not just any kind of *interruption* of work, but the *celebration* of the marvels which God has wrought.

Insofar as this remembrance is alive, *full of thanksgiving and of the praise of God,* human rest on the Lord's Day takes on its full meaning. It is then that men and women enter the depths of God's rest and can experience a tremor of the Creator's joy when, after the creation, he saw that all he had made "was very good" (Genesis 1:31).

FROM THE SABBATH TO SUNDAY

18.   Because the Third Commandment depends upon the remembrance of God's saving works and because Christians saw the definitive time inaugurated by Christ as a new beginning, they made the first day after the Sabbath a festive day, for that was the day on which the Lord rose from the dead. The paschal mystery of Christ is the full revelation of the mystery of the world's origin, the climax of the history of salvation and the anticipation of the eschatological fulfilment of the world. What God accomplished in creation and wrought for his

people in the Exodus has found its fullest expression in Christ's death and resurrection, though its definitive fulfillment will not come until the *Parousia*, when Christ returns in glory. In him, the spiritual meaning of the Sabbath is fully realized, as Saint Gregory the Great declares: "For us, the true Sabbath is the person of our Redeemer, our Lord Jesus Christ."[14] This is why the joy with which God, on humanity's first Sabbath, contemplated all that was created from nothing, is now expressed in the joy with which Christ, on Easter Sunday, appeared to his disciples, bringing the gift of peace and the gift of the Spirit (cf. John 20:19–23). It was in the paschal mystery that humanity, and with it the whole creation, "groaning in birth-pangs until now" (Romans 8:22), came to know its new exodus into the freedom of God's children who can cry out with Christ, "Abba, Father!" (Romans 8:15; Galatians 4:6). In the light of this mystery, the meaning of the Old Testament precept concerning the Lord's Day is recovered, perfected and fully revealed in the glory which shines on the face of the Risen Christ (cf. 2 Corinthians 4:6). We move from the "Sabbath" to the "first day after the Sabbath," from the seventh day to the first day: The *dies Domini* becomes the *dies Christi!*

CHAPTER II
DIES CHRISTI

THE DAY OF THE RISEN LORD
AND OF THE GIFT OF THE HOLY SPIRIT

THE WEEKLY EASTER

19.   "We celebrate Sunday because of the venerable resurrection of our Lord Jesus Christ, and we do so not only at Easter but also at each turning of the week": So wrote Pope Innocent I at the beginning of the fifth century,[15] testifying to an already well established practice which had evolved from the early years after the Lord's resurrection. Saint Basil speaks of "holy Sunday, honored by the Lord's Resurrection, the first fruits of all the other days";[16] and Saint Augustine calls Sunday "a sacrament of Easter."[17]

The intimate bond between Sunday and the resurrection of the Lord is strongly emphasized by all the churches of East and West. In the tradition of the Eastern churches in particular, every Sunday is the *anastasimos hemera,* the day of resurrection,[18] and this is why it stands at the heart of all worship.

In the light of this constant and universal tradition, it is clear that, although the Lord's Day is rooted in the very work of creation and even more in the mystery of the biblical rest of God, it is nonetheless to the resurrection of Christ that we must look in order to understand fully the Lord's Day. This is what the Christian Sunday does, leading the faithful each week to ponder and live the event of Easter, true source of the world's salvation.

20.   According to the common witness of the gospels, the resurrection of Jesus Christ from the dead took place on "the first day after the Sabbath" (Mark 16:2, 9; Luke 24:1; John 20:1). On the same day, the Risen Lord appeared to the two

disciples of Emmaus (cf. Luke 24:13–35) and to the eleven apostles gathered together (cf. Luke 24:36; John 20:19). A week later—as the Gospel of John recounts (cf. 20:26)—the disciples were gathered together once again, when Jesus appeared to them and made himself known to Thomas by showing him the signs of his passion. The day of Pentecost—the first day of the eighth week after the Jewish Passover (cf. Acts 2:1), when the promise made by Jesus to the apostles after the resurrection was fulfilled by the outpouring of the Holy Spirit (cf. Luke 24:49; Acts 1:4–5)—also fell on a Sunday. This was the day of the first proclamation and the first baptisms: Peter announced to the assembled crowd that Christ was risen and "those who received his word were baptized" (Acts 2:41). This was the epiphany of the church, revealed as the people into which are gathered in unity, beyond all their differences, the scattered children of God.

THE FIRST DAY OF THE WEEK

21.   It was for this reason that, from apostolic times, "the first day after the Sabbath," the first day of the week, began to shape the rhythm of life for Christ's disciples (cf. 1 Corinthians 16:2). "The first day after the Sabbath" was also the day upon which the faithful of Troas were gathered "for the breaking of bread," when Paul bade them farewell and miraculously restored the young Eutychus to life (cf. Acts 20:7–12). The Book of Revelation gives evidence of the practice of calling the first day of the week "the Lord's Day" (1:10). This would now be a characteristic distinguishing Christians from the world around them. As early as the beginning of the second century, it was noted by Pliny the Younger, governor of Bithynia, in his report on the Christian practice "of gathering together on a set day before sunrise and singing among themselves a hymn to Christ as to a god."[19] And when Christians spoke of the "Lord's Day," they did so giving to this term the full sense of the Easter proclamation: "Jesus Christ is Lord" (Philippians 2:11; cf. Acts 2:36; 1 Corinthians 12:3). Thus Christ was given the same title which the Septuagint used to translate what in the revelation of the Old Testament was the unutterable name of God: YHWH.

22.   In those early Christian times, the weekly rhythm of days was generally not part of life in the regions where the gospel spread, and the festive days of the Greek and Roman calendars did not coincide with the Christian Sunday. For Christians, therefore, it was very difficult to observe the Lord's Day on a set day each week. This explains why the faithful had to gather before sunrise.[20] Yet fidelity to the weekly rhythm became the norm, since it was based upon the New Testament and was tied to Old Testament revelation. This is eagerly underscored by the apologists and the Fathers of the church in their writings and preaching where, in speaking of the paschal mystery, they use the same scriptural texts which, according to the witness of Saint Luke (cf. 24:27, 44–47), the Risen Christ himself would have explained to the disciples. In the light of these texts, the celebration of the day of the resurrection acquired a doctrinal and symbolic value capable of expressing the entire Christian mystery in all its newness.

23.   It was this newness that the catechesis of the first centuries stressed as it sought to show the prominence of Sunday relative to the Jewish Sabbath. It was on the Sabbath that the Jewish people had to gather in the synagogue and to rest in the way prescribed by the Law. The apostles, and in particular Saint Paul, continued initially to attend the synagogue so that there they might proclaim Jesus Christ, commenting upon "the words of the prophets which are read every Sabbath" (Acts 13:27). Some communities observed the Sabbath while also celebrating Sunday. Soon, however, the two days began to be distinguished ever more clearly, in reaction chiefly to the insistence of those Christians whose origins in Judaism made them inclined to maintain the obligation of the old Law. Saint Ignatius of Antioch writes:

> If those who were living in the former state of things have come to a new hope, no longer observing the Sabbath but keeping the Lord's Day, the day on which our life has appeared through him and his death . . . that mystery from which we have received our faith and in which we persevere in order to be judged disciples of Christ, our only Master, how could we then live without him, given that the prophets too, as his disciples in the Spirit, awaited him as master?[21]

Saint Augustine notes in turn: "Therefore the Lord too has placed his seal on his day, which is the third after the Passion. In the weekly cycle, however, it is the eighth day after the seventh, that is after the Sabbath, and the first day of the week."[22] The distinction of Sunday from the Jewish Sabbath grew ever stronger in the mind of the church, even though there have been times in history when, because the obligation of Sunday rest was so emphasized, the Lord's Day tended to become more like the Sabbath. Moreover, there have always been groups within Christianity which observe both the Sabbath and Sunday as "two brother days."[23]

THE DAY OF THE NEW CREATION

24.   A comparison of the Christian Sunday with the Old Testament vision of the Sabbath prompted theological insights of great interest. In particular, there emerged the unique connection between the resurrection and creation. Christian thought spontaneously linked the resurrection, which took place on "the first day of the week," with the first day of that cosmic week (cf. Genesis 1:1–2:4) which shapes the creation story in the Book of Genesis: the day of the creation of light (cf. 1:3–5). This link invited an understanding of the resurrection as the beginning of a new creation, the first fruits of which is the glorious Christ, "the first born of all creation" (Colossians 1:15) and "the first born from the dead" (Colossians 1:18).

25.   In effect, Sunday is the day above all other days that summons Christians to remember the salvation which was given to them in baptism and which has made them new in Christ. "You were buried with him in baptism, in which you were also raised with him through faith in the working of God, who raised him from the dead" (Colossians 2:12; cf. Romans 6:4–6). The liturgy underscores this baptismal dimension of Sunday, both in calling for the celebration of baptisms—as well

as at the Easter Vigil—on the day of the week "when the Church commemorates the Lord's Resurrection,"[24] and in suggesting as an appropriate penitential rite at the start of Mass the sprinkling of holy water, which recalls the moment of baptism in which all Christian life is born.[25]

THE EIGHTH DAY: IMAGE OF ETERNITY

26.   By contrast, the Sabbath's position as the seventh day of the week suggests for the Lord's Day a complementary symbolism, much loved by the Fathers. Sunday is not only the first day, it is also "the eighth day," set within the seven-fold succession of days in a unique and transcendent position which evokes not only the beginning of time but also its end in "the age to come." Saint Basil explains that Sunday symbolizes that truly singular day which will follow the present time, the day without end which will know neither evening nor morning, the imperishable age which will never grow old; Sunday is the ceaseless foretelling of life without end which renews the hope of Christians and encourages them on their way.[26] Looking toward the last day, which fulfills completely the eschatological symbolism of the Sabbath, Saint Augustine concludes the *Confessions* describing the *eschaton* as "the peace of quietness, the peace of the Sabbath, a peace with no evening."[27] In celebrating Sunday, both the "first" and the "eighth" day, the Christian is led toward the goal of eternal life.[28]

THE DAY OF CHRIST-LIGHT

27.   This Christocentric vision sheds light upon another symbolism which Christian reflection and pastoral practice ascribed to the Lord's Day. Wise pastoral intuition suggested to the church the christianization of the notion of Sunday as "the day of the sun," which was the Roman name for the day and which is retained in some modern languages.[29] This was in order to draw the faithful away from the seduction of cults that worshiped the sun, and to direct the celebration of the day to Christ, humanity's true "sun." Writing to the pagans, Saint Justin uses the language of the time to note that Christians gather together "on the day named after the sun,"[30] but for believers the expression had already assumed a new meaning which was unmistakably rooted in the gospel.[31] Christ is the light of the world (cf. John 9:5; also 1:4–5, 9), and, in the weekly reckoning of time, the day commemorating his resurrection is the enduring reflection of the epiphany of his glory. The theme of Sunday as the day illuminated by the triumph of the Risen Christ is also found in the Liturgy of the Hours[32] and is given special emphasis in the *Pannichida*, the vigil which in the Eastern liturgies prepares for Sunday. From generation to generation as she gathers on this day, the church makes her own the wonderment of Zechariah as he looked upon Christ, seeing in him the dawn which gives "light to those who sit in darkness and in the shadow of death" (Luke 1:78–79), and she echoes the joy of Simeon when he takes in his arms the divine Child who has come as the "light to enlighten the Gentiles" (Luke 2:32).

28.   Sunday, the day of light, could also be called the day of "fire," in reference to the Holy Spirit. The light of Christ is intimately linked to the "fire" of the Spirit, and the two images together reveal the meaning of the Christian Sunday.[33] When he appeared to the apostles on the evening of Easter, Jesus breathed upon them and said: "Receive the Holy Spirit. If you forgive the sins of any, they are forgiven; if you retain the sins of any, they are retained" (John 20:22–23). The outpouring of the Spirit was the great gift of the Risen Lord to his disciples on Easter Sunday. It was again Sunday when, fifty days after the resurrection, the Spirit descended in power, as "a mighty wind" and "fire" (Acts 2:2–3), upon the apostles gathered with Mary. Pentecost is not only the founding event of the church, but is also the mystery which for ever gives life to the church.[34] Such an event has its own powerful liturgical moment in the annual celebration which concludes "the great Sunday,"[35] but it also remains a part of the deep meaning of every Sunday because of its intimate bond with the paschal mystery. The "weekly Easter" thus becomes, in a sense, the "weekly Pentecost," when Christians relive the apostles' joyful encounter with the Risen Lord and receive the life-giving breath of his Spirit.

THE DAY OF FAITH

29.   Given these different dimensions which set it apart, Sunday appears as the supreme *day of faith*. It is the day when, by the power of the Holy Spirit, who is the church's living "memory" (cf. John 14:26), the first appearance of the Risen Lord becomes an event renewed in the "today" of each of Christ's disciples. Gathered in his presence in the Sunday assembly, believers sense themselves called like the apostle Thomas: "Put your finger here, and see my hands. Put out your hand, and place it in my side. Doubt no longer, but believe" (John 20:27). Yes, Sunday is the day of faith. This is stressed by the fact that the Sunday eucharistic liturgy, like the liturgy of other solemnities, includes the profession of faith. Recited or sung, the Creed declares the baptismal and paschal character of Sunday, making it the day on which in a special way the baptized renew their adherence to Christ and his gospel in a rekindled awareness of their baptismal promises. Listening to the word and receiving the Body of the Lord, the baptized contemplate the Risen Jesus present in the "holy signs" and confess with the apostle Thomas: "My Lord and my God!" (John 20:28).

AN INDISPENSABLE DAY!

30.   It is clear then why, even in our own difficult times, the identity of this day must be protected and above all must be lived in all its depth. An Eastern writer of the beginning of the third century recounts that as early as then the faithful in every region were keeping Sunday holy on a regular basis.[36] What began as a spontaneous practice later became a juridically sanctioned norm. The Lord's Day has structured the history of the church through two thousand years: How could we think that it will not continue to shape her future? The pressures of today can make it harder to fulfill the Sunday obligation; and, with a mother's sensitivity, the church looks to the circumstances of each of her

children. In particular, she feels herself called to a new catechetical and pastoral commitment in order to ensure that, in the normal course of life, none of her children are deprived of the rich outpouring of grace which the celebration of the Lord's Day brings. It was in this spirit that the Second Vatican Council, making a pronouncement on the possibility of reforming the church calendar to match different civil calendars, declared that the church "is prepared to accept only those arrangements which preserve a week of seven days with a Sunday."[37] Given its many meanings and aspects, and its link to the very foundations of the faith, the celebration of the Christian Sunday remains, on the threshold of the third millennium, an indispensable element of our Christian identity.

CHAPTER III
DIES ECCLESIAE
THE EUCHARISTIC ASSEMBLY: HEART OF SUNDAY

THE PRESENCE OF THE RISEN LORD

31. "I am with you always, to the end of the age" (Matthew 28:20). This promise of Christ never ceases to resound in the church as the fertile secret of her life and the wellspring of her hope. As the day of resurrection, Sunday is not only the remembrance of a past event: It is a celebration of the living presence of the Risen Lord in the midst of his own people.

For this presence to be properly proclaimed and lived, it is not enough that the disciples of Christ pray individually and commemorate the death and resurrection of Christ inwardly, in the secrecy of their hearts. Those who have received the grace of baptism are not saved as individuals alone, but as members of the mystical body, having become part of the People of God.[38] It is important therefore that they come together to express fully the very identity of the church, the *ekklesia*, the assembly called together by the Risen Lord who offered his life "to reunite the scattered children of God" (John 11:52). They have become one in Christ (cf. Galatians 3:28) through the gift of the Spirit. This unity becomes visible when Christians gather together: It is then that they come to know vividly and to testify to the world that they are the people redeemed, drawn "from every tribe and language and people and nation" (Revelation 5:9). The assembly of Christ's disciples embodies from age to age the image of the first Christian community, which Luke gives as an example in the Acts of the Apostles when he recounts that the first baptized believers "devoted themselves to the apostles' teaching and fellowship, to the breaking of bread and the prayers" (2:42).

THE EUCHARISTIC ASSEMBLY

32. The eucharist is not only a particularly intense expression of the reality of the church's life, but also in a sense its "fountainhead."[39] The eucharist feeds and forms the church: "Because there is one bread, we who are many are one body, for we all partake of the one bread" (1 Corinthians 10:17). Because of this vital link with the sacrament of the Body and Blood of the Lord, the mystery of the church is savored, proclaimed and lived supremely in the eucharist.[40]

This ecclesial dimension intrinsic to the eucharist is realized in every eucharistic celebration. But it is expressed most especially on the day when the whole community comes together to commemorate the Lord's resurrection. Significantly, the *Catechism of the Catholic Church* teaches that "the Sunday celebration of the Lord's Day and his eucharist is at the heart of the church's life."[41]

33.   At Sunday Mass, Christians relive with particular intensity the experience of the apostles on the evening of Easter when the Risen Lord appeared to them as they were gathered together (cf. John 20:19). In a sense, the People of God of all times were present in that small nucleus of disciples, the first fruits of the church. Through their testimony, every generation of believers hears the greeting of Christ, rich with the messianic gift of peace, won by his blood and offered with his Spirit: "Peace be with you!" Christ's return among them "a week later" (John 20:26) can be seen as a radical prefiguring of the Christian community's practice of coming together every seven days, on "the Lord's Day" or Sunday, in order to profess faith in his resurrection and to receive the blessing which he had promised: "Blessed are those who have not seen and yet believe" (John 20:29). This close connection between the appearance of the Risen Lord and the eucharist is suggested in the Gospel of Luke in the story of the two disciples of Emmaus, whom Christ approached and led to understand the scriptures and then sat with at table. They recognized him when he "took the bread, said the blessing, broke it and gave it to them" (24:30). The gestures of Jesus in this account are his gestures at the Last Supper, with the clear allusion to the "breaking of bread," as the eucharist was called by the first generation of Christians.

THE SUNDAY EUCHARIST

34.   It is true that, in itself, the Sunday eucharist is no different from the eucharist celebrated on other days, nor can it be separated from liturgical and sacramental life as a whole. By its very nature, the eucharist is an epiphany of the church;[42] and this is most powerfully expressed when the diocesan community gathers in prayer with its pastor: "The church appears with special clarity when the holy People of God, all of them, are actively and fully sharing in the same liturgical celebrations—especially when it is the same eucharist—sharing one prayer at one altar, at which the bishop is presiding, surrounded by his presbyters and his ministers."[43] This relationship with the bishop and with the entire church community is inherent in every eucharistic celebration, even when the bishop does not preside, regardless of the day of the week on which it is celebrated. The mention of the bishop in the eucharistic prayer is the indication of this.

But because of its special solemnity and the obligatory presence of the community, and because it is celebrated "on the day when Christ conquered death and gave us a share in his immortal life,"[44] the Sunday eucharist expresses with greater emphasis its inherent ecclesial dimension. It becomes the paradigm for other eucharistic celebrations. Each community, gathering all its members for the "breaking of the bread," becomes the place where the mystery of the church is concretely made present. In celebrating the eucharist, the community opens itself to communion with the universal church,[45] imploring the Father to "remember the church throughout the world" and make her grow in the unity of all the faithful with the pope and with the pastors of the particular churches, until love is brought to perfection.

THE DAY OF THE CHURCH

35.   Therefore, the *dies Domini* is also the *dies Ecclesiae*. This is why on the pastoral level the community aspect of the Sunday celebration should be particularly stressed. As I have noted elsewhere, among the many activities of a parish, "none is as vital or as community-forming as the Sunday celebration of the Lord's Day and his eucharist."[46] Mindful of this, the Second Vatican Council recalled that efforts must be made to ensure that there is "within the parish, a lively sense of community, in the first place through the community celebration of Sunday Mass."[47] subsequent liturgical directives made the same point, asking that on Sundays and holy days the eucharistic celebrations held normally in other churches and chapels be coordinated with the celebration in the parish church, in order "to foster the sense of the church community, which is nourished and expressed in a particular way by the community celebration on Sunday, whether around the bishop, especially in the cathedral, or in the parish assembly, in which the pastor represents the bishop."[48]

36.   The Sunday assembly is the privileged place of unity: It is the setting for the celebration of the *sacramentum unitatis* which profoundly marks the church as a people gathered "by" and "in" the unity of the Father, of the Son and of the Holy Spirit.[49] For Christian families, the Sunday assembly is one of the most outstanding expressions of their identity and their "ministry" as "domestic churches,"[50] when parents share with their children at the one table of the word and of the bread of life. We do well to recall in this regard that it is first of all the parents who must teach their children to participate in Sunday Mass; they are assisted in this by catechists, who are to see to it that initiation into the Mass is made a part of the formation imparted to the children entrusted to their care, explaining the important reasons behind the obligatory nature of the precept. When circumstances suggest it, the celebration of Masses for children, in keeping with the provisions of the liturgical norms,[51] can also help in this regard.

    At Sunday Masses in parishes, insofar as parishes are "eucharistic communities,"[52] it is normal to find different groups, movements, associations and even the smaller religious communities present in the parish. This allows everyone to experience in common what they share most deeply, beyond the particular spiritual paths which, by discernment of church authority,[53] legitimately distinguish them. This is why on Sunday, the day of gathering, small group Masses are not to be encouraged: It is not only a question of ensuring that parish assemblies are not without the necessary ministry of priests, but also of ensuring that the life and unity of the church community are fully safeguarded and promoted.[54] Authorization of possible and clearly restricted exceptions to this general guideline will depend upon the wise discernment of the pastors of the particular churches, in view of special needs in the area of formation and pastoral care, and keeping in mind the good of individuals or groups—especially the benefits which such exceptions may bring to the entire Christian community.

37.   As the church journeys through time, the reference to Christ's resurrection and the weekly recurrence of this solemn memorial help to remind us of *the pilgrim and eschatological character of the People of God.* Sunday after Sunday the church moves toward the final "Lord's Day," that Sunday which knows no end. The expectation of Christ's coming is inscribed in the very mystery of the church[55] and is evidenced in every eucharistic celebration. But, with its specific remembrance of the glory of the Risen Christ, the Lord's Day recalls with greater intensity the future glory of his "return." This makes Sunday the day on which the church, showing forth more clearly her identity as "Bride," anticipates in some sense the eschatological reality of the heavenly Jerusalem. Gathering her children into the eucharistic assembly and teaching them to wait for the "divine Bridegroom," she engages in a kind of "exercise of desire,"[56] receiving a foretaste of the joy of the new heavens and new earth, when the holy city, the new Jerusalem, will come down from God, "prepared as a bride adorned for her husband" (Revelation 21:2).

THE DAY OF HOPE

38.   Viewed in this way, Sunday is not only the day of faith, but is also *the day of Christian hope.* To share in "the Lord's Supper" is to anticipate the eschatological feast of the "marriage of the Lamb" (Revelation 19:9). Celebrating this memorial of Christ, risen and ascended into heaven, the Christian community waits "in joyful hope for the coming of our Savior, Jesus Christ."[57] Renewed and nourished by this intense weekly rhythm, Christian hope becomes the leaven and the light of human hope. This is why the prayer of the faithful responds not only to the needs of the particular Christian community but also to those of all humanity; and the church, coming together for the eucharistic celebration, shows to the world that she makes her own "the joys and hopes, the sorrows and anxieties of people today, especially of the poor and all those who suffer."[58] With the offering of the Sunday eucharist, the church crowns the witness which her children strive to offer every day of the week by proclaiming the gospel and practicing charity in the world of work and in all the many tasks of life; thus she shows forth more plainly her identity "as a sacrament, or sign and instrument of intimate union with God and of the unity of the entire human race."[59]

THE TABLE OF THE WORD

39.   As in every eucharistic celebration, the Risen Lord is encountered in the Sunday assembly at the twofold table of the word and of the bread of life. The table of the word offers the same understanding of the history of salvation and especially of the paschal mystery which the risen Jesus himself gave to his disciples: It is Christ who speaks, present as he is in his word "when sacred scripture is read in the church."[60] At the table of the bread of life, the Risen Lord becomes really, substantially and enduringly present through the memorial of his passion and resurrection, and the bread of life is offered as a pledge of future glory. The Second Vatican Council recalled that "the liturgy of the word and the liturgy of the eucharist are so closely joined together that they form a single act

of worship."[61] The Council also urged that "the table of the word of God be more lavishly prepared for the faithful, opening to them more abundantly the treasures of the Bible."[62] It then decreed that, in Masses of Sunday and holy days of obligation, the homily should not be omitted except for serious reasons.[63] These timely decrees were faithfully embodied in the liturgical reform about which Paul VI wrote, commenting upon the richer offering of biblical readings on Sundays and holy days: "All this has been decreed so as to foster more and more in the faithful 'that hunger for hearing the word of the Lord' (Amos 8:11) which, under the guidance of the Holy Spirit, spurs the People of the New Covenant on toward the perfect unity of the church."[64]

40.   In considering the Sunday eucharist more than thirty years after the Council, we need to assess how well the word of God is being proclaimed and how effectively the People of God have grown in knowledge and love of sacred scripture.[65] There are two aspects of this—that of *celebration* and that of *personal appropriation*—and they are very closely related. At the level of celebration, the fact that the Council made it possible to proclaim the word of God in the language of the community taking part in the celebration must awaken a new sense of responsibility toward the word, allowing "the distinctive character of the sacred text" to shine forth "even in the mode of reading or singing."[66] At the level of personal appropriation, the hearing of the word of God proclaimed must be well prepared in the souls of the faithful by an apt knowledge of scripture and, where pastorally possible, by *special initiatives designed to deepen understanding of the biblical readings*, particularly those used on Sundays and holy days. If Christian individuals and families are not regularly drawing new life from the reading of the sacred text in a spirit of prayer and docility to the church's interpretation,[67] then it is difficult for the liturgical proclamation of the word of God alone to produce the fruit we might expect. This is the value of initiatives in parish communities that bring together during the week those who take part in the eucharist—priest, ministers and faithful[68]—in order to prepare the Sunday liturgy, reflecting beforehand upon the word of God that will be proclaimed. The objective sought here is that the entire celebration—praying, singing, listening, and not just the preaching—should express in some way the theme of the Sunday liturgy, so that all those taking part may be penetrated more powerfully by it. Clearly, much depends on those who exercise the ministry of the word. It is their duty to prepare the reflection on the word of the Lord by prayer and study of the sacred text, so that they may then express its contents faithfully and apply them to people's concerns and to their daily lives.

41.   It should also be borne in mind that the *liturgical proclamation of the word of God*, especially in the eucharistic assembly, is not so much a time for meditation and catechesis as *a dialogue between God and his people,* a dialogue in which the wonders of salvation are proclaimed and the demands of the covenant are continually restated. On their part, the People of God are drawn to respond to this dialogue of love by giving thanks and praise, also by demonstrating their fidelity to the task of continual conversion. The Sunday assembly commits us therefore to an inner renewal of our baptismal promises, which are in a sense implicit in the recitation of the Creed, and are an explicit part of the

liturgy of the Easter Vigil and whenever baptism is celebrated during Mass. In this context, the proclamation of the word in the Sunday eucharistic celebration takes on the solemn tone found in the Old Testament at moments when the covenant was renewed, when the Law was proclaimed and the community of Israel was called—like the people in the desert at the foot of Sinai (cf. Exodus 19:7–8; 24:3, 7)—to repeat its "yes," renewing its decision to be faithful to God and to obey his commandments. In speaking his word, God awaits our response: a response which Christ has already made for us with his "Amen" (cf. 2 Corinthians 1:20–22), and which echoes in us through the Holy Spirit so that what we hear may involve us at the deepest level.[69]

THE TABLE OF THE BODY OF CHRIST

42.   The table of the word leads naturally to the table of the eucharistic bread and prepares the community to live its many aspects, which in the Sunday eucharist assume an especially solemn character. As the whole community gathers to celebrate "the Lord's Day," the eucharist appears more clearly than on other days as the great "thanksgiving" in which the Spirit-filled church turns to the Father, becoming one with Christ and speaking in the name of all humanity. The rhythm of the week prompts us to gather up in grateful memory the events of the days which have just passed, to review them in the light of God and to thank him for his countless gifts, glorifying him "through Christ, with Christ and in Christ, in the unity of the Holy Spirit." The Christian community thus comes to a renewed awareness of the fact that all things were created through Christ (cf. Colossians 1:16; John 1:3), and that in Christ, who came in the form of a slave to take on and redeem our human condition, all things have been restored (cf. Ephesians 1:10), in order to be handed over to God the Father, from whom all things come to be and draw their life. Then, giving assent to the eucharistic doxology with their "Amen," the People of God look in faith and hope toward the eschatological end, when Christ "will deliver the kingdom to God the Father . . . so that God may be everything to everyone" (1 Corinthians 15:24, 28).

43.   This ascending movement is inherent in every eucharistic celebration and makes it a joyous event, overflowing with gratitude and hope. But it emerges particularly at Sunday Mass because of its special link with the commemoration of the resurrection. By contrast, this eucharistic rejoicing that "lifts up our hearts" is the fruit of God's descending movement toward us, which remains for ever etched in the essential sacrificial element of the eucharist, the supreme expression and celebration of the mystery of the kenosis, the descent by which Christ "humbled himself, and became obedient unto death, even death on a Cross" (Philippians 2:8).

The Mass in fact *truly makes present the sacrifice of the cross.* Under the species of bread and wine, upon which has been invoked the outpouring of the Spirit who works with absolutely unique power in the words of consecration, Christ offers himself to the Father in the same act of sacrifice by which he offered himself on the cross. "In this divine sacrifice which is accomplished in the

Mass, the same Christ who offered himself once and for all in a bloody manner on the altar of the Cross is contained and is offered in an unbloody manner."[70] To his sacrifice Christ unites the sacrifice of the church: "In the eucharist the sacrifice of Christ becomes also the sacrifice of the members of his Body. The lives of the faithful, their praise, sufferings, prayer and work, are united with those of Christ and with his total offering, and so acquire a new value."[71] The truth that the whole community shares in Christ's sacrifice is especially evident in the Sunday gathering, which makes it possible to bring to the altar the week that has passed, with all its human burdens.

EASTER BANQUET AND FRATERNAL GATHERING

44. The communal character of the eucharist emerges in a special way when it is seen as the Easter banquet in which Christ himself becomes our nourishment. In fact, "for this purpose Christ entrusted to the church this sacrifice: so that the faithful might share in it, both spiritually, in faith and charity, and sacramentally, in the banquet of holy communion. Sharing in the Lord's Supper is always communion with Christ, who offers himself for us in sacrifice to the Father."[72] This is why the church *recommends that the faithful receive communion when they take part in the eucharist*, provided that they are properly disposed and, if aware of grave sin, have received God's pardon in the sacrament of reconciliation,[73] in the spirit of what Saint Paul writes to the community at Corinth (cf. 1 Corinthians 11:27–32). Obviously, the invitation to eucharistic communion is more insistent in the case of Mass on Sundays and holy days.

It is also important to be ever mindful that communion with Christ is deeply tied to communion with our brothers and sisters. The Sunday eucharistic gathering is an *experience of brotherhood*, which the celebration should demonstrate clearly, while ever respecting the nature of the liturgical action. All this will be helped by gestures of welcome and by the tone of prayer, alert to the needs of all in the community. The sign of peace—in the Roman Rite significantly placed before eucharistic communion—is a particularly expressive gesture which the faithful are invited to make as a manifestation of the People of God's acceptance of all that has been accomplished in the celebration[74] and of the commitment to mutual love that is made in sharing the one bread, with the demanding words of Christ in mind: "If you are offering your gift at the altar, and there remember that your brother has something against you, leave your gift there before the altar and go; first be reconciled with your brother, and then come and offer your gift" (Matthew 5:23–24).

FROM MASS TO "MISSION"

45. Receiving the bread of life, the disciples of Christ ready themselves to undertake with the strength of the Risen Lord and his Spirit *the tasks which await them in their ordinary life.* For the faithful who have understood the meaning of what they have done, the eucharistic celebration does not stop at the church door. Like the first witnesses of the resurrection, Christians who gather each Sunday to experience and proclaim the presence of the Risen Lord are called to

evangelize and bear witness in their daily lives. Given this, the prayer after communion and the concluding rite—the final blessing and the dismissal—need to be better valued and appreciated, so that all who have shared in the eucharist may come to a deeper sense of the responsibility that is entrusted to them. Once the assembly disperses, Christ's disciples return to their everyday surroundings with the commitment to make their whole life a gift, a spiritual sacrifice pleasing to God (cf. Romans 12:1). They feel indebted to their brothers and sisters because of what they have received in the celebration, not unlike the disciples of Emmaus who, once they had recognized the Risen Christ "in the breaking of the bread" (cf. Luke 24:30–32), felt the need to return immediately to share with their brothers and sisters the joy of meeting the Lord (cf. Luke 24:33–35).

THE SUNDAY OBLIGATION

46.   Since the eucharist is the very heart of Sunday, it is clear why, from the earliest centuries, the pastors of the church have not ceased to remind the faithful of *the need to take part in the liturgical assembly*. "Leave everything on the Lord's Day," urges the third century text known as the *Didascalia*, "and run diligently to your assembly, because it is your praise of God. Otherwise, what excuse will they make to God, those who do not come together on the Lord's Day to hear the word of life and feed on the divine nourishment which lasts forever?"[75] The faithful have generally accepted this call of the pastors with conviction of soul and, although there have been times and situations when this duty has not been perfectly met, one should never forget the genuine heroism of priests and faithful who have fulfilled this obligation even when faced with danger and the denial of religious freedom, as can be documented from the first centuries of Christianity up to our own time.

In his *First Apology*, addressed to the Emperor Antoninus and the Senate, Saint Justin proudly described the Christian practice of the Sunday assembly, which gathered in one place Christians from both the city and the countryside.[76] When, during the persecution of Diocletian, their assemblies were banned with the greatest severity, many were courageous enough to defy the imperial decree and accepted death rather than miss the Sunday eucharist. This was the case of the martyrs of Abitina, in proconsular Africa, who replied to their accusers: "Without fear of any kind we have celebrated the Lord's Supper, because it cannot be missed; that is our law"; "We cannot live without the Lord's Supper." As she confessed her faith, one of the martyrs said: "Yes, I went to the assembly and I celebrated the Lord's Supper with my brothers and sisters, because I am a Christian."[77]

47.   Even if in the earliest times it was not judged necessary to be prescriptive, the church has not ceased to confirm this obligation of conscience, which rises from the inner need felt so strongly by the Christians of the first centuries. It was only later, faced with the half-heartedness or negligence of some, that the church had to make explicit the duty to attend Sunday Mass: More often than not, this was done in the form of exhortation, but at times the church had to resort to specific canonical precepts. This was the case in a number of local Councils from the fourth century onward (as at the Council of Elvira of 300, which speaks

not of an obligation but of penalties after three absences)[78] and most especially from the sixth century onward (as at the Council of Agde in 506).[79] These decrees of local councils led to a universal practice, the obligatory character of which was taken as something quite normal.[80]

The Code of Canon Law of 1917 for the first time gathered this tradition into a universal law.[81] The present Code reiterates this, saying that "on Sundays and other holy days of obligation the faithful are bound to attend Mass."[82] This legislation has normally been understood as entailing a grave obligation: This is the teaching of the *Catechism of the Catholic Church*,[83] and it is easy to understand why if we keep in mind how vital Sunday is for the Christian life.

48.   Today, as in the heroic times of the beginning, many who wish to live in accord with the demands of their faith are being faced with difficult situations in various parts of the world. They live in surroundings that are sometimes decidedly hostile and at other times—more frequently in fact—indifferent and unresponsive to the gospel message. If believers are not to be overwhelmed, they must be able to count on the support of the Christian community. This is why they must be convinced that it is crucially important for the life of faith that they should come together with others on Sundays to celebrate the Passover of the Lord in the sacrament of the new covenant. It is the special responsibility of the bishops, therefore, "to ensure that Sunday is appreciated by all the faithful, kept holy and celebrated as truly 'the Lord's Day,' on which the church comes together to renew the remembrance of the Easter mystery in hearing the word of God, in offering the sacrifice of the Lord, in keeping the day holy by means of prayer, works of charity and abstention from work."[84]

49.   Because the faithful are obliged to attend Mass unless there is a grave impediment, pastors have the corresponding duty to offer to everyone the real possibility of fulfilling the precept. The provisions of church law move in this direction, as for example in the faculty granted to priests, with the prior authorization of the diocesan bishop, to celebrate more than one Mass on Sundays and holy days,[85] the institution of evening Masses[86] and the provision that allows the obligation to be fulfilled from Saturday evening onwards, starting at the time of First Vespers of Sunday.[87] From a liturgical point of view, in fact, holy days begin with First Vespers.[88] Consequently, the liturgy of what is sometimes called the "vigil Mass" is in effect the "festive" Mass of Sunday, at which the celebrant is required to preach the homily and recite the prayer of the faithful.

Moreover, pastors should remind the faithful that when they are away from home on Sundays they are to take care to attend Mass wherever they may be, enriching the local community with their personal witness. At the same time, these communities should show a warm sense of welcome to visiting brothers and sisters, especially in places which attract many tourists and pilgrims, for whom it will often be necessary to provide special religious assistance.[89]

A JOYFUL CELEBRATION IN SONG

50. Given the nature of Sunday Mass and its importance in the lives of the faithful, it must be prepared with special care. In ways dictated by pastoral experience and local custom in keeping with liturgical norms, efforts must be made to ensure that the celebration has the festive character appropriate to the day commemorating the Lord's resurrection. To this end, it is important to devote attention to the *songs used by the assembly*, since singing is a particularly apt way to express a joyful heart, accentuating the solemnity of the celebration and fostering the sense of a common faith and a shared love. Care must be taken to ensure the quality both of the texts and of the melodies so that what is proposed today as new and creative will conform to liturgical requirements and be worthy of the church's tradition which, in the field of sacred music, boasts a priceless heritage.

A CELEBRATION INVOLVING ALL

51. There is a need too to ensure that all those present, children and adults, take an active interest, by encouraging their involvement at those points where the liturgy suggests and recommends it.[90] Of course, it falls to only those who exercise the priestly ministry to effect the eucharistic sacrifice and to offer it to God in the name of the whole people.[91] This is the basis of the distinction, which is much more than a matter of discipline, between the task proper to the celebrant and that which belongs to deacons and the non-ordained faithful.[92] Yet the faithful must realize that, because of the common priesthood received in baptism, "they participate in the offering of the eucharist."[93] Although there is a distinction of roles, they still "offer to God the divine victim and themselves with him. Offering the sacrifice and receiving holy communion, they take part actively in the liturgy,"[94] finding in it light and strength to live their baptismal priesthood and the witness of a holy life.

OTHER MOMENTS OF THE CHRISTIAN SUNDAY

52. Sharing in the eucharist is the heart of Sunday, but the duty to keep Sunday holy cannot be reduced to this. In fact, the Lord's Day is lived well if it is marked from beginning to end by grateful and active remembrance of God's saving work. This commits each of Christ's disciples to shape the other moments of the day—those outside the liturgical context: family life, social relationships, moments of relaxation—in such a way that the peace and joy of the Risen Lord will emerge in the ordinary events of life. For example, the relaxed gathering of parents and children can be an opportunity not only to listen to one another but also to share a few formative and more reflective moments. Even in lay life, when possible, why not make provision for special *times of prayer*—especially the solemn celebration of Vespers, for example—or *moments of catechesis*, which on the eve of Sunday or on Sunday afternoon might prepare for or complete the gift of the eucharist in people's hearts?

This rather traditional way of keeping Sunday holy has perhaps become more difficult for many people, but the church shows her faith in the strength of the Risen Lord and the power of the Holy Spirit by making it known that today more than ever she is unwilling to settle for minimalism and mediocrity at the level of faith. She wants to help Christians to do what is most correct and pleasing to the Lord. And despite the difficulties, there are positive and encouraging signs. In many parts of the church, a new need for prayer in its many forms is being felt, and this is a gift of the Holy Spirit. There is also a rediscovery of ancient religious practices, such as pilgrimages; often the faithful take advantage of Sunday rest to visit a shrine where, with the whole family perhaps, they can spend time in a more intense experience of faith. These are moments of grace that must be fostered through evangelization and guided by genuine pastoral wisdom.

SUNDAY ASSEMBLIES WITHOUT A PRIEST

53.   There remains the problem of parishes which do not have the ministry of a priest for the celebration of the Sunday eucharist. This is often the case in young churches, where one priest has pastoral responsibility for faithful scattered over a vast area. However, emergency situations can also arise in countries of long-standing Christian tradition, where diminishing numbers of clergy make it impossible to guarantee the presence of a priest in every parish community. In situations where the eucharist cannot be celebrated, the church recommends that the Sunday assembly come together even without a priest,[95] in keeping with the indications and directives of the Holy See which have been entrusted to the episcopal conferences for implementation.[96] Yet the objective must always remain the celebration of the sacrifice of the Mass, the one way in which the Passover of the Lord becomes truly present, the only full realization of the eucharistic assembly over which the priest presides *in persona Christi,* breaking the bread of the word and the eucharist. At the pastoral level, therefore, everything has to be done to ensure that the sacrifice of the Mass is made available as often as possible to the faithful who are regularly deprived of it, either by arranging the presence of a priest from time to time, or by taking every opportunity to organize a gathering in a central location accessible to scattered groups.

RADIO AND TELEVISION

54.   Finally, the faithful who because of sickness, disability or some other serious cause are prevented from taking part should as best they can unite themselves with the celebration of Sunday Mass from afar, preferably by means of the readings and prayers for that day from the Missal, as well as through their desire for the eucharist.[97] In many countries, radio and television make it possible to join in the eucharistic celebration broadcast from some sacred place.[98] Clearly, this kind of broadcast does not in itself fulfill the Sunday obligation, which requires participation in the fraternal assembly gathered in one place, where eucharistic communion can be received. But for those who cannot take part in the eucharist and who are therefore excused from the obligation, radio and television are a precious help, especially if accompanied by the generous service of extraordinary ministers who bring the eucharist to the sick, also bringing them the greeting and solidarity of the whole community. Sunday Mass thus produces rich fruits for these Christians too, and they are truly enabled to experience Sunday as the Lord's Day and the church's day.

CHAPTER IV
DIES HOMINIS
SUNDAY: DAY OF JOY, REST AND SOLIDARITY

THE FULL JOY OF CHRIST

55. "Blessed be he who has raised the great day of Sunday above all other days. The heavens and the earth, angels and people give themselves over to joy."[99] This cry of the Maronite liturgy captures well the intense acclamations of joy that have always characterized Sunday in the liturgy of both East and West. Moreover, historically—even before it was seen as a day of rest, which in any case was not provided for in the civil calendar—Christians celebrated the weekly day of the Risen Lord primarily as a day of joy. "On the first day of the week, you shall all rejoice," urges the *Didascalia*.[100] This was also emphasized by liturgical practice, through the choice of appropriate gestures.[101] Voicing an awareness widespread in the church, Saint Augustine describes the joy of the weekly Easter: "Fasting is set aside and prayers are said standing as a sign of the Resurrection, which is also why the alleluia is sung on every Sunday."[102]

56. Beyond particular ritual forms, which can vary in time depending upon church discipline, there remains the fact that Sunday, as a weekly echo of the first encounter with the Risen Lord, is unfailingly marked by the joy with which the disciples greeted the Master: "The disciples rejoiced to see the Lord" (John 20:20). This was the confirmation of the words that Jesus spoke before the Passion and that resound in every Christian generation: "You will be sorrowful, but your sorrow will turn to joy" (John 16:20). Had not he himself prayed for this, that the disciples would have "the fullness of his joy" (cf. John 17:13)? The festive character of the Sunday eucharist expresses the joy that Christ communicates to his church through the gift of the Spirit. Joy is precisely one of the fruits of the Holy Spirit (cf. Romans 14:17; Galatians 5:22).

57. Therefore, if we wish to rediscover the full meaning of Sunday, we must rediscover this aspect of the life of faith. Certainly, Christian joy must mark the whole of life, and not just one day of the week. But in virtue of its significance as *the day of the Risen Lord*, celebrating God's work of creation and "new creation," Sunday is the day of joy in a very special way, indeed the day most suitable for learning how to rejoice and to rediscover the true nature and deep roots of joy. This joy should never be confused with shallow feelings of satisfaction and pleasure, which inebriate the senses and emotions for a brief moment, but then leave the heart unfulfilled and perhaps even embittered. In the Christian view, joy is much more enduring and consoling; as the saints attest, it can hold firm even in the dark night of suffering.[103] It is, in a certain sense, a virtue to be nurtured.

58. Yet there is no conflict whatever between Christian joy and true human joys, which in fact are exalted and find their ultimate foundation precisely in the joy of the glorified Christ, the perfect image and revelation of humanity as God intended. As my revered predecessor Paul VI wrote in his Exhortation on Christian joy: "In essence, Christian joy is a sharing in the unfathomable joy, at

once divine and human, found in the heart of the glorified Christ."[104] Pope Paul concluded his Exhortation by asking that, on the Lord's Day, the church should witness powerfully to the joy experienced by the apostles when they saw the Lord on the evening of Easter. To this end, he urged pastors to insist

> upon the need for the baptized to celebrate the Sunday eucharist in joy. How could they neglect this encounter, this banquet which Christ prepares for us in his love? May our sharing in it be most worthy and joyful! It is Christ, crucified and glorified, who comes among his disciples, to lead them all together into the newness of his resurrection. This is the climax, here below, of the covenant of love between God and his people: the sign and source of Christian joy, a stage on the way to the eternal feast.[105]

This vision of faith shows the Christian Sunday to be a true "time for celebration," a day given by God to men and women for their full human and spiritual growth.

THE FULFILLMENT OF THE SABBATH

59.   This aspect of the Christian Sunday shows in a special way how it is the fulfillment of the Old Testament Sabbath. On the Lord's Day, which—as we have already said—the Old Testament links to the work of creation (cf. Genesis 2:1–3; Exodus 20:8–11) and the Exodus (cf. Deuteronomy 5:12–15), the Christian is called to proclaim the new creation and the new covenant brought about in the paschal mystery of Christ. Far from being abolished, the celebration of creation becomes more profound within a Christocentric perspective, being seen in the light of the God's plan "to unite all things in [Christ], things in heaven and things on earth" (Ephesians 1:10). The remembrance of the liberation of the Exodus also assumes its full meaning as it becomes a remembrance of the universal redemption accomplished by Christ in his death and resurrection. More than a "replacement" for the Sabbath, therefore, Sunday is its fulfillment, and in a certain sense its extension and full expression in the ordered unfolding of the history of salvation, which reaches its culmination in Christ.

60.   In this perspective, the biblical theology of the Sabbath can be recovered in full, without compromising the Christian character of Sunday. It is a theology which leads us ever anew and in unfailing awe to the mystery of the beginning, when the eternal Word of God, by a free decision of love, created the world from nothing. The work of creation was sealed by the blessing and consecration of the day on which God ceased "from all the work which he had done in creation" (Genesis 2:3). This day of God's rest confers meaning upon time, which in the sequence of weeks assumes not only a chronological regularity but also, in a manner of speaking, a theological resonance. The constant return of the *shabbat* ensures that there is no risk of time being closed in upon itself, since, in welcoming God and his *kairoi*—the moments of his grace and his saving acts—time remains open to eternity.

61.   As the seventh day blessed and consecrated by God, the *shabbat* concludes the whole work of creation and is therefore immediately linked to the work of the sixth day, when God made man and woman "in his image and likeness" (cf.

Genesis 1:26). This very close connection between the "day of God" and the "day of humanity" did not escape the Fathers in their meditation on the biblical creation story. Saint Ambrose says in this regard:

> Thanks, then, to the Lord our God who accomplished a work in which he might find rest. He made the heavens, but I do not read that he found rest there; he made the stars, the moon, the sun, and neither do I read that he found rest in them. I read instead that he made man and woman and that then he rested, finding in them those to whom he could offer the forgiveness of sins.[106]

Thus there will be for ever a direct link between the "day of God" and the "day of humanity." When the divine commandment declares: "Remember the Sabbath day in order to keep it holy" (Exodus 20:8), the rest decreed in order to honor the day dedicated to God is not at all a burden imposed upon men and women, but rather an aid to help them to recognize their life-giving and liberating dependence upon the Creator, and at the same time their calling to cooperate in the Creator's work and to receive his grace. In honoring God's "rest," men and women fully discover themselves, and thus the Lord's Day bears the profound imprint of God's blessing (cf. Genesis 2:3), by virtue of which, we might say, it is endowed in a way similar to the animals and to humanity itself, with a kind of "fruitfulness" (cf. Genesis 1:22, 28). This fruitfulness is apparent above all in filling and, in a certain sense, "multiplying" time itself, deepening in men and women the joy of living and the desire to foster and communicate life.

62.   It is the duty of Christians therefore to remember that although the practices of the Jewish Sabbath are gone, surpassed as they are by the fulfillment that Sunday brings, the underlying reasons for keeping the Lord's Day holy—inscribed solemnly in the Ten Commandments—remain valid, though they need to be reinterpreted in the light of the theology and spirituality of Sunday:

> Remember the Sabbath day to keep it holy, as the LORD your God commanded you. Six days you shall labor, and do all your work; but the seventh day is a Sabbath to the LORD your God. Then you shall do no work, you, or your son, or your daughter, or your servant, or your maid, or your ox, or your ass, or any of your beasts, or the foreigner within your gates, that your servant and maid may rest as well as you. You shall remember that you were a servant in the land of Egypt, and the LORD your God brought you out from there with a mighty hand and an outstretched arm. Therefore the LORD your God commanded that you keep the Sabbath day. (Deuteronomy 5:12–15)

Here the Sabbath observance is closely linked with the liberation which God accomplished for his people.

63.   Christ came to accomplish a new "exodus," to restore freedom to the oppressed. He performed many healings on the Sabbath (cf. Matthew 12:9–14 and parallels), certainly not to violate the Lord's Day, but to reveal its full meaning: "The Sabbath was made for people, not people for the Sabbath" (Mark 2:27). Opposing the excessively legalistic interpretation of some of his contemporaries

and developing the true meaning of the biblical Sabbath, Jesus, as "Lord of the Sabbath" (Mark 2:28), restores to the Sabbath observance its liberating character, carefully safeguarding the rights of God and the rights of human beings. This is why Christians, called as they are to proclaim the liberation won by the blood of Christ, felt that they had the authority to transfer the meaning of the Sabbath to the day of the resurrection. The passover of Christ has in fact liberated human beings from a slavery more radical than any weighing upon an oppressed people—the slavery of sin, which alienates us from God, and alienates us from our very selves and from others, constantly sowing within history the seeds of evil and violence.

THE DAY OF REST

64.   For several centuries, Christians observed Sunday simply as a day of worship, without being able to give it the specific meaning of Sabbath rest. Only in the fourth century did the civil law of the Roman Empire recognize the weekly recurrence, determining that on "the day of the sun" the judges, the people of the cities and the various trade corporations would not work.[107] Christians rejoiced to see thus removed the obstacles which until then had sometimes made observance of the Lord's Day heroic. They could now devote themselves to prayer in common without hindrance.[108]

It would therefore be wrong to see in this legislation of the rhythm of the week a mere historical circumstance with no special significance for the church and which she could simply set aside. Even after the fall of the Empire, the Councils did not cease to insist upon the arrangements regarding Sunday rest. In countries where Christians are in the minority and where the festive days of the calendar do not coincide with Sunday, it is still Sunday that remains the Lord's Day, the day on which the faithful come together for the eucharistic assembly. But this involves real sacrifices. For Christians it is not normal that Sunday, the day of joyful celebration, should not also be a day of rest, and it is difficult for them to keep Sunday holy if they do not have enough free time.

65.   By contrast, the link between the Lord's Day and the day of rest in civil society has a meaning and importance that go beyond the distinctly Christian point of view. The alternation between work and rest, built into human nature, is willed by God himself, as appears in the creation story in the Book of Genesis (cf. 2:2–3; Exodus 20:8–11): Rest is something sacred, because it is a way for men and women to withdraw from the sometimes excessively demanding cycle of earthly tasks in order to renew an awareness that everything is the work of God. There is a risk that the prodigious power over creation which God gives to human beings can lead them to forget that God is the Creator upon whom everything depends. It is all the more urgent to recognize this dependence in our own time, when science and technology have so incredibly increased the power that men and women exercise through their work.

66.   Finally, it should not be forgotten that even in our own day work is very oppressive for many people, either because of miserable working conditions and long hours—especially in the poorer regions of the world—or because of

the persistence in economically more developed societies of too many cases of injustice and exploitation. When, through the centuries, she has made laws concerning Sunday rest,[109] the church has had in mind above all the work of servants and workers, certainly not because this work was any less worthy when compared to the spiritual requirements of Sunday observance, but rather because it needed greater regulation to lighten its burden and thus enable everyone to keep the Lord's Day holy. In this matter, my predecessor Pope Leo XIII in his encyclical *Rerum Novarum* spoke of Sunday rest as a worker's right which the State must guarantee.[110]

In our own historical context there remains the obligation to ensure that everyone can enjoy the freedom, rest and relaxation that human dignity requires, together with the associated religious, family, cultural and interpersonal needs that are difficult to meet if there is no guarantee of at least one day of the week on which people can *both* rest and celebrate. Naturally, this right of workers to rest presupposes their right to work and, as we reflect on the question of the Christian understanding of Sunday, we cannot but recall with a deep sense of solidarity the hardship of countless men and women who, because of the lack of jobs, are forced to remain inactive on workdays as well.

67.   Through Sunday rest, daily concerns and tasks can find their proper perspective: The material things about which we worry give way to spiritual values; in a moment of encounter and less pressured exchange, we see the true face of the people with whom we live. Even the beauties of nature—too often marred by the desire to exploit, which turns against us—can be rediscovered and enjoyed to the full. As the day on which people are at peace with God, with themselves and with others, Sunday becomes a moment when people can look anew upon the wonders of nature, allowing themselves to be caught up in that marvelous and mysterious harmony which, in the words of Saint Ambrose, weds the many elements of the cosmos in a "bond of communion and peace" by "an inviolable law of concord and love."[111] Men and women then come to a deeper sense, as the apostle says, that "everything created by God is good and nothing is to be rejected if it is received with thanksgiving, for then it is consecrated by the word of God and prayer" (1 Timothy 4:4–5). If after six days of work—reduced in fact to five for many—people look for time to relax and to pay more attention to other aspects of their lives, this corresponds to an authentic need which is in full harmony with the vision of the gospel message. Believers are therefore called to satisfy this need in a way consistent with the manifestation of their personal and community faith, as expressed in the celebration and sanctification of the Lord's Day.

Therefore, also in the particular circumstances of our own time, Christians will naturally strive to ensure that civil legislation respects their duty to keep Sunday holy. In any case, they are obliged in conscience to arrange their Sunday rest in a way that allows them to take part in the eucharist, refraining from work and activities that are incompatible with the sanctification of the Lord's Day, with its characteristic joy and necessary rest for spirit and body.[112]

68.   In order that rest may not degenerate into emptiness or boredom, it must offer spiritual enrichment, greater freedom, opportunities for contemplation and fraternal communion. Therefore, among the forms of culture and entertainment that society offers, the faithful should choose those that are most in keeping with a life lived in obedience to the precepts of the Gospel. Sunday rest then becomes prophetic, affirming not only the absolute primacy of God, but also the primacy and dignity of the person with respect to the demands of social and economic life, and anticipating in a certain sense the "new heavens and the new earth," in which liberation from slavery to needs will be final and complete. In short, the Lord's Day thus becomes in the truest sense *the day of humanity* as well.

A DAY OF SOLIDARITY

69.   Sunday should also give the faithful an opportunity to devote themselves to works of mercy, charity and apostolate. To experience the joy of the Risen Lord deep within is to share fully the love that pulses in his heart: There is no joy without love! Jesus himself explains this, linking the "new commandment" with the gift of joy: "If you keep my commandments, you will remain in my love, just as I have kept the Father's commandments and remain in his love. I have told you this that my own joy may be in you and your joy may be complete. This is my commandment: that you love one another as I have loved you" (John 15:10–12).

      The Sunday eucharist, therefore, not only does not absolve the faithful from the duties of charity, but on the contrary commits them even more "to all the works of charity, of mercy, of apostolic outreach, by means of which it is seen that the faithful of Christ are not of this world and yet are the light of the world, giving glory to the Father in the midst of the people."[113]

70.   Ever since apostolic times, the Sunday gathering has in fact been for Christians a moment of fraternal sharing with the very poor. "On the first day of the week, each of you is to put aside and save whatever extra you earn" (1 Corinthians 16:2), says Saint Paul, referring to the collection organized for the poor churches of Judaea. In the Sunday eucharist, the believing heart opens wide to embrace all aspects of the church. But the full range of the apostolic summons needs to be accepted: Far from trying to create a narrow "gift" mentality, Paul calls rather for a demanding *culture of sharing*, to be lived not only among the members of the community itself but also in society as a whole.[114] More than ever, we need to listen once again to the stern warning that Paul addresses to the community at Corinth, guilty of having humiliated the poor in the fraternal *agape* which accompanied "the Lord's Supper": "When you meet together, it is not the Lord's Supper that you eat. For in eating, each one goes ahead with his own meal, and one is hungry and another is drunk. What! Do you not have houses to eat and drink in? Or do you despise the church of God and humiliate those who have nothing?" (1 Corinthians 11:20–22). James is equally forceful in what he writes: "If a man with gold rings and in fine clothing

comes into your assembly and a poor man in shabby clothing also comes in, and you pay attention to the one who wears the fine clothing and say, 'Take a seat here, please,' while you say to the poor man, 'Stand there,' or, 'Sit at my feet,' have you not made distinctions among yourselves, and become judges with evil thoughts?" (2:2–4).

71.   The teachings of the apostles struck a sympathetic chord from the earliest centuries, and evoked strong echoes in the preaching of the Fathers of the church. Saint Ambrose addressed words of fire to the rich who presumed to fulfill their religious obligations by attending church without sharing their goods with the poor, and who perhaps even exploited them: "You who are rich, do you hear what the Lord God says? Yet you come into church not to give to the poor but to take instead."[115] Saint John Chrysostom is no less demanding:

> Do you wish to honor the body of Christ? Do not ignore him when he is naked. Do not pay him homage in the temple clad in silk only then to neglect him outside where he suffers cold and nakedness. He who said: "This is my body," is the same One who said: "You saw me hungry and you gave me no food," and "Whatever you did to the least of my brothers you did also to me." . . . What good is it if the eucharistic table is overloaded with golden chalices, when he is dying of hunger? Start by satisfying his hunger, and then with what is left you may adorn the altar as well.[116]

These words effectively remind the Christian community of the duty to make the eucharist the place where fraternity becomes practical solidarity, where the last are the first in the minds and attention of the brothers and sisters, where Christ himself—through the generous gifts of the rich to the very poor—may somehow prolong in time the miracle of the multiplication of the loaves.[117]

72.   The eucharist is an event and program of true brotherhood. From the Sunday Mass there flows a tide of charity destined to spread into the whole life of the faithful, beginning by inspiring the very way in which they live the rest of Sunday. If Sunday is a day of joy, Christians should declare by their actual behavior that we cannot be happy "on our own." They look around to find people who may need their help. It may be that in their neighborhood or among those they know there are sick people, elderly people, children or immigrants, who precisely on Sundays feel more keenly their isolation, need and suffering. It is true that commitment to these people cannot be restricted to occasional Sunday gestures. But presuming a wider sense of commitment, why not make the Lord's Day a more intense time of sharing, encouraging all the inventiveness of which Christian charity is capable? Inviting to a meal people who are alone, visiting the sick, providing food for needy families, spending a few hours in voluntary work and acts of solidarity—these would certainly be ways of bringing into people's lives the love of Christ received at the eucharistic table.

73.   Lived in this way, not only the Sunday eucharist but the whole of Sunday becomes a great school of charity, justice and peace. The presence of the Risen Lord in the midst of his people becomes an undertaking of solidarity, a compelling force for inner renewal, an inspiration to change the structures of sin in

which individuals, communities and at times entire peoples are entangled. Far from being an escape, the Christian Sunday is a prophecy inscribed on time itself, a prophecy obliging the faithful to follow in the footsteps of the One who came "to preach good news to the poor, to proclaim release to captives and new sight to the blind, to set at liberty those who are oppressed, and to proclaim the acceptable year of the Lord" (Luke 4:18–19). In the Sunday commemoration of Easter, believers learn from Christ, and remembering his promise, "I leave you peace, my peace I give you" (John 14:27), they become in their turn *builders of peace*.

CHAPTER V
DIES DIERUM
SUNDAY: THE PRIMORDIAL FEAST,
REVEALING THE MEANING OF TIME

CHRIST THE ALPHA AND OMEGA OF TIME

74. In Christianity time has a fundamental importance. Within the dimension of time the world was created; within it the history of salvation unfolds, finding its culmination in the "fullness of time" of the Incarnation, and its goal in the glorious return of the Son of God at the end of time. In Jesus Christ, the Word made flesh, time becomes a dimension of God, who is himself eternal.[118]

In the light of the New Testament, the years of Christ's earthly life truly constitute the *center of time*; this center reaches its apex in the resurrection. It is true that Jesus is God made human from the very moment of his conception in the womb of the Blessed Virgin, but only in the resurrection is his humanity wholly transfigured and glorified, thus revealing the fullness of his divine identity and glory. In his speech in the synagogue at Antioch in Pisidia (cf. Acts 13:33), Paul applies the words of Psalm 2 to the resurrection of Christ: "You are my son, this day I have begotten you" (v. 7). It is precisely for this reason that, in celebrating the Easter Vigil, the church acclaims the risen Christ as "the Beginning and End, the Alpha and Omega." These are the words spoken by the celebrant as he prepares the paschal candle, which bears the number of the current year. These words clearly attest that "Christ is the Lord of time; he is its beginning and its end; every year, every day and every moment are embraced by his incarnation and resurrection, and thus become part of the 'fullness of time.'"[119]

75. Since Sunday is the weekly Easter, recalling and making present the day upon which Christ rose from the dead, it is also the day that reveals the meaning of time. It has nothing in common with the cosmic cycles according to which natural religion and human culture tend to impose a structure on time, succumbing perhaps to the myth of eternal return. The Christian Sunday is wholly other! Springing from the resurrection, it cuts through human time, the months, the years, the centuries, like a directional arrow that points them toward their target: Christ's Second Coming. Sunday foreshadows the last day, the day of the *Parousia*, which in a way is already anticipated by Christ's glory in the event of the resurrection.

In fact, everything that will happen until the end of the world will be no more than an extension and unfolding of what happened on the day when the battered body of the crucified Lord was raised by the power of the Spirit and became in turn the wellspring of the Spirit for all humanity. Christians know that there is no need to wait for another time of salvation, since, however long the world may last, they are already living in *the last times.* Not only the church, but the cosmos itself and history are ceaselessly ruled and governed by the glorified Christ. It is this life-force that propels creation, "groaning in birth-pangs until now" (Romans 8:22), toward the goal of its full redemption. Human-kind can have only a faint intuition of this process, but Christians have the key and the certainty. Keeping Sunday holy is the important witness that they are called to bear, so that every stage of human history will be upheld by hope.

SUNDAY IN THE LITURGICAL YEAR

76. With its weekly recurrence, the Lord's Day is rooted in the most ancient tradition of the church and is vitally important for the Christian. But there was another rhythm that soon established itself: *the annual liturgical cycle.* Human psychology in fact desires the celebration of anniversaries, associating the return of dates and seasons with the remembrance of past events. When these events are decisive in the life of a people, their celebration generally creates a festive atmosphere that breaks the monotony of daily routine.

Now, by God's design, the great saving events upon which the church's life is founded were closely linked to the annual Jewish feasts of Passover and Pentecost, and were prophetically foreshadowed in them. Since the second century, the annual celebration of Easter by Christians—having been added to the weekly Easter celebration—allowed a more ample meditation on the mystery of Christ crucified and risen. Preceded by a preparatory fast, celebrated in the course of a long vigil, extended into the fifty days leading to Pentecost, the feast of Easter—"solemnity of solemnities"—became the day *par excellence* for the initiation of catechumens. Through baptism they die to sin and rise to a new life because Jesus "was put to death for our sins and raised for our justification" (Romans 4:25; cf. 6:3–11). Intimately connected to the paschal mystery, the solemnity of Pentecost takes on special importance, celebrating as it does the coming of the Holy Spirit upon the apostles gathered with Mary and inaugurating the mission to all peoples.[120]

77. A similar commemorative logic guided the arrangement of the entire liturgical year. As the Second Vatican Council recalls, the church wished to extend throughout the year

> the entire mystery of Christ, from the Incarnation and Nativity to the Ascension, to the day of Pentecost and to the waiting in blessed hope for the return of the Lord. Remembering in this way the mysteries of redemption, the church opens to the faithful the treasury of the Lord's power and merits, making them present in some sense to all times, so that the faithful may approach them and be filled by them with the grace of salvation.[121]

After Easter and Pentecost, the most solemn celebration is undoubtedly the Nativity of the Lord, when Christians ponder the mystery of the incarnation and contemplate the Word of God who deigns to assume our humanity in order to give us a share in his divinity.

78.   Likewise, "in celebrating this annual cycle of the mysteries of Christ, the holy church venerates with special love the Blessed Virgin Mary, Mother of God, united forever with the saving work of her Son."[122] In a similar way, by inserting into the annual cycle the commemoration of the martyrs and other saints on the occasion of their anniversaries, "the church proclaims the Easter mystery of the saints who suffered with Christ and with him are now glorified."[123] When celebrated in the true spirit of the liturgy, the commemoration of the saints does not obscure the centrality of Christ, but on the contrary extols it, demonstrating as it does the power of the redemption wrought by him. As Saint Paulinus of Nola sings, "All things pass, but the glory of the saints endures in Christ, who renews all things, while he himself remains unchanged."[124] The intrinsic relationship between the glory of the saints and that of Christ is built into the very arrangement of the liturgical year, and is expressed most eloquently in the fundamental and sovereign character of Sunday as the Lord's Day. Following the seasons of the liturgical year in the Sunday observance which structures it from beginning to end, the ecclesial and spiritual commitment of Christians comes to be profoundly anchored in Christ, in whom believers find their reason for living and from whom they draw sustenance and inspiration.

79.   Sunday emerges therefore as the natural model for understanding and celebrating these feast days of the liturgical year, which are of such value for the Christian life that the church has chosen to emphasize their importance by making it obligatory for the faithful to attend Mass and to observe a time of rest, even though these feast days may fall on variable days of the week.[125] Their number has been changed from time to time, taking into account social and economic conditions, and also how firmly they are established in tradition, and how well they are supported by civil legislation.[126]

The present canonical and liturgical provisions allow each episcopal conference, because of particular circumstances in one country or another, to reduce the list of holy days of obligation. Any decision in this regard needs to receive the special approval of the Apostolic See,[127] and in such cases the celebration of a mystery of the Lord, such as the Epiphany, the Ascension or the Solemnity of the Body and Blood of Christ, must be transferred to Sunday, in accordance with liturgical norms, so that the faithful are not denied the chance to meditate upon the mystery.[128] Pastors should also take care to encourage the faithful to attend Mass on other important feast days celebrated during the week.[129]

80.   There is a need for special pastoral attention to the many situations where there is a risk that the popular and cultural traditions of a region may intrude upon the celebration of Sundays and other liturgical feast days, mingling the spirit of genuine Christian faith with elements that are foreign to it and may distort it. In such cases, catechesis and well-chosen pastoral initiatives need to

clarify these situations, eliminating all that is incompatible with the gospel of Christ. At the same time, it should not be forgotten that these traditions—and, by analogy, some recent cultural initiatives in civil society—often embody values that are not difficult to integrate with the demands of faith. It rests with the discernment of pastors to preserve the genuine values found in the culture of a particular social context and especially in popular piety, so that liturgical celebration—above all on Sundays and holy days—does not suffer but rather may actually benefit.[130]

CONCLUSION

81.   The spiritual and pastoral riches of Sunday, as it has been handed on to us by tradition, are truly great. When its significance and implications are understood in their entirety, Sunday in a way becomes a synthesis of the Christian life and a condition for living it well. It is clear therefore why the observance of the Lord's Day is so close to the church's heart, and why in the church's discipline it remains a real obligation. Yet more than as a precept, the observance should be seen as a need rising from the depths of Christian life. It is crucially important that all the faithful should be convinced that they cannot live their faith or share fully in the life of the Christian community unless they take part regularly in the Sunday eucharistic assembly. The eucharist is the full realization of the worship which humanity owes to God, and it cannot be compared to any other religious experience. A particularly efficacious expression of this is the Sunday gathering of the entire community, obedient to the voice of the Risen Lord who calls the faithful together to give them the light of his word and the nourishment of his Body as the perennial sacramental wellspring of redemption. The grace flowing from this wellspring renews humankind, life and history.

82.   It is with this strong conviction of faith, and with awareness of the heritage of human values that the observance of Sunday entails, that Christians today must face the enticements of a culture that has accepted the benefits of rest and free time, but that often uses them frivolously and is at times attracted by morally questionable forms of entertainment. Certainly, Christians are no different from other people in enjoying the weekly day of rest; but at the same time they are keenly aware of the uniqueness and originality of Sunday, the day on which they are called to celebrate their salvation and the salvation of all humanity. Sunday is the day of joy and the day of rest precisely because it is the Lord's Day, the day of the risen Lord.

83.   Understood and lived in this fashion, Sunday in a way becomes the soul of the other days, and in this sense we can recall the insight of Origen that the perfect Christian "is always in the Lord's Day, and is always celebrating Sunday."[131] Sunday is a true school, an enduring program of church pedagog—an irreplaceable pedagogy, especially with social conditions now marked more and more by a fragmentation and cultural pluralism that constantly test the fidelity of individual Christians to the practical demands of their faith. In many parts of the world, we see a "diaspora" Christianity, which is put to the test because

the scattered disciples of Christ can no longer easily maintain contact with one another, and lack the support of the structures and traditions proper to Christian culture. In a situation of such difficulty, the opportunity to come together on Sundays with fellow believers, exchanging gifts of brotherhood, is an indispensable help.

84.   Sustaining Christian life as it does, Sunday has the additional value of being a testimony and a proclamation. As a day of prayer, communion and joy, Sunday resounds throughout society, emanating vital energies and reasons for hope. Sunday is the proclamation that time, in which he who is the Risen Lord of history makes his home, is not the grave of our illusions but the cradle of an ever new future, an opportunity given to us to turn the fleeting moments of this life into seeds of eternity. Sunday is an invitation to look ahead; it is the day on which the Christian community cries out to Christ, "*Marana tha:* Come, O Lord!" (1 Corinthians 16:22). With this cry of hope and expectation, the church is the companion and support of human hope. From Sunday to Sunday, enlightened by Christ, she goes forward toward the unending Sunday of the heavenly Jerusalem, which "has no need of the sun or moon to shine upon it, for the glory of God is its light and its lamp is the Lamb" (Revelation 21:23).

85.   As she strains toward her goal, the church is sustained and enlivened by the Spirit. It is he who awakens memory and makes present for every generation of believers the event of the resurrection. He is the inward gift uniting us to the Risen Lord and to our brothers and sisters in the intimacy of a single body, reviving our faith, filling our hearts with charity and renewing our hope. The Spirit is unfailingly present to every one of the church's days, appearing unpredictably and lavishly with the wealth of his gifts. But it is in the Sunday gathering for the weekly celebration of Easter that the church listens to the Spirit in a special way and reaches out with him to Christ in the ardent desire that he return in glory: "The Spirit and the Bride say, 'Come!'" (Revelation 22:17). Precisely in consideration of the role of the Spirit, I have wished that this exhortation aimed at rediscovering the meaning of Sunday should appear in this year which, in the immediate preparation for the Jubilee, is dedicated to the Holy Spirit.

86.   I entrust this Apostolic Letter to the intercession of the Blessed Virgin, that it may be received and put into practice by the Christian community. Without in any way detracting from the centrality of Christ and his Spirit, Mary is always present in the church's Sunday. It is the mystery of Christ itself which demands this: Indeed, how could she who is *Mater Domini* and *Mater Ecclesiae* fail to be uniquely present on the day which is both *dies Domini* and *dies Ecclesiae?*

As they listen to the word proclaimed in the Sunday assembly, the faithful look to the Virgin Mary, learning from her to keep it and ponder it in their hearts (cf. Luke 2:19). With Mary, they learn to stand at the foot of the cross, offering to the Father the sacrifice of Christ and joining to it the offering of their own lives. With Mary, they experience the joy of the resurrection, making their own the words of the Magnificat, which extol the inexhaustible gift of divine mercy in the inexorable flow of time: "His mercy is from age to age upon those who fear him" (Luke 1:50). From Sunday to Sunday, the pilgrim people follow in the footsteps of Mary, and her maternal intercession gives special power and fervor to the prayer that rises from the church to the most holy Trinity.

87. Dear brothers and sisters, the imminence of the Jubilee invites us to a deeper spiritual and pastoral commitment. Indeed, this is its true purpose. In the Jubilee year, much will be done to give it the particular stamp demanded by the ending of the second millennium and the beginning of the third since the incarnation of the Word of God. But this year and this special time will pass, as we look to other jubilees and other solemn events. As the weekly solemnity, however, Sunday will continue to shape the time of the church's pilgrimage, until that Sunday which will know no evening.

Therefore, dear brother bishops and priests, I urge you to work tirelessly with the faithful to ensure that the value of this sacred day is understood and lived ever more deeply. This will bear rich fruit in Christian communities, and will not fail to have a positive influence on civil society as a whole.

In coming to know the church, which every Sunday joyfully celebrates the mystery from which she draws her life, may the men and women of the third millennium come to know the risen Christ. And constantly renewed by the weekly commemoration of Easter, may Christ's disciples be ever more credible in proclaiming the gospel of salvation and ever more effective in building the civilization of love.

My blessing to you all!

From the Vatican, on 31 May, the Solemnity of Pentecost, in the year 1998, the twentieth of my pontificate.

NOTES

1. Cf. Revelation 1:10: *"Kyriake heméra"*; cf. also the *Didache* 14, 1; Saint Ignatius of Antioch, *To the Magnesians* 9, 1–2; SCh 10, 88–89.

2. Pseudo-Eusebius of Alexandria, *Sermon* 16: PG 86, 416.

3. *In Die Dominica Paschae II,* 52: CCL 78, 550.

4. SC, 106.

5. *Ibid.*

6. Cf. Motu Proprio *Mysterii Paschalis* (14 February 1969): AAS 61 (1969), 222–226.

7. Cf. Pastoral Note of the Italian Episcopal Conference *"Il giorno del Signore"* (15 July 1984), 5: *Enchiridion* CEI 3, 1398.

8. SC, 106.

9. Homily for the Solemn Inauguration of the Pontificate (22 October 1978), 5: AAS 70 (1978), 947.

10. *Laborem excercens,* 25: AAS 73 (1981), 639.

11. GS, 34.

12. For our Jewish brothers and sisters, a "nuptial" spirituality characterizes the Sabbath, as appears, for example, in texts of *Genesis Rabbah* such as X, 9 and XI, 8 (cf. J. Neusner, *Genesis Rabbah,* Atlanta: 1985, vol. I, pp. 107, 117). The song *Leka Dôdi* is also nuptial in tone: "Your God will delight in you, as the Bridegroom delights in the Bride . . . In the midst of the faithful of your beloved people, come O Bride, O Shabbat Queen" (cf. *Preghiera serale del sabato,* Rome: A. Toaff, 1968–69, p. 3).

13. Cf. A. J. Heschel, *The Sabbath: Its Meaning for Modern Man* (22nd ed., 1995), pp. 3–24.

14. *"Verum autem sabbatum ipsum redemptorem nostrum Iesum Christum Dominum habemus"*: *Epist.* 13, 1: CCL 140A, 992.

15. *Ep. ad Decentium* XXV, 4, 7: PL 20, 555.

16. *Homiliae in Hexaemeron* II, 8: SCh 26, 184.

17. Cf. *In Io. Ev. Tractatus* XX, 20, 2: CCL 36, 203; *Epist.* 55, 2: CSEL 34, 170–171.

18. The reference to the resurrection is especially clear in Russian, which calls Sunday simply "Resurrection" *(Voskresenie).*

19. *Epist.* 10, 96, 7.

20. Cf. *ibid.* In reference to Pliny's letter, Tertullian also recalls the *coetus antelucani in Apologeticum* 2, 6: CCL 1, 88; *De Corona* 3, 3: CCL 2, 1043.

21. *To the Magnesians* 9, 1–2: SCh 10, 88–89.

22. *Sermon 8 in the Octave of Easter* 4: PL 46, 841. This sense of Sunday as the first day is clear in the Latin liturgical calendar, where Monday is called *feria secunda,* Tuesday *feria tertia* and so on. In Portuguese, the days are named in the same way.

23. Saint Gregory of Nyssa, *De Castigatione:* PG 46, 309. The Maronite liturgy also stresses the link between the Sabbath and Sunday, beginning with the "mystery of Holy Saturday" (cf. M. Hayek, *Maronite [Eglise], Dictionnaire de spiritualité,* [1980] X, 632–644).

24. RBaptC, 9; cf. RCIA, 59.

25. Cf. RomM, Rite of Blessing and Sprinkling of Holy Water.

26. Cf. Saint Basil, *On the Holy Spirit,* 27, 66: SCh 17, 484–485. Cf. also *Letter of Barnabas* 15, 8–9: SC 172, 186–189; Saint Justin, *Dialogue with Trypho* 24, 138: PG 6, 528, 793; Origen, *Commentary on the Psalms,* Psalm 118 (119), 1: PG 12, 1588.

27. *"Domine, praestitisti nobis pacem quietis, pacem sabbati, pacemsine vespera"*: *Confess.,* 13, 50: CCL 27, 272.

28. Cf. Saint Augustine, *Epist.* 55, 17: CSEL 34, 188: *"Ita ergo erit octavus, qui primus, ut prima vita sed aeterna reddatur."*

29. Thus in English "Sunday" and in German *"Sonntag."*

30. *Apologia* I, 67: PG 6, 430.

31. Cf. Saint Maximus of Turin, *Sermo* 44, 1: CCL 23, 178; *Sermo* 53, 2: CCL 23, 219; Eusebius of Caesarea, *Comm. in Ps.* 91: PG 23, 1169–1173.

32. See, for example, the hymn of the Office of Readings: *"Dies aetasque ceteris octava splendet sanctior in te quam, Iesu, consecras primitiae surgentium"* (Week I); and also: *"Salve dies, dierum gloria, dies felix Christi victoria, dies digna iugi laetitia dies prima. Lux divina caecis irradiat, in qua Christus infernum spoliat, mortem vincit et reconciliat summis ima"* (Week II). Similar expressions are found in hymns included in the Liturgy of the Hours in various modern languages.

33. Cf. Clement of Alexandria, *Stromata*, VI, 138, 1–2: PG 9, 364.

34. Cf. John Paul II, Encyclical Letter *Dominum et Vivificantem* (18 May 1986), 22–26: AAS 78 (1986), 829–837.

35. Cf. Saint Athanasius of Alexandria, *Sunday Letters* 1, 10: PG 26, 1366.

36. Cf. Bardesanes, *Dialogue on Destiny*, 46: PS 2, 606–607.

37. SC, Appendix: Declaration on the Reform of the Calendar.

38. Cf. LG, 9.

39. Cf. John Paul II, Letter *Dominicae Cenae* (24 February 1980), 4: AAS 72 (1980), 120; Encyclical Letter *Dominum et Vivificantem* (18 May 1986), 62–64: AAS 78 (1986), 889–894.

40. Cf. John Paul II, VQA, 9: AAS 81 (1989), 905–906.

41. CCC, 2177.

42. Cf. John Paul II, VQA 9: AAS 81 (1989), 905–906.

43. SC, 41; cf. CD, 15.

44. These are the words of the embolism, formulated in this or similar ways in some of the eucharistic prayers of the different languages. They stress powerfully the paschal character of Sunday.

45. Cf. Congregation for the Doctrine of the Faith, Letter to the Bishops of the Catholic Church on Certain Aspects of the Church as Communion *Communionis Notio* (28 May 1992), 11–14: AAS 85 (1993), 844–847.

46. *Speech to the Third Group of the Bishops of the United States of America* (17 March 1998), 4: *L'Osservatore Romano*, 18 March 1998, 4.

47. SC, 42.

48. EM, 26: AAS 59 (1967), 555.

49. Cf. Saint Cyprian, *De Orat. Dom.* 23: PL 4, 553; *De Cath. Eccl. Unitate*, 7: CSEL 31, 215; LG, 4; SC, 26.

50. Cf. John Paul II, Apostolic Exhortation *Familiaris Consortio* (22 November 1981), 57, 61: AAS 74 (1982), 151, 154.

51. Cf. DMC: AAS 66 (1974), 30–46.

52. Cf. EM, 26: AAS 59 (1967), 555–556; Sacred Congregation for Bishops, Directory for the Pastoral Ministry of Bishops *Ecclesiae Imago* (22 February 1973), 86c: *Enchiridion Vaticanum* 4, 2071.

53. Cf. John Paul II, Post-Synodal Apostolic Exhortation *Christifideles Laici* (30 December 1988), 30: AAS 81 (1989), 446–447.

54. Cf. Sacred Congregation for Divine Worship, Instruction *Masses for Particular Groups* (15 May 1969), 10: AAS 61 (1969), 810.

55. Cf. LG, 48–51.

56. *"Haec est vita nostra, ut desiderando exerceamur"*: Saint Augustine, *In Prima Ioan. Tract.* 4, 6: SCh 75, 232.

57. RomM, embolism after the Lord's Prayer.

58. GS, 1.

59. LG, 1; cf. John Paul II, Encyclical Letter *Dominum et Vivificantem* (18 May 1986), 61–64: AAS 78 (1986), 888–894.

60. SC, 7; cf. 33.

61. *Ibid.*, 56; cf. *Ordo Lectionum Missae, Praenotanda*, 10.

62. SC, 51.

63. Cf. *ibid.*, 52; CIC, c. 767, 2; CCEC, c. 614.

64. Apostolic Constitution *Missale Romanum* (3 April 1969): AAS 61 (1969), 220.

65. The Council's Constitution *Sacrosanctum Concilium* speaks of *"suavis et vivus Sacrae Scripturae affectus"* (24).

66. John Paul II, Letter *Dominicae Cenae* (24 February 1980), 10: AAS 72 (1980), 135.

67. Cf. DV, 25.

68. Cf. *Ordo Lectionum Missae, Praenotanda*, Chap. III.

69. Cf. *Ordo Lectionum Missae, Praenotanda*, Chap. I, 6.

70. Ecumenical Council of Trent, Session XXII, Doctrine and Canons on the Most Holy Sacrifice of the Mass, II: DS 1743; cf. CCC, 1366.

71. CCC, 1368.

72. EM, 3b: AAS 59 (1967), 541; cf. Pius XII, Encyclical Letter *Mediator Dei* (20 November 1947), II: AAS 39 (1947), 564–566.

73. Cf. CCC, 1385; cf. also Congregation for the Doctrine of the Faith, Letter to the Bishops of the Catholic Church concerning the Reception of Eucharistic Communion by Divorced and Remarried Faithful (14 September 1994): AAS 86 (1994), 974–979.

74. Cf. Innocent I, *Epist.* 25, 1 to Decentius of Gubbio: PL 20, 553.

75. II, 59, 2–3: ed. F. X. Funk, 1905, pp. 170–171.

76. Cf. *Apologia* I, 67, 3–5: PG 6, 430.

77. *Acta SS. Saturnini, Dativi et aliorum plurimorum Martyrum in Africa*, 7, 9, 10: PL 8, 707, 709–710.

78. Cf. Canon 21, Mansi, *Conc.* II, 9.

79. Cf. Canon 47, Mansi, *Conc.* VIII, 332.

80. Cf. the contrary proposition, condemned by Innocent XI in 1679, concerning the moral obligation to keep the feast day holy: DS 2152.

81. Canon 1248: *"Festis de praecepto diebus Missa audienda est"*; Canon 1247, 1: *"Dies festi sub praecepto in universa Ecclesia sunt . . . omnes et singuli dies dominici."*

82. CIC, c. 1247; CCEC, c. 881, 1, prescribes that "the Christian faithful are bound by the obligation to participate on Sundays and feast days in the Divine Liturgy or, according to the prescriptions or legitimate customs of their own Church *sui iuris*, in the celebration of the divine praises."

83. CCC, 2181: "Those who deliberately fail in this obligation commit a grave sin."

84. Sacred Congregation for Bishops, Directory for the Pastoral Ministry of Bishops Ecclesiae Imago (22 February 1973), 86a: *Enchiridion Vaticanum* 4, 2069.

85. Cf. CIC, c. 905, 2.

86. Cf. Pius XII, Apostolic Constitution *Christus Dominus* (6 January 1953): AAS 45 (1953), 15–24; Motu Proprio *Sacram Communionem* (19 March 1957): AAS 49 (1957), 177–178. Congregation of the Holy Office, Instruction on the Discipline concerning the Eucharistic Fast (6 January 1953): AAS 45 (1953), 47–51.

87. Cf. CIC, c. 1248, 1; CCEC, c. 881, 2.

88. Cf. GNLY, 3.

89. Cf. Sacred Congregation of Bishops, Directory for the Pastoral Ministry of Bishops *Ecclesiae Imago* (22 February 1973), 86: *Enchiridion Vaticanum* 4, 2069–2073.

90. Cf. SC, 14, 26; VQA, 4, 6, 12: AAS 81 (1989), 900–901, 902, 909–910.

91. Cf. LG, 10.

92. Cf. Interdicasterial Instruction on Certain Questions concerning the Collaboration of Lay Faithful in the Ministry of Priests *Ecclesiae de Mysterio* (15 August 1997), 6, 8: AAS 89 (1997), 869, 870–872.

93. LG, 10: *"in oblationem Eucharistiae concurrunt."*

94. *Ibid.*, 11.

95. Cf. CIC, c. 1248, 2.

96. Cf. Sacred Congregation for Divine Worship, Directory for Sunday Celebrations in the Absence of a Priest *Christi Ecclesia* (2 June 1988): *Enchiridion Vaticanum* 11, 442–468; Interdicasterial Instruction on Certain Questions concerning the Collaboration of Lay Faithful in the Ministry of Priests *Ecclesiae de Mysterio* (15 August 1997): AAS 89 (1997), 852–877.

97. Cf. CIC, c. 1248, 2; Congregation for the Doctrine of the Faith, Letter *Sacerdotium Ministeriale* (6 August 1983), III: AAS 75 (1983), 1007.

98. Cf. Pontifical Commission for Social Communications, Instruction *Communio et Progressio* (23 May 1971), 150–152, 157: AAS 63 (1971), 645–646, 647.

99. This is the deacon's proclamation in honor of the Lord's Day: cf. the Syriac text in the *Missal of the Church of Antioch of the Maronites* (edition in Syriac and Arabic), Jounieh (Lebanon) 1959, p. 38.

100. V, 20, 11: ed. F. X. Funk, 1905, p. 298; cf. *Didache* 14, 1: ed. F X. Funk, 1901, p. 32; Tertullian, *Apologeticum* 16, 11: CCL 1, 116. See in particular the *Epistle of Barnabas*, 15, 9: SCh 172, 188–189: "This is why we celebrate as a joyous feast the eighth day on which Jesus was raised from the dead and, after having appeared, ascended into heaven."

101. Tertullian, for example, tells us that on Sunday it was forbidden to kneel, since kneeling, which was then seen as an essentially penitential gesture, seemed unsuited to the day of joy. Cf. *De Corona* 3, 4: CCL 2, 1043.

102. *Ep.* 55, 28: CSEL 342, 202.

103. Cf. Saint Thérèse of the Child Jesus and the Holy Face, *Derniers entretiens*, 5–6 July 1897, in *Oeuvres complètes*, Paris: Cerf Desclée de Brouwer, 1992, pp. 1024–1025.

104. Apostolic Exhortation *Gaudete in Domino* (9 May 1975), II: AAS 67 (1975), 295.

105. *Ibid.* VII, l.c., 322.

106. *Hex.* 6, 10, 76: CSEL 321, 261.

107. Cf. The Edict of Constantine, 3 July 321: *Codex Theodosianus* II, tit. 8, 1, ed. T. Mommsen, 12, p. 87; *Codex Iustiniani*, 3, 12, 2, ed. P. Krueger, p. 248.

108. Cf. Eusebius of Caesarea, *Life of Constantine*, 4, 18: PG 20, 1165.

109. The most ancient text of this kind is can. 29 of the Council of Laodicea (second half of the fourth century): Mansi, II, 569–570. From the sixth to the ninth century, many Councils prohibited *"opera ruralia."* The legislation on prohibited activities, supported by civil laws, became increasingly detailed.

110. Cf. Encyclical Letter *Rerum Novarum* (15 May 1891): *Acta Leonis XIII* 11 (1891), 127–128.

111. *Hex.* 2, 1, 1: CSEL 321, 41.

112. Cf. CIC, c. 1247; CCEC, c. 881, 1, 4.

113. SC, 9.

114. Cf. also Saint Justin, *Apologia* I, 67, 6: "Each of those who have an abundance and who wish to make an offering gives freely whatever he chooses, and what is collected is given to him who presides and he assists the orphans, the widows, the sick, the poor, the prisoners, the foreign visitors—in a word, he helps all those who are in need": PG 6, 430.

115. *De Nabuthae*, 10, 45: *"Audis, dives, quid Dominus Deus dicat? Et tu ad ecclesiam venis, non ut aliquid largiaris pauperi, sed ut auferas"*: CSEL 322, 492.

116. *Homilies on the Gospel of Matthew*, 50, 3–4: PG 58, 508–509.

117. Saint Paulinus of Nola, *Ep.* 13, 11–12 to Pammachius: CSEL 29, 92–93. The Roman senator is praised because, by combining participation in the eucharist with distribution of food to the poor, he in a sense reproduced the gospel miracle.

118. John Paul II, Apostolic Letter *Tertio Millennio Adveniente* (10 November 1994), 10: AAS 87 (1995), 11.

119. *Ibid.*

120. Cf. CCC, 731–732.

121. SC, 102.

122. *Ibid.*, 103.

123. *Ibid.*, 104.

124. *Carm.* XVI, 3–4: *"Omnia praetereunt, sanctorum gloria durat in Christo qui cuncta novat, dum permanet ipse"*: CSEL 30, 67.

125. Cf. CIC, c. 1247; CCEC, c. 881, 1, 4.

126. By general law, the holy days of obligation in the Latin church are the feasts of the Nativity of the Lord, the Epiphany, the Ascension, the Body and Blood of Christ, Mary Mother of God, the Immaculate Conception, the Assumption, Saint Joseph, Saints Peter and Paul and All Saints: cf. CIC, c. 1246. The holy days of obligation in all the Eastern churches are the feasts of the Nativity of the Lord, the Epiphany, the Ascension, the Dormition of Mary Mother of God and Saints Peter and Paul: cf. CCEC, c. 880, 3.

127. Cf. CIC, c. 1246, 2; for the Eastern Churches, cf. CCEC, c. 880, 3.

128. Cf. GNLY, 5, 7: *Enchiridion Vaticanum* 3, 895, 897.

129. Cf. *Caeremoniale Episcoporum*, ed. typica 1995, 230.

130. Cf. *ibid.*, 233.

131. *Contra Celsum* VIII, 22: SCh 150, 222–224.

CIRCULAR LETTER *PASCHALE SOLEMNITATIS*

ON PREPARING
AND
CELEBRATING
THE PASCHAL FEASTS

CONGREGATION FOR DIVINE WORSHIP
1988

OVERVIEW OF *PASCHALE SOLEMNITATIS:* ON PREPARING AND CELEBRATING THE PASCHAL FEASTS

John F. Baldovin, SJ

I have often thought that the reformed rites of the Roman church had not so much been tried and failed, as not tried at all. This circular letter on the paschal feasts may provide an antidote to the lack of confidence in the power and beauty of our reformed rites.

The seasons of Lent and Easter are clearly the most significant portion of the liturgical year. They comprise six weeks of preparation and seven weeks of celebration, with the paschal Triduum as the centerpiece. This is a rich and complex time for the church's liturgy. Some local communities find in it an opportunity to be creative and experimental; others seem defeated by the complexity (especially of the Triduum) and opt for minimal celebration.

In 1988 the Congregation for Divine Worship issued the circular letter *Paschale solemnitatis* (on preparing and celebrating the paschal feasts), which was intended to steer a middle course between both extremes. A "circular letter" is in the mode of an "instruction"; it does not provide new legislation on the liturgy but rather comments on and confirms what is already in the liturgical books. This circular letter is concerned in particular with the tendency in some places to celebrate the solemn Vigil of Easter as if it were another Saturday evening celebration of the eucharist, contrary to the very concept of a vigil (#3).

SOME PRINCIPLES OF GOOD LITURGY

In several instances the circular letter repeats and confirms what simply must be regarded as some basic principles of good liturgy, whether celebrated during the paschal season or not.

First, the letter emphasizes the importance of the chants of the people and ministers in the Holy Week celebrations "because they add to the solemnity of these days and also because *texts are more effective when sung*" (#42; emphasis added). There follows a charge that episcopal conferences should prepare musical settings for these texts; included are a number of examples of texts that should be sung during Holy Week (for example, the Good Friday intercessions and the acclamations that accompany the procession with the holy oils). The principle that many texts are more effective when sung is certainly one that applies to liturgy in general.

Second, in at least two places the letter insists that the celebrations of the paschal Triduum are communal in nature. They are not meant to be devotional exercises for the benefit of the individual faithful or for small groups; rather, they are to manifest the nature of the church as the assembly of the baptized. Therefore, small religious communities and other groups of the faithful are encouraged to join in the Triduum celebrations in "neighboring principal churches" (#43; see #16 with regard to Lent). This encouragement is repeated with regard to the

Mass of the Lord's Supper on Holy Thursday (#47); the paschal Vigil is likewise understood as a time to manifest "a sense of ecclesial community" (#94). One might suggest that this principle of the communal nature of the liturgy, a principle that favors small groups (even of religious) gathering together for liturgical celebrations, applies as well to Sunday celebrations of the eucharist. Such celebrations are meant to be epiphanies of the church gathered, not simply occasions of pious exercise for individuals or small groups.

LENT

The letter reiterates the two-fold purpose of Lent found in the Constitution on the Sacred Liturgy *Sacrosanctum concilium* (#109) and the *General Norms for the Liturgical Year and the Calendar* (#27), which stipulate that Lent is a time of purification and enlightenment. It should be noted, however, that those two documents place the primary emphasis on Lent as a time of preparation for Christian initiation; penance is secondary. The circular letter, however, seems determined to emphasize the importance of the penitential nature of the season, which may have been lost or de-emphasized in the course of the reform (see #14–15).

In addition to the final preparation of the catechumens, the letter recommends a lenten catechesis for those baptized as Catholics who have not celebrated confirmation or received first communion. Lent is also understood as a time of preparation for the celebration of the sacrament of penance (#9–10).

The letter recommends the ancient Roman tradition of "stational" churches as a model for larger gatherings of the faithful around the bishop on special occasions during Lent (#16). It also recommends the use of the litany of the saints during the procession on the First Sunday of Lent (#23).

The letter also notes that, in accord with the decision of the relevant national conference of bishops, crosses and images may be covered in churches from the Fifth Sunday of Lent through the celebration of Good Friday (crosses) and the beginning of the Easter Vigil (images).

HOLY WEEK

The second major section of the circular letter deals with Holy Week. It should be noted that the letter differentiates between the first days of Holy Week and the Triduum, which has pride of place in the document.

Passion Sunday

In line with the *Missal of Paul VI*, the letter insists that the solemn procession with palms take place only once on Passion (Palm) Sunday (#29). Presumably the reason for this directive is to accentuate the communal nature of the liturgy. On the other hand, one wonders if the directive is realistic in light of large parish communities that have a number of Sunday Masses with equally high attendance.

Preference is given to the "choral" recitation or singing of the passion narrative by three persons. Here, pastors and directors of liturgy should use caution. It is indeed traditional, as the letter affirms, to present the passion narrative in choral fashion (see #33). However, one can question whether proclaiming the passion in this manner respects the genre of the passion as *narrative*. In a number of churches, the passion is read as a narrative with pauses for the singing of a passion chorale or passion hymn.

The letter also reiterates the sacramentary's directive that candles and incense are not to be used in the proclamation of the passion (#33). The reason for this, in the formulation of the German scholar of liturgy Anton Baumstark, is "the retention of the most ancient practices on the most solemn days." Similarly, the stark entrance with prostration at the beginning of the solemn liturgy of Good Friday, as well as refraining from the use of the organ from the Gloria on Holy Thursday up to the Gloria at the Vigil, reflects the same principle.

Chrism Mass

The Chrism Mass takes place on Thursday of Holy Week or, given the circumstances of the diocese, some other day close to the Triduum. Most dioceses seem to opt for one of the earlier days of Holy Week. The unity of presbyters with their bishop is highlighted by the letter (#35). At the same time, the faithful are encouraged to participate in this celebration. It has become common in a number of dioceses for representatives of parishes to participate in this liturgy in order to bring the holy oils back to the community in a solemn fashion at the beginning of the Mass of the Lord's Supper (#36). Thus, a visible connection is made between the local church as diocese and the parish church as the venue of Christian initiation.

The letter notes that penitential services are to be encouraged during Holy Week, but they must take place before the beginning of the Triduum and not immediately prior to the Mass of the Lord's Supper (#37).

TRIDUUM

The circular letter next turns to the Triduum. It reaffirms that the Triduum begins with the Mass of the Lord's Supper on Holy Thursday and lasts until Evening Prayer on Easter Sunday (#38). Many people think that the Triduum ends with the paschal Vigil. It would be wonderful if various communities could recapture the powerful beauty of Easter Evening Prayer.

Citing the *Ceremonial of Bishops*, the letter strongly recommends that Catholics fast not only on Good Friday but also on Holy Saturday as a means of preparation for the great feast of Easter (#39). The writers of the letter might have added that fasting on Holy Saturday can be a powerful way for the faithful to exercise solidarity with the candidates for initiation at the Vigil.

The letter also recommends the public celebration of the Office of Readings and Morning Prayer on the mornings of Good Friday and Holy Saturday (#40). These offices, which constitute the so-called Tenebrae (meaning "darkness," a reference to the practice of gradually extinguishing candles during the prayer until none remain lit), were for a long time celebrated on the evenings of Holy Thursday and Good Friday. (The church has a long tradition of anticipating services at earlier times; witness the pre-1953 Easter "vigil" on Holy Saturday morning, done to end the fast as soon as possible.) Tenebrae can be a profound experience of prayer. The reading of the second century homily assigned for the

Office of Readings on Holy Saturday is itself a sufficient reason for the celebration of this office.

One important aspect of the Triduum that is not emphasized in this document is its unity. Each of the three major celebrations—the Mass of the Lord's Supper, the solemn liturgy of Good Friday, the paschal Vigil—flow from and to the others, creating one great celebration of the one paschal mystery of the passion, death and resurrection of the Lord.

The Mass of the Lord's Supper

The circular letter stresses three "themes" that are commemorated in the Mass of the Lord's Supper that should find a place in the homily: the institution of the eucharist, the institution of the priesthood, and the command of love of neighbor, expressed in the washing of feet (#45). In my opinion, however, it would be wiser not to put too much stress on the institution of the ordained priesthood, since doing so might detract from the fact that the Lord's Supper is, in a sense, the prophecy of the Lord's death and resurrection ritualized in the sacrificial meal and humble service.

In addition to the washing of feet, the procession with and reposition of the blessed sacrament is a unique feature of this night's liturgy. The letter makes it clear that the place of reposition is not to look like a tomb (#55), as if the liturgy of Holy Thursday is some kind of historical reconstruction of the events of Jesus' last days. The chapel of reposition is rather a place to keep the eucharistic bread for communion on Good Friday. In fact, in churches where there is no solemn liturgy on Good Friday, the blessed sacrament may not be reposed (#54). The letter further recommends a kind of solemn vigil with the reading of portions of the Last Supper discourse (John 13—17) in the course of the evening up until midnight.

Some other aspects of the commentary on the Mass of the Lord's Supper are noteworthy. First, the collection of alms at this celebrations is expressly for the poor and might represent the fruits of lenten penance (#52). Secondly, and a practice that might well be observed at every Sunday eucharist, communion for the sick and homebound is appropriately "borne directly from the altar . . . so that in this way [those receiving] may be more closely united to the celebrating church" (#53).

Good Friday

Good Friday is one of the most solemnly observed days in the Christian calendar. The letter restates the sacramentary's direction that no sacraments are to be celebrated on this day (#66)—with the 1977 clarification of the Congregation for Divine Worship that the sacraments of penance and anointing of the sick are permitted. This direction is repeated for Holy Saturday (#75). It should be noted, however, that penance services as such are recommended during Lent (#15) and not during the paschal Triduum. It is preferable for pastoral reasons to arrange for the celebration of the sacrament of penance in its various forms before the beginning of the Triduum.

The circular letter places great stress on the nature of the veneration of the cross at the solemn liturgy. The cross is to be of "appropriate size and beauty" (#68), and only one cross should be used "as this contributes to the full symbolism of the rite" (#69). The letter expresses a strong preference for the individual veneration of the cross by the faithful, even though simultaneous public veneration is allowed.

The Paschal Vigil

The longest section of the circular letter is devoted to the Vigil. It is clear from the beginning of the letter that one of its major concerns is the poor way in which many communities celebrate this highpoint of the church's liturgical year. This is to be a true vigil, not an extended Saturday evening Mass. The letter emphasizes the nocturnal character of the Vigil, beginning after nightfall and ending before dawn. (In parts of the Northern Hemisphere this will require attention to the change from standard to daylight savings time in the spring.)

The letter rounds out its treatment of the Vigil by stressing the importance of the symbols used and the value of using all of the Old Testament readings. One of the more important points relates to the celebration of the eucharist proper, which can tend to seem like an afterthought in such a long liturgy as the Vigil. Communion at the Vigil is correctly understood as the culmination of the Christian initiation of those baptized on this holy night.

Easter Sunday and Pentecost

As mentioned above, the circular letter highly recommends the celebration of Evening Prayer on Easter Sunday as a way of bringing the Triduum to a solemn close. It also stresses the unity of the great 50 days of Easter, concluding with Pentecost, as the church's "great Sunday." It recommends a special vigil for Pentecost, not so much a baptismal vigil as one that reflects the disciples' waiting for the gift of the Holy Spirit (#107).

The letter recognizes the value of giving pride of place to the neophytes throughout the entire 50 days of Easter, as well as the importance of traditional practices attached to Eastertime, such as pastoral visitation and the blessing of homes.

CONCLUSION

In some ways *Paschale solemnitatis* does not add much that is new in terms of directives for the celebration of the liturgy during the holiest season of the year. On the other hand, it is a valuable reminder of the importance of treating our Christian worship with great care and seriousness, honoring the communal character of the liturgy in general and entering into our rites with conviction.

OUTLINE

ON PREPARING AND CELEBRATING THE PASCHAL FEASTS

PREFACE

1.   The Easter solemnity, revised and restored by Pius XII in 1951, and then the Order of Holy Week in 1955 were favorably received by the church of the Roman rite.[1]

The Second Vatican Council, especially in the *Constitution on the Sacred Liturgy*, repeatedly drawing upon tradition, called attention to Christ's paschal mystery and pointed out that it is the fount from which all sacraments and sacramentals draw their power.[2]

2.   Just as the week has its beginning and climax in the celebration of Sunday, which always has a paschal character, so the summit of the whole liturgical year is in the sacred Easter triduum of the passion and resurrection of the Lord,[3] which is prepared for by the period of Lent and prolonged for 50 days.

3.   In many parts of the Christian world the faithful followers of Christ, with their pastors, attach great importance to the celebration of this rite and participate in it with great spiritual gain.

However, in some areas where initially the reform of the Easter Vigil was received enthusiastically it would appear that with the passage of time this enthusiasm has begun to wane. The very concept of the Vigil has almost come to be forgotten in some places, with the result that it is celebrated as if it were an evening Mass, in the same way and at the same time as the Mass celebrated on Saturday evening in anticipation of the Sunday.

It also happens that the celebrations of the triduum are not held at the correct times. This is because certain devotions and pious exercises are held at more convenient times, and so the faithful participate in them rather than in the liturgical celebrations.

Without any doubt, one of the principal reasons for this state of affairs is the inadequate formation given to the clergy and the faithful regarding the paschal mystery as the center of the liturgical year and of Christian life.[4]

4.   The holiday period that today in many places coincides with Holy Week and certain attitudes held by present-day society concur to present difficulties for the faithful to participate in these celebrations.

5.   With these points in mind, the Congregation for Divine Worship, after due consideration, thinks that it is a fitting moment to recall certain elements, doctrinal and pastoral, and various norms that have already been published concerning Holy Week. All those details which are given in the liturgical books concerning Lent, Holy Week, the Easter triduum and paschal time retain their full force unless otherwise stated in this document.

It is the aim of this document that the great mystery of our redemption be celebrated in the best possible way so that the faithful may participate in it with ever greater spiritual advantage.[5]

I. LENTEN SEASON

6.   "The annual Lenten season is the fitting time, to climb the holy mountain of Easter.

"The Lenten season has a double character, namely to prepare both catechumens and faithful to celebrate the paschal mystery. The catechumens, both with the rite of election and scrutinies and by catechesis, are prepared for the celebration of the sacraments of Christian initiation; the faithful, ever more attentive to the word of God and prayer, prepare themselves by penance for the renewal of their baptismal promises."[6]

A) CONCERNING THE RITE OF CHRISTIAN INITIATION

7.   The whole rite of Christian initiation has a markedly paschal character, since it is therein that the sacramental participation in the death and resurrection of Christ takes place for the first time. Therefore Lent should have its full character as a time of purification and enlightenment, especially through the scrutinies and by the presentations; naturally the paschal Vigil should be regarded as the proper time to celebrate the sacraments of initiation.[7]

8.   Communities that do not have any catechumens should not however fail to pray for those who in the forthcoming Paschal Vigil will receive the sacraments of Christian initiation. Pastors should draw the attention of the faithful to those moments of significant importance to their spiritual life, nourished by their baptismal profession of faith, and which they will be invited to renew in the Easter Vigil, "the fullness of the Lenten observance."[8]

9.   In Lent there should be catechesis for those adults who, although baptized when infants, were not brought up in the faith and consequently have not been confirmed nor have they received the eucharist. During this period, penitential services should be arranged to help prepare them for the sacrament of reconciliation.[9]

10.   The Lenten season is also an appropriate time for the celebration of penitential rites on the model of the scrutinies for unbaptized children who are at an age to be catechized, and also for children already baptized, before being admitted to the sacrament of penance.[10]

The bishop should have particular care to foster the catechumenate of both adults and children and, according to circumstances, to preside at the prescribed rites, with the devout participation of the local community.[11]

B) CELEBRATIONS DURING THE LENTEN SEASON

11.   The Sundays of Lent take precedence over all feasts and all solemnities. Solemnities occurring on these Sundays are observed on the preceding Saturday.[12] The weekdays of Lent have precedence over obligatory memorials.[13]

12.   The catechesis on the paschal mystery and the sacraments should be given a special place in the Sunday homilies; the text of the lectionary should be carefully explained, particularly the passages of the Gospel that illustrate the diverse aspects of baptism and of the other sacraments, and of the mercy of God.

13.   Pastors should frequently and as fully as possible explain the word of God in homilies on weekdays, in celebrations of the word of God, in penitential celebrations,[14] in various reunions, in visiting families or on the occasion of blessing families. The faithful should try and attend weekday Mass, and where this is not possible, they should at least be encouraged to read the lessons, either with their family or in private.

14.   "The Lenten season should retain something of its penitential character."[15] "As regards catechesis, it is important to impress on the minds of the faithful not only the social consequences of sin, but also that aspect of the virtue of penance that involves the detestation of sin as an offense against God."[16]

The virtue and practice of penance form a necessary part of the preparation for Easter: From that inner conversion of heart should spring the practice of penance, both for the individual Christian and of the whole community, which while being adapted to the conditions of the present time, should nevertheless witness to the evangelical spirit of penance and also be to the advantage of others.

The role of the church in penitential practices is not to be neglected and encouragement given to pray for sinners, and this intention should be included in the prayer of the faithful.[17]

15.   "The faithful are to be encouraged to participate in an ever more intense and fruitful way in the Lenten liturgy and in penitential celebrations. They are to be clearly reminded that both according to the law and tradition they should approach the sacrament of penance during this season so that with purified heart they may participate in the paschal mysteries. It is appropriate that during Lent the sacrament of penance be celebrated according to the rite for the reconciliation of several penitents with individual confession and absolution, as given in the *Roman Ritual.*"[18]

Pastors should devote themselves to the ministry of reconciliation and provide sufficient time for the faithful to avail themselves of this sacrament.

16.   "All Lenten observances should be of such a nature that they also witness to the life of the local church and foster it. The Roman tradition of the "stational" churches can be recommended as a model for gathering the faithful in one place. In this way the faithful can assemble in larger numbers, especially under the leadership of the bishop of the diocese, or at the tombs of the saints, or in the principal churches of the city or sanctuaries, or some place of pilgrimage that has a special significance for the diocese."[19]

17.   "In Lent the altar should not be decorated with flowers, and musical instruments may be played only to give necessary support to the singing."[20] This is in order that the penitential character of the season be preserved.

18.   Likewise, from the beginning of Lent until the Paschal Vigil, Alleluia is to be omitted in all celebrations, even on solemnities and feasts.[21]

19.   The chants to be sung in celebrations, especially of the eucharist, and also at devotional exercises should be in harmony with the spirit of the season and the liturgical texts.

20.   Devotional exercises which harmonize with the Lenten season are to be encouraged, for example, the Stations of the Cross; they should help foster the liturgical spirit with which the faithful can prepare themselves for the celebration of Christ's paschal mystery.

C) PARTICULAR DETAILS CONCERNING THE DAYS OF LENT

21.   "On the Wednesday before the first Sunday of Lent, the faithful receive the ashes, thus entering into the time established for the purification of their souls. This sign of penance, a traditionally biblical one, has been preserved among the church's customs until the present day. It signifies the human condition of the sinner, who seeks to express his [or her] guilt before the Lord in an exterior manner and by so doing express his [or her] interior conversion, led on by the confident hope that the Lord will be merciful. This same sign marks the beginning of the way of conversion, which is developed through the celebration of the sacraments of penance during the days before Easter."[22]

The blessing and imposition of ashes should take place either in the Mass or outside of the Mass. In the latter case, it is to be part of a Liturgy of the Word and conclude with the prayer of the faithful.[23]

22.   Ash Wednesday is to be observed a day of penance in the whole church, one of both abstinence and fasting.[24]

23.   The first Sunday of Lent marks the beginning of the annual Lenten observance.[25] In the Mass of this Sunday, there should be some distinctive elements that underline this important moment; eg., the entrance procession with litanies of the saints.[26] During the Mass of the first Sunday in Lent, the bishop should celebrate the rite of election in the cathedral or in some other church as seems appropriate.[27]

24.   The Gospel pericopes of the Samaritan woman, of the man blind from birth and the resurrection of Lazarus are assigned to the third, fourth and fifth Sundays of Lent of Year A. Of particular significance in relation to Christian initiation, they can also be read in Years B and C, especially in places where there are catechumens.[28]

25.   On the fourth Sunday of Lent (*Laetare* Sunday), and on solemnities and feasts, musical instruments may be played and the altar decorated with flowers. Rose-colored vestments may be worn on this Sunday.[29]

26.   The practice of covering the crosses and images in the church may be observed if the episcopal conference should so decide. The crosses are to be covered until the end of the celebration of the Lord's Passion on Good Friday. Images are to remain covered until the beginning of the Easter Vigil.[30]

II. HOLY WEEK

27.   During Holy Week, the church celebrates the mysteries of salvation accomplished by Christ in the last days of his life on earth, beginning with his messianic entrance into Jerusalem.

The Lenten season lasts until the Thursday of this week. The Easter triduum begins with the evening Mass of the Lord's Supper, is continued through Good Friday with the celebration of the passion of the Lord and Holy Saturday, to reach its summit in the Easter Vigil and concludes with Vespers of Easter Sunday.

"The days of Holy Week, from Monday to Thursday inclusive, have precedence over all other celebrations."[31] It is not fitting that baptisms and confirmations be celebrated on these days.

A) PASSION SUNDAY (PALM SUNDAY)

28.   Holy Week begins on Passion (or Palm) Sunday, which joins the foretelling of Christ's regal triumph and the proclamation of the passion. The connection between both aspects of the paschal mystery should be shown and explained in the celebration and catechesis this day.[32]

29.   The commemoration of the entrance of the Lord into Jerusalem has, according to ancient custom, been celebrated with a solemn procession in which the faithful in song and gesture imitate the Hebrew children who went to meet the Lord singing hosanna.[33]

The procession may take place only once, before the Mass which has the largest attendance, even if this should be in the evening either of Saturday or Sunday. The congregation should assemble in a secondary church or chapel or in some other suitable place distinct from the church to which the procession will move.

In this procession the faithful carry palm or other branches. The priest and the ministers, also carrying branches, precede the people.[34]

The palms or branches are blessed so that they can be carried in the procession. The palms should be taken home, where they will serve as a reminder of the victory of Christ, which they celebrated in the procession.

Pastors should make every effort to ensure that this procession in honor of Christ the King be so prepared and celebrated that it is of great spiritual significance in the life of the faithful.

30.   The *Missal,* in order to commemorate the entrance of the Lord into Jerusalem, in addition to the solemn procession described above, gives two other forms, not simply for convenience, but to provide for those situations when it will not be possible to have the procession.

The second form is that of a solemn entrance, when the procession cannot take place outside of the church. The third form is a simple entrance such as is used at all Masses on this Sunday that do not have the solemn entrance.[35]

31.   Where the Mass cannot be celebrated, there should be a celebration of the word of God on the theme of the Lord's messianic entrance and passion, either on Saturday evening or on Sunday at a convenient time.[36]

32.   During the procession, the choir and people should sing the chants proposed in the *Roman Missal,* especially Psalms 23 and 46, as well as other appropriate songs in honor of Christ, the King.

33.   The Passion narrative occupies a special place. It should be sung or read in the traditional way, that is, by three persons who take the part of Christ, the narrator and the people. The Passion is proclaimed by deacons or priests, or by lay readers. In the latter case, the part of Christ should be reserved to the priest.

The proclamation of the Passion should be without candles and incense; the greeting and the signs of the cross are omitted; only a deacon asks for the blessing, as he does before the Gospel.[37] For the spiritual good of the faithful, the Passion should be proclaimed in its entirety, and the readings that proceed it should not be omitted.

34.   After the Passion has been proclaimed, a homily is to be given.

B) THE CHRISM MASS

35.   The Chrism Mass, which the bishop concelebrates with his presbyterium, and at which the holy chrism is consecrated and the oils blessed, manifests the communion of the priests with their bishop in the same priesthood and ministry of Christ.[38] At this Mass, the priests who celebrate with the bishop should come from different parts of the diocese, thus showing in the consecration of the chrism to be his witnesses and cooperators, just as in their daily ministry they are his helpers and counselors.

The faithful are also to be encouraged to participate in the Mass and to receive the sacrament of the eucharist.

Traditionally the Chrism Mass is celebrated on the Thursday of Holy Week. If, however, it should prove to be difficult for the clergy and people to gather with the bishop, this rite can be transferred to another day, but one always close to Easter.[39] The chrism and the oil of catechumens is to be used in the celebration of the sacraments of initiation on Easter night.

36.   There should be only one celebration of the Chrism Mass, given its significance in the life of the diocese, and it should take place in the cathedral or, for pastoral reasons, in another church[40] which has a special significance.

The holy oils can be brought to the individual parishes before the celebration of the evening Mass of the Lord's Supper, or at some other suitable time. This can be a means of catechizing the faithful about the use and effects of the holy oils and chrism in Christian life.

C) THE PENITENTIAL CELEBRATIONS IN LENT

37.   It is fitting that the Lenten season should be concluded, both for the individual Christian as well as for the whole Christian community, with a penitential celebration, so that they may be helped to prepare to celebrate more fully the paschal mystery.[41]

These celebrations, however, should take place before the Easter triduum and should not immediately precede the evening Mass of the Lord's Supper.

III. THE EASTER TRIDUUM IN GENERAL

38.   The greatest mysteries of the redemption are celebrated yearly by the church, beginning with the evening Mass of the Lord's Supper on Holy Thursday and ending with Vespers of Easter Sunday. This time is called "the triduum of the crucified, buried and risen";[42] it is also called the "Easter triduum" because during it is celebrated the paschal mystery, that is, the passing of the Lord from this world to his Father. The church, by the celebration of this mystery through liturgical signs and sacramentals, is united to Christ, her spouse, in intimate communion.

39.   The Easter fast is sacred on the first two days of the triduum, in which according to ancient tradition the church fasts "because the Spouse has been taken away."[43] Good Friday is a day of fasting and abstinence; it is also recommended that Holy Saturday be so observed so that the church, with uplifted and welcoming heart, be ready to celebrate the joys of the Sunday of the resurrection.[44]

40.   It is recommended that there be a communal celebration of the office of readings and morning prayer on Good Friday and Holy Saturday. It is fitting that the bishop should celebrate the office in the cathedral, with as far as possible the participation of the clergy and people.[45]

This office, formerly called *"Tenebrae,"* held a special place in the devotion of the faithful as they meditated upon the passion, death and burial of the Lord while awaiting the announcement of the resurrection.

41.   For the celebration of the Easter triduum, it is necessary that there be a sufficient number of ministers and assistants, who should be prepared so that they know what their role is in the celebration. Pastors must ensure that the meaning of each part of the celebration be explained to the faithful so that they may participate more fully and fruitfully.

42.   The chants of the people, and also of the ministers and the celebrating priest, are of special importance in the celebration of Holy Week and particularly of the Easter triduum because they add to the solemnity of these days and also because the texts are more effective when sung.

The episcopal conferences are asked, unless provision has already been made, to provide music for those parts that it can be said should always be sung, namely:

a) The general intercessions of Good Friday; the deacon's invitation and the acclamation of the people.

b) Chants for the showing and veneration of the cross.

c) The acclamations during the procession with the paschal candle and the Easter proclamation, the responsorial "Alleluia," the litany of the saints and the acclamation after the blessing of water.

Since the purpose of sung texts is also to facilitate the participation of the faithful, they should not be lightly omitted; such texts should be set to music. If the text for use in the liturgy has not yet been set to music, it is possible, as a temporary measure, to select other similar texts that are set to music. It is, however, fitting that there should be a collection of texts set to music for these celebrations, paying special attention to:

a) Chants for the procession and blessing of palms, and for the entrance into church.

b) Chants to accompany the procession with the holy oils.

c) Chants to accompany the procession with the gifts on Holy Thursday in the evening Mass of the Lord's Supper, and hymns to accompany the procession of the blessed sacrament to the place of repose.

d) The responsorial psalms at the Easter Vigil, and chants to accompany the sprinkling with blessed water.

Music should be provided for the Passion narrative, the Easter proclamation and the blessing of baptismal water; obviously the melodies should be of a simple nature in order to facilitate their use.

In larger churches where the resources permit, a more ample use should be made of the church's musical heritage, both ancient and modern, always ensuring that this does not impede the active participation of the faithful.

43.   It is fitting that small religious communities, both clerical and lay, and other lay groups should participate in the celebration of the Easter triduum in neighboring principal churches.[46]

Similarly, where the number of participants and ministers is so small that the celebrations of the Easter triduum cannot be carried out with the requisite solemnity, such groups of the faithful should assemble in a larger church.

Also, where there are small parishes with only one priest, it is recommended that such parishes should assemble, as far as possible, in a principal church and there participate in the celebrations.

On account of the needs of the faithful, where a pastor has the responsibility for two or more parishes in which the faithful assemble in large numbers, and where the celebrations can be carried out with the requisite care and solemnity, the celebrations of the Easter triduum may be repeated in accord with the given norms.[47]

So that seminary students "might live fully Christ's paschal mystery and thus be able to teach those who will be committed to their care,"[48] they should be given a thorough and comprehensive liturgical formation. It is important that during their formative years in the seminary, they should experience fruitfully the solemn Easter celebrations, especially those over which the bishop presides.[49]

IV. HOLY THURSDAY EVENING MASS OF THE LORD'S SUPPER

44.　With the celebration of Mass on the evening of Holy Thursday, "the church begins the Easter triduum and recalls the Last Supper, in which the Lord Jesus, on the night he was betrayed, showing his love for those who were his own in the world, gave his body and blood under the species of bread and wine, offering to his Father and giving them to the apostles so that they might partake of them, and he commanded them and their successors in the priesthood to perpetuate this offering."[50]

45.　Careful attention should be given to the mysteries that are commemorated in this Mass: the institution of the eucharist, the institution of the priesthood and Christ's command of brotherly love. The homily should explain these points.

46.　The Mass of the Lord's Supper is celebrated in the evening, at a time that is more convenient for the full participation of the whole local community. All priests may concelebrate, even if on this day they have already concelebrated the Chrism Mass or if, for the good of the faithful, they must celebrate another Mass.[51]

47.　Where pastoral considerations require it, the local ordinary may permit another Mass to be celebrated in churches and oratories in the evening, and in the case of true necessity, even in the morning, but only for those faithful who cannot otherwise participate in the evening Mass. Care should nevertheless be taken to ensure that celebrations of this kind do not take place for the benefit of private persons or of small groups and that they are not to the detriment of the main Mass.

According to the ancient tradition of the church, all Masses without the participation of the people are on this day forbidden.[52]

48.   The tabernacle should be completely empty before the celebration.[53] Hosts for the communion of the faithful should be consecrated during that celebration.[54] A sufficient amount of bread should be consecrated to provide also for communion on the following day.

49. For the reservation of the blessed sacrament, a place should be prepared and adorned in such a way as to be conductive to prayer and meditation; that sobriety appropriate to the liturgy of these days is enjoined, to the avoidance or suppression of all abuses.[55]

When the tabernacle is located in a chapel separated from the central part of the church, it is appropriate to prepare there the place of repose and adoration.

50.   During the singing of the hymn *"Gloria in Excelsis,"* in accordance with local custom, the bells may be rung and should thereafter remain silent until the *"Gloria in Excelsis"* of the Easter Vigil, unless the conference of bishops or the local ordinary, for a suitable reason, has decided otherwise.[56] During this same period the organ and other musical instruments may be used only for the purpose of supporting the singing.[57]

51.   The washing of the feet of chosen men which, according to tradition, is performed on this day, represents the service and charity of Christ, who came "not to be served, but to serve."[58] This tradition should be maintained, and its proper significance explained.

52.   Gifts for the poor, especially those collected during Lent as the fruit of penance, may be presented in the offertory procession while the people sing *"Ubi caritas est vera."*[59]

53.   It is more appropriate that the eucharist be borne directly from the altar by the deacons or acolytes or extraordinary ministers at the moment of communion for the sick and infirm who must communicate at home, so that in this way they may be more closely united to the celebrating church.

54.   After the postcommunion prayer, the procession forms, with the cross-bearer at its head. The blessed sacrament, accompanied by lighted candles and incense, is carried through the church to the place of reservation, to the singing of the hymn *"Pange Lingua"* or some other eucharistic song.[60] This rite of transfer of the blessed sacrament may not be carried out if the liturgy of the Lord's Passion will not be celebrated in that same church on the following day.[61]

55.   The blessed sacrament should be reserved in a closed tabernacle or pyx. Under no circumstances may it be exposed in a monstrance.

The place where the tabernacle or pyx is situated must not be made to resemble a tomb, and the expression *tomb* is to be avoided for the chapel of repose is not prepared so as to represent the "Lord's burial" but for the custody of the eucharistic bread that will be distributed in communion on Good Friday.

56.   The faithful should be encouraged after the Mass of the Lord's Supper to spend a suitable period of time during the night in the church in adoration before the blessed sacrament that has been solemnly reserved. Where appropriate, this prolonged eucharistic adoration may be accompanied by the reading of some part of the Gospel of Saint John (chapters 13–17).

From midnight onward, however, the adoration should be made without external solemnity, for the day of the Lord's Passion has begun.[62]

57.   After Mass the altar should be stripped. It is fitting that any crosses in the church be covered with a red or purple veil, unless they have already been veiled on the Saturday before the fifth Sunday of Lent. Lamps should not be lit before the images of saints.

V. GOOD FRIDAY

58.   On this day, when "Christ, our passover was sacrificed,"[63] the church meditates on the Passion of her Lord and Spouse, adores the cross, commemorates her origin from the side of Christ asleep on the cross and intercedes for the salvation of the whole world.

59.   On this day, in accordance with ancient tradition, the church does not celebrate the eucharist: Holy communion is distributed to the faithful during the celebration of the Lord's Passion alone, though it may be brought at any time of the day to the sick who cannot take part in the celebration.[64]

60.   Good Friday is a day of penance to be observed as of obligation in the whole church, and indeed through abstinence and fasting.[65]

61.   All celebration of the sacraments on this day is strictly prohibited, except for the sacraments of penance and anointing of the sick.[66] Funerals are to be celebrated without singing, music or the tolling of bells.

62.   It is recommended that on this day the office of readings and morning prayer be celebrated with the participation of the people in the churches (cf. No. 40).

63.   The celebration of the Lord's Passion is to take place in the afternoon, at about three o'clock. The time will be chosen as shall seem most appropriate for pastoral reasons in order to allow the people to assemble more easily, for example, shortly after midday or in the late evening, however, not later than nine o'clock.[67]

64.   The order for the celebration of the Lord's Passion (the Liturgy of the Word, the adoration of the cross and holy communion), that stems from an ancient tradition of the church, should be observed faithfully and religiously, and may not be changed by anyone on his own initiative.

65.   The priest and ministers proceed to the altar in silence and without any singing. If any words of introduction are to be said, they should be pronounced before the ministers enter.

The priest and ministers make a reverence to the altar, prostrating themselves. This act of prostration, which is proper to the rite of the day, should be strictly observed for it signifies both the abasement of "earthly man,"[68] and also the grief and sorrow of the church.

As the ministers enter, the faithful should be standing, and thereafter should kneel in silent prayer.

66.   The readings are to be read in their entirety. The responsorial psalm and the chant before the Gospel are to be sung in the usual manner. The narrative of the Lord's Passion according to John is sung or read in the way prescribed for the previous Sunday (cf. No. 33). After the reading of the Passion, a homily should be given, at the end of which the faithful may be invited to spend a short time in meditation.[69]

67.   The general intercessions are to follow the wording and form handed down by ancient tradition, maintaining the full range of intentions so as to signify clearly the universal effect of the Passion of Christ, who hung on the cross for the salvation of the whole world. In case of grave public necessity, the local ordinary may permit or prescribe the adding of special intentions.[70]

In this event, it is permitted to the priest to select from the prayers of the missal those more appropriate to local circumstances, in such a way, however, that the series follows the rule for general intercessions.[71]

68.   For veneration of the cross, let a cross be used that is of appropriate size and beauty, and let one or other of the forms for this rite as found in the *Roman Missal* be followed. The rite should be carried out with the splendor worthy of the mystery of our salvation: Both the invitation pronounced at the unveiling of the cross and the people's response should be made in song, and a period of respectful silence is to be observed after each act of veneration, the celebrant standing and holding the raised cross.

69.   The cross is to be presented to each of the faithful individually for their adoration, since the personal adoration of the cross is a most important feature in this celebration, and only when necessitated by large numbers of faithful present should the rite of veneration be made simultaneously by all present.[72]

Only one cross should be used for the veneration, as this contributes to the full symbolism of the rite. During the veneration of the cross, the antiphons, "reproaches" and hymns should be sung, so that the history of salvation be commemorated through song.[73] Other appropriate songs may also be sung (cf. No. 42).

70.   The priest sings the invitation to the Lord's Prayer, which is then sung by all. The sign of peace is not exchanged. The communion rite is as described in the missal.

During the distribution of communion, Psalm 21 or another suitable song may be sung. When communion has been distributed, the pyx is taken to a place prepared for it outside of the church.

71. After the celebration, the altar is stripped, the cross remaining, however, with four candles. An appropriate place (for example, the chapel of repose used for reservation of the eucharist on Maundy Thursday) can be prepared within the church, and there the Lord's cross is placed so that the faithful may venerate and kiss it, and spend some time in meditation.

72. Devotions, such as the Way of the Cross, processions of the Passion and commemorations of the sorrows of the Blessed Virgin Mary are not, for pastoral reasons, to be neglected. The texts and songs used, however, should be adapted to the spirit of the liturgy of this day. Such devotions should be assigned to a time of day that makes it quite clear that the liturgical celebration by its very nature far surpasses them in importance.[74]

VI. HOLY SATURDAY

73. On Holy Saturday, the church is, as it were, at the Lord's tomb, meditating on his passion and death, and on his descent into hell,[75] and awaiting his resurrection with prayer and fasting. It is highly recommended that on this day the office of readings and morning prayer be celebrated with the participation of the people (cf. No. 40).[76] Where this cannot be done, there should be some celebration of the word of God or some act of devotion suited to the mystery celebrated this day.

74. The image of Christ crucified or lying in the tomb, or the descent into hell, which mystery Holy Saturday recalls, as also an image of the sorrowful Virgin Mary, can be placed in the church for the veneration of the faithful.

75. On this day the church abstains strictly from celebration of the sacrifice of the Mass.[77] Holy communion may only be given in the form of viaticum. The celebration of marriages is forbidden, as also the celebration of other sacraments, except those of penance and the anointing of the sick.

76. The faithful are to be instructed on the special character of Holy Saturday.[78] Festive customs and traditions associated with this day on account of former practice of anticipating the Easter celebration on Holy Saturday should be reserved for Easter night and the day that follows.

VII. EASTER SUNDAY OF THE LORD'S RESURRECTION

A) THE EASTER VIGIL

77. According to a most ancient tradition, this night is "one of vigil for the Lord,"[79] and the vigil celebrated during it to commemorate that holy night when the Lord rose from the dead is regarded as the "mother of all holy vigils."[80] For

in the night the church keeps vigil, waiting for the resurrection of the Lord, and celebrates the sacraments of Christian initiation.[81]

1. The Meaning of the Nocturnal Character of the Easter Vigil

78.   "The entire celebration of the Easter Vigil takes place at night. It should not begin before nightfall; it should end before daybreak on Sunday."[82] This rule is to be taken according to its strictest sense. Reprehensible are those abuses and practices which have crept in many places in violation of this ruling, whereby the Easter Vigil is celebrated at the time of day that it is customary to celebrate anticipated Sunday Masses.[83]

Those reasons which have been advanced in some quarters for the anticipation of the Easter Vigil, such as lack of public order, are not put forward in connection with Christmas night nor other gatherings of various kinds.

79.   The Passover vigil, in which the Hebrews kept watch for the Lord's Passover, which was to free them from slavery to pharaoh, is an annual commemoration. It prefigured the true Pasch of Christ that was to come, the night that is of true liberation, in which "destroying the bonds of death, Christ rose as victor from the depths."[84]

80.   From the very outset, the church has celebrated that annual Pasch, which is the solemnity of solemnities, above all by means of a night vigil. For the resurrection of Christ is the foundation of our faith and hope, and through baptism and confirmation we are inserted into the paschal mystery of Christ, dying, buried and raised with him, and with him we shall also reign.[85]

The full meaning of vigil is a waiting for the coming of the Lord.[86]

2. The Structure of the Easter Vigil
and the Significance of Its Different Elements and Parts

81.   The order for the Easter Vigil is so arranged so that after the service of light and the Easter proclamation (which is the first part of the vigil), holy church meditates on the wonderful works that the Lord God wrought for his people from the earliest times (the second part of the Liturgy of the Word) to the moment when, together with those new members reborn in baptism (third part), she is called to the table prepared by the Lord for the church, the commemoration of his death and resurrection, until he comes (fourth part).[87]

This liturgical order must not be changed by anyone on their own initiative.

82.   The first part consists of symbolic acts and gestures which require that they be performed in all their fullness and nobility so that their meaning, as explained by the introductory words of the celebrant and the liturgical prayers, may be truly understood by the faithful.

Insofar as possible, a suitable place should be prepared outside the church for the blessing of the new fire, whose flames should be such that they genuinely dispel the darkness and light up the night.

The paschal candle should be prepared, which for effective symbolism must be made of wax, never be artificial, be renewed each year, be only one in number and be of sufficiently large size so that it may evoke the truth that Christ is the light of the world. It is blessed with the signs and words prescribed in the missal or by the conference of bishops.[88]

83.   The procession by which the people enter the church should be led by the light of the paschal candle alone. Just as the children of Israel were guided at night by a pillar of fire, so similarly Christians follow the risen Christ. There is no reason why to each response "Thanks be to God" there should not be added some acclamation in honor of Christ.

The light from the paschal candle should be gradually passed to the candles that all present should hold in their hands; the electric lighting should be switched off.

84.   The deacon makes the Easter proclamation, which tells by means of a great poetic text the whole Easter mystery, placed in the context of the economy of salvation. In case of necessity, where there is no deacon and the celebrating priest is unable to sing it, a cantor may do so. The bishops' conferences may adapt this proclamation by inserting into it acclamations from the people.[89]

85.   The readings from Sacred Scripture constitute the second part of the vigil. They give an account of the outstanding deeds of the history of salvation, which the faithful are helped to meditate calmly upon by the singing of the responsorial psalm, by a silent pause and by the celebrant's prayer.

The restored order for the vigil has seven readings from the Old Testament, chosen from the law and the prophets, which are everywhere in use according to the most ancient tradition of East and West, and two readings from the New Testament, namely from the apostle and from the Gospel. Thus the church, "beginning with Moses and all the prophets," explains Christ's paschal mystery.[90] Consequently, wherever this is possible, all the readings should be read in order that the character of the Easter Vigil, which demands that it be somewhat prolonged, be respected at all costs.

Where, however, pastoral conditions require that the number of readings be reduced, there should be at least three readings from the Old Testament— taken from the law and the prophets—and the reading from Exodus 14 with its canticle must never be omitted.[91]

86.   The typological import of the Old Testament texts is rooted in the New and is made plain by the prayer pronounced by the celebrating priest after each reading; but it will also be helpful to introduce the people to the meaning of each reading by means of a brief introduction. This introduction may be given by the priest himself or by a deacon.

National or diocesan liturgical commissions will prepare aids for pastors.

Each reading is followed by the singing of a psalm, to which the people respond.

Melodies that are capable of promoting the people's participation and devotion should be provided for these responses.[92] Great care is to be taken that trivial songs do not take the place of the psalms.

87.   After the readings from the Old Testament and the hymn "Gloria in Excelsis," the bells are rung in accordance with local custom, the collect is recited and the celebration moves on to the readings from the New Testament. An exhortation from the apostle on baptism as an insertion into Christ's paschal mystery is read.

Then all stand, and the priest intones the Alleluia three times, each time raising the pitch. The people repeat it after him.[93] If it is necessary, the psalmist or cantor may sing the Alleluia, which the people then take up as an acclamation to be interspersed between the verses of Psalm 117, which is so often cited by the apostles in their Easter preaching.[94] Finally the resurrection of the Lord is proclaimed from the Gospel as the high point of the whole Liturgy of the Word. After the gospel a homily is to be given, no matter how brief.

88.   The third part of the vigil is the liturgy of baptism. Christ's passover and ours are now celebrated. This is given full expression in those churches that have a baptismal font, and more so when the Christian initiation of adults is held, or at least the baptism of infants.[95] Even if there are no candidates for baptism, the blessing of baptismal water should still take place in parish churches. If this blessing does not take place at the baptismal font but in the sanctuary, baptismal water should be carried afterward to the baptistry, there to be kept throughout the whole of paschal time.[96] Where there are neither candidates for baptism nor any need to bless the font, baptism should be commemorated by a blessing of water destined for sprinkling upon the people.[97]

89.   Next follows the renewal of baptismal promises, introduced by some words on the part of the celebrating priest. The faithful reply to the questions put to them, standing and holding lighted candles in their hands. They are then sprinkled with water; in this way the gestures and words recall to them the baptism they have received. The celebrating priest sprinkles the people by passing through the main part of the church while all sing the antiphon *"Vidi aquam"* or another suitable song of a baptismal character.[98]

90.   The celebration of the eucharist forms the fourth part of the Vigil and marks its high point, for it is in the fullest sense the Easter sacrament, that is to say, the commemoration of the sacrifice of the cross and the presence of the risen Christ, the completion of Christian initiation and the foretaste of the eternal Pasch.

91.   Great care should be taken that this eucharistic liturgy is not celebrated in haste; indeed, all the rites and words must be given their full force: the general intercessions in which for the first time the neophytes now as members of the faithful exercise their priesthood;[99] the procession at the offertory in which the neophytes, if there are any, take part; the first, second or third eucharistic prayer,

preferably sung, with their proper embolisms;[100] and finally eucharistic communion, as the moment of full participation in the mystery that is being celebrated. It is appropriate that at communion there be sung Psalm 117 with the antiphon *"Pascha nostrum,"* or Psalm 33 with the antiphon "Alleluia, Alleluia, Alleluia," or some other song of Easter exultation.

92.   It is fitting that in the communion of the Easter Vigil full expression be given to the symbolism of the eucharist, namely by consuming the eucharist under the species of both bread and wine. The local ordinaries will consider the appropriateness of such a concession and its ramifications.[101]

3. Some Pastoral Considerations

93.   The Easter Vigil liturgy should be celebrated in such a way as to offer to the Christian people the riches of the prayers and rites. It is therefore important that the authenticity be respected, that the participation of the faithful be promoted and that the celebration should not take place without servers, readers and choir exercising their role.

94.   It would be desirable if on occasion provision were made for several communities to assemble in one church wherever their proximity one to another or small numbers mean that a full and festive celebration could not otherwise take place.

The celebration of the Easter Vigil for special groups is not to be encouraged, since above all in this vigil the faithful should come together as one and should experience a sense of ecclesial community.

The faithful who are absent from their parish on vacation should be urged to participate in the liturgical celebration in the place where they happen to be.

95.   In announcements concerning the Easter Vigil, care should be taken not to present it as the concluding period of Holy Saturday, but rather it should be stressed that the Easter Vigil is celebrated "during Easter night," and that it is one single act of worship. Pastors should be advised that in giving catechesis to the people they should be taught to participate in the vigil in its entirety.[102]

96.   For a better celebration of the Easter Vigil, it is necessary that pastors themselves have a deeper knowledge of both text and rites, so as to give a proper mystagogical catechesis to the people.

EASTER DAY

97.   Mass is to be celebrated on Easter Day with great solemnity. It is appropriate that the penitential rite on this day take the form of a sprinkling with water blessed at the vigil, during which the antiphon *"Vidi aquam"* or some other song of baptismal character should be sung. The fonts at the entrance to the church should also be filled with the same water.

98.   The tradition of celebrating baptismal Vespers on Easter Day with the singing of psalms during the procession to the font should be maintained where it is still in force and, as appropriate, restored.[103]

99. The paschal candle has its proper place either by the ambo or by the altar and should be lit at least in all the more solemn liturgical celebrations of the season until Pentecost Sunday whether at Mass or at morning and evening prayer. After the Easter season, the candle should be kept with honor in the baptistry, so that in the celebration of baptism the candles of the baptized may be lit from it. In the celebration of funerals, the paschal candle should be placed near the coffin to indicate that the death of a Christian is one's own passover. The paschal candle should not otherwise be lit or placed in the sanctuary outside the Easter season.[104]

VIII. EASTER TIME

100. The celebration of Easter is prolonged throughout the Easter season. The fifty days from Easter Sunday to Pentecost Sunday are celebrated as one feast day, the "great Sunday."[105]

101. The Sundays of this season are regarded as Sundays of Easter and are so termed, and they have precedence over all feasts of the Lord and over all other solemnities. Solemnities that fall on one of these Sundays are anticipated on the Saturday.[106] Celebrations in honor of the Blessed Virgin Mary or the saints that fall during the week may not be transferred to one of these Sundays.[107]

102. For adults who have received Christian initiation during the Easter Vigil, the whole of this period is given over to mystagogical catechesis. Therefore, wherever there are neophytes, the prescriptions of the Rite of Christian Initiation of Adults, [Nos. 244–251], should be observed. Intercession should be made in the eucharistic prayer for the newly baptized through the Easter octave in all places.

103. Throughout the Easter season, the neophytes should be assigned their own special place among the faithful. All neophytes should endeavor to participate at Mass along with their godparents. In the homily and, according to local circumstances, in the general intercessions, mention should be made of them. Some celebration should be held to conclude the period of mystagogical catechesis on or about Pentecost Sunday, depending upon local custom.[108] It is also appropriate that children receive their first communion on one or other of the Sundays of Easter.

104. During Easter time, pastors should instruct the faithful who have been already initiated into the eucharist on the meaning of the church's precept concerning the reception of holy communion during this period.[109] It is also highly recommended that communion be brought to the sick also, especially during the Easter octave.

105. Where there is the custom of blessing houses in celebration of the resurrection, this blessing is to be imparted after the solemnity of Easter, and not before, by the parish priest or other priests or deacons delegated by him. This is an opportunity for exercising a pastoral ministry.[110] The parish priest should go to each house for the purpose of undertaking a pastoral visitation of each family. There, he will speak with the residents, spend a few moments with them in

prayer, using texts to be found in the Book of Blessings.[111] In larger cities, consideration should be given to the gathering of several families for a common celebration for all.

106. According to the differing circumstances of places and peoples, there are found a number of popular practices linked to celebrations of the Easter season, which in some instances attract greater numbers of the people than the sacred liturgy itself. These practices are not in any way to be undervalued, for they are often well adapted to the religious mentality of the faithful. Let episcopal conferences and local ordinaries, therefore, see to it that practices of this kind, which seem to nourish popular piety, be harmonized in the best way possible with the sacred liturgy, in some way derived from it, and lead the people to it.[112]

107. This sacred period of fifty days concludes with Pentecost Sunday, when the gift of the Holy Spirit to the apostles, the beginnings of the church and the start of its mission to all tongues and peoples and nations are commemorated.[113]

Encouragement should be given to the prolonged celebration of Mass in the form of a vigil, whose character is not baptismal as in the Easter Vigil, but is one of urgent prayer, after the example of the apostles and disciples, who persevered together in prayer with Mary, the mother of Jesus, as they awaited the Holy Spirit.[114]

108. "It is proper to the paschal festivity that the whole church rejoices at the forgiveness of sins, which is not only for those who are reborn in holy baptism but also for those who have long been numbered among the adopted children."[115] By means of a more intensive pastoral care and a deeper spiritual effort, all who celebrate the Easter feasts will, by the Lord's grace, experience their effect in their daily lives.[116]

Given at Rome, at the offices of the Congregation for Divine Worship, January 16, 1988.

NOTES

1. Cf. CR, decree *Dominicae Resurrectionis* (February 9, 1951) AAS 43 (1951):128–137; CR, decree *Maxima Redemptionis Nostrae Mysteria* (November 16, 1955) AAS 47 (1955): 838–847.

2. Cf. SC, 5, 6, 61.

3. Cf. GNLY, 18.

4. Cf. CD, 15.

5. Cf. *Maxima Redemptionis Nostrae Mysteria.*

6. Cf. CB, 249.

7. Cf. RCIA, 8; CIC, c. 856.

8. RomM, The Easter Vigil, 46.

9. Cf. RCIA, Chap. 4, esp. n. 303.

10. Cf. RCIA, 330–333.

11. Cf. CB, 250, 406–407; cf. RCIA, 41.

12. Cf. GNLY, 5, 56f, and *Notitiae*, 23 (1987): 397.

13. GNLY, 16b.

14. GIRM, 42; cf. RPen, 36–37.

15. Paul VI, Apostolic Constitution *Paenitemini*, 1; AAS 58 (1966) 183.

16. CB, 251.

17. Cf. CB, 251; SC, 109.

18. Cf. CB, 251.

19. Cf. CB, 260.

20. CB, 252.

21. Cf. GNLY, 28.

22. Cf. CB, 253.

23. Cf. RomM, Ash Wednesday.

24. Apostolic Constitution *Paenitemini*, II, 1; CIC, c. 1251.

25. Cf. RomM, First Sunday of Lent, opening prayer and prayer over the gifts.

26. Cf. CB, 261.

27. Cf. CB, 408–410.

28. Cf. RomM, *Lectionary for Mass* (1981), Intro., 97.

29. Cf. CB, 252.

30. RomM, rubric, Saturday of the fourth week of Lent.

31. Cf. GNLY, 16, a.

32. Cf. CB, 263.

33. Cf. RomM, Passion Sunday (Palm Sunday), 9.

34. Cf. CB, 270.

35. Cf. RomM, Passion Sunday (Palm Sunday), 16.

36. Cf. *ibid.*, 19.

37. Cf. RomM, 22. For a Mass at which a bishop presides, cf. CB, 74.

38. PO, 7.

39. Cf. CB, 275.

40. Cf. CB, 276.

41. Cf. RPen, App. II, 1, 7; cf. above, n. 18.

42. Cf. *Maxima Redemptionis Nostrae Mysteria*; St. Augustine, Ep. 55, 24, PL, 35, 215.

43. Cf. Mark 2:19–20; Tertullian, *De ieiunio*, 2 and 13, *Collected Works of Christian Writers*, Latin series, II, p.1271.

44. Cf. CB, 295; SC, 110.

45. Cf. CB, 296; GILOH, 210.

46. Cf. EM, 26; AAS 59 (1967) 558. N.B. In monasteries of nuns, every effort should be made to celebrate the Easter triduum with the greatest possible ceremony but within the monastery church.

47. Cf. CR, *Ordinationes et declarationes circa ordinem hebdomadae sanctae instauratum* (February 1, 1957), 21; AAS 49 (1957) 91–95.

48. OT, 8.

49. Cf. Congregation for Catholic Education, Instruction on Liturgical Formation in Seminaries (May 17, 1979) 15, 33.

50. Cf. CB, 297.

51. Cf. RomM, Evening Mass of the Lord's Supper.

52. Cf. *ibid.*

53. Cf. RomM, 1.

54. SC, 55; EM, 31.

55. *Maxima Redemptionis Nostrae Mysteria*, 9.

56. Cf. RomM, Evening Mass of the Lord's Supper.

57. Cf. CB, 300.

58. Matthew 20:28.

59. Cf. CB, 303.

60. Cf. RomM, Evening Mass of the Lord's Supper, 15–16.

61. Cf. CR, *Declaration of March 15, 1956*, 3; AAS 48 (1956) 153; *Ordinationes et declarationes circa ordinem hebdomadae sanctae instauratum* 14.

62. Cf. RomM, Evening Mass of the Lord's Supper, 21; *Maxima Redemptionis Nostrae Mysteria*, 8–10.

63. 1 Corinthians 5:7.

64. Cf. RomM, Good Friday, Celebration of the Lord's Passion, 1, 3.

65. Apostolic Constitution *Paenitemini*, II, 2; CIC, c. 1251.

66. RomM, Good Friday, Celebration of the Lord's Passion, 1; CDW, declaration *Ad Missale Romanum*, in *Notitiae* 13 (1977): 602.

67. Cf. RomM, Good Friday, Celebration of the Lord's Passion, 3; *Ordinationes et declarationes circa ordinem hebdomadae sanctae instauratum*, 15.

68. Cf., RomM, Good Friday, Celebration of the Lord's Passion, alternative prayer.

69. Cf. RomM, Good Friday, Celebration of the Lord's Passion, 9; cf. CB, 319.

70. Cf. RomM, Good Friday, Celebration of the Lord's Passion, 12.

71. Cf. GIRM, 46.

72. Cf. RomM, Good Friday, Celebration of the Lord's Passion, 19.

73. Cf. Micah 6:3–4.

74. Cf. SC, 13.

75. Cf. RomM, Holy Saturday; The Apostles' Creed; 1 Peter 3:19.

76. Cf. GILOH, 210.

77. RomM, Holy Saturday.

78. *Maxima Redemptionis Nostrae Mysteria*, 2.

79. Cf. Exodus 12:42.

80. St. Augustine, Sermon 219, PL 38, 1088.

81. CB, 332.

82. Cf. *ibid.*, RomM, The Easter Vigil, 3.

83. EM, 28.

84. RomM, The Easter Vigil, 19, Easter Proclamation.

85. SC, 6; cf. Romans 6:3–6; Ephesians 2:5–6; Colosians 2:12–13; 2 Timothy 2:11–12.

86. "We keep vigil on that night because the Lord rose from the dead; that life . . . where there is no longer the sleep of death, began for us in his flesh; being thus risen, death will be no more nor have dominion . . . . If we have kept vigil for the risen one, he will see that we shall reign with him forever." St. Augustine, *Sermo Guelferbytan*, 5, 4, PLSupp 2, 552.

87. Cf. RomM, Easter Vigil, 7.

88. Cf. *ibid.*, 10–12.

89. Cf. *ibid.*, 17.

90. Luke 24:27; cf. Luke 24:44–45.

91. Cf. RomM, Easter Vigil, 21.

92. Cf. *ibid.*, 23.

93. Cf. CB, 352.

94. Cf. Acts 4:11–12; Matthew 21:42; Mark 12:10; Luke 20:17.

95. Cf. RBaptC, 6.

96. Cf. RomM, Easter Vigil, 48.

97. Cf. *ibid.*, 45.

98. Cf. *ibid.*, 47.

99. Cf. *ibid.*, 49; RCIA, 36.

100. Cf. RomM, Easter Vigil, 53; RomM, Ritual Masses, 3, Baptism.

101. Cf. GIRM, 240–242.

102. Cf. SC, 106.

103. Cf. GILOH, 213.

104. Cf. RomM, Pentecost Sunday, final rubric; RBaptC, General Introduction, 25.

105. Cf. GNLY, 22.

106. Cf. GNLY, 5, 23.

107. Cf. GNLY, 58.

108. Cf. RCIA, 235–239.

109. Cf. CIC, c. 920.

110. *Maxima Redemptionis Nostrae Mysteria*, 24.

111. BB, chaps. 1, 2; Blessing of a family in its own home.

112. Cf. SC, 13.; cf. CDW, *Orientamenti e proposte per la celebrazione dell'anno mariano.* (April 3, 1987) 3, 51–56.

113. Cf. GNLY, 23.

114. It is possible to combine the celebration of first Vespers with the celebration of Mass as provided for in the General Instruction of the Liturgy of the Hours, 96. In order to throw into greater relief the mystery of this day, it is possible to have several readings from Holy Scripture, as proposed in the lectionary. In this case, after the collect the reader goes to the ambo to proclaim the reading. The psalmist or cantor sings the psalm, to which the people respond with the refrain. Then all stand and the priest says, "Let us pray," and after a short silent pause, he says the prayer corresponding to the reading (for example, one of the collects for the ferial days of the seventh week of Easter).

115. St. Leo the Great, *Sermo 6 de Quadragesima*, 1–2, PL 54: 285.

116. Cf. RomM, Saturday of the Seventh Week of Easter, opening prayer.

DIRECTORY FOR THE
APPLICATION OF PRINCIPLES
AND
NORMS ON ECUMENISM

EXCERPTS

PONTIFICAL COUNCIL FOR PROMOTING CHRISTIAN UNITY
1993

OVERVIEW OF *DIRECTORY FOR THE APPLICATION OF PRINCIPLES AND NORMS ON ECUMENISM*

Paul Turner

May a non-Catholic serve as a godparent for a Catholic baptism? May a Catholic be the best man at a non-Catholic wedding? May someone from an Eastern Orthodox church receive communion at a Roman Catholic Mass? May a Catholic receive communion at a non-Catholic church? These and other questions that Catholics often face due to their family, business and other social relationships are answered in the *Directory for the Application of Principles and Norms on Ecumenism* (DE).

The directory, published by the Pontifical Council for Promoting Christian Unity in 1993, updated and expanded the information previously offered in two post-conciliar documents: *A Directory for the Application of the Second Vatican Council's Decisions on Ecumenism* (1967), and its second part, subtitled *Ecumenism in Higher Education* (1970).

Through the Second Vatican Council (1962–1965) the Catholic church entered a time of self-reflection, probing its identity more deeply and refreshing its dialogue with the world. The fruits of the Council's labor became immediately evident in the church's worship, but its complete goals were broader still.

Among the major areas the Council pursued was ecumenism. Other churches and ecclesial communities had already entered the arena. By the beginning of Vatican II, the World Council of Churches had already formed, and some churches were already merging. Formerly, the ecumenical strategy of the Catholic church seemed to have two goals: the conversion of Protestants and an end to the Orthodox schism. The Council Fathers took a broader look at the ecumenical picture, striking a balance between their convictions already noted in the Dogmatic Constitution on the Church *Lumen gentium:* first, that the church of Christ "subsists in the Catholic church"; and second, that "many elements of sanctification and truth are found outside its visible confines" (#8). In doing so, they called for a deep respect for the personal faith of all. The resulting Decree on Ecumenism *Unitatis redintegratio* catapulted the Catholic church into the ecumenical movement. Its opening words called the restoration of unity one of the principal concerns of the Council, and it criticized division among churches as contrary to the will of Christ and a scandal to the world.

The Decree on Ecumenism still captures the heady enthusiasm of the Second Vatican Council. It launched a sweeping agenda for the church by calling for not only the promotion but the practice of ecumenism. It also recognized the distinct concerns issuing from relationships between the Catholic church and other eastern and western churches. By its nature, the document towered with vision while abstaining from specifics.

The specifics of the Decree on Ecumenism fell to post-conciliar work. The Secretariat for Promoting Christian Unity accepted the responsibility and set about developing its *Directory for the Application of the Second Vatican Council's Decisions on Ecumenism*, published in two parts—in 1967 and 1970.

The first part of the directory (1967) dealt with several practical concerns. These included the creation of diocesan and regional ecumenical commissions, necessary for working out the ideals of the Council. It also affirmed the validity of baptism administered by ministers of other churches and ecclesial communities, and promoted sharing among churches where possible.

The second part (1970) laid more groundwork. It presented the general principles that undergird ecumenism and then worked out particular norms for ecumenical formation and collaboration, especially in regard to schools and institutions.

The *Directory for the Application of the Second Vatican Council's Decisions on Ecumenism* served the church well. However, other concurrent developments began to influence ecumenical progress. Most significantly, the *Code of Canon Law* for the Roman Catholic church was revised in 1983, and the *Code of Canons of the Eastern Churches* was published in 1990. It also became evident that the directory had not adequately treated topics like marriage between Catholics and other Christians. A more coherent integration of all this material, it seemed, would better serve the cause of ecumenism and the church's commitment to it.

Consequently, in 1985, speaking on the twenty-fifth anniversary of the founding of the Secretariat for Promoting Christian Unity, Pope John Paul II called for the revision of the ecumenical directory. The Secretariat once again assumed the task, and thus began a long process of development and consultation for the generation of the revised document. Before its completion in 1993, DE passed through several committees, received reactions from national conferences of bishops around the world, underwent further refinements with the Congregation for the Doctrine of the Faith, and finally won the approval of Pope John Paul II. On March 25, 1993, DE was promulgated under the auspices of the renamed Pontifical Council for Promoting Christian Unity.

The finished document contains five sections. It opens with a chapter on the search for Christian unity—new theological material rooted in the Second Vatican Council's Decree on Ecumenism and Dogmatic Constitution on the Church. It then treats the organization of the Catholic church in its service to Christian unity, calling for internal commissions and international cooperation. The third section discusses the formation of Catholics in ecumenism, an attempt to widen participation in the ecumenical movement. The fourth gathers the practical matters of communion of life and spiritual activity among the baptized. The final section calls for collaboration, dialogue and common witness to ecumenism.

The excerpt included in this volume of *The Liturgy Documents: A Parish Resource* draws from the fourth and fifth sections of DE, articles 92–160 and 183–187. These articles concern specific matters that pertain to liturgical prayer among the Christian churches and ecclesial communities. The first and lengthier part of the excerpt considers prayer and the sacraments. The document gives special consideration to baptism and marriage. However, in a middle section entitled "Sharing Spiritual Activities and Resources," one finds other substantial concerns: principles for prayer in common; sharing in nonsacramental liturgical worship; and sharing in the sacramental life of the church, especially in the eucharist, but also in reconciliation and anointing of sick. The shorter, second part of the excerpt concerns the development of common scriptural and liturgical texts.

The sacrament of baptism prompts several concerns, including conditions for its validity and the role of godparents. Regarding validity, DE assumes the validity of baptisms in which the minister uses the proper matter and form, and has the same intention as the church. This affirmation represents a change in policy. Formerly, the validity of baptisms performed by other Christians was generally considered doubtful; if other Christians desired acceptance into the Catholic church, the priest usually administered a conditional baptism. In fact, this practice was so common that the formula for conditional baptism appeared in the Roman Ritual together with the standard one for hundreds of years. Today, the baptisms of other Christians in the mainline churches and ecclesial communities are presumed to be valid. If any of those Christians desire the full communion of the Catholic church, they celebrate the Rite of Reception; the priest who receives them also confirms them. If a conditional baptism must be performed, it is to happen in private (#93–95, 99–100).

The question of whether Christians of one denomination may serve as godparents in another has vexed many Catholics. DE explains that baptism is celebrated within a given church or ecclesial community. Only a person within that church or ecclesial community may function as a godparent, but other baptized Christians may serve as witnesses together with the godparent. The prescription advises Catholic parents to seek a Catholic godparent, even if they wish to include a witness of another Christian tradition; it also permits Catholics to serve as witnesses for baptisms in other church communities when the host church provides a godparent (#98).

In sharing spiritual activities and resources, DE encourages Catholics to make full use of what they share in common with others. Many nonsacramental occasions may draw churches together for prayer; the funeral of a member of a non-Catholic church may even be celebrated in a Catholic church (#120–121). Catholics may share buildings and religious objects with members of non-Catholic churches, as long as each community's faith is respected (#137–140). Students from other churches or ecclesial communities in Catholic schools may have access to their own ministers (#141), as may patients of other communities in Catholic hospitals (#142).

The question of sharing other sacraments requires much more nuance, and the possibilities depend first on whether or not an Eastern church is involved. The Catholic church recognizes the sacraments of all Eastern churches. It extends its willingness to share the sacraments with them, but not all Eastern churches are able to extend the same invitation back (#122–128).

The sharing of eucharist, penance and anointing of the sick with Christians of Western churches and ecclesial communities is more difficult. For Catholics, the eucharist is a sign of ecclesial communion; being outside that communion excludes members of other Christian communities from ordinary participation. However, there are occasions when the sharing of these sacraments "may be permitted or even commended" (#129). DE offers four conditions: "that the person be unable to have recourse for the sacrament desired to a minister of his or her own church or eccleisal community, ask for the sacrament of his or her own initiative, manifest Catholic faith in this sacrament and be properly disposed" (#131). Catholics under similar circumstances, however, may only receive from those churches whose sacraments are considered valid (#132). Hence, Catholics cannot accept a reciprocal invitation to communion in a non-Catholic church, even in these extraordinary circumstances.

The sense of "communion" at sacramental worship extends also to certain ministries: The reader and homilist at a Catholic eucharistic liturgy should be Catholic. Outside of eucharistic celebrations they need not be (#133–135). Those who witness marriages as best man, maid of honor, or as another member of the wedding party need not be from the same church as the bride or groom, whether the wedding takes place in a Catholic church or elsewhere (#136)

Marriages between Catholics and members of other churches or ecclesial communities pose special pastoral concerns. Even before marriage, couples should discuss the exercise of their faith as part of their preparation for the celebration of the sacrament. One should be firm in one's own faith and learn about the faith of the partner; still, respecting the partner's faith should not invite indifference about one's own. The pastors of each partner should collaborate before the wedding. The couple is exhorted to pray together (#143–149).

Of primary concern in marriage is the faith of the children. The Catholic party is asked to promise to do all in his or her power to raise the children in the Catholic faith, beginning with baptism. The non-Catholic party is to be informed of this promise, but is not asked to assent or sign anything. The Catholic parent is to act always with respect for the religious freedom and conscience of the other parent when sharing the Catholic faith with the children (#150–151).

The wedding ceremony should affirm the significance of the sacrament. Marriages between Catholics and Eastern Christians should stress what the faiths share in common. A Catholic who wishes to marry a member of another church or ecclesial community is still bound by the canonical form of marriage but may obtain a dispensation for various reasons, including "the maintaining of family harmony, obtaining parental consent to the marriage, the recognition of the particular religious commitment of the non-Catholic partner or his/her blood relationship with a minister of another church or ecclesial community" (#154). Still, a single public ceremony is required; a couple may not give consent twice (#156). The Catholic minister may join or be joined by the minister of another community at the wedding; the visiting minister may recite a prayer, proclaim a reading, offer an exhortation or give a blessing (#157–158). DE states that the wedding between a Catholic and a person from another church or ecclesial community will ordinarily not take place within the context of a celebration of the eucharist. If the non-Catholic partner desires communion at the wedding, the norms found in article 131 still apply (#159–160). The bishops of South Africa notably clarified these permissions after DE was published.

The last excerpt included here (#183–187) comes from the closing section of DE and deals with common Bible work and common liturgical texts. Since DE calls on Christians to seek occasions for common prayer, it also encourages the recognition of Bible and liturgy texts that many ecclesial communities might hold in common.

When Catholics in all parts of the world are drawn on a regular basis into conversation and commerce with those of other beliefs, they find the experience both rich and challenging. The *Directory for the Application of Principles and Norms on Ecumenism* aims to help Catholics enter that experience strong in their faith yet committed to the cause of ecumenism.

OUTLINE

DIRECTORY FOR THE APPLICATION OF PRINCIPLES AND NORMS ON ECUMENISM—EXCERPTS

IV. COMMUNION IN LIFE AND SPIRITUAL ACTIVITY AMONG THE BAPTIZED

A. SACRAMENT OF BAPTISM

92.   By the sacrament of baptism a person is truly incorporated into Christ and into his church and is reborn to a sharing of the divine life.[103] Baptism, therefore, constitutes the sacramental bond of unity existing among all who through it are reborn. Baptism, of itself, is the beginning, for it is directed toward the acquiring of fullness of life in Christ. It is thus ordered to the profession of faith, to the full integration into the economy of salvation and to eucharistic communion.[104] Instituted by the Lord himself, baptism, by which one participates in the mystery of his death and resurrection, involves conversion, faith, the remission of sin and the gift of grace.

93.   Baptism is conferred with water and with a formula that clearly indicates that baptism is done in the name of the Father, Son and Holy Spirit. It is therefore of the utmost importance for all the disciples of Christ that baptism be administered in this manner by all and that the various churches and ecclesial communities arrive as closely as possible at an agreement about its significance and valid celebration.

94.   It is strongly recommended that the dialogue concerning both the significance and the valid celebration of baptism take place between Catholic authorities and those of other churches and ecclesial communities at the diocesan or episcopal conference levels. Thus it should be possible to arrive at common statements through which they express mutual recognition of baptisms as well as procedures for considering cases in which a doubt may arise as to the validity of a particular baptism.

95.   In arriving at these expressions of common agreement, the following points should be kept in mind:

a) Baptism by immersion or by pouring, together with the Trinitarian formula, is of itself valid. Therefore, if the rituals, liturgical books or established customs of a church or ecclesial community prescribe either of these ways of baptism, the sacrament is to be considered valid unless there are serious reasons for doubting that the minister has observed the regulations of his/her own community or church.

b) The minister's insufficient faith concerning baptism never of itself makes baptism invalid. Sufficient intention in a minister who baptizes is to be presumed, unless there is serious ground for doubting that the minister intended to do what the church does.

c) Wherever doubts arise about whether or how water was used,[105] respect for the sacrament and deference toward these ecclesial communities require that serious investigation of the practice of the community concerned be made before any judgment is passed on the validity of its baptism.

96. According to the local situation and as occasion may arise, Catholics may, in common celebration with other Christians, commemorate the baptism which unites them by renewing the engagement to undertake a full Christian life which they have assumed in the promises of their baptism and by pledging to cooperate with the grace of the Holy Spirit in striving to heal the divisions which exist among Christians.

97. While by baptism a person is incorporated into Christ and his church, this is only done in practice in a given church or ecclesial community. Baptism, therefore, may not be conferred jointly by two ministers belonging to different churches or ecclesial communities. Moreover, according to Catholic liturgical and theological tradition, baptism is celebrated by just one celebrant. For pastoral reasons, in particular circumstances the local ordinary may sometimes permit, however, that a minister of another church or ecclesial community take part in the celebration by reading a lesson, offering a prayer, etc. Reciprocity is possible only if a baptism celebrated in another community does not conflict with Catholic principles or discipline.[106]

98. It is the Catholic understanding that godparents, in a liturgical and canonical sense, should themselves be members of the church or ecclesial community in which the baptism is being celebrated. They do not merely undertake a responsibility for the Christian education of the person being baptized (or confirmed) as a relative or friend; they are also there as representatives of a community of faith, standing as guarantees of the candidate's faith and desire for ecclesial communion.

a) However, based on the common baptism and because of ties of blood or friendship, a baptized person who belongs to another ecclesial community may be admitted as a witness to the baptism, but only together with a Catholic godparent.[107] A Catholic may do the same for a person being baptized in another ecclesial community.

b) Because of the close communion between the Catholic church and the Eastern Orthodox churches, it is permissible for a just cause for an Eastern faithful to act as godparent together with a Catholic godparent at the baptism of a

Catholic infant or adult, so long as there is provision for the Catholic education of the person being baptized and it is clear that the godparent is a suitable one.

A Catholic is not forbidden to stand as godparent in an Eastern Orthodox church if he/she is so invited. In this case, the duty of providing for the Christian education binds in the first place the godparent who belongs to the church in which the child is baptized.[108]

99.   Every Christian has the right for conscientious religious reasons freely to decide to come into full Catholic communion.[109] The work of preparing the reception of an individual who wishes to be received into full communion with the Catholic church is of its nature distinct from ecumenical activity.[110] The Rite of Christian Initiation of Adults provides a formula for receiving such persons into full Catholic communion. However, in such cases, as well as in cases of mixed marriages, the Catholic authority may consider it necessary to inquire as to whether the baptism already received was validly celebrated. The following recommendations should be observed in carrying out this inquiry.

a) There is no doubt about the validity of baptism as conferred in the various Eastern churches. It is enough to establish the fact of the baptism. In these churches the sacrament of confirmation (chrismation) is properly administered by the priest at the same time as baptism. There it often happens that no mention is made of confirmation in the canonical testimony of baptism. This does not give grounds for doubting that this sacrament was also conferred.

b) With regard to Christians from other churches and ecclesial communities, before considering the validity of baptism of an individual Christian, one should determine whether an agreement on baptism (as mentioned above, No. 94) has been made by the churches and ecclesial communities of the regions or localities involved and whether baptism has in fact been administered according to this agreement. It should be noted, however, that the absence of a formal agreement about baptism should not automatically lead to doubt about the validity of baptism.

c) With regard to these Christians, where an official ecclesiastical attestation has been given there is no reason for doubting the validity of the baptism conferred in their churches and ecclesial communities unless, in a particular case, an examination clearly shows that a serious reason exists for having a doubt about one of the following: the matter and form and words used in the conferral of baptism, the intention of an adult baptized or the minister of the baptism.[111]

d) If, even after careful investigation, a serious doubt persists about the proper administration of the baptism and it is judged necessary to baptize conditionally, the Catholic minister should show proper regard for the doctrine that baptism may be conferred only once by explaining to the person involved both why in this case he is baptizing conditionally and what is the significance of the rite of conditional baptism. Furthermore, the rite of conditional baptism is to be carried out in private and not in public.[112]

e) It is desirable that synods of Eastern Catholic churches and episcopal conferences issue guidelines for the reception into full communion of Christians baptized into other churches and ecclesial communities. Account is to be taken of the fact that they are not catechumens and of the degree of knowledge and practice of the Christian faith which they may have.

100. According to the rite of Christian Initiation of Adults, those adhering to Christ for the first time are normally baptized during the Paschal Vigil. Where the celebration of this rite includes the reception into full communion of those already baptized, a clear distinction must be made between them and those who are not yet baptized.

101. In the present state of our relations with the ecclesial communities of the Reformation of the 16th century, we have not yet reached agreement about the significance or sacramental nature or even of the administration of the sacrament of confirmation. Therefore, under present circumstances, persons entering into full communion with the Catholic church from one of these communities are to receive the sacrament of confirmation according to the doctrine and rite of the Catholic church before being admitted to eucharistic communion.

B. SHARING SPIRITUAL ACTIVITIES AND RESOURCES

GENERAL PRINCIPLES

102. Christians may be encouraged to share in spiritual activities and resources, i.e. to share that spiritual heritage they have in common in a manner and to a degree appropriate to their present divided state.[113]

103. The term "sharing in spiritual activities and resources" covers such things as prayer offered in common, sharing in liturgical worship in the strict sense as described below in No. 116, as well as common use of sacred places and of all necessary objects.

104. The principles which should direct this spiritual sharing are the following:

a) In spite of the serious difficulties which prevent full ecclesial communion, it is clear that all those who by baptism are incorporated into Christ share many elements of the Christian life. There thus exists a real even if imperfect communion among Christians which can be expressed in many ways, including sharing in prayer and liturgical worship,[114] as will be indicated in the paragraph which follows.

b) According to Catholic faith, the Catholic Church has been endowed with the whole of revealed truth and all the means of salvation as a gift which cannot be lost.[115] Nevertheless, among the elements and gifts which belong to the Catholic Church (e.g., the written word of God, the life of grace, faith, hope and charity etc.) many can exist outside its visible limits. The churches and ecclesial communities not in full communion with the Catholic Church have by no means been deprived of significance and value in the mystery of salvation, for the Spirit of Christ has not refrained from using them as means of salvation.[116]

In ways that vary according to the condition of each church or ecclesial community, their celebrations are able to nourish the life of grace in their members who participate in them and provide access to the communion of salvation.[117]

c) The sharing of spiritual activities and resources, therefore, must reflect this double fact:

> 1) The real communion in the life of the Spirit which already exists among Christians and is expressed in their prayer and liturgical worship.

> 2) The incomplete character of this communion because of differences of faith and understanding which are incompatible with an unrestricted mutual sharing of spiritual endowments.

d) Fidelity to this complex reality makes it necessary to establish norms for spiritual sharing which take into account the diverse ecclesial situations of the churches and ecclesial communities involved, so that as Christians esteem and rejoice in the spiritual riches they have in common they are also made more aware of the necessity of overcoming the separations which still exist.

e) Since eucharistic concelebration is a visible manifestation of full communion in faith, worship and community life of the Catholic Church, expressed by ministers of that church, it is not permitted to concelebrate the eucharist with ministers of other churches or ecclesial communities.[118]

105. There should be a certain "reciprocity" since sharing in spiritual activities and resources, even with defined limits, is a contribution, in a spirit of mutual good will and charity, to the growth of harmony among Christians.

106. It is recommended that consultations on this sharing take place between appropriate Catholic authorities and those of other communions to seek out the possibilities for lawful reciprocity according to the doctrine and traditions of different communities.

107. Catholics ought to show a sincere respect for the liturgical and sacramental discipline of other churches and ecclesial communities, and these in their turn are asked to show the same respect for Catholic discipline. One of the objectives of the consultation mentioned above should be a greater mutual understanding of each other's discipline and even an agreement on how to manage a situation in which the discipline of one church calls into question or conflicts with the discipline of another.

PRAYER IN COMMON

108. Where appropriate, Catholics should be encouraged, in accordance with the church's norms, to join in prayer with Christians of other churches and ecclesial communities. Such prayers in common are certainly a very effective means of petitioning for the grace of unity, and they are a genuine expression of the ties which still bind Catholics to these other Christians.[119] Shared prayer is in itself a way to spiritual reconciliation.

109. Prayer in common is recommended for Catholics and other Christians so that together they may put before God the needs and problems they share— e.g., peace, social concerns, mutual charity among people, the dignity of the family, the effects of poverty, hunger and violence, etc. The same may be said of occasions when, according to circumstances, a nation, region or community wishes to make a common act of thanksgiving or petition to God, as on a national holiday, at a time of public disaster or mourning, on a day set aside for remembrance of those who have died for their country, etc. This kind of prayer is also recommended when Christians hold meetings for study or common action.

110. Shared prayer should, however, be particularly concerned with the restoration of Christian unity. It can center, e.g., on the mystery of the church and its unity, on baptism as a sacramental bond of unity or on the renewal of personal and community life as a necessary means to achieving unity. Prayer of this type is particularly recommended during the Week of Prayer for Christian Unity or in the period between Ascension and Pentecost.

111. Representatives of the churches, ecclesial communities or other groups concerned should cooperate and prepare together such prayer. They should decide among themselves the way in which each is to take part, choose the themes and select the scripture readings, hymns and prayers.

a) In such a service there is room for any reading, prayer and hymn which manifests the faith or spiritual life shared by all Christian people. There is a place for an exhortation, address or biblical meditation drawing on the common Christian inheritance and able to promote mutual good will and unity.

b) Care should be taken that the versions of holy scripture used be acceptable to all and be faithful translations of the original text.

c) It is desirable that the structure of these celebrations should take account of the different patterns of community prayer in harmony with the liturgical renewal in many churches and ecclesial communities, with particular regard being given to common heritage of hymns, of texts taken from lectionaries and of liturgical prayers.

d) When services are arranged between Catholics and those of an Eastern church, particular mention should be given to the liturgical discipline of each church, in accordance with No. 115 below.

112. Although a church building is a place in which a community is normally accustomed to celebrating its own liturgy, the common services mentioned above may be celebrated in the church of one or other of the communities concerned if that is acceptable to all the participants. Whatever place is used should be agreeable to all, be capable of being properly prepared and be conducive to devotion.

113. Where there is a common agreement among the participants, those who have a function in a ceremony may use the dress proper to their ecclesiastical rank and to the nature of the celebration.

114. Under the direction of those who have proper formation and experience, it may be helpful in certain cases to arrange for spiritual sharing in the form of days of recollection, spiritual exercises, groups for the study and sharing of traditions of spirituality, and more stable associations for a deeper exploration of a common spiritual life. Serious attention must always be given to what has been said concerning the recognition of the real differences of doctrine which exist as well as to the teaching and discipline of the Catholic Church concerning sacramental sharing.

115. Since the celebration of the eucharist on the Lord's Day is the foundation and center of the whole liturgical year,[120] Catholics—but those of Eastern churches according to their own law[121]—are obliged to attend Mass on that day and on days of precept.[122] It is not advisable therefore to organize ecumenical services on Sundays, and it must be remembered that even when Catholics participate in ecumenical services or in services of other churches and ecclesial communities, the obligation of participating at Mass on these days remains.

SHARING IN NONSACRAMENTAL LITURGICAL WORSHIP

116. By liturgical worship is meant worship carried out according to books, prescriptions and customs of a church or ecclesial community presided over by a minister or delegate of that church or community. This liturgical worship may be of a nonsacramental kind or may be the celebration of one or more of the Christian sacraments. The concern here is nonsacramental worship.

117. In some situations, the official prayer of a church may be preferred to ecumenical services specially prepared for the occasion. Participation in such celebrations as morning or evening prayer, special vigils, etc., will enable people of different liturgical traditions—Catholic, Eastern, Anglican and Protestant—to understand each other's community prayer better and to share more deeply in traditions which often have developed from common roots.

118. In liturgical celebrations taking place in other churches and ecclesial communities, Catholics are encouraged to take part in the psalms, responses, hymns and common actions of the church in which they are guests. If invited by their hosts, they may read a lesson or preach.

119. Regarding assistance at liturgical worship of this type, there should be a meticulous regard for the sensibilities of the clergy and people of all the Christian communities concerned, as well as for local customs that may vary according to time, place, persons and circumstances. In a Catholic liturgical celebration, ministers of other churches and ecclesial communities may have the place and liturgical honors proper to their rank and their role, if this is judged desirable. Catholic clergy invited to be present at a celebration of another church or ecclesial community may wear the appropriate dress or insignia of their ecclesiastical office if it is agreeable to their hosts.

120. In the prudent judgment of the local ordinary, the funeral rites of the Catholic Church may be granted to members of a non-Catholic Church or ecclesial community unless it is evidently contrary to their will and provided that their own minister is unavailable[123] and that the general provisions of canon law do not forbid it.[124]

121. Blessings ordinarily given for the benefit of Catholics may also be given to other Christians who request them, according to the nature and object of the blessing. Public prayer for other Christians, living or dead, and for the needs and intentions of other churches and ecclesial communities and their spiritual heads may be offered during the litanies and other invocations of a liturgical service, but not during the eucharistic anaphora. Ancient Christian liturgical and ecclesiological tradition permits the specific mention in the eucharistic anaphora only of the names of persons who are in full communion with the church celebrating the eucharist.

SHARING IN SACRAMENTAL LIFE, ESPECIALLY THE EUCHARIST

a) With Members of Various Eastern Churches

122. Between the Catholic Church and the Eastern churches not in full communion with it, there is still a very close communion in matters of faith.[125] Moreover, "through the celebration of the eucharist of the Lord in each of these churches, the church of God is built up and grows in stature" and "although separated from us, these churches still possess true sacraments, above all—by apostolic succession—the priesthood and the eucharist."[126] This offers ecclesiological and sacramental grounds, according to the understanding of the Catholic church, for allowing and even encouraging some sharing in liturgical worship, even of the eucharist, with these churches, "given suitable circumstances and the approval of church authorities."[127] It is recognized, however, that Eastern Churches, on the basis of their own ecclesiological understanding, may have more restrictive disciplines in this matter, which others should respect. Pastors should carefully instruct the faithful so that they will be clearly aware of the proper reasons for this kind of sharing in liturgical worship and of the variety of discipline which may exist in this connection.

123. Whenever necessity requires or a genuine spiritual advantage suggests, and provided that the danger of error or indifferentism is avoided, it is lawful for any Catholic for whom it is physically or morally impossible to approach a Catholic minister, to receive the sacraments of penance, eucharist and anointing of the sick from a minister of an Eastern church.[128]

124. Since practice differs between Catholics and Eastern Christians in the matter of frequent communion, confession before communion and the eucharistic fast, care must be taken to avoid scandal and suspicion among Eastern Christians through Catholics not following the Eastern usage. A Catholic who legitimately wishes to communicate with Eastern Christians must respect the Eastern discipline as much as possible and refrain from communicating if that church restricts sacramental communion to its own members to the exclusion of others.

125. Catholic ministers may lawfully administer the sacraments of penance, eucharist and the anointing of the sick to members of the Eastern churches who ask for these sacraments of their own free will and are properly disposed. In these particular cases also, due consideration should be given to the discipline of the Eastern churches for their own faithful, and any suggestion of proselytism should be avoided.[129]

126. Catholics may read lessons at a sacramental liturgical celebration in the Eastern churches if they are invited to do so. An Eastern Christian may be invited to read the lessons at similar services in Catholic churches.

127. A Catholic minister may be present and take part in the celebration of a marriage being properly celebrated between Eastern Christians or between a Catholic and an Eastern Christian in the Eastern church if invited to do so by the Eastern church authority and if it is in accord with the norms given below concerning mixed marriages, where they apply.

128. A member of an Eastern church may act as bridesmaid or best man at a wedding in a Catholic Church; a Catholic also may be bridesmaid or best man at a marriage properly celebrated in Eastern church. In all cases this practice must conform to the general discipline of both churches regarding the requirements for participating in such marriages.

b) With Christians of Other Churches and Ecclesial Communities.

129. A sacrament is an act of Christ and of the church through the Spirit.[130] Its celebration in a concrete community is the sign of the reality of its unity in faith, worship and community life. As well as being signs, sacraments—most specially the eucharist—are sources of the unity of the Christian community and of spiritual life, and are means for building them up. Thus eucharistic communion is inseparably linked to full ecclesial communion and its visible expression.

At the same time, the Catholic Church teaches that by baptism members of other churches and ecclesial communities are brought into a real, even if imperfect, communion with the Catholic Church[131] and that "baptism, which constitutes the sacramental bond of unity existing among all who through it are reborn . . . is wholly directed toward the acquiring of fullness of life in Christ."[132] The eucharist is, for the baptized, a spiritual food which enables them to overcome sin and to live the very life of Christ, to be incorporated more profoundly in him and share more intensely in the whole economy of the mystery of Christ.

It is in the light of these two basic principles, which must always be taken into account together, that in general the Catholic Church permits access to its eucharistic communion and to the sacraments of penance and anointing of the sick only to those who share its oneness in faith, worship and ecclesial life.[133] For the same reasons it also recognizes that in certain circumstances, by way of exception and under certain conditions, access to these sacraments may be permitted or even commended for Christians of other churches and ecclesial communities.[134]

130. In case of danger of death, Catholic ministers may administer these sacraments when the conditions given below (No. 131) are present. In other cases, it is strongly recommended that the diocesan bishop, taking into account any norms which may have been established for this matter by the episcopal conference or by the synods of Eastern Catholic churches, establish general norms for judging situations of grave and pressing need and for verifying the conditions mentioned below (No. 131).[135] In accord with canon law,[136] these general norms are to be established only after consultation with at least the local competent authority of the other interested church or ecclesial community. Catholic ministers will judge individual cases and administer these sacraments only in accord with these established norms, where they exist. Otherwise they will judge according to the norms of this directory.

131. The conditions under which a Catholic minister may administer the sacraments of the eucharist, of penance and of the anointing of the sick to a baptized person who may be found in the circumstances given above (No. 130) are that the person be unable to have recourse for the sacrament desired to a minister of his or her own church or ecclesial community, ask for the sacrament of his or her own initiative, manifest Catholic faith in this sacrament and be properly disposed.[137]

132. On the basis of the Catholic doctrine concerning the sacraments and their validity, a Catholic who finds himself or herself in the circumstances mentioned above (Nos. 130 and 131) may ask for these sacraments only from a minister in whose church these sacraments are valid or from one who is known to be validly ordained according to the Catholic teaching on ordination.

133. The reading of Scripture during a eucharistic celebration in the Catholic Church is to be done by members of that church. On exceptional occasions and for a just cause, the bishop of the diocese may permit a member of another church or ecclesial community to take on the task of reader.

134. In the Catholic eucharistic liturgy the homily which forms part of the liturgy itself is reserved to the priest or deacon, since it is the presentation of the mysteries of faith and the norms of Christian living in accordance with Catholic teaching and tradition.[138]

135. For the reading of Scripture and preaching during other than eucharistic celebrations, the norms given above (No. 118) are to be applied.

136. Members of other churches or ecclesial communities may be witnesses at the celebration of marriage in a Catholic Church. Catholics may also be witnesses at marriages which are celebrated in other churches or ecclesial communities.

SHARING OTHER RESOURCES FOR SPIRITUAL LIFE AND ACTIVITY

137. Catholic churches are consecrated or blessed buildings which have an important theological and liturgical significance for the Catholic community. They are therefore generally reserved for Catholic worship. However, if priests,

ministers or communities not in full communion with the Catholic Church do not have a place or the liturgical objects necessary for celebrating worthily their religious ceremonies, the diocesan bishop may allow them the use of a church or a Catholic building and also lend them what may be necessary for their services. Under similar circumstances, permission may be given to them for interment or for the celebration of services at Catholic cemeteries.

138. Because of developments in society, the rapid growth of population and urbanization, and for financial motives, where there is a good ecumenical relationship and understanding between the communities the shared ownership or use of church premises over an extended period of time may become a matter of practical interest.

139. When authorization for such ownership or use is given by the diocesan bishop according to any norms which may be established by the episcopal conference or the Holy See, judicious consideration should be given to the reservation of the blessed sacrament so that this question is resolved on the basis of a sound sacramental theology with the respect that is due, while also taking account of the sensitivities of those who will use the building, e.g. by construction a separate room or chapel.

140. Before making plans for a shared building, the authorities of the communities concerned should first reach agreement as to how their various disciplines will be observed, particularly in regard to the sacraments. Furthermore, a written agreement should be made which will clearly and adequately take care of all questions which may arise concerning financial matters and the obligations arising from church and civil law.

141. In Catholic schools and institutions every effort should be made to respect the faith and conscience of students or teachers who belong to other churches or ecclesial communities. In accordance with their own approved statutes, the authorities of these schools and institutions should take care that clergy of other communities have every facility for giving spiritual and sacramental ministration to their own faithful who attend such schools or institutions. As far as circumstances allow, with the permission of the diocesan bishop these facilities can be offered on the Catholic premises, including the church or chapel.

142. In hospitals, homes for the aged and similar institutions conducted by Catholics, the authorities should promptly advise priests and ministers of other communities of the presence of their faithful, and afford them every facility to visit these persons and give them spiritual and sacramental ministrations under dignified and reverent conditions, including the use of the chapel.

C. MIXED MARRIAGES

143. This section of the Ecumenical Directory does not attempt to give an extended treatment of all the pastoral and canonical questions connected with

either the actual celebration of the sacrament of Christian marriage or the pastoral care to be given to Christian families, since such questions form part of the general pastoral care of every bishop or regional conference of bishops. What follows below focuses on specific issues related to mixed marriages and should be understood in the context. The term *mixed marriage* refers to any marriage between a Catholic and a baptized Christian who is not in full communion with the Catholic church.[139]

144. In all marriages, the primary concern of the church is to uphold the strength and stability of the indissoluble marital union and the family life that flows from it. The perfect union of persons and full sharing of life which constitutes the married state are more easily assured when both partners belong to the same faith community. In addition, practical experience and the observations obtained in various dialogues between representatives of churches and ecclesial communities indicate that mixed marriages frequently present difficulties for the couples themselves and for the children born to them in maintaining their Christian faith and commitment, and for the harmony of family life. For all these reasons, marriage between persons of the same ecclesial community remains the objective to be recommended and encouraged.

145. In view, however, of the growing number of mixed marriages in many parts of the world, the church includes within its urgent pastoral solicitude couples preparing to enter, or already having entered, such marriages. These marriages, even if they have their own particular difficulties, "contain numerous elements that could well be made good use of and developed both for their intrinsic value and for the contribution they can make to the ecumenical movement. This is particularly true when both parties are faithful to their religious duties. Their common baptism and the dynamism of grace provide the spouses in these marriages with the basis and motivation for expressing unity in the sphere of moral and spiritual values."[140]

146. It is the abiding responsibility of all, especially priests and deacons and those who assist them in pastoral ministry, to provide special instruction and support for the Catholic party in living his or her faith as well as for the couples in mixed marriages both in the preparation for the marriage, in its sacramental celebration and for the life together that follows the marriage ceremony. This pastoral care should take into account the concrete spiritual condition of each partner, their formation in their faith and their practice of it. At the same time respect should be shown for the particular circumstances of each couple's situation, the conscience of each partner and the holiness of the state of sacramental marriage itself. Where judged useful, diocesan bishops, synods of Eastern Catholic churches or episcopal conferences could draw up more specific guidelines for this pastoral care.

147. In fulfilling this responsibility, where the situation warrants it positive steps should be taken, if possible, to establish contacts with the minister of the other church or ecclesial community, even if this may not always prove easy. In general,

mutual consultation between Christian pastors for supporting such marriages and upholding their values can be a fruitful field of ecumenical collaboration.

148. In preparing the necessary marriage preparation programs, the priest or deacon and those who assist him should stress the positive aspects of what the couple share together as Christians in the life of grace, in faith, hope and love, along with the other interior gifts of the Holy Spirit.[141] Each party, while continuing to be faithful to his or her Christian commitment and to the practice of it, should seek to foster all that can lead to unity and harmony, without minimizing real differences and while avoiding an attitude of religious indifference.

149. In the interest of greater understanding and unity, both parties should learn more about their partner's religious convictions and the teaching and religious practices of the church or ecclesial community to which he or she belongs. To help them live the Christian inheritance they have in common, they should be reminded that prayer together is essential for their spiritual harmony and that reading and study of the sacred Scriptures are especially important. In the period of preparation, the couple's effort to understand their individual religious and ecclesial traditions, and serious consideration of the differences that exist can lead to greater honesty, charity and understanding of these realities and also of the marriage itself.

150. When, for a just and reasonable cause, permission for a mixed marriage is requested, both parties are to be instructed on the essential ends and properties of marriage which are not to be excluded by either party. Furthermore, the Catholic party will be asked to affirm, in the form established by the particular law of the Eastern Catholic churches or by the episcopal conference, that he or she is prepared to avoid the dangers of abandoning the faith and to promise sincerely to do all in his/her power to see that the children of the marriage be baptized and educated in the Catholic Church. The other partner is to be informed of these promises and responsibilities.[142] At the same time it should be recognized that the non-Catholic partner may feel a like obligation because of his/her own Christian commitment. It is to be noted that no formal written or oral promise is required of this partner in canon law.

Those who wish to enter into a mixed marriage should, in the course of the contacts that are made in this connection, be invited and encouraged to discuss the Catholic baptism and education of the children they will have and where possible come to a decision on this question before the marriage.

In order to judge the existence or otherwise of a "just and reasonable cause" with regard to granting permission for this mixed marriage, the local ordinary will take account, among other things, of an explicit refusal on the part of the non-Catholic party.

151. In carrying out this duty of transmitting the Catholic faith to the children the Catholic parent will do so with respect for the religious freedom and conscience of the other parent and with due regard for the unity and permanence of the marriage and for the maintenance of the communion of the family. If,

notwithstanding the Catholic's best efforts, the children are not baptized and brought up in the Catholic Church, the Catholic parent does not fall subject to the censure of canon law.[143] At the same time, his/her obligation to share the Catholic faith with the children does not cease. It continues to make its demands, which could be met, for example, by playing an active part in contributing to the Christian atmosphere of the home; doing all that is possible by word and example to enable the other members of the family to appreciate the specific values of the Catholic tradition; taking whatever steps are necessary to be well informed about his/her own faith so as to be able to explain and discuss it with them; praying with the family for the grace of Christian unity as the Lord wills it.

152. While keeping clearly in mind that doctrinal differences impede full sacramental and canonical communion between the Catholic Church and the various Eastern churches, in the pastoral care of marriages between Catholics and Eastern Christians particular attention should be given to the sound and consistent teaching of the faith which is shared by both and to the fact that in the Eastern churches are to be found "true sacraments, and above all, by apostolic succession, the priesthood and the eucharist, whereby they are still joined to us in closest intimacy."[144] If proper pastoral care is given to persons involved in these marriages, the faithful of both communions can be helped to understand how children born of such marriages will be initiated into and spiritually nourished by the sacramental mysteries of Christ. Their formation in authentic Christian doctrine and ways of Christian living would, for the most part, be similar in each church. Diversity in liturgical life and private devotion can be made to encourage rather than hinder family prayer.

153. A marriage between a Catholic and a member of an Eastern church is valid if it has taken place with the celebration of a religious rite by an ordained minister, as long as any other requirements of law for validity have been observed. For lawfulness in these cases, the canonical form of celebration is to be observed.[145] Canonical form is required for the validity of marriages between Catholics and Christians of churches and ecclesial communities.[146]

154. The local ordinary of the Catholic partner, after having consulted the local ordinary of the place where the marriage will be celebrated, may for grave reasons and without prejudice to the law of the Eastern churches[147] dispense the Catholic partner from the observance of the canonical form of marriage.[148] Among these reasons for dispensation may be considered the maintaining of family harmony, obtaining parental consent to the marriage, the recognition of the particular religious commitment of the non-Catholic partner or his/her blood relationship with a minister of another church or ecclesial community. Episcopal conferences are to issue norms by which such a dispensation may be granted in accordance with a common practice.

155. The obligation imposed by some churches or ecclesial communities for the observance of their own form of marriage is not a motive for automatic dispensation from the Catholic canonical form. Such particular situations should form the subject of dialogue between the churches, at least at the local level.

156. One must keep in mind that if the wedding is celebrated with a dispensation from canonical form some public form of celebration is still required for validity.[149] To emphasize the unity of marriage, it is not permitted to have two separate religious services in which the exchange of consent would be expressed twice, or even one service which would celebrate two such exchanges of consent jointly or successively.[150]

157. With the previous authorization of the local ordinary, and if invited to do so, a Catholic priest or deacon may attend or participate in some way in the celebration of mixed marriages in situations where the dispensation from canonical form has been granted. In these cases there may be only one ceremony in which the presiding person receives the marriage vows. At the invitation of this celebrant, the Catholic priest or deacon may offer other appropriate prayers, read from the Scriptures, give a brief exhortation and bless the couple.

158. Upon request of the couple, the local ordinary may permit the Catholic priest to invite the minister of the party of the other church or ecclesial community to participate in the celebration of the marriage, to read from the Scriptures, give a brief exhortation and bless the couple.

159. Because of problems concerning eucharistic sharing which may arise from the presence of non-Catholic witnesses and guests, a mixed marriage celebrated according to the Catholic form ordinarily takes place outside the eucharistic liturgy. For a just cause, however, the diocesan bishop may permit the celebration of the eucharist.[151] In the latter case, the decision as to whether the non-Catholic party of the marriage may be admitted to eucharistic communion is to be made in keeping with the general norms existing in the matter both for Eastern Christians[152] and for other Christians,[153] taking into account the particular situation of the reception of the sacrament of Christian marriage by two baptized Christians.

160. Although the spouses in a mixed marriage share the sacraments of baptism and marriage, eucharistic sharing can only be exceptional and in each case the norms stated above concerning the admission of a non-Catholic Christian to eucharistic communion,[154] as well as those concerning the participation of a Catholic in eucharistic communion in an other church,[155] must be observed.

V. ECUMENICAL COOPERATION, DIALOGUE AND COMMON WITNESS

COMMON BIBLE WORK

183. The word of God that is written in the Scriptures nourishes the life of the church in manifold ways[170] and is "a precious instrument in the mighty hand of God for attaining to that unity which the Savior holds out to all men."[171] Veneration of the Scriptures is a fundamental bond of unity between Christians, one that holds firm even when the churches and communities to which they

belong are not in full communion with each other. Everything that can be done to make members of the churches and ecclesial communities read the word of God, and to do that together when possible (e.g., Bible Weeks), reinforces this bond of unity that already unites them, helps them to be open to the unifying action of God and strengthens the common witness to the saving word of God which they give to the world. The provision and diffusion of suitable editions of the Bible is a prerequisite to the hearing of the word. While the Catholic Church continues to produce editions of the Bible that meet her own specific standards and requirements, it also cooperates willingly with other churches and ecclesial communities in the making of translations and in the publication of common editions in accordance with what was foreseen by the Second Vatican Council and is provided for in the Code of Canon Law.[172] It sees ecumenical cooperation in this field as a valuable form of common service and common witness in the church and to the world.

184. The Catholic Church is involved in this cooperation in many ways and at different levels. The Pontifical Council for Promoting Christian Unity was involved in the setting up, in 1969, of the World Catholic Federation for the Biblical Apostolate (now Catholic Biblical Federation), as an international Catholic organization of a public character to further the pastoral implementation of *Dei Verbum*, Ch. VI. In accordance with this objective, whenever local circumstances allow, collaboration at the level of local churches as well as at the regional level, between the ecumenical officer and the local sections of the federation should be strongly encouraged.

185. Through the general secretariat of the Catholic Biblical Federation, the Pontifical Council for Promoting Christian Unity maintains and develops relations with the United Bible Societies, an international Christian organization which has published jointly with the secretariat "Guidelines for Interconfessional Cooperation in Translating the Bible."[173] This document sets out the principles, methods and concrete orientations of this special type of collaboration in the biblical field. This collaboration has already yielded good results. Similar contacts and cooperation between institutions devoted to the publication and use of the Bible are encouraged on all levels of the life of the church. They can help cooperation between the churches and ecclesial communities in missionary work, catechetics and religious education, as well as in common prayer and study. They can often result in the joint production of a Bible that may be used by several churches and ecclesial communities in a given cultural area, or for specific purposes such as study or liturgical life.[174] Cooperation of this kind can be an antidote to the use of the Bible in a fundamentalist way or for sectarian purposes.

186. Catholics can share the study of the Scriptures with members of other churches and ecclesial communities in many different ways and on many different levels. This sharing goes from the kind of work that can be done in neighborhood or parochial groups to that of scholarly research among professional exegetes. In order to have ecumenical value, at whatever level it is done, this work needs to be grounded on faith and to nourish faith. It will often bring home

to the participants how the doctrinal positions of different churches and ecclesial communities, and differences in their approaches to the use and exegesis of the Bible, lead to different interpretations of particular passages. It is helpful for Catholics when the editions of the Scriptures that they use actually draw attention to passages in which the doctrine of the church is at issue. They will want to face up to any difficulties and disagreements that come from the ecumenical use of the Scriptures with an understanding of and a loyalty to the teaching of the church. But this need not prevent them from recognizing how much they are at one with other Christians in the interpretation of the Scriptures. They will come to appreciate the light that the experience and traditions of the different churches can throw on parts of the Scriptures that are especially significant for them. They will become more open to the possibility of finding new starting points in the Scriptures themselves for discussion about controversial issues. They will be challenged to discover the meaning of God's word in relation to contemporary human situations that they share with their fellow Christians. Moreover, they will experiences with joy the unifying power of God's word.

COMMON LITURGICAL TEXTS

187. Churches and ecclesial communities whose members live within a culturally homogeneous area should draw up together, where possible, a text of the most important Christian prayers (the Lord's Prayer, Apostles' Creed, Nicene-Constantinopolitan Creed, a Trinitarian doxology, the Glory to God in the Highest). These would be for regular use by all the churches and ecclesial communities or at least for use when they pray together on ecumenical occasions. Agreement on a version of the psalter for liturgical use, or at least of some of the more frequently used psalms would also be desirable; a similar agreement for common scriptural readings for liturgical use should also be explored. The use of liturgical and other prayers that come from the period of the undivided church can help to foster an ecumenical sense. Common hymn books, or at least common collections of hymns to be included in the books of the different churches and ecclesial communities, as well as cooperation in developing liturgical music, are also to be recommended. When Christians pray together with one voice, their common witness reaches to heaven as well as being heard on earth.

NOTES

103. Cf. UR, 22.

104. Cf. UR, 22.

105. With regard to all Christians, consideration should be given to the danger of invalidity when baptism is administered by sprinkling, especially of several people at once.

106. Cf. Ecumenical Directory (1967).

107. Cf. CIC, c. 874.2. According to the explanation given by the *Acta Commissionis* (Communicationes 5, 1983, p. 182) the wording *communitas ecclesialis* does not include the Eastern Orthodox churches not in full communion with the Catholic church *(Notatur insuper ecclesias Orientales Orthodoxas in schemate sub nomine communitatis ecclesialis non venire).*

108. Cf. Ecumenical Directory, 48; CCEC, c. 685.3.

109. Cf. UR, 4; CCEC, c. 896–901.

110. Cf. UR, 4.

111. CIC, c. 869.2.

112. Cf. CIC, c. 869.1 and .3.

113. UR, 8.

114. Cf. UR, 3 and 8; see also n. 116 below.

115. Cf. LG, 8; UR, 4.

116. Cf. UR, 3.

117. Cf. UR, 3, 15, 22.

118. Cf. CIC, c. 908; CCEC, c. 702.

119. Cf. UR, 8.

120. Cf. SC, 106.

121. Cf. CCEC, c. 881.1; CIC, c. 1247.

122. Cf. CIC, c. 1247; CCEC, c. 881.1.

123. Cf. CIC, c. 1183.3; CCEC, c. 876.2.

124. Cf. CIC, c. 1184; CCEC, c. 887.

125. Cf. UR, 14.

126. UR, 22.

127. UR, 22.

128. Cf. CIC, c. 844.2 and CCEC, c. 671.2.

129. Cf. CIC, c. 844.3 and cf. n. 106 above.

130. Cf. CIC, c. 840 and CCEC, c. 667.

131. Cf. UR, 3.

132. UR, 22.

133. Cf. UR, 8; CIC, c. 844.1 and CCEC, c. 671.1.

134. Cf. CIC, c. 844.4 and CCEC, c. 671.4.

135. For the establishing of these norms we refer to the following documents: "On Admitting Other Christians to Eucharistic Communion in the Catholic Church" (1972) and "Note Interpreting the Instruction on Admitting Other Christians to Eucharistic Communion Under Certain Circumstances" (1973).

136. Cf. CIC, c. 844.5 and CCEC, c. 671.5.

137. Cf. CIC, c. 844.4 and CCEC, c. 671.4.

138. Cf. CIC, c. 767 and CCEC, c. 614.4.

139. Cf. CIC, c. 1124 and CCEC, c. 813.

140. Cf. John Paul II, apostolic exhortation *Familiaris consortio* (on the family), Nov. 22, 1981: 78.

141. Cf. UR, 3.

142. Cf. CIC, cc. 1125, 1126 and CCEC, cc. 814, 815.

143. Cf. CIC, c. 1366 and CCEC, c. 1439.

144. Cf. UR, 15.

145. Cf. CIC, c. 1127.1 and CCEC, c. 834.2.

146. Cf. CIC, c. 1127.1 and CCEC, c. 834.1.

147. Cf. CCEC, c. 835.

148. Cf. CIC, c. 1127.2.

149. Cf. *ibid.*

150. Cf. CIC, c. 1127.3 and CCEC, c. 839.

151. RMarr, 8.

152. Cf. above, n. 125.

153. Cf. above, nn. 129–131.

154. Cf. above, nn. 125, 130 and 131.

155. Cf. above, n. 132.

170. Cf. DV, Ch. 6.

171. UR, 21.

172. Cf. CIC, c. 825.2 and CCEC, c. 655.1.

173. New revised edition 1987 of the first 1968 version. Published in Information Service of the SPCU, 65 (1987): 140–145.

174. In accordance with the norms laid down in CIC, cc. 825–827, 838 and in CCEC, cc. 655–659 and the decree of the Congregation for the Doctrine of the Faith *Ecclesiae Pastorum de Ecclesiae Pastorum Vigilantia Circa Libros* (March 19, 1975) in AAS 1975, 281–184.

INCULTURATION
AND THE
ROMAN LITURGY:
FOURTH INSTRUCTION FOR
THE RIGHT APPLICATION
OF THE CONCILIAR CONSTITUTION
ON THE LITURGY (nn. 37–40)

CONGREGATION FOR DIVINE WORSHIP
AND THE DISCIPLINE OF THE SACRAMENTS
1994

OVERVIEW OF *INCULTURATION AND THE ROMAN LITURGY*

Mark R. Francis, CSV

Inculturation and the Roman Liturgy (IRL) was issued in 1994 by the Congregation for Divine Worship and the Discipline of the Sacraments as a commentary on articles 37–40 of the Constitution on the Sacred Liturgy *Sacrosanctum concilium* (SC), which deal with the process of liturgical inculturation. For this reason, its purpose is very focused: to offer principles and norms for implementing those articles entitled, "Norms for Adapting the Liturgy to the Culture and Traditions of Peoples."

SUMMARY

IRL is divided into four major sections, preceded by a rather lengthy introduction (#1–8), which explains the principles underlying the process of liturgical inculturation. The first section (#9–20) reviews evidence of inculturation throughout salvation history. It traces the influence of culture on the expression of the faith, as reflected in the Old and New Testaments, and in the church's proclamation of the Good News in new cultural and historical contexts.

The second section (#21–32) considers the theological aspects of liturgical inculturation, such as the intrinsic relationship between the liturgy and the expression of faith. These considerations are followed by a discussion of preliminary conditions necessary for inculturating the liturgy: an effective presentation of the scriptures linked with an accurate assessment of the cultural context. The section ends by discussing the particular responsibility of national conferences of bishops in promoting responsible liturgical inculturation.

The third section (#33–51) deals directly with inculturation. It first speaks of the overarching goal of inculturation, which is the participation of the faithful in the liturgy. It underscores the importance of the unity of the Roman rite and reaffirms that inculturation takes place under the authority of the Holy See, the local conference of bishops and the local ordinary. The second part of this section lists the modes of adaptation: language, music, gesture and posture, movement, art and environment, and the relation of the liturgy to popular devotions. The final articles of this section raise a word of caution regarding inculturation, especially in multicultural contexts and in societies in the midst of rapid social change.

The fourth and final section (#52–69) looks specifically at how national conferences of bishops may adapt the liturgy within the norms set by the liturgical books. Issues of translation, adaptation of the eucharistic celebration, the sacraments of initiation, the marriage rite, funerals, blessings, the liturgical year and the Liturgy of the Hours are discussed. The second part of this section deals with the procedure to be followed when more radical adaptation of the liturgy is needed. This possibility is described in article 40 of SC and involves the approval of the Holy See.

The appearance of this document was surprising to those who felt the renewal of the liturgy had already been accomplished. That the Congregation for Divine Worship and the Discipline of the Sacraments would issue a document in 1994 on four articles from the 1963 Constitution on the Liturgy—a full 31 years after that document was promulgated—seemed curious indeed. The Congregation evidently saw a need to promote and guide the process of liturgical inculturation being carried out around the world. This also explains its subtitle: "Fourth Instruction for the Right Application of the Conciliar Constitution on the Liturgy (nn. 37–40)."

It is necessary to remember that after the promulgation of SC, a committee (the Consilium) was created in order to implement the liturgical renewal mandated by the Council. Three instructions were issued by the Consilium to this end: *Inter oecumenici* (1964), *Tres abhinc annos* (1967) and *Liturgicae instaurationes* (1970). It should also be noted that this same Consilium issued a particular instruction to translators, known by its French title *Comme le prévoit* (1969). The Consilium was dissolved in the 1970s after having completed its work with the publication of the *Roman Missal* and other liturgical books. Thus, this document is deliberately offered in continuity with the previous three general instructions on implementing the reform of the liturgy.

This instruction, however, as it is meant to comment on SC, needs to be interpreted in light of subsequent and more mature conciliar and magisterial reflections on the issue of culture and faith, notably the Decree on the Missionary Activity of the Church *Ad gentes* and the Pastoral Constitution on the Church in the Modern World *Gaudium et spes*. Other sources of magisterial teaching also contain important developments in the church's understanding of the interrelation of culture and the expression of faith. For example, two encyclicals, *Evangelii nuntiandi* (1975) of Pope Paul VI and *Redemptoris missio* (1991) of Pope John Paul II, articulate well the growing awareness of the church's need to go beyond the more superficial aspects of what was originally called "adaptation" by SC. The conscious decision to change terminology from "adaptation" to "inculturation" reflects this new sensitivity.

Perhaps the most influential post-conciliar document guiding the overall implementation of liturgical renewal was the instruction on the translation of liturgical texts, *Comme le prévoit*, mentioned above. It highlights the nature of worship as communication and advances the discussion of inculturation by championing the principle of a dynamic rather than a literal translation of the Latin texts. Even more importantly, the final article of *Comme le prévoit* refers implicitly to inculturation when it declares that "texts translated from another language are clearly not sufficient for the celebration of a renewed liturgy" and calls for new prayers composed in modern languages.

The principles and norms of this instruction must also be read in the light of the more than 30 years of experience in implementing liturgical renewal—a renewal that has necessarily involved inculturation. For example, the Holy See's approval of the so-called Zairian rite (the Roman rite for the dioceses of Zaire, now called the Congo) in 1987, following almost 20 years of effort by the bishops of Zaire, seems to serve as an implicit model for the instruction's understanding of liturgical inculturation. Clearly it was not written as if the church were just beginning the process of liturgical renewal.

INCULTURATION AS DIALOGUE

While IRL is very careful to stress the need for catechesis on the liturgy in order for the "young churches" to deepen their understanding of the liturgical heritage of the Roman church, this catechesis is done to initiate a dialogue with the received liturgical tradition in order that young churches "find in their own cultural heritage appropriate forms which can be integrated into the Roman rite where this is judged useful and necessary" (#33). The dialogical nature of the inculturation process needs to be emphasized here, since it is at the heart of the definition of inculturation found in article 8 of IRL, as developed by John Paul II in his encyclicals *Redemptoris missio* (#52) and *Catechesi tradendae* (#53). Inculturation is not only "an intimate transformation of the authentic cultural values by their integration into Christianity and the implantation of Christianity into different human cultures," but also an introduction of peoples "together with their cultures, into [the church's] own community." Thus, this introduction of new peoples into the Body of Christ necessarily implies that the church as a whole will be enriched and transformed by the new insights into faith and Christian witness lived in the new Christian settings and expressed in the liturgy.

IRL's emphasis on the full, conscious and active participation of the laity in the liturgy as the overarching goal of inculturation is significant (#35). In emphasizing the assembly's central role in renewing the liturgy by quoting article 21 of SC, IRL continues to guide the process of inculturation along the path indicated by Vatican II.

What does this mean practically? If, after serious catechesis on the liturgy and scripture, the liturgy as presented in the typical editions of the liturgical books is not comprehensible to people of a given culture, or if it does not allow the assembly in that culture to take part in the rites with ease, the church local and universal not only has the option but the real obligation to inculturate the rites. This is a reaffirmation of article 40 of SC, which allows for radical adaptations of the liturgy if the cultural context is such that the rites would not be understandable to the faithful. Not only is the relevance of the rite important here, but the church's very identity and the effectiveness of its primary mission of proclaiming God's salvation in Christ is at stake.

THE SUBSTANTIAL UNITY OF THE ROMAN RITE

IRL emphasizes that one of its goals, after that of ensuring the assembly's understanding and participation, is to preserve the "substantial unity of the Roman rite" (#36). This phrase is taken from article 38 of SC. A definition of this "substantial unity" is not contained in SC, but it is now defined in IRL as being expressed in two kinds of liturgical books: "the typical editions of liturgical books published by authority of the supreme pontiff" and the liturgical books "approved by the episcopal conferences for their areas and confirmed by the Apostolic See" (#36).

Interestingly, the duly approved "local interpretations" of the official Latin liturgical books, although far from uniform in many respects, are regarded as instruments of the substantial unity of the Roman rite. Rather than a call to inflexible uniformity, the "substantial unity of the Roman rite" is thus being interpreted by this document in a rather broad manner. Admittedly, the document has a concern for abusive and unauthorized modification of the rites (#37) and the inappropriate juxtaposition of Christian rites with non-Christian practices, known as syncretism (#47). It also states quite plainly that its understanding of liturgical inculturation "does not foresee the creation of new families of rites." Rather, "inculturation responds to the needs of a particular culture and leads to adaptations which still remain part of the Roman rite" (#36). However, a hallmark of the typical editions of the liturgical books is pastoral flexibility (see, for example, footnote 82 of IRL).

The manner in which the current second generation of typical editions takes into account the suggestions made by language groups and episcopal conferences offers an important context for speaking of "substantial unity." Surely this unity is not found in mere translation of the Latin typical editions, but in implementing the flexibility already built into the approved rites. The most famous example of this is found in the rite for Zaire, mentioned above. In this version of the eucharistic liturgy, whole sections of the Mass are transposed and new liturgical ministers are added. This flexibility is also evident in the approval of the revised *Rite of Christian Initiation of Adults* (1987) and the *Order of Christian Funerals* (1989), prepared by the International Commission on English in the Liturgy. Therefore, this "substantial unity of the Roman rite" seems to consist in fidelity to the wide range of options supplied by the duly approved liturgical books. In this, IRL is faithful to the spirit of Vatican II in moving beyond the rigid rubricism of the Tridentine period to a unity based on a diversity of liturgical possibilities sensitive to the cultural reality of the assembly.

MULTICULTURAL CONCERNS

IRL shows sensitivity to some of the problems that involve inculturation in a multicultural context. Article 49 notes that the relationship between the various ethnic groups in a multicultural society is very complex and constantly changing. National conferences of bishops should "respect the riches of each culture and those who advance their cause, but they should not ignore or neglect a minority culture or one with which they are not familiar." The goal, however, is to arrive at a balanced attempt "which respects the individual rights of groups or tribes, but without carrying to extremes the localization of the liturgical celebrations" (#50). IRL also warns against an artificial folklorism that equates inculturation with proposing long-abandoned customs in order to shore-up cultural identity in an artificial way—especially for political purposes (#49).

IRL's acknowledgement of the existence of popular devotions in local churches is important (#45). It is just as important not to read its seemingly comprehensive prohibition against the "introduction of devotional practices into liturgical celebrations under the pretext of inculturation" without nuance. For example, the Congregation cannot have in mind the blessing of a wreath at the beginning of Mass on the First Sunday of Advent in North America, nor the *santo encuentro* (holy meeting) of statues of the risen Jesus with his mother at the entrance of the church on Easter morning, as practiced by Hispanics and Filipinos. Although both of these practices do not appear in the *editio typica* of the *Roman Missal,* they come directly from popular religious practice and have been approved by the respective conferences of bishops.

CONCLUSION

While the IRL's presentation of principles and norms is far from specific regarding the method or methods a national episcopal conference is to employ in inculturating the liturgy, this document presents the necessity of continuing the work of inculturation. It is unfortunate, though, that while the document insists that inculturation is a more appropriate word for what SC had in mind, it reverts to the use of "adaptation" in the last sections of the text. This lack of coherence in the document may reflect the ambivalence that many in the Congregation for Divine Worship and the Discipline of the Sacraments still seem to feel regarding the complex and sometimes messy nature of the process of inculturation.

Whatever its shortcomings, IRL recognizes the need for evaluating the liturgy in light of the vision proclaimed by the Second Vatican Council. This very pastoral vision seeks to take into account the many cultural contexts in which the Roman rite is celebrated, in order to more effectively proclaim the suffering, death and resurrection of Jesus Christ.

OUTLINE

INCULTURATION AND THE ROMAN LITURGY

INTRODUCTION

1.　Legitimate differences in the Roman rite were allowed in the past and were foreseen by the Second Vatican Council in the Constitution on the Sacred Liturgy *Sacrosanctum Concilium*, especially in the missions.[1] "Even in the liturgy the church has no wish to impose a rigid uniformity in matters that do not affect the faith or the good of the whole community."[2] It has known and still knows many different forms and liturgical families, and considers that this diversity, far from harming her unity, underlines its value.[3]

2.　In his apostolic letter *Vicesimus Quintus Annus*, the Holy Father Pope John Paul II described the attempt to make the liturgy take root in different cultures as an important task for liturgical renewal.[4] This work was foreseen in earlier instructions and in liturgical books, and it must be followed up in the light of experience, welcoming where necessary cultural values "which are compatible with the true and authentic spirit of the liturgy, always respecting the substantial unity of the Roman rite as expressed in the liturgical books."[5]

A) NATURE OF THIS INSTRUCTION

3.　By order of the supreme pontiff, the Congregation for Divine Worship and the Discipline of the Sacraments has prepared this instruction: The norms for the adaptation of the liturgy to the temperament and conditions of different peoples, which were given in Articles 37–40 of the constitution *Sacrosanctum Concilium*, are here defined; certain principles expressed in general terms in those articles are explained more precisely, the directives are set out in a more appropriate way and the order to be followed is clearly set out, so that in future this will be considered the only correct procedure. Since the theological principles relating to questions of faith and inculturation have still to be examined in depth, this congregation wishes to help bishops and episcopal conferences to consider or put into effect, according to the law, such adaptations as are already foreseen in the liturgical books; to re-examine critically arrangements that have already been made; and if in certain cultures pastoral need requires that form of adaptation of the liturgy which the constitution calls "more profound" and at the same time considers "more difficult," to make arrangements for putting it into effect in accordance with the law.

B) PRELIMINARY OBSERVATIONS

4.　The constitution *Sacrosanctum Concilium* spoke of the different forms of liturgical adaptation.[6] Subsequently the magisterium of the church has used the term *inculturation* to define more precisely "the incarnation of the Gospel in autonomous cultures and at the same time the introduction of these cultures into the life of the church."[7] Inculturation signifies "an intimate transformation of the authentic cultural values by their integration into Christianity and the implantation of Christianity into different human cultures."[8]

The change of vocabulary is understandable, even in the liturgical sphere. The expression *adaptation*, taken from missionary terminology, could lead one to think of modifications of a somewhat transitory and external nature.[9] The term *inculturation* is a better expression to designate a double movement: "By inculturation, the church makes the Gospel incarnate in different cultures and at the same times introduces peoples, together with their cultures, into her own community."[10] On the one hand the penetration of the Gospel into a given sociocultural milieu "gives inner fruitfulness to the spiritual qualities and gifts proper to each people . . . , strengthens these qualities, perfects them and restores them in Christ."[11]

On the other hand, the church assimilates these values, when they are compatible with the Gospel, "to deepen understanding of Christ's message and give it more effective expression in the liturgy and in the many different aspects of the life of the community of believers."[12] This double movement in the work of inculturation thus expresses on the component elements of the mystery of the incarnation.[13]

5.   Inculturation thus understood has its place in worship as in other areas of the life of the church.[14] It constitutes one of the aspects of the inculturation of the Gospel, which calls for true integration[15] in the life of faith of each people of the permanent values of a culture rather than their transient expressions. It must, then, be in full solidarity with a much greater action, a unified pastoral strategy which takes account of the human situation.[16] As in all forms of the work of evangelization, this patient and complex undertaking calls for methodical research and ongoing discernment.[17] The inculturation of the Christian life and of liturgical celebrations must be the fruit of a progressive maturity in the faith of the people.[18]

6.   The present instruction has different situations in view. There are in the first place those countries which do not have a Christian tradition or where the Gospel has been proclaimed in modern times by missionaries who brought the Roman rite with them. It is now more evident that "coming into contact with different cultures, the church must welcome all that can be reconciled with the Gospel in the tradition of a people to bring to it the riches of Christ and to be enriched in turn by the many different forms of wisdom of the nations of the earth."[19]

7.   The situation is different in the countries with a long-standing Western Christian tradition, where the culture has already been penetrated for a long time by the faith and the liturgy expressed in the Roman rite. That has helped the welcome given to liturgical reform in these countries, and the measures of adaptation envisaged in the liturgical books were considered, on the whole, sufficient to allow for legitimate local diversity (cf. below Nos. 53–61). In some

countries, however, where several cultures coexist, especially as a result of immigration, it is necessary to take account of the particular problems which this poses (cf. below No. 49).

8. It is necessary to be equally attentive to the progressive growth both in countries with a Christian tradition and in others of a culture marked by indifference or disinterest in religion.[20] In the face of this situation, it is not so much a matter of inculturation, which assumes that there are pre-existent religious values and evangelizes them, but rather a matter of insisting on liturgical formation[21] and finding the most suitable means to reach spirits and hearts.

I. PROCESS OF INCULTURATION THROUGHOUT THE HISTORY OF SALVATION

9. Light is shed upon the problems being posed about the inculturation of the Roman rite in the history of salvation. The process of inculturation was a process which developed in many ways.

The people of Israel throughout its history preserved the certain knowledge that it was the chosen people of God, the witness of his action and love in the midst of the nations. It took from neighboring peoples certain forms of worship, but its faith in the God of Abraham, Isaac and Jacob subjected these borrowings to profound modifications, principally changes of significance but also often changes in the form, as it incorporated these elements into its religious practice in order to celebrate the memory of God's wonderful deeds in its history.

The encounter between the Jewish world and Greek wisdom gave rise to a new form of inculturation: the translation of the Bible into Greek introduced the word of God into a world that had been closed to it and caused, under divine inspiration, and enrichment of the Scriptures.

10. "The law of Moses, the prophets and the psalms" (cf. Luke 24:27 and 44) was a preparation for the coming of the Son of God upon earth. The Old Testament, comprising the life and culture of the people of Israel, is also the history of salvation.

On coming to the earth the Son of God, "born of a woman, born under the law" (Galatians 4:4), associated himself with social and cultural conditions of the people of the alliance, with whom he lived and prayed.[22] In becoming a man he became a member of a people, a country and an epoch "and in a certain way, he thereby united himself to the whole human race."[23] For "we are all one in Christ, and the common nature of our humanity takes life in him. It is for this that he was called the 'new Adam.'"[24]

11. Christ, who wanted to share our human condition (cf. Hebrews 2:14), died for all in order to gather into unity the scattered children of God (cf. John 11:52). By his death he wanted to break down the wall of separation between mankind, to make Israel and the nations one people. By the power of his resurrection he

drew all people to himself and created out of them a single new man (cf. Ephesians 2:14–16; John 12:32). In him a new world has been born (cf. 2 Corinthians 5:16–17), and everyone can become a new creature. In him, darkness has given place to light, promise became reality and all the religious aspirations of humanity found their fulfillment. By the offering that he made of his body, once for all (cf. Hebrews 10:10), Christ Jesus brought about the fullness of worship in spirit and in truth in the renewal which he wished for his disciples (cf. John 4:23–24).

12.   "In Christ . . . the fullness of divine worship has come to us."[25] In him we have the high priest, taken from among men (cf. Hebrews 5:15; 10:19–21), put to death in the flesh but brought to life in the spirit (cf. 1 Peter 3;18). As Christ and Lord, he has made out of the new people "a kingdom of priests for God his Father" (cf. Revelation 1:6; 5:9–10).[26] But before inaugurating by the shedding of his blood the paschal mystery,[27] which constitutes the essential element of Christian worship,[28] Christ wanted to institute the eucharist, the memorial of his death and resurrection, until he comes again. Here is to be found the fundamental principle of Christian liturgy and the kernel of its ritual expression.

13.   At the moment of his going to his Father, the risen Christ assures his disciples of his presence and sends them to proclaim the Gospel to the whole of creation, to make disciples of all nations and baptize them (cf. Matthew 28:15; Mark 16:15; Acts 1:8). On the day of Pentecost, the coming of the Holy Spirit created a new community with the human race, uniting all in spite of the differences of language, which were a sign of division (cf. Acts 2:1–11). Henceforth the wonders of God will be made known to people of every language and culture (cf. Acts 10:44–48). Those redeemed by the blood of the Lamb and united in fraternal communion (cf. Acts 2:42) are called from "every tribe, language, people and nation" (cf. Revelation 5:9).

14.   Faith in Christ offers to all nations the possibility of being beneficiaries of the promise and of sharing in the heritage of the people of the covenant (cf. Ephesians 3:6), without renouncing their culture. Under the inspiration of the Holy Spirit, following the example of St. Peter (cf. Acts 10), St. Paul opened the doors of the church, not keeping the Gospel within the restrictions of the Mosaic law but keeping what he himself had received of the tradition which came from the Lord (cf. 1 Corinthians 11:23). Thus, from the beginning, the church did not demand of converts who were uncircumcised "anything beyond what was necessary" according to the decision of the apostolic assembly of Jerusalem (cf. Acts 15:28).

15.   In gathering together to break the bread on the first day of the week, which became the day of the Lord (cf. Acts 20:7; Revelation 1:10), the first Christian communities followed the command of Jesus who, in the context of the memorial of the Jewish pasch, instituted the memorial of his passion. In continuity with the unique history of salvation, they spontaneously took the forms and texts of Jewish worship and adapted them to express the radical newness of

Christian worship.[29] Under the guidance of the Holy Spirit, discernment was exercised between what could be kept and what was to be discarded of the Jewish heritage of worship.

16.   The spread of the Gospel in the world gave rise to other types of ritual in the churches coming from the gentiles, under the influence of different cultural traditions. Under the constant guidance of the Holy Spirit, discernment was exercised to distinguish those elements coming from "pagan" cultures which were incompatible with Christianity from those which could be accepted in harmony with apostolic tradition and in fidelity to the gospel of salvation.

17.   The creation and the development of the forms of Christian celebration developed gradually according to local conditions in the great cultural areas where the good news was proclaimed. Thus were born distinct liturgical families of the churches of the West and of the East. Their rich patrimony preserves faithfully the Christian tradition in its fullness.[30] The church of the West has sometimes drawn elements of its liturgy from the patrimony of the liturgical families of the East.[31] The church of Rome adopted in its liturgy the living language of the people, first Greek and then Latin, and, like other Latin churches, accepted into its worship important events of social life and gave them a Christian significance. During the course of the centuries, the Roman rite has known how to integrate texts, chants, gestures and rites from various sources[32] and to adapt itself in local cultures in mission territories,[33] even if at certain periods a desire for liturgical uniformity obscured this fact.

18.   In our own time, the Second Vatican Council recalled that the church "fosters and assumes the ability, resources and customs of each people. In assuming them, the church purifies, strengthens and ennobles them. . . . Whatever good lies latent in the religious practices and cultures of diverse peoples, it is not only saved from destruction but it is also cleansed, raised up and made perfect unto the glory of God, the confounding of the devil, and the happiness of mankind."[34] So the liturgy of the church must not be foreign to any country, people or individual, and at the same time it should transcend the particularity of race and nation. It must be capable of expressing itself in every human culture, all the while maintaining its identity through fidelity to the tradition which comes to it from the Lord.[35]

19.   The liturgy, like the Gospel, must respect cultures, but at the same time invite them to purify and sanctify themselves.

In adhering to Christ by faith, the Jews remained faithful to the Old Testament, which led to Jesus, the Messiah of Israel; they knew that he had fulfilled the Mosaic alliance, as the mediator of the new and eternal covenant, sealed in his blood on the cross. They knew that, by his one perfect sacrifice, he is the authentic high priest and the definitive temple (cf. Hebrews 6–10), and the prescriptions of circumcision (cf. Galatians 5:1–6), the Sabbath (cf. Matthew 12:8 and similar),[36] and the sacrifices of the temple (cf. Hebrews 10) became of only relative significance.

In a more radical way Christians coming from paganism had to renounce idols, myths, superstitions (cf. Acts 19:18–19; 1 Corinthians 10:14–22; 2:20–22; 1 John 5:21) when they adhered to Christ.

But whatever their ethnic or cultural origin, Christians have to recognize the promise, the prophecy and the history of their salvation in the history of Israel. They must accept as the word of God the books of the Old Testament as well as those of the New.[37] They welcome the sacramental signs, which can only be understood fully in the context of Holy Scripture and the life of the church.[38]

20.   The challenge which faced the first Christians, whether they came from the chosen people or from a pagan background, was to reconcile the renunciations demanded by faith in Christ with fidelity to the culture and traditions of the people to which they belonged.

And so it will be for Christians of all times, as the words of St. Paul affirm: "We proclaim Christ crucified, scandal for the Jews, foolishness for the pagans" (1 Corinthians 1:23).

The discernment exercised during the course of the church's history remains necessary, so that through the liturgy the work of salvation accomplished by Christ may continue faithfully in the church by the power of the Spirit in different countries and times and in different human cultures.

II. REQUIREMENTS AND PRELIMINARY CONDITIONS FOR LITURGICAL INCULTURATION

A) REQUIREMENTS EMERGING FROM THE NATURE OF THE LITURGY

21.   Before any research on inculturation begins, it is necessary to keep in mind the nature of the liturgy. It "is, in fact the privileged place where Christians meet God and the one whom he has sent, Jesus Christ" (cf. John 17:3).[39] It is at once the action of Christ the priest and the action of the church which is his body, because in order to accomplish his work of glorifying God and sanctifying mankind, achieved through visible signs, he always associates with himself the church, which, through him and in the Holy Spirit, gives the Father the worship which is pleasing to him.[40]

22.   The nature of liturgy is intimately linked up with the nature of the church; indeed, it is above all in the liturgy that the nature of the church is manifested.[41] Now the church has specific characteristics which distinguish it from every other assembly and community.

It is not gathered together by a human decision, but is called by God in the Holy Spirit and responds in faith to his gratuitous call (ekklesia derives from klesis, "call"). This singular characteristic of the church is revealed by its coming together as a priestly people, especially on the Lord's day, by the word which God addresses to his people and by the ministry of the priest, who through the sacrament of orders acts in the person of Christ the head.[42]

Because it is catholic, the church overcomes the barriers which divide humanity: By baptism all become children of God and form in Christ Jesus one people where "there is neither Jew nor Greek, neither slave nor free, neither male nor female" (Galatians 3:28). Thus church is called to gather all peoples, to speak the languages, to penetrate all cultures.

Finally, the church is a pilgrim on the earth far from the Lord (cf. 2 Corinthians 5:6): It bears the marks of the present time in the sacraments and in its institutions, but is waiting in joyful hope for the coming of Jesus Christ (cf. Titus 2:13).[43] This is expressed in the prayers of petition: It shows that we are citizens of heaven (cf. Philippians 3:20), at the same time attentive to the needs of mankind and of society (cf. 1 Timothy 2:1–4).

23.   The church is nourished on the word of God written in the Old and New Testaments. When the church proclaims the word in the liturgy, it welcomes it as a way in which Christ is present: "It is he who speaks when the sacred Scriptures are read in church."[44] For this reason the word of God is so important in the celebration of the liturgy[45] that the holy Scripture must not be replaced by any other text, no matter how venerable it may be.[46] Likewise the Bible is the indispensable source of the liturgy's language, of its signs and of its prayer, especially in the psalms.[47]

24.   Since the church is the fruit of Christ's sacrifice, the liturgy is always the celebration of the paschal mystery of Christ, the glorification of God the Father and the sanctification of mankind by the power of the Holy Spirit.[48] Christian worship thus finds its most fundamental expression when every Sunday throughout the whole world Christians gather around the altar under the leadership of the priest, celebrate the eucharist, listen to the word of God, and recall the death and resurrection of Christ, while awaiting his coming in glory.[49] Around this focal point, the paschal mystery is made present in different ways in the celebration of each of the sacraments.

25.   The whole life of the liturgy gravitates in the first place around the eucharistic sacrifice and the other sacraments given by Christ to his church.[50] The church has the duty to transmit them carefully and faithfully to every generation. In virtue of its pastoral authority, the church can make dispositions to provide for the good of the faithful, according to circumstances, times and places.[51] But it has no power over the things which are directly related to the will of Christ and which constitute the unchangeable part of the liturgy.[52] To break the link that the sacraments have with Christ, who instituted them, and with the very beginnings of the church,[53] would no longer be to inculturate them, but to empty them of their substance.

26.   The church of Christ is made present and signified in a given place and in a given time by the local or particular churches, which through the liturgy reveal the church in its true nature.[54] That is why every particular church must be united with the universal church not only in belief and sacramentals, but also in those practices received through the church as part of the uninterrupted apostolic tradition.[55] This includes, for example, daily prayer,[56] sanctification of

Sunday and the rhythm of the week, the celebration of Easter and the unfolding of the mystery of Christ throughout the liturgical year,[57] the practice of penance and fasting,[58] the sacraments of Christian initiation, the celebration of the memorial of the Lord and the relationship between the Liturgy of the Word and the eucharistic liturgy, the forgiveness of sins, the ordained ministry, marriage and the anointing of the sick.

27.   In the liturgy the faith of the church is expressed in a symbolic and communitarian form: This explains the need for a legislative framework for the organization of worship, the preparation of texts and the celebration of rites.[59] The reason for the preceptive character of this legislation throughout the centuries and still today is to ensure the orthodoxy of worship; that is to say, not only to avoid errors, but also to pass on the faith in the integrity so that the "rule of prayer" *(lex orandi)* of the church may correspond to the "rule of faith" *(lex credendi).*[60]

However deep inculturation may go, the liturgy cannot do without legislation and vigilance on the part of those who have received this responsibility in the church: the Apostolic See and, according to the prescriptions of the law, the episcopal conference for its territory and the bishop for his diocese.[61]

B) PRELIMINARY CONDITIONS FOR INCULTURATION OF THE LITURGY

28.   The missionary tradition of the church has always sought to evangelize people in their own language. Often indeed, it was the first apostles of a country who wrote down languages which up till then had only been oral. And this is right, as it is by the mother language, which conveys the mentality and the culture of a people, that one can reach the soul, mold it in the Christian spirit and allow to share more deeply in the prayer of the church.[62]

After the first evangelization, the proclamation of the word of God in the language of a country remains very useful for the people in their liturgical celebrations. The translation of the Bible, or at least of the biblical texts used in the liturgy, is the first necessary step in the process of the inculturation of the liturgy.[63]

So that the word of God may be received in a right and fruitful way, "it is necessary to foster a taste for holy Scripture, as is witnessed by the ancient traditions of the rites of both East and West."[64] Thus inculturation of the liturgy presupposes the reception of the sacred Scripture into a given culture.[65]

29.   The different situations in which the church finds itself are an important factor in judging the degree of liturgical inculturation that is necessary. The situation of countries that were evangelized centuries ago and where the Christian faith continues to influence the culture is different from countries which were evangelized more recently or where the Gospel has not penetrated deeply into cultural values.[66] Different again is the situation of a church where Christians are a minority of the population. A more complex situation is found when the population has different languages and cultures. A precise evaluation of the situation is necessary in order to achieve satisfactory solutions.

30.   To prepare an inculturation of the liturgy, episcopal conferences should call upon people who are competent both in the liturgical tradition of the Roman rite and in the appreciation of local cultural values. Preliminary studies of a historical, anthropological, exegetical and theological character are necessary. But these need to be examined in the light of the pastoral experience of the local clergy, especially those born in the country.[67] The advice of "wise people" of the country, whose human wisdom is enriched by the light of the Gospel, would also be valuable. Liturgical inculturation should try to satisfy the needs of traditional culture[68] and at the same time take account of the needs of those affected by an urban and industrial culture.

C) THE RESPONSIBILITY OF THE EPISCOPAL CONFERENCE

31.   Since it is a question of local culture, it is understandable that the constitution *Sacrosanctum Concilium* assigned special responsibility in this matter to the "various kinds of competent territorial bodies of bishops legitimately established."[69] In regard to this, episcopal conferences must consider "carefully and prudently what elements taken from the traditions and cultures of individual peoples may properly be admitted into divine worship."[70] They can sometimes introduce "into the liturgy such elements as are not bound up with superstition and error . . . provided they are in keeping with the true and authentic spirit of the liturgy."[71]

32.   Conferences may determine, according to the procedure given below (cf. Nos. 62 and 65–69), whether the introduction into the liturgy of elements borrowed from the social and religious rites of a people, and which form a living part of their culture, will enrich their understanding of liturgical actions without producing negative effects on their faith and piety. They will always be careful to avoid the danger of introducing elements that might appear to the faithful as the return to a period before evangelization (cf. below, No. 47).

In any case, if changes in rites or texts are judged to be necessary, they must be harmonized with the rest of the liturgical life and, before being put into practice, still more before being made mandatory, they should first be presented to the clergy and then to the faithful in such a way as to avoid the danger of troubling them without good reason (cf. below, Nos. 46 and 69).

III. PRINCIPLES AND PRACTICAL NORMS FOR INCULTURATION OF THE ROMAN RITE

33.   As particular churches, especially the young churches, deepen their understanding of the liturgical heritage they have received from the Roman church which gave them birth, they will be able in turn to find in their own cultural heritage appropriate forms which can be integrated into the Roman rite where this is judged useful and necessary.

The liturgical formation of the faithful and the clergy, which is called for by the constitution *Sacrosanctum Concilium*,[72] ought to help them to understand the meaning of the texts and the rites given in the present liturgical books. Often this will mean that elements which come from the tradition of the Roman rite do not have to be changed or suppressed.

A) GENERAL PRINCIPLES

34.   In the planning and execution of the inculturation of the Roman rite, the following points should be kept in mind: 1) the goal of inculturation; 2) the substantial unity of the Roman rite; 3) the competent authority.

35.   The goal which should guide the inculturation of the Roman rite is that laid down by the Second Vatican Council as the basis of the general restoration of the liturgy: "Both texts and rites should be so drawn up that they express more clearly the holy things they signify and so that the Christian people, as far as possible, may be able to understand them with ease and to take part in the rites fully, actively and as befits a community."[73]

Rites also need "to be adapted to the capacity of the faithful and that there should not be a need for numerous explanations for them to be understood."[74] However, the nature of the liturgy always has to be borne in mind, as does the biblical and traditional character of its structure and the particular way in which it is expressed (cf. above, Nos. 21–27).

36.   The process of inculturation should maintain the substantial unity of the Roman rite.[75] This unity is currently expressed in the typical editions of liturgical books, published by authority of the supreme pontiff and in the liturgical books approved by the episcopal conferences for their areas and confirmed by the Apostolic See.[76] The work of inculturation does not foresee the creation of new families of rites; inculturation responds to the needs of a particular culture and leads to adaptations which still remain part of the Roman rite.[77]

37.   Adaptations of the Roman rite, even in the field of inculturation, depend completely on the authority of the church. This authority belongs to the Apostolic See, which exercises it through the Congregation for Divine Worship and the Discipline of the Sacraments;[78] it also belongs, within the limits fixed by law, to episcopal conferences[79] and to the diocesan bishop.[80] "No other person, not even if he is a priest, may on his own initiative add, remove or change anything in the liturgy."[81] Inculturation is not left to the personal initiative of celebrants or to the collective initiative of an assembly.[82]

Likewise concessions granted to one region cannot be extended to other regions without the necessary authorization, even if an episcopal conference considers that there are sufficient reasons for adopting such measures in its own area.

B) ADAPTATIONS WHICH CAN BE MADE

38.   In an analysis of a liturgical action with a view to its inculturation, it is necessary to consider the traditional value of the elements of the action and in particular their biblical or patristic origin (cf. above, Nos. 21–26), because it is not sufficient to distinguish between what can be changed and what is unchangeable.

39.   Language, which is a means of communication between people. In liturgical celebrations its purpose is to announce to the faithful the good news of salvation[83] and to express the church's prayer to the Lord. For this reason it must always express, along with the truths of the faith, the grandeur and holiness of the mysteries which are being celebrated.

Careful consideration therefore needs to be given to determine which elements in the language of the people can properly be introduced into liturgical celebrations, and in particular whether it is suitable or not to use expressions from non-Christian religions. It is just as important to take account of the different literary genres used in the liturgy: biblical texts, presidential prayers, psalmody, acclamations, refrains, responsories, hymns and litanies.

40.   Music and singing, which express the soul of people, have pride of place in the liturgy. And so singing must be promoted, in the first place singing the liturgical text, so that the voices of the faithful may be heard in the liturgical actions themselves.[84] "In some parts of the world, especially mission lands, there are people who have their own musical traditions, and these play a great part in their religious and social life. Due importance is to be attached to their music and a suitable place given to it, not only in forming their attitude toward religion, but also in adapting worship to their native genius."[85]

It is important to note that a text which is sung is more deeply engraved in the memory than when it is read, which means that it is necessary to be demanding about the biblical and liturgical inspiration and the literary quality of texts which are meant to be sung.

Musical forms, melodies and musical instruments could be used in divine worship as long as they "are suitable, or can be made suitable, for sacred use, and provided they are in accord with the dignity of the place of worship and truly contribute to the uplifting of the faithful."[86]

41.   The liturgy is an action, and so gesture and posture are especially important. Those which belong to the essential rites of the sacraments and which are required for their validity must be preserved just as they have been approved or determined by the supreme authority of the church.[87]

The gestures and postures of the celebrating priest must express his special function: He presides over the assembly in the person of Christ.[88]

The gestures and postures of the assembly are signs of its unity and express its active participation and foster the spiritual attitude of the participants.[89] Each culture will choose those gestures and bodily postures which express the attitude of humanity before God, giving them a Christian significance, having some relationship if possible, with the gestures and postures of the Bible.

42.   Among some peoples, singing is instinctively accompanied by hand clapping, rhythmic swaying and dance movements on the part of the participants. Such forms of external expression can have a place in the liturgical actions of these peoples on condition that they are always the expression of true communal prayer of adoration, praise, offering and supplication, and not simply a performance.

43. The liturgical celebration is enriched by the presence of art, which helps the faithful to celebrate, meet God and pray. Art in the church, which is made up of all peoples and nations, should enjoy the freedom of expression as long as it enhances the beauty of the buildings and liturgical rites, investing them with the respect and honor which is their due.[90] The arts should also be truly significant in the life and tradition of the people.

The same applies to the shape, location and decoration of the altar,[91] the place for the proclamation of the word of God[92] and for baptism,[93] all the liturgical furnishings, vessels, vestments and colors.[94] Preference should be given to materials, forms and colors which are in use in the country.

44. The constitution *Sacrosanctum Concilium* has firmly maintained the constant practice of the church of encouraging the veneration by the faithful of images of Christ, the Virgin Mary and the saints,[95] because the honor "given to the image is given to its subject."[96] In different cultures believers can be helped in their prayer and in their spiritual life by seeing works of art which attempt, according to the genius of the people, to express the divine mysteries.

45. Alongside liturgical celebrations and related to them, in some particular churches there are various manifestations of popular devotion. These were sometimes introduced by missionaries at the time of the initial evangelization, and they often develop according to local custom.

The introduction of devotional practices into liturgical celebrations under the pretext of inculturation cannot be allowed "because by its nature, (the liturgy) is superior to them."[97]

It belongs to the local ordinary[98] to organize such devotions, to encourage them as supports for the life and faith of Christians, and to purify them when necessary, because they need to be constantly permeated by the Gospel.[99] He will take care to ensure that they do not replace liturgical celebrations or become mixed up with them.[100]

C) NECESSARY PRUDENCE

46. "Innovations should only be made when the good of the church genuinely and certainly requires them; care must be taken that any new forms adopted should in some way grow organically from forms already existing."[101] This norm was given in the constitution *Sacrosanctum Concilium* in relation to the restoration of the liturgy, and it also applies, in due measure, to the inculturation of the Roman rite. In this field changes need to be gradual and adequate explanation given in order to avoid the danger of rejection or simply an artificial grafting onto previous forms.

47. The liturgy is the expression of faith and Christian life, and so it is necessary to ensure that liturgical inculturation is not marked, even in appearance, by religious syncretism. This would be the case if the places of worship, the liturgical objects and vestments, gestures and postures let it appear as if rites had the same significance in Christian celebrations as they did before evangelization.

The syncretism will be still worse if biblical readings and chants (cf. above, No. 26) or the prayers were replaced by texts from other religions, even if these contain an undeniable religious and moral value.[102]

48. The constitution *Sacrosanctum Concilium* envisaged the admission of rites or gestures according to local custom into rituals of Christian initiation, marriage and funerals.[103] This is a stage of inculturation, but there is also the danger that the truth of the Christian rite and the expression of the Christian faith could be easily diminished in the eyes of the faithful. Fidelity to traditional usages must be accompanied by purification and, if necessary, a break with the past. The same applies, for example, to the possibility of Christianizing pagan festivals or holy places, or to the priest using the signs of authority reserved to the heads of civil society or for the veneration of ancestors. In every case it is necessary to avoid any ambiguity. Obviously the Christian liturgy cannot accept magic rites, superstition, spiritism, vengeance or rites with a sexual connotation.

49. In a number of countries there are several cultures which coexist and sometimes influence each other in such a way as to lead gradually to the formation of a new culture, while at times they seek to affirm their proper identity or even oppose each other in order to stress their own existence. It can happen that customs may have little more than folkloric interest. The episcopal conference will examine each case individually with care: They should respect the riches of each culture and those who defend them, but they should not ignore or neglect a minority culture with which they are not familiar. They should weigh the risk of a Christian community becoming inward looking and also the use of inculturation for political ends. In those countries with a customary culture, account must also be taken of the extent to which modernization has affected the people.

50. Sometimes there are many languages in use in the one country, even though each one may be spoken only by a small group of persons or a single tribe. In such cases a balance must be found which respects the individual rights of these groups or tribes but without carrying to extremes the localization of the liturgical celebrations. It is also sometimes possible that a country may be moving toward the use of a principal language.

51. To promote liturgical inculturation in a cultural area bigger than one country, the episcopal conferences concerned must work together and decide the measures which have to be taken so that "as far as possible, there are not notable ritual differences in regions bordering on one another."[104]

IV. AREAS OF ADAPTATION IN THE ROMAN RITE

52. The constitution *Sacrosanctum Concilium* had in mind an inculturation of the Roman rite when it gave norms for the adaptation of the liturgy to the mentality and needs of different peoples, when it provided for a degree of adaptation in the liturgical books (cf. below, Nos. 53–61), and also when it envisaged the possibility of more profound adaptations in some circumstances, especially in mission countries (cf. below, Nos. 63–64).

A) ADAPTATIONS IN THE LITURGICAL BOOKS

53.   The first significant measure of inculturation is the translation of liturgi-cal books into the language of the people.[105] The completion of translations and their revision, where necessary, should be effected according to the directives given by the Holy See on this subject.[106] Different literary genres are to be respected, and the content of the texts of the Latin typical edition is to be pre-served; at the same time the translations must be understandable to participants (cf. above, No. 39), suitable for proclamation and singing, with appropriate responses and acclamations by the assembly.

All peoples, even the most primitive, have a religious language which is suitable for expressing prayer, but liturgical language has its own special char-acteristics: It is deeply impregnated by the Bible; certain words in current Latin use (memoria, sacramentum) took on a new meaning in the Christian faith. Certain Christian expressions can be transmitted from one language to another, as has happened in the past, for example in the case of ecclesia, evangelium, baptisma, eucharistia.

Moreover, translators must be attentive to the relationship between the text and the liturgical action, aware of the needs of oral communication and sensitive to the literary qualities of the living language of the people. The quali-ties needed for liturgical translations are also required in the case of new com-positions, when they are envisaged.

54.   For the celebration of the eucharist, the Roman Missal, "while allowing . . . for legitimate differences and adaptations according to the prescriptions of the Second Vatican Council," must remain "a sign and instrument of unity"[107] of the Roman rite in different languages. The General Instruction on the Roman Missal foresees that "in accordance with the constitution on the liturgy, each conference of bishops has the power to lay down norms for its own territory that are suited to the traditions and character of peoples, regions and different communities."[108] The same also applies to the gestures and postures of the faithful,[109] the way in which the altar and the book of the gospels are venerated,[110] the texts of the opening chants,[111] the song at the preparation of the gifts[112] and the communion song,[113] the rite of peace,[114] conditions regulating communion with the chalice,[115] the materials for the construction of the altar and liturgical furni-ture,[116] the material and form of sacred vessels,[117] liturgical vestments.[118] Epis-copal conferences can also determine the manner of distributing communion.[119]

55.   For the other sacraments and for sacramentals, the Latin typical edition of each ritual indicates the adaptations which pertain to the episcopal confer-ences[120] or to individual bishops in particular circumstances.[121] These adapta-tions concern texts, gestures and sometimes the ordering of the rite. When the typical edition gives alternative formulas, conferences of bishops can add other formulas of the same kind.

56.   For the rites of Christian initiation, episcopal conferences are "to examine with care and prudence what can properly be admitted from the traditions and

character of each people"[122] and "in mission countries to judge whether initiation ceremonies practiced among the people can be adapted into the rite of Christian initiation and to decide whether they should be used."[123] It is necessary to remember, however, that the term *initiation* does not have the same meaning or designate the same reality when it is used of social rites of initiation among certain people or when it is contrary to the process of Christian initiation, which leads through the rites of the catechumenate to incorporation into Christ in the church by means of the sacraments of baptism, confirmation and eucharist.

57. In many places it is the marriage rite that calls for the greatest degree of adaptation so as not to be foreign to social customs. To adapt it to the customs of different regions and peoples, each episcopal conference has the "faculty to prepare its own proper marriage rite, which must always conform to the law which requires that the ordained minister or the assisting layperson,[124] according to the case, must ask for and obtain the consent of the contracting parties and give them the nuptial blessing."[125] This proper trite must obviously bring out clearly the Christian meaning of marriage, emphasize the grace of the sacrament and underline the duties of the spouses.[126]

58. Among all peoples, funerals are always surrounded with special rites, often of great expressive value. To answer to the needs of different countries, the Roman Ritual offers several forms of funerals.[127] Episcopal conferences must choose those which correspond best to local customs.[128] They will wish to preserve all that is good in family traditions and local customs, and ensure that funeral rites manifest the Christian faith in the resurrection and bear witness to the true values of the Gospel.[129] It is in this perspective that funeral rituals can incorporate the customs of different cultures and respond as best they can to the needs and traditions of each region.[130]

59. The blessing of persons, places or things touches the everyday life of the faithful and answers their immediate needs. They offer many possibilities for adaptation, for maintaining local customs and admitting popular usages.[131] Episcopal conferences will be able to employ the foreseen dispositions and be attentive to the needs of the country.

60. As regards the liturgical year, each particular church and religious family adds its own celebrations to those of the universal church, after approval by the Apostolic See.[132] Episcopal conferences can also, with the prior approval of the Apostolic See, suppress the obligation of certain feasts or transfer them to a Sunday.[133] They also decide the time and manner of celebrating rogationtide and ember days.[134]

61. The Liturgy of the Hours has as its goal the praise of God and the sanctification by prayer of the day and all human activity. Episcopal conferences can make adaptations in the second reading of the office of readings, hymns and intercessions and in the final Marian antiphons.[135]

62.   When an episcopal conference prepares its own edition of liturgical books, it decides about the translations and also the adaptations which are envisaged by the law.[136] The acts of the conference, together with the final vote, are signed by the president and secretary of the conference and sent to the Congregation for Divine Worship and the Discipline of the Sacraments, along with two copies of the approved text.

Moreover along with the complete dossier should be sent:

a) A succinct and precise explanation of the reasons for the adaptations that have been introduced.

b) Indications as to which sections have been taken from other already approved liturgical books and which are newly composed.

After the recognition by the Apostolic See has been received according to the law,[137] the episcopal conference promulgates the decree and determines the date when the new text comes into force.

B) ADAPTATIONS ENVISAGED BY NO. 40 OF THE CONCILIAR CONSTITUTION
ON THE LITURGY

63.   Apart from the adaptations provided for in the liturgical books, it may be that "in some places and circumstances an even more radical adaptation of the liturgy is needed, and this entails greater difficulties."[138] This is more than the sort of adaptations envisaged by the general instructions and the *praenotanda* of the liturgical books.

It presupposes that an episcopal conference has exhausted all the possibilities of adaptation offered by the liturgical books; that it has made an evaluation of the adaptations already introduced and maybe revised them before proceeding to more far-reaching adaptations.

The desirability or need for an adaptation of this sort can emerge in one of the areas mentioned above (cf. Nos. 53–61) without the others being affected. Moreover, adaptations of this kind do not envisage a transformation of the Roman rite, but are made within the context of the Roman rite.

64.   In some places when there are still problems about the participation of the faithful, a bishop or several bishops can set out their difficulties to their colleagues in the episcopal conferences and examine with them the desirability of introducing more profound adaptations, if the good of souls truly requires it.[139]

It is the function of episcopal conferences to propose to the Apostolic See the modifications it wishes to adopt following the procedure set out below.[140]

The Congregation for Divine Worship and the Discipline of the Sacraments is ready to receive the proposals of episcopal conferences and examine them, keeping in mind the good of the local churches concerned and the common good of the universal church, and to assist the process of inculturation where it is desirable or necessary. It will do this in accordance with the principles laid down in this instruction (cf. above, Nos. 33–51), and in a spirit of confident collaboration and shared responsibility.

Procedure

65.   The episcopal conference will examine what has to be modified in liturgical celebrations because of the traditions and mentality of peoples. It will ask the national or regional liturgical commission to study the matter and examine the different aspects of the elements of local culture and their eventual inclusion in the liturgical celebrations. The commission is to ensure that it receives the appropriate expert advice. It may be sometimes opportune to ask the advice of members of non-Christian religions about the religious or civil value of this or that element (cf. above, Nos. 30–32).

If the situation requires it, this preliminary examination will be made in collaboration with the episcopal conferences of neighboring countries or those with the same culture (cf. above, Nos. 33–51).

66.   The episcopal conference will present the proposal to the congregation before any experimentation takes place. The presentation should include a description of the innovations proposed, the reasons for their adoption, the criteria used, the times and places chosen for a preliminary experiment and an indication which groups will make it, and finally the acts of the discussion and the vote of the conference.

After an examination of the proposal carried out together by the episcopal conference and the congregation, the latter will grant the episcopal conference a faculty to make an experiment for a definite period of time, where this is appropriate.[141]

67.   The episcopal conference will supervise the process of experimentation,[142] normally with the help of the national or regional liturgical commission. The conference will also take care to ensure that the experimentation does not exceed the limits of time and place that were fixed. It will also ensure pastors and the faithful know about the limited and provisional nature of the experiment, and it will not give it publicity of a sort which could have an effect on the liturgical practice of the country. At the end of the period of experimentation, the episcopal conference will decide whether it matches up to the goal that was proposed or whether it needs revision, and it will communicate its conclusions to the congregation along with full information about the experiment.

68.   After examining the dossier, the congregation will issue a decree giving its consent, possibly with some qualifications, so that the changes can be introduced into the territory covered by the episcopal conference.

69.   The faithful, both lay people and clergy, should be well informed about the changes and prepared for their introduction into the liturgical celebrations. The changes are to be put into effect as circumstances require, with a transition period if this is appropriate (cf. above, No. 61).

CONCLUSION

70.   The Congregation for Divine Worship and the Discipline of the Sacraments presents these rules to the episcopal conferences to govern the work of liturgical inculturation envisaged by the Second Vatican Council as a response to the pastoral needs of peoples of different cultures. Liturgical inculturation should be carefully integrated into a pastoral plan for the inculturation of the Gospel into the many different human situations that are to be found. The Congregation for Divine Worship and the Discipline of the Sacraments hopes that each particular church, especially the young churches, will discover that the diversity of certain elements of liturgical celebrations can be a source of enrichment, while respecting the substantial unity of the Roman rite, the unity of the whole church and the integrity of the faith transmitted to the saints for all time (cf. Jude 3).

The present instruction was prepared by the Congregation for Divine Worship and the Discipline of the Sacraments, by order of His Holiness Pope John Paul II, who approved it and ordered that it be published.

From the Congregation for Divine Worship and the Discipline of the Sacraments, January 25, 1994.

NOTES

1. Cf. SC, 38; cf. also no. 40.

2. SC, 37.

3. Cf. OE, 2; SC, 3 and 4; CCC, 1200–1206, especially 1204–1206.

4. Cf. VQA, 16: AAS 81 (1989), 912.

5. *Ibid.*

6. SC, 37–40.

7. John Paul II, Encyclical *Slavorum Apostoli*, June 2,1985, No. 21: AAS 77 (1985), 802–803; discourse to the Pontifical Council for Culture, plenary assembly, January 17, 1987, No. 5: AAS 79 (1987), 1204–1205.

8. RM, 52: AAS 83 (1991), 300.

9. Cf. *ibid.*, and Synod of Bishops, Final Report *Exeunte Coetu Secundo*, December 7, 1985, D 4.

10. RM, 52.

11. GS, 58.

12. GS, 58.

13. Cf. CT, 53: AAS 71 (1979), 1319.

14. Cf. CCEC, c. 584.2: *"Evangelizatio gentium ita fiat, ut servata integritate fidei et morum Evangelium se in cultura singulorum populorum exprimere possit, in catechesi scilicet, in ritibus propriis liturgicis, in arte sacra in iure particulari ac demum in tota vita ecclesiali."*

15. Cf. CT, 53: "concerning evangelization in general, we can say that it is a call to bring the strength of the Gospel to the heart of culture and cultures. . . . It is in this way that it can propose to cultures the knowledge of the mystery hidden and help them to make of their own living tradition original expressions of life, celebration and Christian thought."

16. Cf. RM, 52: "Inculturation is a slow process covering the whole of missionary life and involves all who are active in the mission *ad gentes* and Christian communities in the measure that they are developing." Discourse to Pontifical Council for Culture plenary assembly: "I strongly reaffirm the need to mobilize the whole church into a creative effort toward a renewed evangelization of both people and cultures. It is only by a joint effort that the church will be able to bring the hope of Christ into the heart of cultures and present-day ways of thinking."

17. Cf. Pontifical Biblical Commission, *Foi et culture a la lumiere de la Bible*, 1981; and International Theological Commission, "Faith and Inculturation," 1988.

18. Cf. John Paul II, discourse to the bishops of Zaire, April 12, 1983, No. 5: AAS 75 (1983), 620: "How is it that a faith which has truly matured, is deep and firm, does not succeed in expressing itself in a language, in a catechesis, in theological reflection, in prayer, in the liturgy, in art, in the institutions which are truly related to the African soul of your compatriots? There is the key to the important and complex question of the liturgy, to mention just one area. Satisfactory progress in this domain can only be the fruit of a progressive growth in faith, linked with spiritual discernment, theological clarity, a sense of the universal church."

19. Discourse to Pontifical Council for Culture, 5: "In coming into contact with the cultures, the church must welcome all that in the traditions of peoples is compatible with the Gospel, to give all the riches of Christ to them and to enrich itself of the varied wisdom of the nations of the earth."

20. Cf. discourse to the Pontifical Council for Culture, 5; cf. also VQA, 17.

21. Cf. SC, 19 and 35.

22. Cf. AG, 10.

23. GS, 22.

24. St. Cyril of Alexandria, *In Ioannem*, I 14: PG, 73, 162C.

25. SC, 5.

26. Cf. LG, 10.

27. Cf. RomM, Fifth Weekday of the Passion of the Lord, 5: Prayer One: *". . . per suum cruorem instituit paschale mysterium."*

28. Cf. Paul VI, apostolic letter *Mysterii Paschalis*, February 14, 1969: AAS 61 (1969), 222–226.

29. Cf. CCC, 1096.

30. Cf. CCC, 1200–1203.

31. Cf. UR, 14–15.

32. Texts: cf. the sources of the prayers, the prefaces and the eucharistic prayers of the RomM; chants: for example the antiphons for Jan. 1, baptism of the Lord; Sept. 8, the *Improperia* of Good Friday, the hymns of the Liturgy of the Hours; gestures: for example the sprinkling of holy water, use of incense, genuflection, hands joined; rites: for example Palm Sunday procession, the adoration of the cross on Good Friday, the rogations.

33. Cf. in the past St. Gregory the Great, *Letter to Mellitus:* Reg. XI, 59: CIC 140A, 961–962; John VIII, Bull *Industriae Tuae*, June 26, 880: PL, 126, 904; Congregation for the Propagation of the Faith, Instruction to the Apostolic Vicars of China and Indochina (1654): *Collectanea S.C. de Propaganda Fide*, I 1 Rome, 1907, No. 135; instruction *Plane Compertum*, December 8, 1939: AAS 32 (1940), 2426.

34. LG, 17 also 13.

35. Cf. CT, 52–53; RM, 53–54; CCC 1204–1206.

36. Cf., also St. Ignatius of Antioch, Letter to the Magnesians, 9: Funk 1, 199: "We have seen how former adherents of the ancient customs have since attained to a new hope; so that they have given up keeping the sabbath, and now order their lives by the Lord's day instead."

37. Cf. DV, 14–16; *Ordo Lectionum Missae* ed. *typica altera Praenotanda*, 5: "It is the same mystery of Christ that the church announces when she proclaims the Old and New Testament in the celebration of the liturgy. The New Testament is, indeed, hidden in the Old and, in the New the Old is revealed. Because Christ is the center and fullness of all Scripture, as also of the whole liturgical celebration"; CCC, 120–123, 128–130, 1093–1095.

38. Cf. CCC, 1093–1096.

39. VQA, 7.

40. Cf. SC, 5–7.

41. Cf. SC, 2; VQA, 9.

42. Cf. PO, 2.

43. Cf. LG, 48; SC, 2 and 8.

44. SC, 7.

45. Cf. SC, 24.

46. Cf. *Ordo Lectionem Missae Praenotanda*, 12: "It is not allowed to suppress or reduce either the biblical readings in the celebration of Mass or the chants that are drawn from sacred Scripture. It is absolutely forbidden to replace these readings by other nonbiblical readings. It is through the word of God in the Scriptures that 'God continues to speak to his people' (SC, 33), and it is through familiarity with the Holy Scripture that the people of God, made docile by the Holy Spirit in the light of faith, can by their life and way of living witness to Christ before the whole world."

47. Cf. CCC, 2585–2589.

48. Cf. SC, 7.

49. Cf. SC, 6, 47, 56, 102, 106; cf. GIRM, 1, 7, 8.

50. Cf. SC, 6.

51. Cf. Council of Trent, Session 21, Chap. 2: Denz-Schonm. 1728; SC, 48ff, 62ff.

52. Cf. SC, 21.

53. Cf. CDF, *Inter Insigniores*, October 15, 1976: AAS 69 (1977), 107–108.

54. Cf. LG, 28; also no. 26.

55. Cf. St. Irenaeus, *Against the Heresies*, III, 2, 1–3; 3, 1–2: SCh, 211, 24–31; cf. St. Augustine, *Letter to Januarius* 54, 1: PL 33, 200: "But regarding those other observances which we keep and all the world keeps, and which do not derive from Scripture but from tradition, we are given to understand that they have been ordained or recommended to be kept by the apostles themselves or by the plenary councils, whose authority is well founded in the church"; cf. RM, 53–4; cf. CDF, *Letter to Bishops of the Catholic Church on Certain Aspects of the Church Understood as Communion*, May 28, 1992, Nos. 7–10.

56. Cf. SC, 83.

57. Cf. SC, 102, 106 and App.

58. Cf. Paul VI, apostolic constitution *Paenitemini*, February 17, 1966: AAS 58 (1966), 177–198.

59. Cf. SC, 22; 26; 28; 40, 43 and 128; CIC, c. 2 and *passim*.

60. Cf. GIRM, 2; Paul VI, *Discourse to the Consilium for the Application of the Constitution on the Liturgy*, October 13, 1966: AAS 58 (1966), 1146; October 14, 1968: AAS 60 (1968), 734.

61. Cf. SC, 22; 36; 40; 44–46; CIC, cc. 47ff and 838.

62. Cf. RM, 53.

63. Cf. SC, 35 and 36; CIC, c. 825.1.

64. SC, 24.

65. Cf. SC; CT, 55.

66. In SC, attention is drawn to Nos. 38 and 40: "above all in the missions."

67. Cf. AG, 16 and 17.

68. Cf. AG, 19.

69. SC, 22; cf. AG, 39 and 40; CIC, cc. 447–448ff.

70. SC, 40.

71. SC, 37.

72. Cf. SC, 14–19.

73. SC, 21.

74. Cf. SC, 34.

75. Cf. SC., 37–40.

76. Cf. VQA, 16.

77. Cf. John Paul II, discourse to the plenary assembly of the Congregation for Divine Worship and the Discipline of the Sacraments, January 26, 1991, No. 3: AAS 83 (1991), 940: "This is not to suggest to the particular churches that they have a new task to undertake following the application of liturgical reform, that is to say, adaptation or inculturation. Nor is it intended to mean inculturation as the creation of alternative rites. . . . It is a of collaborating so that the Roman rite, maintaining its own identity, may incorporate suitable adaptations."

78. Cf. SC, 22; CIC, cc. 838.1 and 838.2; John Paul II, apostolic constitution *Pastor Bonus*, 62, 64.3: AAS 80 (1988), 876–877; VQA, 19.

79. Cf. SC, 22 and cc. 447ff and 838.1 and 838.3; VQA, 20.

80. Cf. SC, 22, and CIC, cc. 838.1 and 838.4; VQA, 21.

81. Cf. SC, 22.

82. The situation is different when, in the liturgical books published after the constitution, the introductions and the rubrics envisaged adaptations and the possibility of leaving a choice to the pastoral sensitivity of the one presiding, for example, when it says "if it is opportune," "in these or similar terms," "also," "according to circumstances," "either . . . or," "if convenient," "normally," "the most suitable form can be chosen." In making a choice, the celebrant should seek the good of the assembly, taking into account the spiritual preparation and mentality of the participants rather than his own or the easiest solution. In celebrations for particular groups, other possibilities are available. Nonetheless, prudence and discretion are always called for in order to avoid the breaking up of the local church into little "churches" or "chapels" closed in upon themselves.

83. Cf. CIC, cc. 762–772, esp. c. 769.

84. Cf. SC, 118; also No. 54: While allowing that "a suitable place be allotted to the language of the country" in the chants, "steps should be taken so that the faithful may also be able to say or sign together in Latin those parts of the ordinary of the Mass which pertain to them," especially the Our Father, cf. GIRM, 19.

85. SC, 119.

86. SC., 120.

87. Cf. CIC, c. 841.

88. Cf. SC, 33; CIC, c. 899.2.

89. Cf. SC, 30.

90. Cf. SC, 123–124; CIC, c. 1216.

91. Cf. GIRM, 259–270; CIC, cc. 1235–1239, esp. c. 1236.

92. Cf. GIRM, 272.

93. Cf. *De Benedictionibus Ordo Benedictionis Baptisterii seu Fontis Baptismalis*, 832–837.

94. Cf. GIRM, 287–310.

95. Cf. SC, 125; LG, 67; CIC, c. 1188.

96. Council of Nicea II: Denz.-Schonm. 601; cf. St. Basil, "On the Holy Spirit," XVIII, 45; SCh 17, 194.

97. SC, 13.

98. Cf. CIC, c. 839.2.

99. VQA, 18.

100. Cf. *ibid.*

101. SC, 23.

102. These texts can be used profitably in the homily because it is one of the tasks of the homily "to show the points of convergence between revealed divine wisdom and noble human thought, seeking the truth by various paths" (John Paul II, apostolic letter *Dominicae Cenae*, February 24, 1980, No. 10: AAS 72 (1980), 137.

103. SC, 65, 77, 81. Cf. *Ordo Initiationis Christianae Adultorum, Praenotanda,* 30–31, 79–81, 88–89; *Ordo Celebrandi Matrimonium, editio typica altera, Praenotanda,* 41–44; *Ordo Exsequiarum, Praenotanda,* 21–22.

104. SC, 23.

105. Cf. SC, 36; 54; 63.

106. Cf. VQA, 20.

107. Cf. Paul VI, apostolic constitution *Missale Romanum,* April 3, 1969: AAS 61 (1969), 221.

108. GIRM, 6; cf. also *Ordo Lectionum Missae, editio typica altera, Praenotanda,* 111–118.

109. GIRM, 22.

110. Cf. GIRM, 232.

111. Cf. GIRM, 26.

112. Cf. GIRM, 50.

113. Cf. GIRM, 56 i.

114. Cf. GIRM, 56 b.

115. Cf. GIRM, 242.

116. Cf. GIRM, 263 and 288.

117. Cf. GIRM, 290.

118. Cf. GIRM, 304, 305, 308.

119. Cf. *De Sacra Communione et de Cultu Mysterii Eucharistici Extra Missam, Praenotanda,* 21.

120. Cf. *Ordo Initiationis Christianae Adultorum, Praenotanda Generalia,* 30–33; *Praenotanda,* 12, 20,47, 64–65; *Ordo,* 312; Appendix, 12; *Ordo Baptismi Parvulorum, Praenotanda,* 8, 23–25; *Ordo Confirmationis, Praenotanda,* 11–12, 16–17; *De Sacra Communione et de Cultu Mysterii Eucharistici Extra Missam, Praenotanda,* 12; *Ordo Paenitentiae, Praenotanda,* 35b, 38; *Ordo Unctionis Infirmorum Eorumque Pastoralis Curae, Praenotanda,* 38–39; *Ordo Celebrandi Matrimonium, editio typica altera, Praenotanda,* 39–44; *De Ordinatione Episcopi Presbyterorum et Diaconorum, editio typica altera, Praenotanda,* 11; *De Benedictionibus, Praenotanda Generalia,* 39.

121. Cf. *Ordo Initiationis Christianae Adultorum, Praenotanda,* 66; *Ordo Baptismi Parvulorum, Praenotanda,* 26; *Ordo Paenitentiae, Praenotanda,* 39; *Ordo Celebrandi Matrimonium, editio typica altera, Praenotanda,* 36.

122. *Ordo Initiationis Christianae Adultorum, Praenotanda Generalis,* 30.2.

123. *Ibid.,* 31; cf. SC, 65.

124. Cf. CIC, cc. 1108 and 1112.

125. SC, 77; *Ordo Celebrandi Matrimonium, editio typica altera, Praenotanda,* 42.

126. Cf. SC, 77.

127. Cf. *Ordo Exsequiarum Praenotanda,* 4.

128. Cf. *ibid.,* 9 and 21.1–21.3.

129. Cf. *ibid.,* 2.

130. Cf. SC, 81.

131. Cf. SC, 79; *De Benedictionibus, Praenotanda Generalia,* 39; *Ordo Professionis Religiosae, Praenotanda,* 12–15.

132. Cf. GNLY, 49, 55; CDW, Instruction *Calendaria Particularia,* June 24, 1970: AAS, 62 (1970), 349–370.

133. Cf. CIC, c. 1246.2.

134. Cf. GNLY, 46.

135. GILOH, 92, 162, 178, 184.

136. Cf. CIC, cc. 455.2 and 838.3; that is also the case for a new edition, cf. VQA, 20.

137. CIC, c. 838.3

138. SC, 40.

139. Cf. Congregation for Bishops, *Directory on the Pastoral Ministry of Bishops,* February 22, 1973, No. 84.

140. Cf. SC, 40.

141. Cf. SC, 40.

142. Cf. SC, 40.

GOD'S MERCY
ENDURES FOREVER
GUIDELINES ON THE PRESENTATION
OF JEWS AND JUDAISM
IN CATHOLIC PREACHING

BISHOPS' COMMITTEE ON THE LITURGY
NATIONAL CONFERENCE OF CATHOLIC BISHOPS
1988

OVERVIEW OF *GOD'S MERCY ENDURES FOREVER*

Gerard S. Sloyan

In June 1985, the Vatican Commission for Religious Relations with Jews issued its *Notes on the Correct Way to Present the Jews and Judaism in Preaching and Catechesis of the Roman Catholic Church.* In response to this document, the U.S. Bishops' Committee on the Liturgy was charged with the preparation of a statement and a set of guidelines concerning the presentation of Jews and Judaism in Catholic preaching. *God's Mercy Endures Forever* is that statement. Authorized for publication in 1988, it is a relatively brief statement, only 32 numbered articles, but offers clear guidelines for preachers. The following essay offers an introduction and some background to the issues presented in this valuable document.

It is hard to generalize about the contemporary presentation of Jews and Judaism in Roman Catholic preaching. This is primarily due to the fact that the Catholic church is global, made up of a great number of people and cultures, many of whom have never even met a Jew or given much thought to Judaism. But most Catholics in the United States and Canada have, and the Jews they have contact with are rightly sensitive to Christian speech and action in their regard.

The chief problem with Catholic preaching about Jews and Judaism, as with Protestant and Orthodox preaching, is that it is based on the Bible. This fact constitutes a cruel paradox. One might expect that God's inspired word would be incapable of leading those who believe in it down wrong paths. It is, however, the word of God in the words of human beings, presumably men, and the Holy Spirit appears to have done nothing to curb the passions or prejudices of the authors of both Testaments. They have, of course, been marvelously influenced by the Spirit, and have given the church words that clothe God's word in a way that has produced boundless good. But the Deuteronomist, the Chronicler, the prophets, the sages and psalmists, the evangelists, the writers of letters and treatises, all were men of their times. Those times were long ago, millennia in some cases. Yet these ancient writings are the only words many Christians have heard about Jews and the religion of Israel.

The Hebrew culture that produced the Bible was often oppressed by neighboring peoples or foreign empires. The ancient Hebrews themselves did some oppressing as well, especially of the Canaanite tribes. According to the Christian scriptures, the Jews of the first century CE persecuted their own Jewish neighbors who believed in Jesus.

This means that preachers must be assiduous students of the Bible, lest they betray it by failing to explore the kind of writing it is, both in its place and time, and in its contemporary hearers' lives. This does not mean that biblical wisdom can only be discovered once the husk of historical setting and cultural outlook is stripped away. That would do violence to the inspired word of God. Instead, at every turn, preachers must search for the context of what was written, although it will not always be possible to uncover it. Still, the sacred writings must not be allowed to create false understandings in the minds of the hearers when preached from the pulpit. That will inevitably be the case if the preachers have erroneous understandings themselves.

The readings provided in the *Lectionary for Mass* have more often than not been isolated from their contexts. The hope is that they will not create needless problems in the hearers' minds when proclaimed alone. However, this can raise as many problems as it solves. For example, the lectionary spares Catholic assemblies from the invective of Jeremiah against Egypt, Philistia, Moab, Ammon, Edom, Damascus, Arabia, Elam and Babylon. Since all these peoples are long dead, we tend to think that no harm is done. However, there are still living Egyptians, Syrians and Arabians. The learned among them know very well what the Bible of the Jews and Christians has to say about their fore-bears. However, some of these peoples are less sensitive to the portrayal of their ancestors in the Bible because, over the course of history, they have become predominantly Christian. Jews, however, are highly sensitive to the way their ancestors are treated in the Christian scriptures and in pulpit expositions of both Testaments. What accounts for this sensitivity, and how are Jews and Judaism to be presented in Christian preaching?

THE HISTORICAL CONTEXT OF THE NEW TESTAMENT WRITINGS

An important thing for homilists to be aware of is that no attempt was made at interreligious understanding in the ancient world, much less dialogue. The religious "other" was wrong by definition. Jesus, a Jew, referred to a Syrian woman of the Phoenician coast as a dog (Mark 7:27), and no one was shocked by the casual opprobrium. It was mutual. Secondly, the Jewish penchant for religious argument was such that Jesus probably had the backing of other Jews in his exchanges with the Pharisees. Many of his contemporaries felt oppressed by the demand that, in addition to keeping the written Torah, the oral law must be kept as well. That is why, despite their bitterness, one should not make too much of the reported confrontations in the gospels.

As accounts of these polemics reach us two thousand years later, we need to understand that they were more a phenomenon of the evangelists' day than the time of Jesus. After the destruction of Jerusalem (ca. 70 CE), strong lines were drawn separating Jews and non-Jews. We have in the gospels (written and edited between ca. 70 and 100 CE) strong echoes of this debate. Similarly, Saint Paul had his own test for who was a true Jew (see Romans 2:28–29), without respect to faith in Christ. For their part, the earliest believers in Jesus' resurrection, all of them Jewish, soon began to accept non-Jews into their company, including Samaritans (see John 4:39–42; Acts 8:25) and Gentiles who lived beyond the borders of the land of Israel.

The protestations of the early Christians that theirs was the correct understanding of the religion of Israel met with increasing hostility. Jews wondered how the Judaism of those who believed in Jesus could be authentic. They not only proclaimed Jesus—a man executed by the Romans on a political charge—as Israel's Messiah, but they increasingly failed to observe the authentic signs of Judaism: circumcision and the laws of ritual purity.

This is why the gospels of Matthew (ca. 85 CE) and John (ca. 90–100 CE) report the struggles of the late first century as they do. They do not describe a pitched battle between "Jews" and "Christians," but a debate within Judaism itself: Who had the true understanding of the faith of Israel? Was it the rabbis, who fell heirs to the Pharisees after the destruction of Jerusalem? Or was it the Jews who believed that Jesus was the Messiah?

In churches like those evangelized by Paul and his companions, and in the churches of Rome, Alexandria and Edessa, the situation grew more complicated. Non-Jews were accepting the gospel in great numbers, and Jews were resisting the claim that they should have been the first to believe. Both a religion and a political identity were at stake; Jews could not accept their religious traditions and their peoplehood being invaded by Gentiles. They must have thought that their God had deserted them in a new and strange way.

All of this means that Catholic preaching should not be attempted by those who have not studied the origins of Christianity in depth. Most who complete a formal course in theology have trouble replacing the stereotypes of their youth with a dependable picture of the 100-year period called the "apostolic age." They continue to think that "the Jews," who above all should have accepted the gospel, stubbornly refused to. They are encouraged in this line of thinking by some passages in Paul's letters and by the Acts of the Apostles, which contains Stephen's proclamation that his fellow Jews are a "a stiff-necked people, uncircumcised in heart and ears . . . always oppos[ing] the Holy Spirit" (Acts 7:51).

Many homilists, like many other Christians, believe that the chief priests and the elders engineered Jesus' death, while a cowardly Pilate reluctantly acquiesced, as the gospels seem to indicate. Their source, it should be noted, is not so much the word of scripture as the writings of the church Fathers. These giants of theology had a talent for interpreting certain passages of the New Testament incorrectly; they were infuriated by the refusal of the Jews of their own day to accept the gospel. Thus, the anti-Judaism of Christianity was established by five centuries of patristic biblical commentary. Serious efforts are being made in our day to turn back the tide, but it will not be easy. This inaccurate reading of history, Jewish and Christian, is pervasive; it is a problematic inheritance by any standard.

IMPLICATIONS FOR THE HOMILIST

What measures can preachers take when expounding biblical passages—the essence of a homily—to be sure that they do not slip unconsciously into anti-Jewish speech? Some suggestions follow below.

Maintain the Integrity of the First Testament

First, although the *Lectionary for Mass* operates on a typological principle in its search for prefigurations of Jesus in the First Testament, these correspondences must not be presumed to be the First Testament author's intent, not even his unconscious intent. Believers in Jesus Christ will understandably see the gospel prefigured in earlier biblical writings. The evangelists did this deliberately in the way they framed and phrased their narratives. When the gospel writers,

Saint Paul or the authors of the other epistles cite passages from the Hebrew scriptures, they most often do it illustratively, in the manner of the rabbis of the Hellenistic period. If, for example, Matthew (or, less frequently, John) claims that a biblical passage or event is fulfilled in Christ, he is giving a specific instance of the general principle that all of Israel's history has come to fruition in Christ. Such is the faith of the church. This does not mean, however, that the author of the book of Exodus had Jesus' passion in mind when he wrote that no bone of a Passover lamb should be broken (Exodus 12:46, quoted in John 19:36), or that Zechariah was describing the onlookers at Calvary as he wrote, "when they look on the one whom they have pierced, they shall mourn for him, as one mourns for an only child . . . a firstborn" (Zechariah 12:10, quoted in John 19:37).

The first reading at Sunday Mass must always be explained as God's revelation to Israel, important in itself, for that is what it is. It should not be presented as totally subordinate to God's revelation in Jesus Christ, as if the Holy Spirit were at work in the people of Israel over centuries only to prepare for something else.

The Christian conviction that the culmination of Israel's history is realized in Jesus must be maintained, but Christians must never claim that Israel's history became insignificant with Jesus' appearance. Above all, Mosaic Law must not be presented as burdensome or impossible to fulfill; Saul of Tarsus did not find it so. Only certain interpretations of the Law are defined as such in the gospels. To this day, the Law is the glory and the joy of observant Jews, among whom it is variously interpreted. Some signs of Jewish identity, like circumcision and the kosher laws, were abrogated for Gentile and Jewish believers in Christ, but the bulk of Mosaic Law (apart from the archaic prescriptions incomprehensible even to the Jews of Jesus' day) continues to apply to Christians. The grace and truth that came with Jesus Christ neither abrogated nor minimized all that God did and does for Israel, the people of God's special love.

Preach the Message of the Prophets

When the lectionary readings contain the pronouncements leveled by the prophets against their Jewish contemporaries, Christian preachers need to know that these passages must be understood as applicable to the *contemporary Christian* situation. Homilists have inherited the mantle of the Jewish prophets and must wear it responsibly in admonishing *their own* people.

Avoid Generalizations

The unflattering portrait of the Pharisees in the gospels must not be taken as an accurate picture of them as a group. Saint Paul, who spoke proudly of having been of their number, never spoke ill of them in his correspondence. The gospels contrast Jesus' teaching with that of the narrowest and most demanding of the Pharisees, a contrast in which they are bound to come off badly.

Study Jewish Sources and Images

Because the Bible is a storehouse of images, preachers are right to draw on them constantly in proclaiming the gospel. The Semitic imagery of both Testaments is rich. Modern Westerners must master that imagery, not in the archaic speech of older Bible translations but in the timelessness of Semitic metaphor. This is an important part of laying hold of the church's Jewish heritage.

CONCLUSION

Above all, it is important to remember that, in our theology, the church of Christ is the continuation of the people of Israel. "Just as the people of Israel in the flesh, who wandered in the desert, were already called the church of God . . . so too, the new Israel [an unfortunate phrase—G.S.S.], which advances in this present era in search of a future and permanent city . . . is also called the church of Christ" (LG, 9). In the final analysis, then, there is no "we" and "they," only "us."

OUTLINE

GOD'S MERCY ENDURES FOREVER

INTRODUCTION

On June 24, 1985, the solemnity of the Birth of John the Baptist, the Holy See's Commission for Religious Relations with the Jews issued its *Notes on the Correct Way to Present the Jews and Judaism in Preaching and Catechesis of the Roman Catholic Church* (hereafter, 1985 *Notes*). The 1985 *Notes* rested on a foundation of previous Church statements, addressing the tasks given Catholic homilists by the Second Vatican Council's *Declaration on the Relationship of the Church to Non-Christian Religions (Nostra Aetate)*, no. 4.

On December 1, 1974, for example, the Holy See had issued *Guidelines and Suggestions for Implementing the Conciliar Declaration "Nostra Aetate,"* no. 4 (hereafter, 1974 *Guidelines*). The second and third sections of this document placed central emphasis on the important and indispensable role of the homilist in ensuring that God's Word be received without prejudice toward the Jewish people or their religious traditions, asking "with respect to liturgical readings," that "care be taken to see that homilies based on them will not distort their meaning, especially when it is a question of passages which seem to show the Jewish people as such in unfavorable light" (1974 *Guidelines*, no. 2).

In this country, the National Conference of Catholic Bishops, in 1975, similarly urged catechists and homilists to work together to develop among Catholics increasing "appreciation of the Jewishness of that heritage and rich spirituality which we derive from Abraham, Moses, the prophets, the psalmists, and other spiritual giants of the Hebrew Scriptures" (*Statement on Catholic-Jewish Relations*, November 20, 1975, no. 12).

Much progress has been made since then. As it continues, sensitivities will need even further sharpening, founded on the Church's growing understanding of biblical and rabbinic Judaism.

It is the purpose of these present *Guidelines* to assist the homilist in these continuing efforts by indicating some of the major areas where challenges and opportunities occur and by offering perspectives and suggestions for dealing with them.

JEWISH ROOTS OF THE LITURGY

1. "Our common spiritual heritage [with Judaism] is considerable. To assess it carefully in itself and with due awareness of the faith and religious life of the Jewish people as they are professed and practiced still today, can greatly help us to understand better certain aspects of the life of the Church. Such is the case with the liturgy, whose Jewish roots remain still to be examined more deeply,

and in any case should be better known and appreciated by the faithful" (Pope John Paul II, March 6, 1982).

2.   Nowhere is the deep spiritual bond between Judaism and Christianity more apparent than in the liturgy. The very concepts of a liturgical cycle of feasts and the *lectio continua* principle of the lectionary that so mark Catholic tradition are adopted from Jewish liturgical practice. Easter and Pentecost have historical roots in the Jewish feasts of Passover and Shavuot. Though their Christian meaning is quite distinct, an awareness of their original context in the story of Israel is vital to their understanding, as the lectionary readings themselves suggest. Where appropriate, such relationships should be pointed out. The homilist, as a "mediator of meaning" (NCCB Committee on Priestly Life and Ministry, *Fulfilled in Your Hearing*, 1982) interprets for the liturgical assembly not only the Scriptures but their liturgical context as well.

3.   The central action of Christian worship, the eucharistic celebration, is likewise linked historically with Jewish ritual. The term for Church, *ecclesia*, like the original sense of the word *synagogue*, is an equivalent for the Hebrew *keneset* or *kenessiyah* (assembly). The Christian understanding of *ecclesia* is based on the biblical understanding of *qahal* as the formal "gathering" of the people of God. The Christian *ordo* (order of worship) is an exact rendering of the earliest rabbinic idea of prayer, called a *seder*, that is, an "order" of service. Moreover, the Christian *ordo* takes its form and structure from the Jewish *seder*: the Liturgy of the Word, with its alternating biblical readings, doxologies, and blessings; and the liturgical form of the Eucharist, rooted in Jewish meal liturgy, with its blessings over bread and wine. Theologically, the Christian concept of *anamnesis* coincides with the Jewish understanding of *zikkaron* (memorial reenactment). Applied to the Passover celebration, *zikkaron* refers to the fact that God's saving deed is not only recalled but actually relived through the ritual meal. The synoptic gospels present Jesus as instituting the Eucharist during a Passover *seder* celebrated with his followers, giving to it a new and distinctly Christian "memory."

4.   In addition to the liturgical seasons and the Eucharist, numerous details of prayer forms and ritual exemplify the Church's continuing relationship with the Jewish people through the ages. The liturgy of the hours and the formulas of many of the Church's most memorable prayers, such as the "Our Father," continue to resonate with rabbinic Judaism and contemporary synagogue prayers.

HISTORICAL PERSPECTIVES AND CONTEMPORARY PROCLAMATION

5.   The strongly Jewish character of Jesus' teaching and that of the primitive Church was culturally adapted by the growing Gentile majority and later blurred by controversies alienating Christianity from emerging rabbinic Judaism at the end of the first century. "By the third century, however, a de-Judaizing process had set in which tended to undervalue the Jewish origins of the Church, a tendency that has surfaced from time to time in devious ways throughout Christian history" (*Statement on Catholic-Jewish Relations*, no. 12).

6.   This process has manifested itself in various ways in Christian history. In the second century, Marcion carried it to its absurd extreme, teaching a complete opposition between the Hebrew and Christian Scriptures and declaring that different Gods had inspired the two Testaments. Despite the Church's condemnation of Marcion's teachings, some Christians over the centuries continued to dichotomize the Bible into two mutually contradictory parts. They argued, for example, that the New Covenant "abrogated" or "superseded" the Old, and that the Sinai Covenant was discarded by God and replaced with another. The Second Vatican Council, in *Dei Verbum* and *Nostra Aetate*, rejected these theories of the relationship between the Scriptures. In a major address in 1980, Pope John Paul II linked the renewed understanding of Scripture with the Church's understanding of its relationship with the Jewish people, stating that the dialogue, as "the meeting between the people of God of the Old Covenant, never revoked by God, is at the same time a dialogue within our Church, that is to say, a dialogue between the first and second part of its Bible" (Pope John Paul II, Mainz, November 17, 1980).

7.   Another misunderstanding rejected by the Second Vatican Council was the notion of collective guilt, which charged the Jewish people *as a whole* with responsibility for Jesus' death (cf. nos. 21–25 below, on Holy Week). From the theory of collective guilt, it followed for some that Jewish suffering over the ages reflected divine retribution on the Jews for an alleged "deicide." While both rabbinic Judaism and early Christianity saw in the destruction of the Jerusalem Temple in AD 70 a sense of divine punishment (see Luke 19:42–44), the theory of collective guilt went well beyond Jesus' poignant expression of his love as a Jew for Jerusalem and the destruction it would face at the hands of Imperial Rome. Collective guilt implied that because "the Jews" had rejected Jesus, God had rejected them. With direct reference to Luke 19:44, the Second Vatican Council reminded Catholics that "nevertheless, now as before, God holds the Jews most dear for the sake of their fathers; he does not repent of the gifts he makes or of the calls he issues," and established as an overriding hermeneutical principle for homilists dealing with such passages that "the Jews should not be represented as rejected by God or accursed, as if this followed from Holy Scripture" (*Nostra Aetate*, no. 4; cf. 1985 *Notes*, VI:33).

8.   Reasons for increased sensitivity to the ways in which Jews and Judaism are presented in homilies are multiple. First, understanding of the biblical readings and of the structure of Catholic liturgy will be enhanced by an appreciation of their ancient sources and their continuing spiritual links with Judaism. The Christian proclamation of the saving deeds of the One God through Jesus was formed in the context of Second Temple Judaism and cannot be understood thoroughly without that context. It is a proclamation that, at its heart, stands in solidarity with the continuing Jewish witness in affirming the One God as Lord of history. Further, false or demeaning portraits of a repudiated Israel may undermine Christianity as well. How can one confidently affirm the truth of God's covenant with all humanity and creation in Christ (see Romans 8:21) without at the same time affirming God's faithfulness to the Covenant with Israel that also lies at the heart of the biblical testimony?

9.   As Catholic homilists know, the liturgical year presents both opportunities and challenges. One can show the parallels between the Jewish and Catholic liturgical cycles. And one can, with clarity, confront misinterpretations of the meaning of the lectionary readings, which have been too familiar in the past. Specifically, homilists can guide people away from a triumphalism that would equate the pilgrim Church with the Reign of God, which is the Church's mission to herald and proclaim. Likewise, homilists can confront the unconscious transmission of anti-Judaism through cliches that derive from an unhistorical overgeneralization of the self-critical aspects of the story of Israel as told in the Scriptures (e.g., "hardheartedness" of the Jews, "blindness," "legalism," "materialism," "rejection of Jesus," etc.). From Advent through Passover/Easter, to Yom Kippur and Rosh Hashana, the Catholic and Jewish liturgical cycles spiral around one another in a stately progression of challenges to God's people to repent, to remain faithful to God's call, and to prepare the world for the coming of God's Reign. While each is distinct and unique, they are related to one another. Christianity is engrafted on and continues to draw sustenance from the common root, biblical Israel (Romans 11:13–24).

10.   In this respect, the 1985 *Notes*, stressing "the unity of the divine plan" (no. 11), caution against a simplistic framing of the relationship of Christianity and Judaism as "two parallel ways of salvation" (no. 7). The Church proclaims the universal salvific significance of the Christ-event and looks forward to the day when "there shall be one flock and one shepherd" (John 10:16; cf. Isaiah 66:2; Zephaniah 3:9; Jeremiah 23:3; Ezra 11:17; see also no. 31e below). So intimate is this relationship that the Church "encounters the mystery of Israel" when "pondering her own mystery" (1974 *Guidelines*, no.5).

ADVENT: THE RELATIONSHIP BETWEEN THE SCRIPTURES

11.   The lectionary readings from the prophets are selected to bring out the ancient Christian theme that Jesus is the "fulfillment" of the biblical message of hope and promise, the inauguration of the "days to come" described, for example, by the daily Advent Masses, and on Sundays by Isaiah in cycle A and Jeremiah in cycle C for the First Sunday of Advent. This truth needs to be framed very carefully. Christians believe that Jesus is the promised Messiah who has come (see Luke 4:22), but also know that his messianic kingdom is not yet fully realized. The ancient messianic prophecies are not merely temporal predictions but profound expressions of eschatological hope. Since this dimension can be misunderstood or even missed altogether, the homilist needs to raise clearly the hope found in the prophets and heightened in the proclamation of Christ. This hope includes trust in what is promised but not yet seen. While the biblical prophecies of an age of universal *shalom* are "fulfilled" (i.e, irreversibly inaugurated) in Christ's coming, the fulfillment is not yet completely worked out in each person's life or perfected in the world at large (1974 *Guidelines*, no. 2). It is the mission of the Church, as also that of the Jewish people, to proclaim and to work to prepare the world for the full flowering of God's Reign, which is, but is "not yet" (cf. 1974 *Guidelines*, II). Both the Christian "Our Father" and the Jewish *Kaddish* exemplify this message. Thus, both Christianity and Judaism seal their worship with a common hope: "Thy kingdom come!"

12.   Christians proclaim that the Messiah has indeed come and that God's Reign is "at hand." With the Jewish people, we await the complete realization of the messianic age.

> In underlining the eschatological dimension of Christianity, we shall reach a greater awareness that the people of God of the Old and the New Testament are tending toward a like end in the future: the coming or return of the Messiah—even if they start from two different points of view (1985 Notes, nos. 18–19).

13.   Other difficulties may be less theologically momentous but can still be troublesome. For example, the reading from Baruch in cycle C or from Isaiah in cycle A for the Second Sunday of Advent can leave the impression that pre-Jesus Israel was wholly guilt-ridden and in mourning, and Judaism virtually moribund. In fact, in their original historical settings, such passages reveal Judaism's remarkable capacity for self-criticism. While Israel had periods of deep mourning (see Lamentations) and was justly accused of sinfulness (e.g., see Jeremiah), it also experienced periods of joy, return from Exile, and continuing *teshuvah*, turning back to God in faithful repentance. Judaism was and is incredibly complex and vital, with a wide variety of creative spiritual movements vying for the people's adherence.

14.   The reform of the liturgy initiated by the Second Vatican Council reintroduced regular readings from the Old Testament into the lectionary. For Catholics, the Old Testament is that collection that contains the Hebrew Scriptures and the seven deuterocanonical books. Using postbiblical Jewish sources, with respect for the essential differences between Christian and Jewish traditions of biblical interpretation, can enliven the approach to the biblical text (cf. nos. 31a and 31i below). The opportunity also presents a challenge for the homilist. Principles of selection of passages vary. Sometimes the readings are cyclic, providing a continuity of narrative over a period of time. At other times, especially during Advent and Lent, a reading from the prophets or one of the historical books of the Old Testament and a gospel pericope are "paired," based on such liturgical traditions as the *sensus plenior* (fuller meaning) or, as is especially the case in Ordinary Time, according to the principle of *typology*, in which biblical figures and events are seen as "types" prefiguring Jesus (see no. 31e below).

15.   Many of these pairings represent natural associations of similar events and teachings. Others rely on New Testament precedent and interpretation of the messianic psalms and prophetic passages. Matthew 1:23, for example, quotes the Septuagint, which translates the Hebrew *almah* (young woman) as the Greek for *virgin* in its rendering of Isaiah 7:14. The same biblical text, therefore, can have more than one valid hermeneutical interpretation, ranging from its original historical context and intent to traditional Christological applications. The 1985 *Notes* describe this phenomenon as flowing from the "unfathomable riches" and "inexhaustible content" of the Hebrew Bible. For Christians, the unity of the Bible depends on understanding all Scripture in the light of Christ. Typology is one form, rooted in the New Testament itself, of expressing this unity of Scripture and of the divine plan (see no. 31e below). As such, it "should

not lead us to forget that it [the Hebrew Bible] retains its own value as Revelation that the New Testament often does no more than resume" (1985 *Notes*, no. 15; cf. *Dei Verbum*, 14–18).

LENT: CONTROVERSIES AND CONFLICTS

16.   The Lenten lectionary presents just as many challenges. Prophetic texts such as Joel (Ash Wednesday), Jeremiah's "new covenant" (cycle B, Fifth Sunday), and Isaiah (cycle C, Fifth Sunday) call the assembly to proclaim Jesus as the Christ while avoiding negativism toward Judaism.

17.   In addition, many of the New Testament texts, such as Matthew's references to "hypocrites in the synagogue" (Ash Wednesday), John's depiction of Jesus in the Temple (cycle B, Third Sunday), and Jesus' conflicts with the Pharisees (e.g., Luke, cycle C, Fourth Sunday) can give the impression that the Judaism of Jesus' day was devoid of spiritual depth and essentially at odds with Jesus' teaching. References to earlier divine punishments of the Jews (e.g., 1 Corinthians, cycle C, Third Sunday) can further intensify a false image of Jews and Judaism as a people rejected by God.

18.   In fact, however, as the 1985 *Notes* are at pains to clarify (sec. III and IV), Jesus was observant of the Torah (e.g, in the details of his circumcision and purification given in Luke 2:21–24), he extolled respect for it (see Matthew 5:17–20), and he invited obedience to it (see Matthew 8:4). Jesus taught in the synagogues (see Matthew 4:23 and 9:35; Luke 4:15–18; John 18:20) and in the Temple, which he frequented, as did the disciples even after the Resurrection (see Acts 2:46; 3:1ff). While Jesus showed uniqueness and authority in his interpretation of God's word in the Torah—in a manner that scandalized some Jews and impressed others—he did not oppose it, nor did he wish to abrogate it.

19.   Jesus was perhaps closer to the Pharisees in his religious vision than to any other group of his time. The 1985 *Notes* suggest that this affinity with Pharisaism may be a reason for many of his apparent controversies with them (see no. 27). Jesus shared with the Pharisees a number of distinctive doctrines: the resurrection of the body; forms of piety such as almsgiving, daily prayer, and fasting; the liturgical practice of addressing God as Father; and the priority of the love commandment (see no. 25). Many scholars are of the view that Jesus was not so much arguing against "the Pharisees" as a group, as he was condemning excesses of some Pharisees, excesses of a sort that can be found among some Christians as well. In some cases, Jesus appears to have been participating in internal Pharisaic debates on various points of interpretation of God's law. In the case of divorce (see Mark 10:2–12), an issue that was debated hotly between the Pharisaic schools of Hillel and Shammai, Jesus goes beyond even the more stringent position of the House of Shammai. In other cases, such as the rejection of a literal interpretation of the *lex talionis* ("An eye for an eye . . . "), Jesus' interpretation of biblical law is similar to that found in some of the prophets and ultimately adopted by rabbinic tradition as can be seen in the *Talmud*.

20.   After the church had distanced itself from Judaism (cf. no. 5 above), it tended to telescope the long historical process whereby the gospels were set down some generations after Jesus' death. Thus, certain controversies that may actually have taken place between church leaders and rabbis toward the end of the first century were "read back" into the life of Jesus:

> Some [New Testament] references hostile or less than favorable to Jews have their historical context in conflicts between the nascent Church and the Jewish community. Certain controversies reflect Christian-Jewish relations long after the time of Jesus. To establish this is of capital importance if we wish to bring out the meaning of certain gospel texts for the Christians of today. All this should be taken into account when preparing catechesis and homilies for the weeks of Lent and Holy Week (1985 *Notes*, no. 29; see no. 26 below).

HOLY WEEK: THE PASSION NARRATIVES

21.   Because of the tragic history of the "Christ-killer" charge as providing a rallying cry for anti-Semites over the centuries, a strong and careful homiletic stance is necessary to combat its lingering effects today. Homilists and catechists should seek to provide a proper context for the proclamation of the passion narratives. A particularly useful and detailed discussion of the theological and historical principles involved in presentations of the passions can be found in *Criteria for the Evaluation of Dramatizations of the Passion* issued by the Bishops' Committee for Ecumenical and Interreligious Affairs (March 1988).

22.   The message of the liturgy in proclaiming the passion narratives in full is to enable the assembly to see vividly the love of Christ for each person, despite their sins, a love that even death could not vanquish. "Christ in his boundless love freely underwent his passion and death because of the sins of all so that all might attain salvation" (*Nostra Aetate,* no. 4). To the extent that Christians over the centuries made Jews the scapegoat for Christ's death, they drew themselves away from the paschal mystery. For it is only by dying to one's sins that we can hope to rise with Christ to new life. This is a central truth of the Catholic faith stated by the *Catechism* of the Council of Trent in the sixteenth century and reaffirmed by the 1985 *Notes* (no. 30).

23.   It is necessary to remember that the passion narratives do not offer eyewitness accounts or a modern transcript of historical events. Rather, the events have had their meaning focused, as it were, through the four theological "lenses" of the gospels. By comparing what is shared and what distinguishes the various gospel accounts from each other, the homilist can discern the core from the particular optics of each. One can then better see the significant theological differences between the passion narratives. The differences also are part of the inspired Word of God.

24.   Certain historical essentials are shared by all four accounts: a growing hostility against Jesus on the part of some Jewish religious leaders (note that the Synoptic gospels do not mention the Pharisees as being involved in the events leading to Jesus' death, but only the "chief priests, scribes, and elders");

the Last Supper with the disciples; betrayal by Judas; arrest outside the city (an action conducted covertly by the Roman and Temple authorities because of Jesus' popularity among his fellow Jews); interrogation before a high priest (not necessarily a Sanhedrin trial); formal condemnation by Pontius Pilate (cf. The Apostles' and Nicene Creeds, which mention *only* Pilate, even though some Jews were involved); crucifixion by Roman soldiers; affixing the title "King of the Jews" on the cross; death; burial; and resurrection. Many other elements, such as the crowds shouting "His blood be on us and on our children" in Matthew, or the generic use of the term "the Jews" in John, are unique to a given author and must be understood within the context of the author's overall theological scheme. Often, these unique elements reflect the perceived needs and emphases of the author's particular community at the end of the first century, *after* the split between Jews and Christians was well underway. The bitterness toward synagogue Judaism seen in John's gospel (e.g., John 9:22;16:2) most likely reflects the bitterness felt by John's own community after its "parting of the ways" with the Jewish community, and the martyrdom of St. Stephen illustrates that verbal disputes could, at times, lead to violence by Jews against fellow Jews who believed in Jesus.

25.   Christian reflection on the passion should lead to a deep sense of the need for reconciliation with the Jewish community today. Pope John Paul II has said:

> Considering history in the light of the principles of faith in God, we must also reflect on the catastrophic event of the *Shoah* . . .
>
> Considering this mystery of the suffering of Israel's children, their witness of hope, of faith, and of humanity under dehumanizing outrages, the Church experiences ever more deeply her common bond with the Jewish people and with their treasure of spiritual riches in the past and in the present (*Address to Jewish Leadership*, Miami, September 11, 1987).

THE EASTER SEASON

26.   The readings of the Easter season, especially those from the book of Acts, which is used extensively throughout this liturgical period, require particular attention from the homilist in light of the enduring bond between Jews and Christians. Some of these readings from Acts (e.g, cycles A and B for the Third and Fourth Sundays of Easter) can leave an impression of collective Jewish responsibility for the crucifixion ("You put to death the author of life . . . " Acts 3:15). In such cases, the homilist should put before the assembly the teachings of *Nostra Aetate* in this regard (see no. 22 above), as well as the fact noted in Acts 3:17 that what was done by some individual Jews was done "out of ignorance" so that no unwarranted conclusion about collective guilt is drawn by the hearers. The Acts may be dealing with a reflection of the Jewish-Christian relationship as it existed toward the end of the first century (when Acts was composed) rather than with the actual attitudes of the post-Easter Jerusalem Church. Homilists should desire to convey the spirit and enthusiasm of the early Church that marks these Easter season readings. But in doing so, statements about Jewish responsibility have to be kept in context. This is part of the reconciliation between Jews and Christians to which we are all called.

27.   Pope John Paul II's visit to the Chief Rabbi of Rome on Good Friday, 1987, gives a lead for pastoral activities during Holy Week in local churches. Some dioceses and parishes, for example, have begun traditions such as holding a "Service of Reconciliation" with Jews on Palm Sunday, or inviting Holocaust survivors to address their congregations during Lent.

28.   It is becoming familiar in many parishes and Catholic homes to participate in a Passover Seder during Holy Week. This practice can have educational and spiritual value. It is wrong, however, to "baptize" the Seder by ending it with New Testament readings about the Last Supper or, worse, turn it into a prologue to the Eucharist. Such mergings distort both traditions. The following advice should prove useful:

> When Christians celebrate this sacred feast among themselves, the rites of the *haggadah* for the seder should be respected in all their integrity. The seder . . . should be celebrated in a dignified manner and with sensitivity to those to whom the seder truly belongs. The primary reason why Christians may celebrate the festival of Passover should be to acknowledge common roots in the history of salvation. Any sense of restaging the Last Supper of the Lord Jesus should be avoided . . . . The rites of the Triduum are the [Church's] annual memorial of the events of Jesus' dying and rising (Bishops' Committee on the Liturgy *Newsletter*, March 1980, p.12).

Seders arranged at or in cooperation with local synagogues are encouraged.

29.   Also encouraged are joint memorial services commemorating the victims of the *Shoah* (Holocaust). These should be prepared for with catechetical and adult education programming to ensure a proper spirit of shared reverence. Addressing the Jewish community of Warsaw, Pope John Paul II stressed the uniqueness and significance of Jewish memory of the *Shoah*: "More than anyone else, it is precisely you who have become this saving warning. I think that in this sense you continue your particular vocation, showing yourselves to be still the heirs of that election to which God is faithful. This is your mission in the contemporary world before . . . all of humanity" (Warsaw, June 14, 1987). On the Sunday closest to *Yom ha Shoah*, Catholics should pray for the victims of the Holocaust and their survivors. The following serve as examples of petitions for the general intercessions at Mass:

- For the victims of the Holocaust, their families, and all our Jewish brothers and sisters, that the violence and hatred they experienced may never again be repeated, we pray to the Lord.

- For the Church, that the Holocaust may be a reminder to us that we can never be indifferent to the sufferings of others, we pray to the Lord.

- For our Jewish brothers and sisters, that their confidence in the face of long-suffering may spur us on to a greater faith and trust in God, we pray to the Lord.

30.   The challenges that peak in the seasons of Advent, Lent, and Easter are present throughout the year in the juxtaposition of the lectionary readings. There are many occasions when it is difficult to avoid a reference either to Jews or Judaism in a homily based upon a text from the Scriptures. For all Scripture, including the New Testament, deals with Jews and Jewish themes.

31.   Throughout the year, the following general principles will be helpful:

a) Consistently affirm the value of the whole Bible. While "among all the Scriptures, even those of the New Testament, the Gospels have a special pre-eminence" (*Dei Verbum*, 18), the Hebrew Scriptures are the word of God and have validity and dignity in and of themselves (ibid., 15). Keep in view the intentions of the biblical authors (ibid., 19).

b) Place the typology inherent in the lectionary in a proper context, neither overemphasizing nor avoiding it. Show that the meaning of the Hebrew Scriptures for their original audience is not limited to nor diminished by New Testament applications (1985 *Notes*, II).

c) Communicate a reverence for the Hebrew Scriptures and avoid approaches that reduce them to a propaedeutic or background for the New Testament. It is God who speaks, communicating himself through divine revelation (*Dei Verbum*, 6).

d) Show the connectedness between the Scriptures. The Hebrew Bible and the Jewish tradition founded on it must not be set against the New Testament in such a way that the former seems to constitute a religion of only retributive justice, fear, and legalism, with no appeal to love of God and neighbor (cf. Deuteronomy 6:5; Leviticus 19:18,32; Hosea 11:1–9; Matthew 22:34–40).

e) Enliven the eschatological hope, the "not yet" aspect of the *kerygma*. The biblical promises are realized in Christ. But the Church awaits their perfect fulfillment in Christ's glorious return when all creation is made free (1974 *Guidelines*, II).

f) Emphasize the Jewishness of Jesus and his teachings and highlight the similarities of the teachings and highlight the similarities of the teachings of the Pharisees with those of Christ (1985 *Notes*, III and IV).

g) Respect the continuing validity of God's covenant with the Jewish people and their responsive faithfulness, despite centuries of suffering, to the divine call that is theirs (1985 *Notes*, VI).

h) Frame homilies to show that Christians and Jews together are "trustees and witnesses of an ethic marked by the Ten Commandments, in the observance of which humanity finds its truth and freedom" (John Paul II, Rome Synagogue, April 13, 1986).

i) Be free to draw on Jewish sources (rabbinic, medieval, and modern) in expounding the meaning of the Hebrew Scriptures and the apostolic writings. The 1974 *Guidelines* observe that "the history of Judaism did not end with the destruction of Jerusalem, but went on to develop a religious tradition . . . rich in religious values." The 1985 *Notes* (no. 14) thus speak of Christians "profiting discerningly from the traditions of Jewish readings" of the sacred texts.

32.   The 1985 *Notes* describe what is central to the role of the homilist: "Attentive to the same God who has spoken, hanging on the same word, we have to witness to one same memory and one common hope in him who is master of history. We must also accept our responsibility to prepare the world for the coming of the Messiah by working together for social justice, respect for the rights of persons and nations, and for social and international reconciliation. To this we are driven, Jews and Christians, by the command to love our neighbor, by a common hope for the kingdom of God, and by the great heritage of the prophets" (1985 *Notes*, no. 19; see also Leviticus 19:18, 32).

PLENTY GOOD ROOM:
THE SPIRIT AND TRUTH OF
AFRICAN AMERICAN
CATHOLIC WORSHIP

SECRETARIAT FOR THE LITURGY
AND SECRETARIAT FOR BLACK CATHOLICS
NATIONAL CONFERENCE OF CATHOLIC BISHOPS
1990

OVERVIEW OF *PLENTY GOOD ROOM*

J-Glenn Murray, SJ

A PASTORAL LETTER

Happily, from Saint Paul's first letter to the faith community at Thessalonika even to our own day, bishops have rarely missed the opportunity to write a letter in response to pastoral cares and concerns. *Plenty Good Room: The Spirit and Truth of African American Catholic Worship* (PGR) is such a letter. Its general concern is cultural adaptation of the liturgy (inculturation), specifically as it applies to the African American Catholic community.

In a well-known passage, the Constitution on the Sacred Liturgy *Sacrosanctum concilium* (SC) states:

> Even in the liturgy the Church has no wish to impose a rigid uniformity in matters that do not affect the faith or the good of the whole community; rather, the Church respects and fosters the genius and talents of the various races and peoples. (#37)

Though this passage is now commonplace to us, when it was promulgated it signaled a recovery of a long-standing though dormant practice of the church: inculturation, that is, "the incarnation of the Gospel in the autonomous cultures and at the same time the introduction of these cultures into the life of the Church."[1]

Until recent times and the advent of the discerning writings of many a social scientist and liturgist, inculturation was not given much thought or sway. In fact, most of us thought of Western European cultures as the only "real" cultures. All others were somehow "elementary" at best and "primitive," "barbaric" and "uncivilized" at worst. As a result, there was no need to adapt the liturgy to other cultures. Very few of us think this way anymore. "In the contemporary view, no one culture is normative, and all races and ethnic group are to be taken seriously" (PGR, 40).

Though culture is like an ocean, surrounding us as water does a fish, it is not easily defined. For our purposes, let me try to put it simply (I hope without being simplistic): Culture comprises the practices (mores, customs, traditions, way of life, rituals) and texts (stories, symbols, art) that signify or produce meaning, or serve as the occasion for its production.[2] From such an understanding, one that I believe underlies much of the thinking of the church leaders at the Second Vatican Council, it should be apparent why the concern for inculturation of the liturgy would arise. How can we gather to worship the living God and come to know the significance and meaning of "who and whose we are" in this corporate act of worship without raising the issue of culture? PGR is a beginning attempt at the dialogue.

THE WORK OF MANY HUMAN HANDS

Presumably, Saint Paul wrote his pastoral letters alone. Such is not the case with this letter. It was written by the Black Liturgy Subcommittee, formed initially under the auspices of the Bishops' Committee on the Liturgy, and later, the Black Catholic Secretariat.

As each of Saint Paul's letters has a history, so does this particular pastoral letter. The late Archbishop James Patterson Lyke, OFM, then an auxiliary bishop of the diocese of Cleveland, urged by his friend and spirited revivalist, the late Sister Thea Bertha Bowman, FSPA, began to look at the experiences of Black Catholic worship in predominantly Black parishes. He was concerned that the various styles of celebration found there needed some evaluation, guidance and incorporation within the wider church. Consequently, he proposed the writing of a pastoral letter that would examine the nature of liturgical adaptation and chart various ways of implementing some concrete liturgical revisions on the local level.

The need for these liturgical revisions was so urgent that the subcommittee, with the expert help of Bishop Wilton Daniel Gregory (an African American bishop with a doctorate in sacred liturgy) went about drafting and publishing *In Spirit and Truth: Black Catholic Reflections on the Order of Mass* (IST) in 1988. For those who had engaged in the options and choices presented within the document, IST was a welcomed addition; for those who had done very little adaptation, IST was particularly threatening; for those who had gone beyond those adaptations, IST was largely useless. Something more was needed, something that included a pastoral articulation of the theological foundations of the proposed cultural adaptations of IST.

After many listening sessions, much gathering of information, and a good deal of discussion, discernment and prayer from within and outside the subcommittee, it was decided that one person would have to draft such a pastoral. The subcommittee gave the task to the late Father Donald Michael Clark, a priest and liturgist of the archdiocese of Detroit. The result was a very poetic piece, and the subcommittee, though moved deeply, was not completely satisfied. The subcommittee then turned to Father William Leonard Norvel, SSJ.

As the first draft was poetic, Father Norvel's draft was challenging. While most were using the conciliar term "adaptation," Father Norvel was calling for "inculturation." He wanted no transitory or external modifications; rather, he called for nothing less than the transformation of both the culture and the church. The subcommittee knew he had arrived at the heart of the matter, though they still felt that something was missing.

At that point the subcommittee turned to Bishop Edward Kenneth Braxton, then a priest and campus minister in the archdiocese of Chicago. Bishop Braxton's ministerial schedule at the time was more than full, but he took up the labor of love nonetheless. What he produced was nothing short of brilliant. Not only was it theologically sophisticated, doctrinally nuanced and pastorally sound, it was cogent and cohesive. It was also clearly written for a theologically astute audience. But the committee knew that Braxton's draft had to be the foundational one, for he had laid the basis for the theological arguments that would comprise the final product.

From a synthesis of these three drafts, the final one was written and reviewed attentively by the members of the subcommittee and others interested in the dialogue. Finally, it was sent to all the bishops of the U.S. National Conference of Catholic Bishops for their comments, emendations and final approval. On August 28, 1990, the memorial of Saint Augustine, bishop of Hippo, the letter was released for publication.

As is clear from its history, PGR, approved and published by the Secretariats for the Liturgy and for African American Catholics of the National Conference of Catholic Bishops, is the result of the painstaking work and tender care of a "wisdom community." *Many* bishops, clergy, religious, pastoral ministers, scholars of liturgy and devoted faithful directly contributed to and carefully reviewed this statement of care and concern about liturgy and African American culture. The poetry, challenge, history, theological acumen and pastoral sensitivity is theirs and now ours.

Let us look briefly at what that community said and our bishops approved and published. Perhaps there is no better place to look for the major themes articulated within the document than Bishop Gregory's introduction to PGR, which presents them in a succinct fashion.

FAITH AND CULTURE

> The Church lives in the modern world with a heart that must be ever open to the sounds that voice the joy and hope, the poverty and affliction of humanity. Those sounds are found most eloquently in the cultures of the human family.[3]

This issue of faith and culture, which is at the very heart of PGR, is discussed in some detail in articles 14–23 and 34–42. In article 14 we discover that the wedding of culture and liturgy is not new, for

> [f]rom the beginning, in order to recall and relive the experience of Christ in their midst, the Church, at Jesus' command and under the guidance of the Holy Spirit, engaged and transformed many Jewish rituals, symbols, gestures, and customs beloved by Jesus and his original disciples.

Of particular interest in this section is the history presented in articles 15–23, which outline how the church has benefited from the rituals, symbols, gestures and customs of Jewish, Hellenistic, Roman and Franco-Germanic cultures. Moreover, this section details the decline of this process at the time of the Council of Trent, as well as its re-emergence in the liturgical movements of both the Baroque and Romantic periods. In the midst of this discussion of faith and culture, the document discusses the rather limited view of culture held by many before our current, more expansive one—a consequence of contemporary scholarship (#34–42).

THE GENIUS OF AFRICAN AMERICAN SPIRITUALITY

> For several decades, Black religious music has had a respected place alongside other indigenous American hymnody in Catholic worship. But more recently, African American art, devotional traditions, styles of preaching and praying, rhythm and tempo at worship services also have begun to influence Catholic liturgy.[4]

PGR asserts, and rightly so, that the African American religious experience has its roots in Africa (#69–70), which is still evident today in prayer (#71), sermons (#72), song (#73), fellowship (#74), partnership (#75) and healing (#76). From this experience has grown a spirituality (#78–80) that is best identified as contemplative (#81), holistic (#82), joyful (#83), and communitarian (#84). It is a spirituality deeply rooted in a faith that has a strongly intuitive and emotive base (#85–87). "Whereas the European way might be summarized in Descartes' 'I think, therefore I am,' the African model might be 'I am, I dance the Other, I am'" (#86). Finally, this spirituality comes to full expression in ritual activity (#88) that is concerned with space (#89–90), time (#91), action (#92–94), prayer (#95–96), preaching (#97–100) and sacred song (#101–104).

THOUGH NOT MONOLITHIC, THERE IS A RICH, SHARED EXPERIENCE

> The members of the Black Liturgy Subcommittee are also aware and respectful of the multicultural diversity embraced by the African American religious heritage. While we might speak in general terms regarding elements of Black culture, we realize that such generalities do not exhaust the complexity of our own heritage.[5]

This statement is taken up in PGR in articles 43–68. The document begins by reminding the reader that African Americans are a varied people, living, working, studying, recreating and praying in multiple and diverse ways (#43–45). That having been said, the reader is further reminded that both the African American bishops and social scientists posit that there are characteristics common to Blacks in general and consequently to Black Catholics, "cradle" and "convert" both (#46). These elements developed in the broader context of Africa (#47–48, 50), American Protestantism (#49), scripture (#51–56), the "invisible institution" (#57–60) and spirituals (#61–62). It is also in this same section that the document recognizes and laments the meager efforts at evangelization on the part of the church in the United States (#63–67). "That is why the Church's present efforts at evangelization and liturgical adaptation are all the more necessary and urgent, and yet all the more difficult to accomplish" (#68).

THE CALL FOR LITURGICAL INCULTURATION
IN THE AFRICAN AMERICAN CATHOLIC COMMUNITY

> With the personally expressed encouragement of our Holy Father, John Paul II, we are embarking upon this adventure so that all may better understand and preserve our precious African American heritage for the glory of the Church, which stands to continue benefiting from the gifts of our cultural treasures.[6]

As has been noted above, the long-standing tradition of the church has been to wed the liturgy with the various cultures it has encountered. This tradition, though dormant for many years, has been awakened by the Second Vatican Council, post-conciliar documents and papal writings (#24–28). This tradition has received new vigor in relation to African American Catholics and the call to liturgical inculturation among us (#30–33).

There can be no discussion of liturgical adaptation without a discussion of liturgy and culture. Having already seen what the document said about culture, we turn our attention to its discussion of liturgy. There is perhaps no more succinct, accessible and clear discussion of liturgy and symbolic reality, and liturgy and the Christ event, than that found in articles 1–13 of PGR. It is a section that should be read by anyone interested in liturgy, regardless of the question of inculturation.

A POSSIBLE MODEL

> The Bishops' Committee on the Liturgy has prepared this statement for those who wish to reflect more deeply on the Church's encounter with African American culture in its worship.[7]

The conclusion of PGR makes explicit that this statement is but a beginning in a process that must take years of serious study, prayerful discernment, pastoral sensitivity and approbation by competent authorities (#123). Nevertheless, some model needs to start the conversation. After delineating principles that might govern liturgical inculturation (#109), the pastoral letter proposes one possible "signpost"—*In Spirit and Truth*—that may assist worship in the African American Catholic community at Sunday eucharist (#110–122).

Finally, all involved in the process are reminded of two essentials—serious study and ardent prayer—if this great work is to be done for the glory of God and the building up of the whole Church, in which there is plenty good room!

NOTES

1. John Paul II, encyclical letter *Slavorum Apostoli*, 2 (June 2, 1985), AAS 77 (1985): 802–803; Discourse to the Plenary Assembly of the Pontifical Council for Culture, 5 (January 17, 1987), AAS 79 (1987): 1204–05.

2. See Raymond Williams' discussion of the three broad meanings of culture in *Keywords* (London: Fontana, 1983), 87–90.

3. Wilton D. Gregory, "Introduction," in PGR, vii.

4. *Ibid.*

5. *Ibid.*, viii.

6. *Ibid.*

7. *Ibid.*, vii.

OUTLINE

PLENTY GOOD ROOM: THE SPIRIT AND TRUTH OF AFRICAN AMERICAN CATHOLIC WORSHIP

I. LITURGY AND SYMBOLIC REALITY

You awake us to delight in your praise, for you have made us for yourself, and our heart is restless until it rests in you.[1]

A. AN EXAMINATION OF RITUAL

1.   Public worship, rooted in humanity's response to God's self-revelation, is a rich and complex reality. Although every people attempts to convey its awareness of absolute mystery, dread, awe, wonder, and love in its experience of the holy, ultimately, there are no adequate words for this ineffable mystery. The experience nonetheless is real, and it leads to a profound sense of total dependence, of utter creaturehood in the presence of the Creator. This experience of the absolute majesty of God, the One who dwells in unapproachable light, who is the source of life and goodness, is tempered by the equally powerful sense of the fascinating nearness and familiarity of God, who created all things and fills them with every blessing.[2]

> For without God all of our efforts turn to ashes and our sunrises into darkest nights. Without God, life is a meaningless drama with the decisive scenes missing. But with God we are able to rise from the fatigue of despair to the buoyancy of hope. With God we are able to rise from the midnight of desperation to the daybreak of joy. Saint Augustine was right—we were made for God and we will be restless until we find rest in God.[3]

This is uniquely true in the Christian tradition, because in Jesus Christ the mystery of the divine and of the human are both made manifest.[4] For by his dying and rising, "Jesus revealed the human face of God and transformed the face of humanity."[5] He is, as Saint Paul says, an unshakable "Yes" both to God and to us (see 2 Corinthians 1:18–22).

2.   Liturgy celebrates and evokes that divine reality that is at once remote and intimate, transcendent and immanent, beyond our reach and ever present. As a result, liturgy has an undeniable density and complexity even when worshipers and religious leaders themselves do not advert to it.[6] Liturgy evokes a world that is at once shared with others and is at the same time beyond ordinary life. To borrow the words of Howard Thurman, liturgy "bathes one's whole being with something more wonderful than words can ever tell."[7]

B. SYMBOLS

3.   Precisely because liturgy is concerned with realities of faith that go beyond immediate experience, it celebrates mystery by means of symbols and signs.[8] Liturgical activity, therefore, is not principally concerned about directly producing effects in the world as it is, except insofar as they relate to the coming of God's reign. Thus, in ritual activity, the faithful do not eat and drink only to feed their bodies. They do not sing only to make music. They do not speak only to teach and to learn. They do not pray only to restore psychic equilibrium. By using space, time, action, and speech in a new way, worship turns the attention of the assembly toward realities that would otherwise go unattended.[9] Worship lifts people up and moves them into the soul-stirring, the awe-inspiring, the transcendent, and the inciting[10] so that, ultimately, they may worship in spirit and truth (cf. John 4:24), so that they may not honor Christ in worship clothed in silk vestments, only to pass him by unclothed and frozen outside.[11]

4.   Since liturgy is possible only by reason of humanity's intrinsic symbol-making genius, and because of the depth and complexity of both humanity and its symbols, it is possible for our symbols to be misused and misunderstood in the Sunday liturgy.

5.   First, one cannot arbitrarily make or establish symbols. Symbols are not merely things. Certain realities become symbolic in particular circumstances and only in relation to a human community. In and of themselves bread, wine, water, oil, fire, incense, a cross, a fish, a white robe, an organ melody, a purple cloth, a paragraph from Scripture may not be symbolic. They become symbolic because of their resonating with the members of a given historical, cultural, ethnic, and racial community. They can assume levels of meaning that make sense of birth, life, and death—by means of tradition, community, and grace.[12]

6.   Second, symbols are not to be confused with signs. Signs have conventional meanings established by the community. The purpose of a sign is clear and unambiguous (e.g., a red light means stop, and only stop; a green light means go, and only go). They are signs. There is no ambiguity. This is not the case with symbols. Symbols are necessarily ambiguous, that is, they evoke multiple meanings and associations. Water, for example, is a primal symbol. For different people, in different circumstances, a body of water may evoke very diverse symbolic associations: coolness, calm, life, storm, danger, drowning, flood, death. For this reason, symbols cannot be strictly controlled in an effort to manage and predict exactly what associations and feelings people will have in their presence.[13]

7.   This is why people can participate in the same celebration of the Eucharist on Sunday and find different meanings in the Scriptures proclaimed, the hymns sung, the preparation of the gifts, the eucharistic prayer, the sign of peace, the sharing in the Body and Blood of the Lord. This is also why people of different ethnic and cultural backgrounds may have different subjective responses to the same objective symbolic activity.

8.   Third, it is inadequate to think of symbols primarily as bearers of knowledge or information. While there is a catechetical and instructional dimension to the liturgy, the Eucharist is not the same as a religion class. It is a serious mistake to judge the impact of symbols by what people explicitly understand by them, and even worse by what they can put into words. Moved by symbols, the faithful often know and understand far more than they can say.

9.   The Second Vatican Council and the postconciliar liturgical instructions of the Church enriched the symbols of the liturgy by restoring to the rites much of their original simplicity and beauty. This restoration emphasized the importance of the participation of the assembly, revised all existing rites, expanded the use of Scripture, and encouraged a greater degree of cultural diversity. As a result, the liturgy should be more understandable to the assembly and should invite the participation of all. Moreover, these enriched symbols have an authentic driving force even when they seem beyond comprehension. A person may be particularly moved by the singing of a certain hymn, by an element in one of the rites of Christian initiation, by the ritualized actions of vested ministers, or by the rich ceremonies of Holy Week without fully understanding them in the cognitive sense. Were they asked, "What do these symbols mean?" they might respond, "I don't know. I didn't even know they were symbols!" This would not imply that they have not experienced meaning in their symbolic activity. They have, for symbols are truly multi-dimensional phenomena.

10.   Again, if people are asked why they are deeply moved by the recitation of a poem by Langston Hughes, a sermon preached by Martin Luther King, Jr., jazz played by Mary Lou Williams, music scored by Lionel Hampton, the blues sung by Ray Charles, an aria performed by Marian Anderson, or a ballet choreographed by Alvin Ailey, they might be able to discourse on aesthetic theory, but they might not be able to say why the work moves them so. The interplay between symbol and person is far more than that of cause and effect. Symbols draw upon the accumulated wisdom and heritage of a people. They combine concepts and values, while appealing to memory and imagination. They derive much of their power through association with the collective experience and history of a people. Perhaps one of the reasons why some Catholic assemblies do not experience the full depth of their liturgical prayer is that the seeming ordinariness of their lives and daily work in some way separates them from poetic, artistic, and symbolic language. Such a difficulty might suggest a greater catechesis *through* and *for* the liturgy by "attending to what we and others actually experience in liturgy; reflecting on what our experience and that of others means; applying what we have learned to future liturgies."[14]

II. LITURGY AND THE CHRIST EVENT

A. WHO AND WHAT LITURGY CELEBRATES

11.   Liturgy celebrates the landscapes of human experience: happiness, sadness, renewal, and grief. Liturgy provides rites of passage in human life: birth, maturity, vocation, commitment, old age, death. Liturgy also celebrates the

universal human need for communion, healing, and reconciliation. Christian liturgy embraces all these and far more by celebrating the new meaning that the life, death, and resurrection of Jesus Christ give to the lives of all people. In the liturgy, the Church proclaims the paschal mystery, the paradigmatic event that transforms the past, the present, and the future. In faith, and in fact, the liturgy is the memorial that joins the worshipers to the past experience of the mystery of Christ that radically changed the lives of his followers and altered the history of the world. It is this memorial that directs worshipers into the future, the "not-yet" of Christ's coming in glory.[15]

12. In the liturgy, Christ speaks to each person and each community in their lived conditions. Saint Augustine reminds us: "He [Christ] has ascended without leaving us. While in heaven he is also with us, and while on earth we are also with him."[16] In this manner, people are able to unite the drama of their own sufferings with the paschal mystery of the Lord. The liturgy encourages the people of God, nourished by Christ's Body and Blood and filled with his Holy Spirit,[17] to approach the future with hope and trust. Even though this future is unknown, faith guarantees that Christ will be there. This confident hope embraces everyone's personal history as well as the future of the world. Believers realize that their faith in Christ makes them conscious that they must do everything they can to overcome personal problems and world discord, to be a living sacrifice of praise.[18] The liturgy also reminds them that when they have done all they can, they should not despair, because Christ is still with them. Events and experiences that seem random and confusing to them may be a part of a larger, providential design beyond their complete understanding. It is this Christ event that all Catholics celebrate in the liturgy. It is this Christ event without which we cannot go on living.[19] It is this Christ event that is the hinge event of history, whose meaning surpasses the limits of time and locality.

B. THE ENCOUNTER WITH CHRIST

13. In whatever locality he preached, Jesus preached that the reign of God was at hand (Mark 1:15). Wherever he traveled, Jesus turned people's hearts to God (see Luke 18:42–43). Whenever he proclaimed the Good News, Jesus showed the way to God's prodigal love and mercy (see Luke 15:11–32). Whoever followed him experienced in Jesus the very mystery of God. In him, their longings for a coming High Priest, Prophet, King, Suffering Servant, Savior, and Messiah were all fulfilled. He was the Christ, the Son of the living God (see Matthew 16:13–23). The encounter with Christ changed their lives completely (see Luke 8:1–3). They could never forget the sacred meal that he left them (see 1 Corinthians 11:23–26), the meal that kept the memory of the Passover of the Lord but which they would now eat in memory of the Lord's dying and rising "until he comes" (see 1 Corinthians 11:26).[20] They experienced the devastation of his death (see Matthew 27:45–66) and the joyous reality of his resurrection (see John 20:1–21, 25). These experiences drew them deeper into the mystery of God. They preserved and passed onto others the meaning and truth of their encounter with Christ by means of oral and written accounts, by creeds, and most important, by liturgical symbols and rites (see Acts 2:42). These symbols and rites have been

continually adapted, depending upon the varying cultures encountered. The goal of the adaptations has always been to intensify the experience of the mystery of Christ and God's saving power for all peoples—even to the very ends of the earth (see Matthew 28:16–20).

III. LITURGY AND CULTURE

A. THE ENCOUNTER WITH CHRIST CONTINUED: CULTURAL ADAPTATION OF THE LITURGY THROUGHOUT HISTORY

14.   From the beginning, in order to recall and relive the experience of Christ in their midst, the Church, at Jesus' command and under the guidance of the Holy Spirit, engaged and transformed many Jewish rituals, symbols, gestures, and customs beloved by Jesus and his original disciples.

15.   In this early and fertile Jewish period (c. 33 to c. 100), the Church harvested not only many followers but also words and phrases such as: *alleluia; amen;* "holy, holy, holy"; "it is right and just to give thanks and praise"; and "let us pray." It likewise gave a Christian meaning to the essential structure of the Eucharistic Prayer, intercessory prayer, and the liturgy of the word; baptismal rites, devotion to the saints, and laying on of hands; and designation of Sunday as the weekly day of worship.[21]

16.   As the Church grew, it continued its mission to the very ends of the earth. It encountered and labored among both the Hellenistic and Roman worlds. From this period (c. 100 and c. 321), the Church acquired the wisdom of Justin Martyr, Clement of Alexandria, Tertullian, Hippolytus and other learned doctors; words and phrases such as: *acclamation; advent; agape; anamnesis; canon; epiclesis; ephiphany; eucharist; eulogy; Lord, have mercy; mystery;* and *preface;* the concepts of formulary prayer, sacrament, and silence; the rites of anointing, exorcism; the Church calendar;[22] and the *domus ecclesiae* (house of the Church), which was complete with an atrium where the assembly gathered, a large tank of water where the initiates could be baptized, and a table where the leader presided—all of which became the model space for the assembly's worship.[23]

17.   With the peace established between Constantine and the Church in 313 with the Edict of Milan, the Church gained not only official recognition but also the new and free ideas of those such as Cyril of Jerusalem, Ambrose of Milan, John Chrysostom, and Augustine of Hippo; the concepts of mystagogy and of facing the East during prayer—prayer that was prayed through Christ, with Christ, and in Christ;[24] the continuing development of the Roman and Oriental Rites, baptismal candles, the washing of feet at baptism, and white baptismal garments; imperial court ceremonials; high esteem for the bishop and his office; liturgical vesture and ornaments, especially the pallium and ring; kissing the altar; and the establishment of the solemnity of Christmas—a prime example of cultural adaptation.[25]

18.   As the Church continued to develop, it heralded the Good News of the Christ-event to countless others. In the process of this proclamation, the Church became incarnate in new and varying cultures. From the Franco-Germanic period (c. 590 to c. 1073), the Church renewed its liturgical life and added to it by the families of sacramentaries attributed to Leo the Great, Gelasius, and Gregory the Great; the lyrics of the "Veni Creator" and "Victimae Paschali"; devotion to the saints, liturgical drama, and verbal flourishes in prayer; the procession with palms on Palm Sunday, footwashing on Holy Thursday, the veneration of the cross on Good Friday; the blessing of the new fire, the greeting of the Light of Christ, the "Exultet," the blessing of the baptismal water at the Easter Vigil; Romanesque churches and their rites of dedication.[26] Simultaneously, from the East the Church reaped the bounty of the greatness of Cyril and Methodius in their adapting the Byzantine liturgy to the culture and language of the Slavic peoples.[27] All this activity served as powerful testimony to Saint Peter's early admonition: "In truth, I see that God shows no partiality. Rather, in every nation whoever fears him and acts uprightly is acceptable to him" (Acts 10:34–35).[28]

19.   With the passage of time, the Church continued to grow even further and farther and reached the very limits of the known world. Having converged with the world's manifold cultures and having adapted worthily to them, the Church regrettably, as Anscar Chupungco has stated, entered upon a period of "luxuriant growth in which the liturgy was both reinterpreted and misinterpreted."[29] The first chill in the midwinter of the Church's liturgical adaptation was felt in the political policies of Saint Pope Gregory VII (c. 1021–1085); the unification of the Western liturgies through the agency of mendicant preachers; elaborate liturgical plays, with actors supplanting the solemn liturgical actions of the assembly; the multiplication of Masses, with the attendant diminution of the liturgical ministries coupled with an exaggerated piety toward the Eucharist apart from the eucharistic action and the reception of Holy Communion; and all this to the increased accompaniment of sacring-bells and the song of paid chantry clerks.[30] Of this age, Walter Howard Frere writes:

> Equally unfortunate was the effect on persons. The Mass-priest became dominant. Now, so long as he had a serving boy, he could dispense with deacon and other ministers; he could supersede the congregation also. With the disappearance of the sense of sacrifice there disappeared also not only the layman's communion but also the sense of his lay-priesthood. The ideal layman was the boy who would serve the priest's Mass. Drill superseded worship and the Mass was commercialized. The hour of Low Mass arrived; and the hour of revulsion drew on.[31]

20.   Because of the aforementioned factors, and out of the rapid expansion and sometimes unregulated practices of the Middle Ages, there arose a call for strict uniformity. A heightened rubrical approach followed the Council of Trent, whose principal aim was to curb abuses and institute reforms, not to introduce new adaptations. With the reform of the Roman Misal by Saint Pius V in 1570 and the establishment of the Sacred Congregation of Rites by Sixtus V in 1588, the centralizing effort of Trent was realized, free development of the liturgy in local churches was greatly curtailed, and the cultural accommodation of liturgy came

to a virtual standstill.[32] One need only examine the Chinese Rites controversy to see how creative and daring adaptations of the faith and its practices to the Chinese Confucian culture of the sixteenth and seventeenth centuries came into direct conflict with the Church's desire for unification.[33] Liturgical creativity took avenues other than the Mass: devotion to the Blessed Sacrament, which gave rise to the use of tabernacles, sanctuary lights, elevations, exposition, and benediction.[34]

21.   In reaction to this period of strict uniformity and its consequent alienation of the assembly came the Age of the Baroque with its "flair for festivity, external manifestations of grandeur and triumphalism, especially through pilgrimages and processions, and sensuousness in artistic expression and pious devotions."[35]

22.   In time, some protested the inflexibility of the state of the liturgical life of the post-Tridentine Church as well as the externalism of the Baroque. With this protest developed the advent of Romanticism and its subsequent stress on history. The Church began to reexamine the origins and meaning of liturgical gestures, vestments, vessels, rites, and feasts.

23.   From the nineteenth century onward came renowned liturgists such as Prosper Gueranger, Virgil Michel, Odo Casel, Pius Parsch, Lambert Beauduin, and Romano Guardini; and the great liturgical centers at Solesmes, Beuron, Maredsous, Maria Laach, and Malines.[36] These scholars and outstanding centers of renewed liturgical life provided the foundation of the Liturgical Movement of the early 1900s, which culminated in Pius XII's encyclical on the sacred liturgy, *Mediator Dei*, in 1947; the reformation of the Holy Week Rites in 1955; and finally, the magna carta of contemporary liturgical renewal, the *Constitution on the Sacred Liturgy* of the Second Vatican Council, which was promulgated by Paul VI on December 4, 1963.[37]

B. CULTURAL ADAPTATION AND THE SECOND VATICAN COUNCIL

24.   Throughout much of its history, the Church was firmly committed to cultural adaptation in public worship for the good of the people of God. The same is true of the Church today. The *Constitution on the Sacred Liturgy*, the principal guide for the pastoral adaptation of the liturgy, reminds us of the communal and unifying nature of the liturgy:

> Liturgical services are not private functions, but are celebrations belonging to the Church, which is the "sacrament of unity," namely, the holy people united and ordered under their bishops.[38]

Yet, recognizing the diversity of Christian communities, the missionary nature of the Church, and the exigencies of evangelization, the Church teaches that liturgical rites may be adapted to the temperaments and traditions of different ethnic, language, cultural, and racial groups. With due respect for the common good and unity of faith, the Church does not wish to impart a rigid uniformity upon liturgical expression. Rather, when local customs are free of superstition and error, they may be admitted into the liturgy "provided they are in keeping with the true and authentic spirit of the liturgy."[39]

25.   While clearly calling for the safeguarding of the substantial unity of the Roman Rite, the Church insists that there be legitimate variations and adaptations to different groups, regions, and peoples in drawing up rites, determining rubrics, and revising liturgical books. This is particularly important in areas where the Church is still very young or very small.[40] Therefore, within the limits specified by the liturgical books themselves, specific adaptations may be made in the style of celebrating the sacraments, sacramentals, processions, liturgical language, music, and art by competent territorial ecclesiastical authority.[41]

26.   Because the bishops of the Second Vatican Council, assembled from all over the world, were quite aware of the racial, cultural, and spiritual differences of the people of their local churches and the millions of people yet to hear or respond to the gospel of Christ, they provided for "even more radical adaptations." Such adaptations are always to be guided by the following considerations:

a) The competent, territorial ecclesiastical authority mentioned in art. 22, par. 2, must, in this matter, carefully, and prudently weigh what elements from the traditions and culture of individual peoples may be appropriately admitted into divine worship. They are to propose to the Apostolic See adaptations considered useful or necessary that will be introduced with its consent.

b) To ensure that adaptations are made with all the circumspection they demand, the Apostolic See will grant power to this same territorial ecclesiastical authority to permit and to direct, as the case requires, the necessary preliminary experiments within certain groups suited for the purpose and for a fixed time.

c) Because liturgical laws often involve special difficulties with respect to adaptation, particularly in mission lands,[42] experts in these matters must be employed to formulate them.[43]

27.   The Church further recognized that there is a necessary connection between liturgical adaptations and ongoing catechesis. The *Constitution on the Sacred Liturgy* expressed well the Church's desire to ensure that no one in the Church feel estranged or alienated, but that those who are invited to the feast may be able to participate fully:

The Church, therefore, earnestly desires that Christ's faithful, when present at this mystery of faith, should not be there as strangers or silent spectators; on the contrary, through a good understanding of the rites and prayers they should take part in the sacred service conscious of what they are doing, with devotion and full involvement. They should be instructed by God's word and be nourished at the table of the Lord's body; they should give thanks to God; by offering the immaculate Victim, not only through the hands of the priest, but also with him, they should learn to offer themselves as well; through Christ the Mediator, they should be formed day by day into an ever more perfect unity with God and with each other, so that finally God may be all in all.[44]

28. In its continuing implementation of the reforms initiated by the Second Vatican Council, the Church has spoken still further on the direct connection between liturgical adaptation and evangelization:

> In the work of evangelization the liturgy clearly holds a place of primary importance: it stands as a high point at which the preached mystery of salvation becomes actual; pastorally it offers to evangelization privileged occasions and a sound and effective formation. . . . The intimate union between evangelization and liturgy also gives rise to the duty of renewing the liturgical celebration; this will unfailingly have a strong impact on the life of the Church.[45]

IV. LITURGICAL ADAPTATION IN THE AFRICAN AMERICAN COMMUNITY

A. THE CALL

29. The aforementioned summary statements about liturgical uniformity, diversity, catechesis, and evangelization should make it clear that the Church is sincerely and fundamentally committed to translating its liturgical rites to the many voices of various people, creating, it is hoped, one song of praise.

30. Nowhere is this commitment more profoundly expressed than in Paul VI's speech to the young churches in Africa:

> The expression, that is, the language and mode of manifesting this one faith, may be manifold; hence, it may be original, suited to the tongue, the style, the character, the genius and the culture of one who professes this one faith. From this point of view, a certain pluralism is not only legitimate, but desirable. An adaptation of the Christian life in the fields of pastoral, ritual, didactic and spiritual activities is not only possible, it is even favored by the Church. The liturgical renewal is a living example of this. And in this sense you may, and you must, have an African Christianity. Indeed you possess human values and characteristic forms of culture which rise up to perfection such as to find in Christianity and for Christianity a true superior fullness and prove to be capable of a richness of expression all its own, and genuinely African. . . . You will be capable of bringing to the Catholic Church the precious and original contribution of "Blackness" which she particularly needs in this historic hour.[46]

31. What Paul VI asked of Africans for the universal Church, the Church in the United States asks of its African American daughters and sons—the gift of "Blackness," a gift so intensely expressive and so alive that it comes from the very depths of the Black soul, a gift not just to improve the work of evangelization but to further the very Catholic nature that is the Church's.[47]

32. This Catholic Church indeed welcomes the genius and talents of African Americans. Witness but a few of the many recent signs of growth and vitality of the Church in that community:

- *Discrimination And Christian Conscience* (1958); *On Racial Harmony* (1963); *A Statement on the National Race Crisis* (1968); *Brothers and Sisters to Us* (1979)[48]—challenging statements and pastoral letters of the National Conference of Catholic Bishops condemning the sin of racism and calling for a commitment to eradicate it;
- the ordination of our African American brothers to the episcopacy and the issuing of *What We Have Seen and Heard*,[49] their illustrative pastoral letter on the nature of evangelization in the African American community;
- the clear inclusion of African American leaders at all levels of church government;
- the establishment of diocesan offices of ministry to the African American community;
- the creation of a Secretariat for Black Catholics at the National Conference of Catholic Bishops;
- the Sixth National Black Catholic Congress, its subsequent compelling Pastoral Plan, and its continuing conferences and workshops to assist those who minister in the African American community;
- the introduction and publication of *Lead Me, Guide Me* (GIA Publications, Inc., 1987), the first African American Catholic hymnal, and *In Spirit and Truth: Black Catholic Reflections on the Order of Mass* (USCC, 1987);
- the secure foundation of quality liturgical programs throughout the United States for African Americans;
- a host of diocesan-wide revivals and festive celebrations commemorating Dr. Martin Luther King, Jr. and Black History Month;
- the ever-increasing creation of African American choirs to employ the wide range of the African American musical heritage; and
- John Paul II's spirited meeting with representatives of the African American Catholic community in New Orleans during his 1987 pastoral visit, where he stated:

> While remaining faithful to her doctrine and discipline, the Church esteems and honors all cultures; she respects them in all her evangelizing efforts among the various people. At the first Pentecost, those present heard the apostles speaking in their own languages (cf. Acts 2:4 ff). With the guidance of the Holy Spirit, we try in every age to bring the gospel convincingly and understandably to people of all races, languages, and cultures. It is important to realize that there is no black Church, no white Church, no American Church; but there is and must be, in the one Church of Jesus Christ, a home for blacks, whites, Americans, every culture and race. What I said on another occasion, I willingly repeat: "The Church is catholic . . . because she is able to present in every human context the revealed truth, preserved by her intact in its divine content, in such a way as to bring it into contact with the lofty thoughts and just expectations of every individual and every people." (*Slavorum Apostoli*, 18)

Dear brothers and sisters, your black cultural heritage enriches the Church and makes her witness of universality more complete. In a real way the Church needs you, just as much as you need the Church, for you are part of the Church and the Church is part of you. . . .[50]

33.   The Church's commitment to and call for liturgical adaptation are clear. The Church's commitment to and call for liturgical adaptation in the African American community are clear and unequivocal. Yet, the continuation of the task at hand is involved and complex.

B. THE EARLY YEARS OF THE CHURCH IN THE UNITED STATES: A DOMINANCE OF WESTERN CULTURE THROUGH MISSIONARY ACTIVITY

34.   Sadly, many Americans, even a number of African American Catholics, perceive and experience the Catholic Church in the United States as an exclusively white European reality. This is due in part to the centuries-old Catholic tradition associated with countries like Italy, France, Spain, Germany, Poland, and Ireland and with the great missionaries of the Church who were noted for having brought the faith from these Christian countries to peoples of distant lands.

35.   In the United States, Catholicism was introduced primarily through the colonizing vigor of the Spanish, French, and English.[51]

36.   Inspired by the drive to announce the reign of God to Native Americans and European settlers, Franciscans, Dominicans, Jesuits, and Sulpicians evangelized Florida, the Southwest, Texas, California, Canada, the Great Lakes region, Maryland, Pennsylvania, and New York.

37.   During this Spanish, French, and English missionary activity, Catholicism was so intimately wed to the culture of the missionaries that, doubtless, many of them could not easily distinguish the Gospel that they preached from their own particular cultural expression of it. As a result, because of its links to Europe and its history, the Church in America, like most American institutions, tended to assume that European cultures were the only cultures and found it extremely difficult to imagine, much less value, cultures other than their own.

38.   Happily, for the better part of this century, there has been a gradual change in the understanding of human experience and human perception, particularly by those who are expert observers and evaluators of culture. There is a greater awareness that European cultures are not normative.

39.   As long as Europe was recognized as the "center of gravity," many people perceived European cultures as the norm, as the only "real" cultures. In scholarly circles and in common parlance, these cultures came to be called "classical." They were viewed as a distillation of the great achievements of ancient Greek philosophy, Roman political systems, and Western European philosophy, art, music, architecture, and social values. And they were viewed as universal, providing the normative understanding of the human condition, the nature of

religion, and the social order. For generations, these "classical" cultures held sway, and in some quarters they continue to hold sway even today as the only authentic expressions of culture. Consequently, the mores, customs, traditions, folkways, rituals, and symbols of people who are not European were rarely, if ever, considered expressions of culture, especially as these people were viewed as "primitive," "barbaric," and "uncivilized." Recent evidence for this can be found, for example, in the way Native, African, and Asian American peoples were portrayed in American film and television from the 1930s until the late 1960s and in the fact that the art and artifacts of Africa have only recently been deemed truly worthy of a place in American and European art museums.

C. CONTEMPORARY UNDERSTANDING OF CULTURE

40.   Fortunately, contemporary understanding of culture is quite different. In the contemporary view, no one culture is normative, and all races and ethnic groups are to be taken seriously. Indeed, all peoples have customs, mores, artistic expressions, and traditions that constitute genuine culture. Furthermore, this contemporary view of culture has a historical perspective. It accepts and embraces diversity and pluralism in a manner that the "classical" cultures never could. European "classical" culture is accepted as one among many expressions of culture.

41.   For centuries, the Church shaped and influenced European cultures in an intimate way, and, most assuredly, European cultures had an equal impact on the Church. The necessary process of ridding what is obsolete in this "classical" view of culture and assimilating what is of value in the contemporary view of culture is painstakingly difficult. Nevertheless, it is just such a process that is essential in promoting liturgical adaptation in the African American community.

42.   The fact that the Church is renewing its recognition of and warmly embracing a plurality of cultures does not mean that it must abandon the rich liturgical and aesthetic traditions developed in Europe.[52] What must happen, and indeed what is already happening, is that the Church welcomes and strongly encourages the equally rich and diverse traditions of all peoples in every time and in every place.

V. THE AFRICAN AMERICAN RELIGIOUS EXPERIENCE IN THE UNITED STATES

A. A VARIED PEOPLE

43.   Before all else, and in order better to understand Roman Catholic worship in the African American community, it must first be stated that the African American community is not monolithic. Even the term "African American" is not universally used. Many people prefer other descriptions, such as "Negro," "African," "Afro-American," "Black," or simply "people of color." Still others think of themselves only as human beings. Race, for them, is a secondary reality that merits neither discrimination nor special treatment.

44. African Americans live, work, study, and recreate in a wide variety of social settings. There is indeed a great diversity in nations of origin, socioeconomic status, religious and political persuasions, historical backgrounds, and life-styles. Strictly speaking, African American enslavement was not the universal experience of all "African" people in the United States. Yet while slavery was not an experience common to all African Americans, racism, which has been part of the social fabric of America since its European colonization and which persists still today in many blatant and covert ways, was.

45. Some African Americans do not wish to be thought of as "African American Catholics." Rather, they simply regard themselves as Catholics. They may cherish the Gregorian *Missa Orbis Factor* or may relish singing traditional hymns and contemporary songs as much as their white counterparts. These traditional Black Catholics should not be treated as "odd, misinformed, or pitiable souls," but they must be respected, for all Catholics are indeed our brothers and sisters in the faith. They, along with many other Catholics, may also need to be reminded that, some twenty-five years after the Second Vatican Council, reform and renewal of the liturgy are at the very heart of the Church's life and mission today. Others, unfortunately, may have to be persuaded to overcome in themselves any subtle forms of self-hatred that is an unsightly fragment of years of sustained racism.

46. Despite this diversity, the vast majority of African American Catholics, both convert and "cradle Catholic," upper middle-class and poor, would attest with their African American brothers in the episcopacy that

> There is a richness in our Black experience that we must share with the entire people of God. These are gifts that are part of an African past. For we have heard with Black ears and have seen with Black eyes and we have understood with an African heart. We thank God for the gifts of our Catholic faith and we give thanks for the gifts of our Blackness. In all humility we turn to the whole Church that it might share our gifts so that "our joy may be complete."

> To be Catholic is to be universal. To be universal is not to be uniform. It does mean, however, that the gifts of individuals and of particular groups become the common heritage shared by all. Just as we lay claim to the gifts of Blackness, so we share these gifts within the Black community at large and within the Church. This will be our part in the building up of the whole Church. This will also be our way of enriching ourselves. "For it is in giving that we receive." Finally, it is our way to witness to our brothers and sisters within the Black community that the Catholic Church is both one and also home to us all.[53]

B. THE BROADER CONTEXT

47. African American religious experience is shaped by African factors as well as by those on these shores. To begin with, several key concepts should be noted:

- that religion is an all-pervasive reality for African peoples;[54]

- that a sense of the holy encompasses the whole mystery of life, beginning before birth and continuing after death;[55]
- that for most Africans, to live is to participate in a religious drama;[56] and
- that African people see themselves as totally immersed in a sacred cosmos.[57]

This was the religious cultural matrix of many African Americans who accepted Christianity in this country.

48.   Although current evidence seems to suggest that those Africans who were enslaved here were not brought from African territories where Christianity may have existed, we must nevertheless remember that Christianity was indeed no stranger to African cultures. Actually, Christianity had been well established in much of North Africa, parts of the Sudan, Egypt, and Ethiopia. This was a dynamic Christianity, one that produced great scholars and theologians like Clement of Alexandria, Tertullian, Origen, Cyprian of Carthage, Augustine of Hippo, and Pope Gelasius. Ethiopia was evangelized in the fourth century by Saint Frumentius, whom Saint Athanasius selected to be bishop. In the sixth century, the Emperor Justinian and the Empress Theodora, respectively, sent two groups of missionaries to evangelize Nubia (modern-day Sudan). Until Islamic armies conquered the area in the seventh century, many North Africans made significant contributions to the Church. The Moslem conquest reduced the Church in North Africa to a mere remnant, and by the year 1000 much of North Africa's Church was extinct.

49.   Once in the United States, enslaved Africans had some contact with the Catholic Church in those areas where Catholics were numerous. In other areas where the slave holders were Protestant, they had little, if any, initial contact with the Catholic Church. These enslaved people responded most favorably, however, to the evangelizing efforts of Methodist and Baptist preachers. The fact that these preachers were willing to allow the enslaved to express freely the religious feelings of their hearts contributed greatly to the growth of the Protestant churches among Africans in the United States. Protestant revivals,[58] camp meetings, and the growth of the "secret church," that is, the church under the trees, the church in chains, the church in the fields—the church not doctrinally, institutionally, nor juridically denominational; that church of the slave quarters and family gatherings, where the spirituals were born, sung, danced, prayed, shouted, sermonized; where the sin-sick soul was healed—all gave the enslaved Africans hope of at least a spiritual escape from their oppression.

C. THE U.S. RELIGIOUS EXPERIENCE IN DETAIL

50.   The experience of the African American religious origins here in the United States bears a deeper scrutiny. The enslaved African women and men brought with them to this continent a concept of the Supreme Being, who was deeply and continually involved in the practical affairs of their daily lives, but in a different way than the Christian God.[59]

> For Africans believed in a God who was not only omnipresent, omniscient, omnipotent, and eternal, they believed in a God, who as Supreme Being,

had a radical moral relationship with humanity. This Being was approach-able through many intermediaries, especially nature—all symbolic representatives of the living, pulsating environment in which humans subsist and through which we are related to the spirits of natural things and the ancestors, but preeminently with the Supreme Being, the God who is above all gods and who is known as Creator, Judge, and Redeemer.[60]

This God and their belief in this God helped them to survive.

SCRIPTURE

51.   When the enslaved began to learn Bible stories, beginning with Adam and Eve and continuing through to the ministry of Jesus; Jesus' suffering, death, and resurrection; and the Day of Judgment,[61] they developed a unique theological vision that spoke directly to their plight. They concluded that the God of the Bible was the same universal guide and ruler of the religion of their forebears:

> God is a God.
> God don't never change!
> God is a God.
> An' He always will be God.
>   (Spiritual: "God Is A God")[62]

This God cared for and rewarded all people who were good and punished all who were wicked. This God was not partial to the enslaved or the free; men or women; black or white; brown, yellow or red; for there would be "plenty good room in my Father's Kingdom" (Spiritual: "Plenty Good Room").[63]

52.   Though uprooted and far from home, the enslaved now found a basic orientation and harmony in the scriptural world. These enslaved people from Africa, now baptized, knew that the God of the Bible was a God of liberation, a God who set captives free, who sent Moses "to tell ole Pharaoh to let my people go" (Spiritual: "Go Down, Moses").[64] They understood that this God did not accept slavery any more than sin. And they decided that, if the God of Hebrew children would work to free them and give them a homeland, and if the God of Jesus Christ so loved the world that the only-begotten Son was given to the world to be its Savior, then this same God must love them too. This God would not leave them in bondage under the taskmaster's whip forever. They would indeed be "free at last. Thank God Almighty we're free at last!" (Spiritual: "Free At Last").[65]

53.   Those few enslaved who were able to read were particularly ignited by the Scriptures and often went from camp to camp sharing the encouraging word of what God had done and what God could indeed still do.

54.   In continuing to tell the Bible's story to each other again and again, the slaves came to recognize more powerfully their own story in the Bible. They were a scattered people of many tribal origins, all of whom involuntarily had been enslaved for the service of another nation. They had cried out to the God of their ancestors for deliverance, and they had been answered by a God they did not at first know. They soon learned that this God was the God of their

ancestors, and entering their lives, this God constituted them a beloved people, a light to the nations (see Isaiah 42:6).

55.   These enslaved Africans discovered their own story in the story of Jesus as well, for he identified with those who were poor, blind, and suffering. Like so many of them, Jesus had been born into an oppressed class, suffered real pain, carried a real cross, died a real human death. But he had overcome it all for their sake. And in his resurrection, Jesus showed himself their Lord and Savior, guaranteeing deliverance to his friends, promising to come again when "the Lord shall bear my spirit home."[66]

56.   Enslaved African people in America accepted Christianity because it explained their unique situation: God saw a suffering people; Jesus took up their burden, and he had changed the world, changed the history of the African American slave, lifting it and pointing it toward divine expectations: the freedom of the children of God (see Romans 8:21).

THE INVISIBLE INSTITUTION

57.   This unique Christian vision of enslaved African Americans resulted in a religion that strengthened them in times of great adversity.[67] This same vision gave birth to the "Black church"—the "invisible institution"[68]—when, out of fear of the African American uprisings, religious services by the enslaved were forbidden unless overseen by whites. This church "became the religion of double blackness, carried on in the shadows and under cover of the night, always in danger of interruption and punishment so severe that it might even mean death."[69] Like any other highly developed religion, the "invisible institution," whose vestiges are visible even today, had its sacred space, sacred time, and sacred action.[70]

58.   Its sacred space was the woods in the evening, groupings around camp fires, secret gatherings in a cabin, stealing away under trees, standing in an open field. These places were called "hush-harbors," places where softly spoken words and sacred chants were secretly, yet boldly uttered.

59.   Its sacred time was a gentle combination of God's time and their own life cycle. It was a time in which one, wearing a white robe, could be fully immersed in the saving waters of baptism and enfolded in the community's love. It was a time where two, who could be sold separately, were made one in the midst of a joyous community. It was a time when one could die, but not be forgotten, ever living in the hearts and minds of a remembering community.

60.   Its sacred action was prayer, preaching, and conversion supported by gesture and sacred song. The Scripture was proclaimed and broken open by one who was "acquainted with the source of sacred knowledge."[71] The preacher's ability to dramatize and apply the sacred texts to the assembly's lives in burning oratory, and sometimes solemnly chanted sermons, had to be unparalleled. It had to lead people to "conversion," a radical change of heart ending in a sense of cleanliness, certainty, and reintegration—the three things every enslaved person was

denied in life.[72] The minister's ability to lift up the assembly by eloquent, poetic prayer, large gestures, and spirited song encouraged the assembly to do the same.

SPIRITUALS

61.   Recalling the melodies of Mother Africa; using the hymnody of a new land; recalling the stories from the Bible; and using clapping, moaning, shouting, waving hands, and dance, this community sang songs of life and death, suffering and sorrow, love and judgment, grace and hope, justice and mercy. They sang ardently and lovingly, often hoping against hope. And in singing these "spirituals" they expressed all manner of things:[73]

- their anguish in slavery ("I've Been Buked And I've Been Scorned");[74]
- their trust in God's mighty arm ("Didn't My Lord Deliver Daniel?");[75]
- their belief in God's care ("Nobody Knows The Trouble I See");[76]
- their identification with Jesus' suffering, a suffering like their own ("Were You There When They Crucified My Lord?");[77]
- their belief in the resurrection ("Soon-a Will Be Done");[78]
- their desire for freedom ("O Freedom");[79]
- their assurance of certain freedom now sung in "double coded" songs ("Steal Away");[80] and
- their need for constant conversion and prayer ("Wade In The Water"; "Standin' In The Need Of Prayer").[81]

62.   What must be noted here is that the Scriptures cited in these "spirituals" were not from the Douai-Rheims translation of the Bible, but from the King James translation. This is yet another one of the many clear reminders to us Roman Catholics that when the "Black church" was developed, most of the enslaved knew almost nothing about the Catholic Church.

EFFORTS AT EVANGELIZATION

63.   Though it is true that in the British colonies, during the seventeenth and eighteenth centuries, Roman Catholics were numerically and culturally an insignificant minority—most being found only in Maryland, in parts of Pennsylvania, and, by the beginning of the nineteenth century, in Kentucky and Louisiana—the Catholic Church, except in some isolated instances, was not at all aggressive in the evangelization of the Africans in America or in supporting the Abolitionist Movement to end slavery. As a result, the Church failed to seize the initiative in the evangelizing and converting of the African American population. This failure was due in great part to the acceptance of slavery as an institution by many of the Christian faithful and clergy. Tragically, there seems to have been no Saint Peter Claver or Bishop Bartolomé de Las Casas to cry out in the wilderness of the United States.

64.   Furthermore, there is one sad fact we can neither excuse nor ignore: the clergy and people of the Church in America did very little to evangelize African

Americans; to expose them to the rich graces and strengths of Catholic life, tradition, and worship; or to lighten the weight of their suffering.

65.   What efforts were made to evangelize African Americans began in earnest with the advent of Mary Elizabeth Lange and the Oblate Sisters of Providence in 1828, in Baltimore; Henriette Delille and the Sisters of the Holy Family in 1842, in New Orleans; the arrival of the Mill Hill Fathers (Josephites) from England in 1871, in Baltimore; and the founding of the Sisters of the Blessed Sacrament by Blessed Katharine Drexel two decades later in Philadelphia.[82]

66.   In the 1920s and 1930s, African Americans migrated to the North in large numbers, hoping to escape the blatant racism in the South and searching for employment. The Jim Crow laws and the no less blatant segregation practiced in all northern cities resulted in "Negro parishes," similar to those already established in the South. Because there was no contact with "white parishes," there was little or limited shared experience of a common church life.

67.   Whenever a parish changed from serving white Americans to serving African Americans, the ordinary policy of most dioceses was to turn parish administration over to religious orders that were willing to take up the special ministry to African Americans. One dubious result of this segregated ministry was that certain religious orders attracted at least a few African American vocations, while most diocesan seminaries and communities of religious women attracted almost none.

68.   Unfortunately, because of this attitude toward African Americans, many in this century believe that the Church saw its work as little more than a burdensome endeavor to educate African Americans out of their "uncivilized and barbaric" traditions and into the European-American culture with which the Church seemed so fundamentally identified. That is why the Church's present efforts at evangelization and liturgical adaptation are all the more necessary and urgent, and yet all the more difficult to accomplish.

VI. THE AFRICAN AMERICAN CHURCH

A. AFRICAN VESTIGES

69.   The religious history of Africans and their descendants in this country is certainly a long and complex one. But, in spite of this troubled history, continuity with a rich African ritual has survived in the "Black church," if only in fragmentary ways, even to this very day. W. E. B. Du Bois, Albert J. Raboteau, and George Ofori-atta-Thomas inform us that ancient West African worship was marked by dramatic prayer, storytelling, teaching, song, poetic intensity, and by postures of praise, beauty of symbol, kinship, and healing. *Griots* (African storytellers) and others—persons who assisted the community in its encounter with the sacred—presided over these rituals, told the ancient story, and reminded the assembled who they were and whose they were.[83]

70. Robert C. Williams, Robert Farris Thompson, and Ulysses D. Jenkins tell us that the enslaved Africans, combining these ancient elements with a new understanding of the God of Jesus, created a ritual process that was dramatic in character, influenced by the shout, and was the means by which conversion and God were experienced. They were thus enabled to follow a more or less orderly means of ritually seeking solutions to their problems—to "sing a song of the LORD in a foreign land" (Psalm 137:4).[84]

B. THE "BLACK CHURCH" TODAY

71. The vestiges of this transformed ritual process are present even now in many African American Protestant traditions. Today, we can still hear dramatic prayer:

> Dear God,
>
> Enable us, we pray, to see your acts and to hear your voice amidst the rumbling and confusion of these earthquaking days. Equip us to seize the time that we may be vigilant in our freedom, committed in our callings, and just in our relations with all. *Amen.*[85]

72. We can still hear the sermon "preached," employing Scripture, drama, sustained tones, intonation, rhythm, call-and-response, congregational identification, and a call to conversion:[86]

> As they went up to the temple to pray, a certain man—don't know the man's name, but the next few words tell us somewhat of his condition—a certain man that was lame from his mother's womb. When he said "a lame man," that made me feel sorry for him because it is a pitiful thing when a person has been useful and now has lost that usefulness.
>
> But when I got to thinking about this man who was lame, and I remember the writer said that he was lame from his mother's womb, that made it all the more pitiful to me. For not only was he a lame man, but he had been lame all his life. And I can think of nothing more pitiful than a lame baby—one who was born into the world and whose parents have ever hoped some day he will be strong and healthy. I can see those parents watching him day in and day out, but he never had any use of his limbs. He grew old in age, but still lame.
>
> I think it was last fall, or some time recently, a teenager was told that one of his legs would have to be amputated. He just hated the idea. "Here I am a teenager, where all of the other children my age are active in getting around, doing this and that; and conditions are such that I will have to lose one of my legs and be a cripple the rest of my life."
>
> Well, it is a pitiful thing to see a teenager lame. But, here, this man had never been able to use his limbs, and had been lame from his mother's womb. This man had to be carried. You know we can understand this man's condition because he couldn't help himself. I know a lot of people in the church that are healthy and strong but still want to be carried. . . . They had to carry this man and they brought him daily and laid him at a gate called Beautiful. Now they carried him daily, it means that he must

have been receiving something that kept him coming back. . . . Look at that man that was made by the hands of God. That man is lame and twisted, and had to be carried.

Well, when he saw Peter and John going into the temple, he got glad because, you know, he had begged so long until he could just look at a person as he approached and he could tell what kind of gift he was going to get. I can understand, somehow, how he felt. At one time I used to hop bells at a hotel. And, you know, after a few years I could look at a guest when he pulled up in front of the door and I could pretty well tell what kind of tip I was going to get. Oh, I could look at his bags, yes, I could . . . I could look at the way he was dressed and I could tell the type, the size of tip I was going to get.

Well, this man had been in this business so long until he could look and size up the kind of gift he was going to get. But this time he underestimated. Yes, he did! He knew he was looking for alms. He was looking for something that he could exchange at the supermarket. Oh, but Peter and John said, "Look on us." And every one of us who is representative of the Lord ought to be able to tell the world to "look on us . . ."[87]

73. We can still hear syncopated, heart-throbbing, feeling-thumping song, as varied as: "Do, Lord, Remember Me"[88] or Andre Crouch's "Soon And Very Soon"[89] or Leon Robert's "Holy, Holy, Holy."[90]

74. We can still hear kinship in warm, heartfelt fellowship:

On Sundays when services are to be held, the congregation gathers long before it is time to begin. As they drop in one or two at a time, there is much merriment. Each new arrival means a round of handshaking and earnest inquiry as to health.[91]

75. We can still hear partnership expressed:

Preacher: "Let the church say Amen!"

Church: "Amen. Praise the Lord. Hallelujah!"

or

"I hear you! Say so. Look out now. Go head!"

76. We can still feel the healing when persons "get the spirit" or "fall out" or are "slain in the Spirit." We see this healing acclaimed in witness, testimony, and spontaneous song as well.

VII. TOWARD AN AUTHENTIC AFRICAN AMERICAN CATHOLIC WORSHIP

A. WORD AND SACRAMENT

77. First, when African American Catholics began to thirst for African American cultural expressions in Roman Catholic worship, they turned to those vestigial African traditions still found in the Protestant churches. Initially, some

Catholics may have attempted to bring whole structures of African American Protestant worship into Catholic liturgy exactly as they experienced them. However, ecclesiological and credal differences, as well as, theological and sociological analyses suggest that most Baptist, Methodist, and Pentecostal practices simply cannot be, and nor should they be, translated into Catholic liturgy. Specifically:

> Though our liturgy is Catholic in that it is open to welcome the spiritual contributions of all peoples which are consistent with our biblical faith and our historical continuity, it is also Catholic in that everything that is done in our worship clearly serves (and does not interrupt) this ritual action of Word and sacrament which has its own rhythm and movement, all built on the directions, rites, and forms of the Roman Catholic liturgy as they are approved and promulgated.[92]

African American Catholics "understand the clear distinction between the Roman Catholic Church as a sacramental-eucharistic community and Christian churches of the Protestant tradition as evangelical."[93]

B. SPIRITUALITY

78.　Second, African American Catholics turned to "Black theology" for inspiration. This theology, which is concerned with the desire of the African American community to know itself and to know God in the context of African American experience, history, and culture, is as old as the first sermon preached by enslaved Africans to their brothers and sisters huddled together in some plantation swamp, and as new as the reflections of James Cone, Major Jones, J. Deotis Roberts, Cecil Cone, and others beginning in the 1960s.[94] It is a theology of, about, and by African Americans. And while the formal proponents of this theology were a group of creative Protestant scholars, African American Catholic thinkers have used it as a point of departure to elaborate theological reflection that is both African American and Catholic.[95] The contributions made to this theology are decidedly significant, but what they added to the discussion on the nature of authentic African American Catholic liturgy is invaluable.

79.　These theologians state that spirituality must be the starting point of a distinctively African American Catholic liturgy. It is a spirituality that is born of moments of the African American sense of "conversion." This conversion is neither "confected" nor produced in liturgy as much as it is nourished and sustained.[96]

80.　The African American bishops, in their pastoral letter, *What We Have Seen And Heard*, spoke eloquently of some of the qualities of an African American spirituality. They called particular attention to its contemplative, holistic, joyful, and communitarian nature.

CONTEMPLATIVE

81. African American spirituality "senses the awe of God's transcendence and the vital intimacy of His closeness."[97] Lifted up into God's presence, African Americans respond by surrendering and basking completely in marvelous mystery, whether in church on bended knee or at home in labor or at rest. This contemplative prayer is central and pervasive in the African American tradition.

HOLISTIC

82. African American spirituality involves the whole person: intellect and emotion, spirit and body, action and contemplation, individual and community, secular and sacred.

> In keeping with our African heritage, we are not ashamed of our emotions. For us, the religious experience is an experience of the whole human being, both the feeling and the intellect, the heart as well as the head. It is a spirituality grounded in the doctrine of the Incarnation—our belief that Jesus is both divine and human.[98]

It is a spirituality needed in a society that produces "progressive dehumanization brought about by a technocratic society."[99]

JOYFUL

83. African American spirituality explodes in the joy of movement, song, rhythm, feeling, color, and sensation. "This joy is a result of our conviction that 'in the time of trouble, He will lead me.' . . . This joy comes from the teaching and wisdom of our mothers and fathers in the Faith."[100]

COMMUNITARIAN

84. African American spirituality means community. Worship is always a celebration of community. Because in this spirituality, "I" takes its meaning from "we"; "community means social concern for human suffering and other people's concerns."[101]

C. EMOTION: A WAY OF LEARNING

85. Third, the qualities of an African American spirituality suggest that this spirituality, which is deeply rooted in faith, has a strongly intuitive and emotive base. Nathan Jones, Jawanza Kunjufu, Alvin Pouissant, Na'im Akbar, and many others tell us that there are many ways of knowing and relating to the world.[102] The intellect is not the only way to experience reality. Reality may be experienced by emotion. Leopold Sedar Senghor expresses it best:

> The elan vital of Black Africans, their self-abandonment to the Other (emotion) is, therefore, animated by reason—reason, note, that is not the reason of "seeing" of European whites, which is more a reason of set categories into which the outside world is forced. African reason is more *logos* (word) than *ratio* (intellect). For *ratio* is compasses, square and sextant, scale and yardstick, whereas *logos* is the living Word, the most specifically human

expression of the neuro-sensorial impression. . . . The Black African logos in its ascent to the *Verbum* (transcendent) removes the rust from reality to bring out its primordial color, grain, texture, sound, and color.[103]

This emotive way of knowing is not based primarily on the sense of sight as in the ocular, print-oriented culture of Europe, but on the African oral tradition, which tends to be poetic rather than literal.

86.   Whereas the European way might be summarized in Descartes' "I think, therefore, I am," the African model might be "I am, I dance the Other, I am." For,

> Africans do not make a distinction between themselves and the Object, whether it be tree or stone, human or beast. . . . They become receptive to the impression it emanates, and, like the blind, take hold of it, full of life, with no attempt to hold it in store, without killing it. . . . Black Africans are children of the third day of creation, pure sensory fields.[104]

87.   Father Clarence Joseph Rivers, noted African American liturgist, informs us that in this way of knowing "there is a natural tendency for interpenetration and interplay, creating a concert or orchestration in which the ear sees, the eye hears, and where one both smells and tastes color; wherein all the senses, unmuted, engage in every experience."[105] This way of knowing does not exclude a discursive dimension. It simply states that emotion is the primary way of knowing among African peoples and their descendants. It attests that objective detachment and analytical explanations are useful, but are not the sole means of communicating faith.[106] And lastly, it asserts that peoples everywhere are not poetic or discursive, but both poetic and discursive.

D. SOME RITUAL EMPHASES

88.   Fourth and finally, this articulated African American spirituality comes to full expression in ritual activity, that activity where the Creator and creation meet; where the assembled look upon the face of God and do not die but are sustained;[107] where special attention is paid to space, time, action, language, preaching, and song.

SPACE

89.   The hush-harbors, places of conversion and wholeness, of prayer and preaching, of solace and forgiveness, of shout and dance, were the places where the enslaved went to worship. It was in these small-group spaces that they responded to the God of their forebears in praise, adoration, and reverence. It was in these places that God brought healing, meaning, sustenance, and wholeness to them as individuals and as a group.[108] Today, the holy ground on which the African American assembly gathers, hears God's life-giving Word, gives thanks in a sacrificial meal, and is sent back into the world must be a hush-harbor. As in former times, these hush-harbors may be anywhere, but they must reflect the assembly whose roots are both African and American, not simply African or American. For as surely as the hush-harbors of old formed the assembly, our

new African American liturgical environments will shape those worshiping today. And as the worshipers are shaped, so the world too is in which they live.

90.   The current hush-harbors must be "houses of the Church." They must be spaces that have "the power to anchor and map our human world and our Christian journey through it."[109] They must be places that give full sway to the rich array of the auditory, tactile, visual, and olfactory senses.[110] They must communicate relations with an African heritage and with the struggle of people today. They must be places that speak clearly to the reality that here in this sacred space is an African American, Roman Catholic people gathered for the celebration of word and sacrament. Consequently, this space must be attentive to and mindful of not only all that the African American community has to say, but all that the Church has to say about environment as well, especially in chapters 5 and 6 of the *General Instruction of the Roman Missal* and the statement of the Bishops' Committee on the Liturgy, *Environment and Art in Catholic Worship.*

TIME

91.   The expressions, "We're going to have a good time" and "We're going to have church," sum up the African American's experience of sacred time. Although it is our duty and salvation always and everywhere to give thanks to God, gathering for liturgy is not simply an obligation. Gathering for liturgy is a time of glory and praise. Gathering for liturgy is "passing time" with the Lord. It is a time to heal the "sin-sick" soul. It is a time to give the Spirit breathing room. It is a time to tell the ancient story, at dawn and at dusk, on Sunday, and in every season. It is preeminently a time for the liturgical re-presentation of the paschal mystery: the dying and rising of Christ, that event of "the life of Jesus of Nazareth who was born, lived, taught, ministered, suffered, was put to death, transcended death paradoxically and was proclaimed and exalted as the Christ. . . . [This event] is celebrated in liturgy in such a way that its interpretation of the past event has a plenitude of meaning for the present. That past event becomes sacred time."[111]

ACTION

92.   Holy hands lifted in prayer, bowed heads, bended knee, jumping, dancing, and shouting were all accepted movements in ancient African American worship, because they were creative (i.e., created by the Spirit, who moves us to do so)(see Romans 8:15). In an African American liturgy today, this movement must still play a vital part, not merely because it is a vestige of an African heritage but because gesture is a long-standing tradition of Roman Catholic worship as well.[112] Gestures reveal our inner feelings, hopes, fears, dreams, and longings for freedom. Furthermore:

> If we attend to our experience of bodily interaction with others, we discover that we become the persons we are through that interaction. We learn from the caring touch of a parent that we are valued and loved, and that incites in us the ability to value and love others in return. The attentive, engrossed look on the face of a conversation partner encourages us to

share and develop the feelings and ideas within us. The forgiving hug of a friend loosens in us an unsuspected power to forgive. A hand stretched out to us in a moment of need teaches us how to rise above self-concern in dealing with others. In other words, we are called forth to become the persons we are by the deeds of others.[113]

93.   In both the Church and the African American community, there is great evidence of the power of posture in prayer.

> Prayer said standing with head and hands upraised becomes prayer of praise and self-commitment. Bended knees and bowed head plead and repent. Raised hands speak of hearts lifted to God. A handshake or an embrace offers a peace which the world cannot give. Hands folded as mirror images of each other bring an inner quiet and peace of soul. Sitting hollows out in us a lap-like receptivity to receive a word in faith.[114]

94.   Crying out soars to heaven and joins in the great seraphic hymn. Waving hands proclaim a deep-down praise and thanks when mere words fail. And being slain in the spirit brings an abiding and quickening rest to a world-weary soul. One caveat:

> The liturgy of the Church has been rich in a tradition of ritual movement and gestures. These actions, subtly, yet really, contribute to an environment which can foster prayer or which can distract from prayer. When the gestures are done in common, they contribute to the unity of the worshiping assembly. Gestures which are broad and full in both a visual and tactile sense, support the entire symbolic ritual. When gestures are done by the presiding minister, they can either engage the entire assembly and bring them into even greater unity, or if done poorly, they can isolate.[115]

LANGUAGE: PRAYER

95.   African American liturgy is marked by a rich narrative quality. Words are important. And how words are used in prayer is critical.

> Prayer in the Black Tradition is the very center of the Christian life of Black people and continues to be the basis of hope. In those days when they dwelt in the dark valley of bondage hope was yet unborn. It was through prayer in which they found solace and temporary escape from their sordid condition. . . . The prayers were so fervent, they seemed to ring up heaven. A significant and cogent feature of the prayers was the theological and sociological aspects. Their God was the same God of Abraham, Isaac, and Jacob; a captain who never lost a battle; a God of unrelenting love and forgiveness. Yet their prayers were always mindful of their brothers and sisters who shared some hope for freedom some day. . . . Today in an unsupportive society, prayer for Black people is still the "soul's sincere desire."[116]

96.   The language of African American liturgy can be proclamatory in "witnessing" and attentive in listening; very personal without being exclusive; immanent while genuinely transcendent; exuberant and profoundly silent. It is a language that promotes the assembly's full active participation.[117]

97.   Words are also important in the art of preaching. James Weldon Johnson has described the role of preaching in African American worship this way:

> The old-time Negro preacher was above all an orator, and in good measure, an actor. He knew the secret of oratory, that at bottom it is a progression of rhythmic words more than anything else. I have witnessed congregations moved to ecstasy by the rhythmic intonations. He was a master of all the modes of eloquence. He often possessed a voice that was a marvelous instrument, a voice he could modulate from a sepulchral whisper to a crashing thunderclap. His discourse was generally kept at a high pitch of fervency, but occasionally he dropped into colloquialisms and, less often, into humor. He preached a personal and anthropomorphic God, a sure-enough heaven and red-hot hell. His imagination was bold and unfettered. He had the power to sweep his hearers before him; and so he himself was often swept away. At such times his language was not prose but poetry.[118]

98.   Preaching frequently becomes a dialogue involving the preacher and the assembly. When the preacher delivers a sermon or makes an important point, the congregation may respond from their hearts: "Amen!"; "Yes, Lord!"; "Thank you, Jesus!" They may hum. And sometimes worshipers may simply raise their hands on high in silent gestures of praise, gratitude, and affirmation. These responses are an acclamation of faith that neither demand nor expect any rubrics.

99.   Because of the African American aesthetic appreciation of the vivid narrative form, the celebration of the Word of God in African American worship must be viewed as an experience of communal storytelling through which salvation history is related to the day-to-day lives of the faithful. The presiding minister is the leader of this storytelling experience. The presiding minister is a person of the "Book" (the Scriptures), whose role is to articulate the tale of the Christ event so that people can relate the salvation experience to their lives.[119]

100. Both preaching and praying are always in need of improvement. Those who are called to minister in the African American community must see it as their sacred trust to develop effective, spirit-filled, sound preaching and prayer. Both are a folk art. Thus, white and African American preacher-presiding ministers alike can benefit by learning more about the techniques of this African American liturgical art and regularly evaluating their ministry.

SACRED SONG

101. The "soul" in African American liturgy calls forth a great deal of musical improvisation and creativity. It also calls forth a greater sense of spontaneity. The African American assembly is not a passive, silent, nonparticipating assembly. It participates by responding with its own interjections and acclamations, with expressions of approval and encouragement.

102. This congregational response becomes a part of the ritualized order of the celebration. The assembly has a sense of when and how to respond in ways that would no more disrupt the liturgy than applause would interrupt a politician's speech or laughter a comedian's monologue. The deadly silence of an unresponsive assembly gives the impression that the Spirit is absent from the community's act of praise.[120]

103. African Americans are heirs to the West African music aesthetic of the call-and-response structure, extensive melodic ornamentation (e.g., slides, slurs, bends, moans, shouts, wails, and so forth), complex rhythmic structures, and the integration of song and dance.[121] As a result, African American sacred song, as Thea Bowman noted, is:

> *holistic:* challenging the full engagement of mind, imagination, memory, feeling, emotion, voice, and body;
>
> *participatory:* inviting the worshiping community to join in contemplation, in celebration, and in prayer;
>
> *real:* celebrating the immediate concrete reality of the worshiping community—grief or separation, struggle or oppression, determination or joy—bringing that reality to prayer within the community of believers;
>
> *spirit-filled:* energetic, engrossing, intense; and
>
> *life-giving:* refreshing, encouraging, consoling, invigorating, sustaining.[122]

African American sacred song is also the song of the people, a people "who share and claim a common history, a common experience, a common oppression, common values, hopes, dreams, and visions."[123]

104. African American Catholic worship may be greatly enhanced by spirituals and gospel music, both of which are representations of this aesthetic. But classical music; anthems; African Christian hymns; jazz; South American, African-Caribbean, and Haitian music may all be used where appropriate. It is not just the style of music that makes it African American, but the African American assembly that sings it and the people whose spirits are uplifted by it.

VIII. AN AFRICAN AMERICAN CATHOLIC WORSHIP MODEL: *IN SPIRIT AND TRUTH*

A. THE IMPORTANCE OF SUNDAY WORSHIP

105. The one Church of Jesus Christ is indeed a home to us all, a place where all cultures meet and contribute to the one Body of Christ. The liturgy is the summit toward which the activity of this family (the Church) is directed; at the same time it is the fount from which all its power flows.[124] Of preeminence is the Church's Sunday Eucharist:

> For on this day Christ's faithful must gather together, so that, by hearing the word of God and taking part in the eucharist, they may call to mind the passion, resurrection, and glorification of the Lord Jesus and may

thank God, who "has begotten them again unto a living hope through the resurrection of Jesus Christ from the dead"(1 Peter 1:3).[125]

106. This Sunday celebration of the dying and rising of Christ has several principal requisites:

a. the gathering of the faithful to manifest the Church, not simply on their own initiative but as called together by God, that is, as the people of God in their organic structure, presided over by a priest, who acts in the person of Christ;

b. their instruction in the paschal mystery through the Scriptures that are proclaimed and that are explained by a priest or deacon;

c. the celebration of the eucharistic sacrifice, by which the paschal mystery is expressed, and which is carried out by the priest in the person of Christ and offered in the name of the entire Christian people.[126]

107. African American Catholics and those ministering with them are most sincerely thankful for and respectful of this Sunday liturgy. While realizing that the Church's eucharistic and sacramental tradition is not the same as that of the Protestant evangelical tradition, many African Americans recognize that a more caring celebration of the Roman Rite encourages a wedding of the Gospel of Jesus Christ and the rich heritage of the African American culture—a process in which the liturgy is not adapted to the culture as much as the liturgical assembly absorbing the best and most fitting cultural elements into itself in a rich diversity of ways and over long periods of time.[127]

108. Currently, there may be no worshiping community to which the Church in the United States can turn as an ideal example of authentic indigenous African American Catholic worship. One parish may have the appropriate balance of choir and congregational participation.[128] Another may have a powerful preaching tradition that does not eclipse an equally important liturgy of the Eucharist. Still another may have found ways to relate heroes from the larger African American experience with more traditional Catholic saints. Yet another may have found ways to respect the diversity of the African American worshiping community itself, taking care not to impose something on older people or younger people or Catholics from different parts of the country.

B. PRINCIPLES OF CULTURAL ADAPTATION

109. Although no model worshiping community presently exists, there are principles, based on the very nature of the liturgy itself, that should guide those African Americans who are in the ardent search of such a model:[129]

- " . . . the liturgy is above all things the worship of the divine majesty" (SC 33 [DOL 1]). It is humanity's personal encounter with God in faith, hope, and love through Christ in the community of the Church;

- Christ and his paschal mystery are at the very center of every liturgical act, whether the liturgy celebrates Baptism, or Eucharist, or the Liturgy of the Hours. The Church continually proclaims Christ and his salvific act of dying and rising;

- the Church prays through Christ, with Christ, and in Christ to God, the Father, in the union of the Holy Spirit;
- "the liturgy is made up of unchangeable elements divinely instituted (e.g., water for baptism, food and drink for eucharist), and elements subject to change" (signs dependent upon the culture and tradition of the people, e.g., the method used for the exchange of peace during the sign of peace);
- "Sacred Scripture is of the greatest importance in the celebration of the liturgy" (SC 24 [DOL 1]), that is, the Word of God is a sacramental that effects what it says. Therefore, non-biblical literature should not be used in the place of God's Word or in such a way as to draw the assembly's attention away from this Word;
- the assembly's full, conscious, and active participation in liturgical celebrations is called for by the very nature of the liturgy (SC 14 [DOL 1]), while respecting the simplicity of the rites and the varying roles of the liturgical ministers within these rites;
- there is an educative and catechetical value present in every liturgy, since each liturgy "contains rich instruction for the faithful. For in the liturgy God is speaking to his people and Christ is still proclaiming his Gospel."(SC 33 [DOL 1]);
- the use of a language that reflects the thought of the people, native symbols, and motifs can help make signs and symbols clear.

C. *IN SPIRIT AND TRUTH:* A MODEL

110. Though no model African American Catholic community exists, there is a signpost—based on a love of the Church's liturgy, an equal love of the powerful, religious traditions of the African American community, and the guidelines articulated above—that may assist in pointing the way to such a worshiping community. That signpost is *In Spirit and Truth: Black Catholic Reflections on the Order of Mass.*

111. The Black Liturgy Subcommittee of the Bishops' Committee on the Liturgy prepared those reflections to assist and enhance the liturgical life of parish communities and to present the many opportunities already present for the accommodation of the liturgy to the "genius and talents" of the many ethnic, cultural, and racial groups that make up the Church in the United States, particularly the African American community.[130]

PRELIMINARY GATHERING

112. Noting the long-standing traditions of "fellowship" and "witnessing" in the Black Church, *In Spirit and Truth* suggests a preliminary gathering:

The purpose of this preliminary gathering is most commonly to help the congregation experience Christ's presence and to build up fellowship within the assembly. . . .[131]

Later, while discussing the sign of peace in the Communion Rite, *In Spirit and Truth* offers this reflection:

The warmth and affection of Black Catholic communities may prompt the extension or enlargement of this ritual [the sign of peace] to the point that it overshadows the sharing of the Bread of life, the richest sign of Christians' oneness in Christ. Extended greetings and signs of communicating affection are more properly given during the *Preliminary Gathering of the Assembly* and not at this time.[132]

113. A preliminary gathering, presided over by a deacon or lay minister, might resemble the following:[133]

• An organ or choral prelude as the assembly gathers.

• A well-known congregational hymn that engenders a sense of fellowship or reflects the theme of that day's Scripture readings.

• A scriptural greeting and testimony.

This is a time when many or a few members of the church stand and utter their praises to God for what God has done. This time need "not be eternal to be immortal (see Matthew 6:7–8). It lifts people from the habit of rote prayers, and it causes them to say in one or two lines exactly the thought they would utter to God."[134]

As an example, the presiding minister might say:

They that hope in the Lord
Will renew their strength,
They will soar as with eagles' wings;
They will run and not grow weary,
Walk and not grow faint (Isaiah 40:31).

What a mighty God we serve! Amen? Amen!
Is there anyone who wishes to witness to the Lord's goodness this morning?

One who gives testimony might say:

Saints of God, I have been coming up the rough side of the mountain all week. Along the way I thought I wouldn't make it. But I kept on praying, and the Lord has brought me through. He has made a way out of no way, and I am here to tell the story! Amen!

or:

This week has been a particularly rough one for me, my friends. But I have survived because the Lord is truly like a mother who forgets not her child. And I'm so glad that God has not forgotten me.

- A Prayer.

    After the leader has discerned when these testimonies should come to an end,[135] he or she may collect all these praises into one prayer, summarizing the concerns of those who have spoken.

- Fellowship.

    This is a time when those who form the assembly may greet one another enthusiastically.[136]

    For example, the leader might say:

    > The Lord's kindness never fails. Let us ready ourselves to receive that kindness in abundance. Let us stand and greet one another in fellowship, for this is the day the Lord has made. Let us rejoice and be glad!

    This preliminary gathering may also take the form of hymn singing, catechesis, instruction for the liturgy, and fellowship.

PRAYER

114. Recalling the African American community's rich tradition of prayer, *In Spirit and Truth* states:

> The invitation *Let us pray* is always addressed to the assembly and never to God. This invitation may be extended and adapted to the needs of the assembly, in the style of alternative opening prayers found in the *Sacramentary*. Any variation in this invitation should focus upon the opening prayer prescribed for the day, which must always be said. . . .[137]

Compare:

> Let us pray
> [to the Father whose kindness never fails]
> (Eighteenth Sunday in Ordinary Time)

with:

> Let us pray
> to the Father whose kindness never fails.
> Let us pray
> to the God of our salvation.
> Let us pray
> for peace and life and guidance
> on our pilgrim way.

or:

> Our God is good, yes? Yes! Amen!
> Our God is gracious, yes? Yes! Amen!
> Our God has helped us, yes? Yes! Amen!
> Helped us travel this lonesome valley, yes? Yes! Amen!
> Then let us open our hearts and bow our heads
> And pray to our God whose kindness never fails.[139]

115. The penitential rite and the general intercessions are additional opportunities for using the beauty and poetry of African American prayer to great effect:[139]

A Possible Penitential Rite for the Eighteenth Sunday in Ordinary Time, Sunday Cycle A[140]

Priest or Deacon:

> Mindful of our many sins
> and hungering for forgiveness,
> let us remember God's mercy
> made manifest in Christ Jesus our Lord.
>
> (pause)
>
> Lord Jesus Christ, you are our Bread of heaven, Lamb of God and Word of life. Lord, have mercy.
>
> Lord Jesus Christ, you are our Rock in a weary land, and our Shelter in the storm. Christ, have mercy.
>
> Lord Jesus Christ, you are our soon-coming King. Lord, have mercy.

A Possible Litany for the General Intercessions for the Eighteenth Sunday in Ordinary Time, Sunday, Cycle A[141]

Priest:

> O brothers and sisters,
> drawn together by Jesus, the Bread of Life,
> and mindful of God's manifold blessings,
> we cry out that the many hungers of the world
> may indeed be satisfied.

Minister:

> For the Church scattered throughout the world and longing to spread the Good New of God's most merciful reign, we pray to the Lord. Lord, have mercy.
>
> For our elected leaders who labor for an abiding justice and a peace unending, we pray to the Lord. Lord, have mercy.
>
> For the homeless who ache for shelter, the poor who hunt for bread, the young who starve for love, we pray to the Lord. Lord, have mercy.
>
> For the broken in mind and body who set their hearts on wholeness, especially those for whom we now pray (pause to allow the congregation to voice names of the sick), we pray to the Lord. Lord, have mercy.
>
> For the dead who yearn for eternal rest, especially those for whom we now pray (pause to allow the congregation to voice names of the dead), we pray to the Lord. Lord, have mercy.

Priest:

> Heavenly Father,
> hear us in what we ask

and perfect us in what we do
and, at last, gather us into your kingdom
where our deepest needs will be satisfied
through Christ our Lord.

SCRIPTURE

116. Keeping in mind the African American community's unbroken love of Scripture, *In Spirit and Truth* observes:

"In the dark days of slavery, reading was forbidden, but for our ancestors the Bible was never a closed book. The stories were told and retold in sermons, spirituals and shouts, proverbs and turns of phrases borrowed freely from the Bible. . . . Thus, when the word of Scripture is proclaimed in the Black community, it is not a new message but a new challenge" (*What We Have Seen And Heard*, pp.4–5). . . .

. . . [Consequently] a reader may, according to his or her talent, lend a spirit of enthusiasm to the proclamation of the Scripture texts. Many Black Americans have long grown accustomed to such a spirited proclamation of God's word. So long as the word of God is announced with faith, clarity, and sincerity such styles may be appropriate in the Eucharist.[142]

HOMILY

117. Acknowledging the fertile past of the African American preaching, *In Spirit and Truth* reminds us:

[T]he homily is an application of the Scripture readings and the meaning of the solemnity or feast to everyday Christian living and continued conversion.

The style and manner of preaching should be influenced by "the composition and expectations of the congregation to which it is addressed and not exclusively by the preference of the preacher" (Bishops' Committee on Priestly Life and Ministry, *Fulfilled in Your Hearing: The Homily in the Sunday Assembly*, p.25:1). . . .

. . . Traditionally, good "Black preaching" is rich in content and expression, relies heavily on the biblical text, and draws generously from story, song, poetry, humor, anecdote, and descriptive language. Good Black preaching balances emotion and content and never descends to crass affectation. . . .[143]

LITURGY OF THE EUCHARIST

118. Remembering the African American community's longing for continual conversion, its desire to stand at the foot of the cross, and the zeal of souls who sing "How great Thou art!" beckons the community to gather around the table of the Lord.[144] *In Spirit and Truth* remarks:[145]

At the last supper Christ instituted the sacrifice and paschal meal that make the sacrifice of the cross to be continuously present in the Church, when the priest, representing Christ the Lord, carries out what the Lord did and handed over to his disciples to do in his memory (*General Instruction of the Roman Missal*, 48). . . .

The eucharistic prayer, also called the anaphora, "a prayer of thanksgiving and sanctification, is the center of the entire celebration" (Bishops' Committee on the Liturgy, *Music in Catholic Worship*, 47).

SACRED SONG

119. Observing the African American community's characteristic for dialogue and acclamation, and its passion for singing the Lord's song, *In Spirit and Truth* urges the examination of the use of music:[146]

- in the Entrance Song;
- at the Gloria;
- as the assembly prepares to hear God's word;
- in the Responsorial Psalm;
- at the Gospel procession;
- after the proclamation of the Gospel;
- in the General Intercessions;
- at the Preparation of the Altar and the Gifts;
- for the acclamations in the Eucharistic Prayer;
- for the Lord's Prayer;[147]
- at the Breaking of the Bread;
- for the Communion procession;
- for the Psalm or Hymn of Praise after Communion; and
- at the Recessional.

GESTURE

120. Understanding the African American community's affection for gesture, *In Spirit and Truth* points out those places where gesture and other movements are appropriate:[148]

- the Entrance Procession;
- the Gospel Procession;
- the Preparation of the Altar and the Gifts;
- the Communion Rite;[149] and
- the Recessional.

SILENCE

121. Appreciating the African American community's sense of profound silence, *In Spirit and Truth* calls to mind the liturgy's call to silence:[150]

- during the Opening Prayer and Prayer after Communion; and
- after Communion.

The liturgical celebration will be served by this additional reminder:

> Silence should be observed at the designated times as part of the celebration. Its function depends on the time it occurs in each part of the celebration. Thus at the penitential rite and again after the invitation to pray, all recollect themselves; at the conclusion of a reading or the homily, all meditate briefly on what has been heard; after communion, all praise God in silent prayer (*General Instruction of the Roman Missal,* 23 [DOL 208]).

WELCOMING OF GUESTS

122. Finally, as was noted earlier, fellowship and hospitality are a fundamental element of the Black Church experience. One manifestation of that hospitality is the warm attention paid to visitors and guests. In many Black churches where this tradition survives, the welcoming of guests is an important part of the pastor's announcements.[151] In keeping with that tradition and noting the placement of announcements at the beginning of the Concluding Rites of the Sunday liturgy,[152] we might suggest the following as one of those brief announcements:

> Mindful of the Lord's words:
> "Anyone who welcomes you, welcomes me," (Matthew 10:40)
> we welcome all our guests.
> To those of you who are Catholic
> and have no church home,
> please feel free to see me or one of our ushers
> about becoming an active member of our church family.
> To those of you who may possibly be seeking membership
> in the Catholic Church, please see me
> about initiating so wondrous a step.
> Again, know that you are all welcome.

D. CONCLUSION

123. *In Spirit and Truth* provides an excellent model and serves as a worthy signpost. But it must be remembered that African American Catholics are in the process of developing and continuing a tradition, a laudatory and difficult task.[153] This task is one in which we welcome from the African American culture all that is "compatible with aspects of the true and authentic spirit of the liturgy, in respect for the substantial unity of the Roman Rite."[154] This task, as John Paul II reminds us, ". . . demands a serious formation in theology, history, and culture as well as a sound judgment in discerning what is necessary or useful and what is not useful or even dangerous to faith. . . ."[155] It will take time for people who are authentically African American and truly Catholic and who know the nature of the liturgy and worship to nurture this tradition. In the meantime, African American Catholics must establish, with the authority of the Congregation for Divine Worship and the Discipline of the Sacraments, the Bishops' Committee on the Liturgy, and their local bishops, various liturgical centers of pastoral sensitivity and academic excellence where liturgists, scholars, artists, musicians, and pastors may continue to dedicate their skills in God's service.[156] Furthermore,

these prayerful men and women might do well to look beyond these shores to Africa. As Bishop Wilton D. Gregory has exhorted:

> It might well be, and in many cases I suspect that it will be true that there is much that the Church in service to African Americans can learn from and use from the Catholic Church in Africa. Our people need to continue to explore the genuine and authentic African heritage that is ours, but has been denied or denigrated for far too long. What we do not need are facile, inaccurate, incomplete, uninformed exposure to certain African traditions which ignore the complexity of their origin used in a Catholic ritual context without proper explanation and reverence for either the ritual or African custom.[157]

124. And finally, African Americans, all, must pray:

> Be in the fleeting word, our Father, the stumbling effort.
> Touch mind and heart and life,
> that as we move from this place
> into the way that we must take,
> we shall not be alone,
> but feel Thy Presence beside us, all the way.[158]

African Americans must pray so as to continue exploring and searching the established traditions of the Church and the powerful gifts of the African American culture, in order to determine what is the best result for the Church—all to the greater honor and glory of God, in whose house there is plenty good room!

NOTES

1. Saint Augustine, *Confessions* 1, i, 1.

2. Cf. Eucharistic Prayer IV; Psalms 145:16 and 136:25.

3. Coretta Scott King, ed., *The Words of Martin Luther King, Jr.* (New York: Newmarket Press, 1987), 64.

4. Cf. Joseph Gelineau, SJ, *Liturgy: Today and Tomorrow* (New York: Paulist Press, 1978).

5. Gilbert Ostdiek, OFM, *Catechesis for Liturgy* (Washington, D.C.: The Pastoral Press, 1986), 50.

6. Cf. Mercea Eliade, *The Sacred and the Profane* (New York: Harper Torchbook, 1959).

7. Howard Thurman, *The Growing Edge* (Richmond, Indiana: Friends United Press, 1956), 117.

8. For an extensive explanation of symbol, see Edward K. Braxton, "Reflections from a Theological Perspective," *This Far by Faith: American Black Catholic Worship and Its African Roots* (Washington, D.C.: The Liturgical Conference, 1977).

9. Cf. *Catechesis for Liturgy.*

10. Sean Swayne, *Gather around the Lord: A Vision for Renewal of the Sunday Eucharist* (Dublin: The Columba Press, 1987), 32–36.

11. Cf. Saint John Chrysostom, *Homilies on the Gospel of Matthew,* Matthew 14:23–24, no. 50, para. 3–4.

12. Cf. Paul Ricoeur, *The Symbolism of Evil* (Boston: Beacon Press, 1967).

13. Cf. *Liturgy: Today and Tomorrow.*

14. *Catechesis for Liturgy,* 13–20

15. Cf. Braxton, *This Far by Faith,* 74.

16. Saint Augustine, *Sermon on the Words of the Gospel,* Luke 7:2, para. 1.

17. Cf. Eucharistic Prayer III; Acts 2:33.

18. Cf. Eucharistic Prayer IV; Romans 12:1, Ephesians 1:14.

19. Cf. *Gather around the Lord,* 12–20.

20. Anscar J. Chupungco, OSB, *Cultural Adaptation of the Liturgy* (New York: Paulist Press, 1982), 7.

21. Theodor Klauser, *A Short History of the Western Liturgy* (Oxford: Oxford University Press, 1979), 4–7.

22. Cf. *ibid.,* 7.

23. Cf. *Cultural Adaptation of the Liturgy,* 11.

24. Cf. *A Short History of the Western Liturgy,* 30–32. This custom of praying through, with, and in Christ is one that is practiced and reaffirmed even to this day:

    > Christ Jesus, High Priest of the new and eternal covenant, taking human nature, introduced into this earthly exile the hymn that is sung throughout all ages in the halls of heaven. He joins the entire human community to himself, associating it with his own singing of this canticle of divine praise (SC, 83).

    Or in short:

    > Jesus sings the only song that is heard in heaven, those whose voices would be heard must sing along with Christ (Austin Fleming, *Preparing for Liturgy* [Washington, D.C.: The Pastoral Press, 1985], 17).

25. Cf. *Cultural Adaptation of the Liturgy,* 20–22. Father Chupungco provides early definitions of *acculturation* and *inculturation.* Acculturation is "the process whereby cultural elements that are compatible with Roman Liturgy are incorporated into it either as substitutes for or illustrations of ritual elements of the Roman Rite." Inculturation is "the process whereby a pre-Christian rite is permanently given a Christian meaning" (*ibid.,* 81–86). In a later work *Liturgies of the Future: The Process and Methods of Inculturation* (Mahwah, N.J.: Paulist Press, 1989), Father Chupungco further develops these definitions.

26. Cf. *ibid.,* 27–29.

27. Cf. Joseph P. Fitzpatrick, SJ, *One Culture Many Cultures: Challenge of Diversity* (Kansas City: Sheed and Ward, 1987), 54–61.

28. Pope Gregory the Great addressed a similar theme in his letter to Augustine of Canterbury:

    You, brother, know the usage of the Roman Church in which you were brought up: hold it very much in affection. But as far as I am concerned, if you have found something more pleasing to Almighty God, either in the Frankish or in any other Church, make a careful choice and institute in the Church of the English—which as yet is new to the faith—the best usages which you have gathered together from many Churches. For we should love things not because of the places where they are found, but places because of the good things they contain. Therefore choose from each particular Church what is godly, religious and sound, and gathering all together as it were into a dish, place it on the table of the English for their customary diet (*Cultural Adaptation of the Liturgy*, 26).

29. *A Short History of the Western Liturgy*, 2.

30. Cf. David A. Novak, "A Brief History of the Eucharist," Address to Eucharistic Ministers in the Diocese of Cleveland (November 12, 1989).

31. Walter Howard Frere, *The Anaphora or Great Eucharistic Prayer* (London: SPCK Press, 1938), 138.

32. Cf. *A Short History of the Western Liturgy*, 117–123.

33. Cf. *One Culture Many Cultures*, 61–91.

34. Cf. *A Short History of the Western Liturgy*, 135–140.

35. *Cultural Adaptation of the Liturgy*, 34.

36. Cf. *A Short History of the Western Liturgy*, 122.

37. Cf. *Cultural Adaptation of the Liturgy*, 37–38.

38. SC, 26.

39. SC, 37.

40. Cf. SC, 38.

41. Cf. SC, 39.

42. ". . . 'Missions' is the name generally given to those special endeavors by which heralds of the Gospel sent by the Church and going out into the whole world fulfill the office of preaching the Gospel and of implanting the Church among peoples or groups not yet believing in Christ" (AG, 6). According to this definition, would not "unchurched" African Americans be considered a valid mission?

43. SC, 40.

44. SC, 48.

45. Secretariat of State, "Letter of Cardinal J. Villot to Bishop R. Alberti, President of the Department of Liturgy of CELAM," On the Occasion of the Second Latin American Meeting on the Liturgy (Caracas, July 12–14, 1977), *Notitiae* 13 (1977): 459–467.

46. Paul VI, "Address at the Closing of the Symposium of African Bishops Given at Kampala," Excerpt on the Liturgy and Different Cultures, (July 31, 1969), AAS 61 (1969): 573–578.

47. Cf. Clarence J. Rivers on the definition of "soul" in *Soulfull Worship* (Washington, D.C.: National Office for Black Catholics, 1974), 14.

48. These statements and pastoral letters are contained in the four-volume *Pastoral Letters of the United States Bishops, 1792–1983* (Washington D.C.: USCC Office for Publishing and Promotion Services, 1984).

49. Jospeh L. Howze, et al., *What We Have Seen and Heard: A Pastoral Letter on Evangelization from the Black Bishops of the United States* [= WWHSH] (Cincinnati: St. Anthony Messenger Press, 1984).

50. "Meeting with Black Catholic Leadership," *Unity in the Work of Service*, 55.

51. Cf. John Tracy Ellis, *American Catholicism* (Chicago: The University of Chicago Press, 1956), 1–39; Dennis R. Clark, *Our Catholic Roots* (New York: Sadlier-Oxford, 1988), 2–27.

52. For a discussion of the relationship between religion and culture see Bernard J. F. Lonergan, SJ, *Method in Theology* (New York: Herder and Herder, 1972).

53. WWHSH, 4.

54. Cf. John S. Mbiti, *African Religions and Philosophy* (New York: Praeger, 1970).

55. Cf. for example, *ibid.*, 100–162.

56. Cf. *ibid.*, 108.

57. Cf. J. S. Mbiti, *Concepts of God in Africa* (New York: Praeger, 1970), 1–154.

58. Cf. Diana L. Hayes, "Black Catholic Revivalism: The Emergence of a New Form of Worship," *The Journal of the Interdenominational Theological Center* XIV:1–2 (Fall 1986/Spring 1987): 87–107.

59. Cf. Gayraud S. Wilmore, *Black Religion and Black Radicalism*, Second Edition (New York: Orbis Books, 1983), 15.

60. *Ibid.*, 16.

61. Cf. Charles B. Copher, "Biblical Characters, Events, Places, and Images Remembered and Celebrated in Black Church Worship," *The Journal of the Interdenominational Theological Center* XIV:1–2 (Fall 1986/Spring 1987): 75–86.

62. See *Songs of Zion* [= SOZ] (Nashville: Abingdon Press, 1981), no. 140.

63. See *Lead Me, Guide Me: The African American Catholic Hymnal* [= LMGM] (Chicago: GIA Publications, Inc., 1987), no. 318.

64. See LMGM, no. 292.

65. See LMGM, no. 293.

66. James H. Cone, *The Spirituals and the Blues: An Interpretation* (New York: Seabury Press, 1972), 54.

67. This strength in times of adversity is true even today:

> Recognizing the necessity for suffering I have tried to make it a virtue. If only to save myself from bitterness. . . . I have lived these last few years with the conviction that unearned suffering is redemptive. . . . So like the Apostle Paul, I can now humbly yet proudly say, 'I bear in my body the marks of the Lord Jesus.' The suffering and agonizing moments through which I have passed over the last few years have also drawn me closer to God. More than ever before, I am convinced of the reality of a personal God (Martin Luther King, Jr., in an interview with the *Christian Century* [April 27, 1960], as quoted in James M. Washington, *A Testament of Hope: The Essential Writings of Martin Luther King, Jr.* [San Francisco: Harper and Row, 1986], 41.)

68. E. Franklin Frazier, *The Negro in America* (New York: Schocken Books, 1974), 23.

69. Catherine L. Albanese, *America: Religions and Religion* (Belmont, Calif.: Wadsworth Publishing Company, 1981), 120.

70. Cf. *ibid.*, 119–123.

71. *The Negro in America*, 24.

72. Cf. Clifton H. Johnson, ed., *God Struck Me Dead: Religious Conversion Experiences and Autobiographies of Ex-Slaves* (Philadelphia: Pilgrim Press, 1969).

73. Cf. James H. Cone, *The Spiritual and the Blues*.

74. See LMGM, no. 53.

75. See SOZ, no. 106

76. See SOZ, no. 170.

77. See LMGM, no. 43.

78. See SOZ, no. 158.

79. See SOZ, no. 102.

80. See LMGM, no. 319.

81. See LMGM, no. 107, 216.

82. Cf. Cyprian Davis, OSB, "Black Catholics in Nineteenth-century America," *U.S. Catholic Historian* 5:1 (1986): 4–17.

83. See George Ofori-atta-Thomas, "African Inheritance in the Black Church Worship," *The Journal of the Interdenominational Theological Center* XIV:1–2 (Fall 1986/Spring 1987): 43–74. See also W.E.B. Du Bois, *The Gift of Black Folk* (Greenwich, Conn.: Fawcett, 1903); and Albert J. Raboteau, *Slave Religion* (Oxford: Oxford University Press, 1978).

84. See Robert C. Williams, "Worship and Anti-structure in Thurman's Vision of the Sacred," *The Journal of the Interdenominational Theological Center* XIV: 1–2 (Fall 1986/Spring 1987): 173. See also Robert Farris Thompson, *Flash of the Spirit* (New York: Vintage Books, 1983); and Ulysses D. Jenkins, *Ancient African Religion and the African-American Church* (Jacksonville, N.C.: Flame International, 1978).

85. See O. Richard Bowyer, Betty L. Hart, Charlotte A. Meade, eds., *Prayer in the Black Tradition* (Nashville: The Upper Room, 1986).

86. Cf. Henry H. Mitchell, *Black Preaching* (San Francisco: Harper and Row, 1979).

87. *Ibid.*, 196–271.

88. See SOZ, no. 119.

89. See LMGM, no. 4.

90. See LMGM, no. 426.

91. *God Struck Me Dead*, 2.

92. See J-Glenn Murray, SJ, "The Liturgy of the Roman Rite and African American Worship," in LMGM.

93. Donald M. Clark, as cited in Bishop James P. Lyke, OFM, "Liturgical Expression in the Black Community," *Worship* 57:1 (January 1983): 20.

94. Cf. Eric Lincoln, *The Black Church Since Frazier* (New York: Schocken, 1974).

95. Cf. Gayraud S. Wilmore and James H. Cone, eds., *Black Theology: A Documented History* (Maryknoll, N.Y.: Orbis Books, 1979).

96. Cf. *Preparing for Liturgy*, 82.

97. WWHSH, 8.

98. *Ibid.*

99. *Ibid.*, 9.

100. *Ibid.*

101. *Ibid.*, 10.

102. Cf. Nathan Jones, *Sharing the Old, Old Story: Educational Ministry in the Black Community* (Winona, MN: Saint Mary's Press, 1982); Jawanza Kunjufu, *Developing Positive Self-Images and Discipline in Black Children* (Chicago: African-American Images, 1984); Alvin F. Poussaint, *Why Blacks Kill Blacks* (New York: Emerson Hall Publishers, 1972); Na'im Akbar, *Chains and Images of Psychological Slavery* (Jersey City: New Mind Productions, 1984); Reginald Lanier Jones, *Black Psychology* (New York: Harper and Row, 1972); and Alfred B. Pasteur and Ivory L. Toldson, *Roots of Soul: The Psychology of Black Expressiveness* (New York: Anchor Press, 1982).

103. Leopold Sedar Senghor, "The Psychology of the African Negro," *Freeing the Spirit*, as cited in Clarence Joseph Rivers, "The Oral African Tradition versus the Ocular Western Tradition," *This Far by Faith*, 41.

104. *Ibid.*

105. "The Oral African Tradition," 45.

106. See *ibid.*, 49.

107. Cf. *Preparing for Liturgy*, 19.

108. Cf. Edward P. Wimberly, "The Dynamics of Black Worship: A Psychological Exploration of the Impulses That Lie at the Roots of Black Worship," *The Journal of the Interdenominational Theological Center*, Volume XIV:1–2 (Fall 1986/Spring 1987):198.

109. *Catechesis for Liturgy*, 70.

110. Cf. EACW, 12.

111. "Reflections from a Theological Perspective," 74.

112. Cf. EACW, 56.

113. *Catechesis for Liturgy*, 126.

114. *Ibid.*, 128.

115. EACW, 56.

116. *Prayer in the Black Tradition*, 13–14.

117. Cf. SC, 30.

118. James Weldon Johnson, *God's Trombones: Seven Negro Sermons in Verse* (New York: The Viking Press, 1969), 5.

119. Cf. Giles Conwill, "Black Preaching and Catholicism," *Ministry among Black Americans* (Indianapolis: Lilly Endowment, Inc., 1980), 31–43.

120. "To promote active participation, the people should be encouraged to take part by means of acclamations, responses, psalmody, antiphons, and songs, as well as by actions, gestures, and bearing. And at the proper times all should observe a reverent silence" (SC, 30).

121. Cf. Portia K. Maultsby, "The Use and Performance of Hymnody, Spirituals and Gospels in the Black Church," *The Journal of the Interdenominational Theological Center* XIV:1–2 (Fall 1986/Spring 1987): 141–160.

122. See Thea Bowman, FSPA, "The Gift of African American Sacred Song," in LMGM, 3.

123. *Ibid.*, 5.

124. Cf. SC, 10.

125. SC, 106.

126. Congregation for Divine Worship, *Directory for Sunday Celebrations in the Absence of a Priest* (June 2, 1988) ICEL trans. (Washington, D.C.: USCC Office for Publishing and Promotion Services, 1988), 12.

127. Cf. Aidan Kavanagh, OSB, *Elements of Rite: A Handbook of Liturgical Style* (New York: Pueblo Publishing Company, 1982), 55–57.

128. Cf. J. Wendell Mapson, Jr., *The Ministry of Music in the Black Church* (Valley Forge: Judson Press, 1984), 43–54.

129. *Cultural Adaptation of the Liturgy*, 63–74.

130. Cf. IST, Preface, 1.

131. IST, 9.

132. IST, 51.

133. Cf. J-Glenn Murray, SJ, "Enfleshing *In Spirit and Truth*," Address Given to the African American Catholic Liturgical Ministers (Los Angeles, February 18, 1988).

134. Harold A. Carter, *The Prayer Tradition of Black People* (Valley Forge: Judson Press, 1976), 123.

135. Cf. *ibid.*, 123.

136. "I advanced towards the people. The church was full. Cries of joy echoed through it: 'Glory to God! God be praised!' Nobody was silent. Shouts were coming from everywhere. I greeted the people, and again they began to cry out in their enthusiasm. Finally, when silence was restored, the readings from the Sacred Scripture were proclaimed." Saint Augustine, *The City of God*, Book 22, VII, 22 as cited in R. Cabie, *The Church at Prayer*, Volume 2 (London: Geoffrey Chapman, 1986), 50.

137. IST, 22.

138. "Enfleshing *In Spirit and Truth*."

139. Cf. IST, 17, 18, 39–40.

140. "Enfleshing *In Spirit and Truth*."

141. *Ibid.*

142. IST, 23, 26.

143. IST, 33–35.

144. See Stuart K. Hine, "How Great Thou Art," in LMGM, no. 181.

145. IST, 41, 44.

146. See IST, 11, 20, 24, 28, 30, 32, 40, 42, 45, 49, 55, 57, 58, 59, 65.

147. Musical settings of the Lord's Prayer should always include the embolism (Deliver us, Lord . . .") a development of the last petition of the Lord's Prayer that begs, on behalf of the entire community of the faithful, deliverance from the power of evil (GIRM, 56a). Given the times of great anxiety in which we live, this embolism surely needs to be prayed.

148. See IST, 12–13, 31, 43, 66.

149. It might be suggested that the assembly stand in *orans* for the Lord's Prayer (see Tertullian, *De oratione*, 14), embrace at the Sign of Peace (GIRM, 56b), and make a proper reverence before the reception of Communion (GIRM, 244c).

150. See IST, 21, 60.

151. Cf. Rawn Harbor, "Music and the Black Church Experience," Talk Given at the Black Catholic Worship Conference (Archdiocese of Detroit, February 3, 1989).

152. Cf. GIRM, 123.

153. Cf. Bishop Wilton D. Gregory, "Black Catholic Liturgy: What Do You Say It Is?" *U.S. Catholic Historian* 7:2–3 (Spring/Summer 1988): 316–319.

154. John Paul II, Apostolic Letter *On the Twenty-fifth Anniversary of the "Constitution on the Sacred Liturgy"* (December 4, 1988) (Washington D.C.: USCC Office for Publishing and Promotion Services, 1989), 16.

155. *Ibid.*

156. Cf. WWHSH, 30–33.

157. Bishop Wilton D. Gregory, "Children of the Same Mother," Talk Given at the Workshop for Pastors Serving in the African American Catholic Community (Atlanta, May 12, 1990), 11–12.

158. *The Growing Edge*, 154.

GUIDELINES FOR
THE CELEBRATION OF
THE SACRAMENTS WITH
PERSONS WITH DISABILITIES

NATIONAL CONFERENCE OF CATHOLIC BISHOPS
1995

OVERVIEW OF *GUIDELINES FOR THE CELEBRATION OF THE SACRAMENTS WITH PERSONS WITH DISABILITIES*

Mary Therese Harrington, SH

Guidelines for the Celebration of the Sacraments with Persons with Disabilities (GSPD) appeared in 1995, although it already had a 25-year history before it came into print. Parents of children with disabilities had been disappointed and angered for years because their children, once baptized, were denied the other sacraments of initiation, not to mention marriage and ordination. Finally, in 1979, one year after the historic 1978 pastoral statement of the U.S Catholic bishops on handicapped people, a group of parents requested that the U.S. National Conference of Catholic Bishops look into the situation. As a result of the parents' action, various pastoral leaders began to collect reports of cases in which sacraments had been denied to persons with disabilities. By 1982 they had collected a sufficient body of data to make it clear that there were in fact a number of problems.

GSPD is a response to these problems, which have not gone away with time. Its introduction identifies GSPD's goal as addressing the inconsistencies in pastoral practice from parish to parish and from diocese to diocese. GSPD draws from the church's ritual books, canonical tradition and experience with persons with disabilities in order to dispel misunderstandings that may impede sound pastoral practice in the celebration of the sacraments.

PRINCIPLES AND SPECIFIC GUIDELINES

The document offers seven general principles and then specifically addresses each of the sacraments. The principles include the recognition that all people are equal in dignity in the sight of God, and that Catholics with disabilities have the right to request the sacraments. In addition, persons with disabilities should have access to the sacraments in their own or nearby parishes. Those who live in residences apart from their families are to be welcomed, as are those who live with their families. Pastors are responsible for providing evangelization, catechesis and more immediate preparation for the celebration of the sacraments. Finally, an accessible parish provides more than physical accommodations. Parish members and staff need to demonstrate a welcoming attitude in order to provide those services that will ensure the inclusion of persons with disabilities in the community of believers.

With these principles in place, the document refers to each sacrament. In the section on baptism, it declares that a disability of itself is never a reason for deferring baptism. It also indicates parents' needs for pastoral care at the time of the baptism of a baby with a disability. It also affirms that persons with disabilities may be sponsors for the sacraments of initiation.

Confirmation is encouraged for all those who have been baptized, even if they have a severe disability. The bishop is obliged to see that the sacrament is conferred on those who properly and reasonably request it.

The eucharist is also to be made available to persons with disabilities. If the person is able to evidence an awareness of the difference between ordinary bread and communion through gesture or reverential silence, even if he or she is not able to verbally distinguish between them, communion is to be offered. The existence of a disability does not disqualify a person from receiving the eucharist.

Likewise, reconciliation is to be made available. As long as the individual is capable of having a sense of contrition, even if he or she cannot describe events precisely in words, the person may receive absolution. Those with profound disabilities may be invited to participate in penitential services with the rest of the community to the extent of their ability. Catholics who are deaf should have an opportunity to confess to a priest in sign language, or through an interpreter of their choice, or in writing.

Persons with disabilities who are ill should have access to the anointing of the sick, although the person should not be anointed because of the disability itself. Persons with disabilities who are ill may also be included in communal celebrations of penance.

Ordination cannot be denied just because a candidate has a disability. However, candidates must possess the personal qualities needed to serve a community of faith. Decisions are to be made according to the gifts and needs of each individual. Counseling and information resources are to be made available for men with disabilities who are discerning a vocation to serve the church in one of the ordained ministries. Those who are responsible for the education and formation of seminarians are to see to it that all students in the seminary are prepared to serve persons with disabilities.

Marriage may be contracted by all who are not prohibited by law from doing so. The local ordinary should make the necessary provisions to ensure the inclusion of persons with disabilities in marriage preparation programs. Each couple must be evaluated according to its competencies and needs. There are to be resource personnel in the diocese who are prepared and able to relate to couples with special needs. Paraplegia is not necessarily an impediment to marriage; in case of doubt, marriage cannot be denied.

THE "USE OF REASON"

The document, the first of its kind in English, provides a good summary of what is already written in canon law and various liturgical texts. It is helpful to have this information at hand in one text. GSPD is sympathetic to those with disabilities and provides a basic platform for advocacy in pastoral settings.

The weakness of the text flows from the limitations of the documents quoted—ritual books and the *Code of Canon Law*. The most glaring difficulty is the recurring reference to the requirement of the "use of reason." This norm, and the associated "age of reason," caused the denial of the sacraments to those with disabilities in the first place, and consequently the need for these guidelines.

GSPD speaks of the "use of reason" on several occasions.

- "All baptized . . . who possess the use of reason may receive the sacrament of confirmation," but "persons who because of developmental or mental difficulties may never attain the use of reason are to be encouraged . . . to receive the sacrament of confirmation" (#16).

- "Only those who have the use of reason are capable of committing serious sin," however, "as long as the individual is capable of having a sense of contrition . . . even if he or she cannot describe the sin precisely in words, the person may receive sacramental absolution" (#23).
- "The anointing of the sick may be conferred if the recipient has sufficient use of reason . . . or if the person has lost the use of reason and would have asked for the sacrament," or "if there is doubt as to whether the sick person has attained the use of reason, the sacrament is to be conferred" (#29).
- Marriage is for those who "possess a sufficient use of reason" (#37).

Obviously, the particular meaning of the "use of reason" is defined by the sacrament being celebrated; for example, what is necessary for anointing of the sick is not the same as what is required for marriage.

"Age of reason" is a related expression to "use of reason" and is often understood to refer to the capabilities of a child of about seven years of age. However, if the child has a developmental disability such as mental retardation, the *chronological* age of seven may not tell the parish priest very much about the strengths and limitations of the child. Because of this problem, some look for the *mental* age of seven as a norm. This does not work very well either, however, because such a gauge of a child's capacity does not usually take into account the child's sense of the sacred, desire for communion, or capacity for intuitive faith.

Most of the cases that precipitated the publication of GSPD were cases in which "use of reason" or "age of reason" were used to deny confirmation, communion, reconciliation, anointing of the sick or marriage. Even though "use of reason" and "age of reason" do not reveal very much about the person's capacity for faith, these norms were used nonetheless to screen out people with disabilities from receiving the sacraments. This is precisely the crux of the pastoral problem of access to the sacraments for persons with disabilities.

We no longer assess human development according to the norm of reason, primarily because not everyone knows what it means. Uncritical recourse to the "age of reason" or the "use of reason" as a way to evaluate ability to participate in the sacraments can have devastating results.

The key to understanding access to the sacraments for persons with disabilities is to look at the sacraments in such a way that God's graciousness comes first. All believers try to respond to God's grace according to their abilities. Even though disabilities can be a source of anguish, shame, grief and dependence, persons with disabilities are made in the image and likeness of God, and share that image and likeness with Jesus Christ, whose own body was broken and cast out before it was made glorious. It is this Christ who initiates grace-filled interaction with all, especially seeking out those who are marginalized or considered not worth the effort. We do not admit people with disabilities to the sacraments out of exceptional charity but out of the realization that vulnerability and interdependence are at the heart of what it means to be human.

The work that remains to be done includes reflecting on experiences of sacramental participation with those who have disabilities, preparing liturgies that include everyone, and going forth with the immense work of hospitality.

Reflection

One learns a great deal from the experience of pastoral care and work with persons with disabilities. However, parish leaders need to reflect on these experiences and ask numerous questions that can push them to be creative, compassionate and authentic. Whatever is done must really respond to the people who are present. Some examples follow below.

- Why did this person with mental illness request this sacrament? What does it mean to him or her? How can we prepare the celebration to include friends of this person? How can this celebration be authentic and liberating?

- Why does this person with blindness find it hard to experience a sense of belonging in a parish and so travel from parish to parish to celebrate the liturgy? Would people with blindness ever like to be together for a celebration? Is it okay for those with similar disabilities to get together to probe their life experiences in the light of the gospel? Must they always adjust to interests of the rest of the world?

- Why does this deaf person prefer to celebrate with other deaf people and avoid attending liturgy with the rest of the family? How can we plan a wedding celebration for a couple that is deaf? What is most helpful? What should we avoid?

- Why does this young family avoid having their baby baptized? The baby has multiple disabilities, and since the birth the family has avoided being with others at church. Why?

- How does a child with autism, who has a very poor sense of time, manage to get his parents' attention to make sure they know he wants to go to church and be with others? What is the connection here between his belonging to a small community of faith for catechesis and liturgy on Sunday?

- Why does this young adult with Down's syndrome love the kiss of peace and become such a delightful encouragement to unity in the assembly? What is going on?

- How is it that three young adults with disabilities who are being confirmed and making their first communion are able to fill the church with all their friends and family?

- Why is this young man in a wheelchair so nervous about asking for the sacrament of marriage, and how can he be put at ease?

- Why is this young man who was born with spina bifida so nervous about considering the priesthood when his friend with a similar disability holds a position of responsibility in a bank?

Hospitality

The work of hospitality begins with an attitude of welcome. The desire to be hospitable immediately faces the reality that genuine hospitality to those with disabilities requires some adjustments. Some people with disabilities may not see, hear, walk or read, and accommodations will be necessary to ensure their full, conscious and active participation in the liturgy. At first, the parish community may recognize a great absence. Some will say, "We don't have any people with disabilities in our parish, so why change anything?" Of course, there will probably never be persons with disabilities present in a parish unless adjustments are made to welcome them and meet their needs.

CONCLUSION

The responsibility to make sacramental life accessible and meaningful to persons with disabilities rests with a parish's leaders. Hopefully, diocesan resources are available to provide encouragement, confidence and competence. But the actual work of inclusion takes place in the parish, one parish at a time. Small communities of faith within a parish can provide a bridge to the larger parish assembly and a place where ongoing sacramental life can be supported by catechesis. When the ministries of catechesis and liturgy work hand in hand, strategies to include everyone can be developed. Then the parish will be blessed by becoming more fully what it is called to be: a community with room for all.

OUTLINE

GUIDELINES FOR THE CELEBRATION OF THE SACRAMENTS WITH PERSONS WITH DISABILITIES

"It is essential that all forms of the liturgy be completely accessible to persons with disabilities since these forms are the essence of the spiritual tie that binds the Christian community together. To exclude members of the parish from these celebrations of the life of the Church, even by passive omission, is to deny the reality of that community. Accessibility involves far more than physical alterations to parish buildings. Realistic provision must be made for persons with disabilities to participate fully in the eucharist and other liturgical celebrations such as the sacraments of reconciliation, confirmation and anointing of the sick" (*Pastoral Statement of U.S. Catholic Bishops on Persons with Disabilities;* November 1978, revised 1989).

PREFACE

Catholics with disabilities, as well as those who minister to or with them, often point out that pastoral practice with regard to the celebration of the sacraments varies greatly from diocese to diocese, even from parish to parish. Inconsistencies arise in such areas as the provision of sign language interpreters for persons who are deaf, in the accessibility of church facilities for persons with mobility problems, and in the availability of catechetical programs for persons with developmental and mental disabilities. Pastoral inconsistencies may occur in other areas as well.

The inconsistencies in pastoral practice often arise from distinct yet overlapping causes. Some result from a misunderstanding about the nature of disabilities. Others arise from an uncertainty about the appropriate application of Church law toward persons with disabilities. Others are born out of fear or misunderstanding. Still others are the result of a studied and honest acceptance of the realistic limitations of a parish's or diocese's available resources.

These guidelines were developed to address many of the concerns raised by priests, pastoral ministers, other concerned Catholics, persons with disabilities, their advocates and their families for greater consistency in pastoral practice in the celebration of the sacraments throughout the country. With this objective in view, the guidelines draw upon the Church's ritual books, its canonical tradition, and its experience in ministering to or with persons with disabilities in order to dispel any misunderstandings that may impede sound pastoral practice in the celebration of the sacraments. It is our hope that the guidelines will complement diocesan policies already in existence.

The bishops of the United States offer the *Guidelines for the Celebration of the Sacraments with Persons with Disabilities* in order to give a more concrete expression to our long-standing concern for "realistic provision" for the means of access to full sacramental participation for Catholic persons with disabilities. While they do not address every conceivable situation that may arise in pastoral practice, the guidelines present a set of general principles to provide access to the sacraments for persons with disabilities. Diocesan staff, pastoral leaders, catechists, parishioners, health care workers and all those who minister to or with Catholics with disabilities are invited and encouraged to reflect upon and accept these guidelines in their continuing effort to bring Christ's healing message and call to justice to the world.

I. GENERAL PRINCIPLES

1.   By reason of their baptism, all Catholics are equal in dignity in the sight of God, and have the same divine calling.

2.   Catholics with disabilities have a right to participate in the sacraments as full functioning members of the local ecclesial community.[1] Ministers are not to refuse the sacraments to those who ask for them at appropriate times, who are properly disposed, and who are not prohibited by law from receiving them.[2]

3.   Parish sacramental celebrations should be accessible to persons with disabilities and open to their full, active and conscious participation, according to their capacity. Pastoral ministers should not presume to know the needs of persons with disabilities, but rather they should consult with them or their advocates before making determinations about the accessibility of a parish's facilities and the availability of its programs, policies, and ministries. These adaptations are an ordinary part of the liturgical life of the parish. While full accessibility may not always be possible for every parish, it is desirable that at least one fully accessible community be available in a given area. Parishes may, in fact, decide to collaborate in the provision of services to persons with disabilities.

4.   Since the parish is the center of the Christian experience for most Catholics, pastoral ministers should make every effort to determine the presence of all Catholics with disabilities who reside within a parish's boundaries. Special effort should be made to welcome those parishioners with disabilities who live in institutions or group homes and are unable to frequent their parish churches or participate in parish activities. However, pastoral ministers should remember that many persons with disabilities still reside with their families. Pastoral visitation, the parish census and the diverse forms of parish and diocesan social communication are just a few of the many ways in which the pastoral staff can work toward the inclusion of all parishioners in the parish's sacramental life.

5.   In accord with Canon 777.4, pastors are responsible to be as inclusive as possible in providing evangelization, catechetical formation and sacramental preparation for parishioners with disabilities. Persons with disabilities, their advocates and their families, as well as those knowledgeable in serving disabled

persons can make a most valuable contribution to these programs. Parish cate-chetical and sacramental preparation programs may need to be adapted for some parishioners with disabilities. Further, parishes should encourage persons with disabilities to participate in all levels of pastoral ministry (e.g. as care ministers, catechists, etc.). Dioceses are encouraged to establish appropriate support services for pastors to facilitate the evangelization, catechetical formation, and sacramen-tal preparation for parishioners with disabilities.

6.   The creation of a fully accessible parish reaches beyond mere physical accommodation to encompass the attitudes of all parishioners toward persons with disabilities. Pastoral ministers are encouraged to develop specific programs aimed at forming a community of believers known for its joyful inclusion of all of God's people around the table of the Lord.

7.   In the course of making pastoral decisions, it is inevitable that pastoral care workers will encounter difficult cases. Dioceses are encouraged to establish appropriate policies for handling such cases which respect the procedural and substantive rights of all involved, and which ensure the necessary provision of consultation.

II. PARTICULAR SACRAMENTS

BAPTISM

8.   Through the sacrament of baptism the faithful are incorporated into Christ and into his church. They are formed into God's people and obtain forgiveness of all their sins. They become a new creation and are called, rightly, the children of God.[3]

9.   Because it is the sacrament of universal salvation, baptism is to be made available to all who freely ask for it, are properly disposed and are not prohibited by law from receiving it. Baptism may be deferred only when there is no reason for hoping that the person will be brought up in the Catholic religion.[4] Disability, of itself, is never a reason for deferring baptism. Persons who lack the use of reason are to be baptized provided at least one parent or guardian consents to it.[5]

10.   So that baptism may be seen as a sacrament of the Church's faith and of admittance into the people of God, it should be celebrated ordinarily in the parish church on a Sunday or, if possible, at the Easter Vigil.[6] The Church, made present in the local community, has an important role to play in the baptism of all of its members. Before and after the celebration of the sacrament, the baptized have the right to the love and help of the community.[7]

11.   Either personally or through others, the pastor is to see to it that the par-ents of an infant who is disabled, or those who take the place of the parents, are properly instructed as to the meaning of the sacrament of baptism and the obli-gations attached to it. If possible, either the pastor or a member of the parish community should visit with the family, offering them the strength and support

of the community which rejoices at the gift of new life, and which promises to nurture the faith of its newest member. It is recommended that preparation programs for baptism gather several families together so that they may commonly be formed by pastoral direction and prayer, and so that they may be strengthened by mutual support.[8]

12.   If the person to be baptized is of catechetical age, the Rite of Christian Initiation may be adapted according to need.[9]

13.   A sponsor is to be chosen who will assist the newly baptized in Christian initiation. Sponsors have a special role in fostering the faith life of the baptized person. As such, they are to be chosen and prepared accordingly. Persons with disabilities may be sponsors for these sacraments of initiation.

CONFIRMATION

14.   Those who have been baptized continue on the path of Christian initiation through the sacrament of confirmation. In this way they receive the Holy Spirit, conforming them more perfectly to Christ and strengthening them so that they may bear witness to Christ for the building up of his body in faith and love.[10]

15.   Parents, those who care for persons with disabilities and shepherds of souls— especially pastors—are to see to it that the faithful who have been baptized are properly instructed to receive the sacrament of confirmation and to approach it at the appropriate time.[11] The diocesan bishop is obliged to see that the sacrament of confirmation is conferred on his subjects who properly and reasonably request it.[12]

16.   All baptized, unconfirmed Catholics who possess the use of reason may receive the sacrament of confirmation if they are suitably instructed, properly disposed and able to renew their baptismal promises.[13] Persons who because of developmental or mental difficulties may never attain the use of reason are to be encouraged either directly or, if necessary, through their parents or guardian, to receive the sacrament of confirmation at the appropriate time.

17.   Confirmation is to be conferred on the faithful between the age of discretion (which is about the age of 7) and 18 years of age, within the limits determined by the diocesan bishop, or when there is a danger of death or in the judgment of the minister a grave cause urges otherwise.

18.   A sponsor for the one to be confirmed should be present. The sponsor assists the confirmed person on the continuing path of Christian initiation.[14] For this reason, it is desirable that the one who undertook the role of sponsor at baptism be the sponsor for confirmation.[15]

EUCHARIST

19.   The eucharist is the most august sacrament, in which Christ the Lord himself is contained, offered, and received, and by which the Church constantly lives and grows. It is the summit and the source of all Christian worship and

life, signifying and effecting the unity of the people of God, providing spiritual nourishment for the recipient and achieving the building up of the Body of Christ. The celebration of the eucharist is the center of the entire Christian life.[16]

20.   Parents, those who take the place of parents and pastors are to see to it that children who have reached the use of reason are correctly prepared and are nourished by the eucharist as early as possible. Pastors are to be vigilant lest any children come to the Holy Banquet who have not reached the use of reason or whom they judge are not sufficiently disposed.[17] It is important to note, however, that the criterion for reception of holy communion is the same for persons with developmental and mental disabilities as for all persons, namely that the person be able to distinguish the Body of Christ from ordinary food, even if this recognition is evidenced through manner, gesture, or reverential silence rather than verbally. Pastors are encouraged to consult with parents, those who take the place of parents, diocesan personnel involved with disability issues, psychologists, religious educators and other experts in making their judgment. If it is determined that a parishioner who is disabled is not ready to receive the sacrament, great care is to be taken in explaining the reasons for this decision. Cases of doubt should be resolved in favor of the right of the baptized person to receive the sacrament. The existence of a disability is not considered in and of itself as disqualifying a person from receiving the eucharist.

21.   Eucharistic celebrations are often enhanced by the exercise of the diverse forms of ministry open to the laity. In choosing those who will be invited to use their gifts in service to the parish community, the parish pastoral staff should be mindful of extending Christ's welcoming invitation to qualified parishioners with disabilities.

RECONCILIATION

22.   In the sacrament of reconciliation, the Christian faithful obtain from the mercy of God pardon for their sins. At the same time they are reconciled with the Church, which they have wounded by their sins and which works for their conversion by charity, example, and prayer.[18]

23.   Only those who have the use of reason are capable of committing serious sin. Nevertheless, even young children and persons with mental disabilities often are conscious of committing acts that are sinful to some degree and may experience a sense of guilt and sorrow. As long as the individual is capable of having a sense of contrition for having committed sin, even if he or she cannot describe the sin precisely in words, the person may receive sacramental absolution. Those with profound mental disabilities, who cannot experience even minimal contrition, may be invited to participate in penitential services with the rest of the community to the extent of their ability.

24.   Catholics who are deaf should have the opportunity to confess to a priest able to communicate with them in sign language, if sign language is their primary means of communication. They may also confess through an approved sign language interpreter of their choice.[19] The interpreter is strictly bound to

respect the seal of confession.[20] When no priest with signing skills is available, nor sign language interpreter requested, Catholics who are deaf should be permitted to make their confession in writing. The written materials are to be returned to the penitent or otherwise properly destroyed.

25.   In the case of individuals with poor communication skills, sorrow for sin is to be accepted even if this repentance is expressed through some gesture rather than verbally. In posing questions and in the assignment of penances, the confessor is to proceed with prudence and discretion, mindful that he is at once judge and healer, minister of justice as well as of mercy.[21]

ANOINTING OF THE SICK

26.   Through the anointing of the sick, the Church commends to the suffering and glorified Lord the faithful who are seriously ill, so that they may be relieved of their suffering and be saved.[22]

27.   Those who have the care of souls and those who are close to the sick are to see to it that the faithful who are in danger due to sickness or old age are supported by the sacrament of anointing at the appropriate time.[23]

28.   Since disability does not necessarily indicate an illness, Catholics with disabilities should receive the sacrament of anointing on the same basis and under the same circumstances as any other member of the Christian faithful.[24]

29.   The anointing of the sick may be conferred if the recipient has sufficient use of reason to be strengthened by the sacrament, or if the sick person has lost the use of reason and would have asked for the sacrament while in control of his or her faculties.[25] If there is doubt as to whether the sick person has attained the use of reason, the sacrament is to be conferred.[26] Persons with disabilities may at times be served best through inclusion in communal celebrations of the sacrament of anointing.[27]

HOLY ORDERS

30.   By divine institution, some among the Christian faithful are constituted sacred ministers through the sacrament of orders. They are consecrated and deputed to shepherd the people of God, each in accord with his own grade of orders, by fulfilling in the person of Christ the functions of teaching, sanctifying, and governing.[28]

31.   The existence of a physical disability is not considered in and of itself as disqualifying a person from holy orders. However, candidates for ordination must possess the necessary spiritual, physical, intellectual, emotional, and psychological qualities and abilities to fulfill the ministerial functions of the order they receive.[29] The proper bishop or competent major superior makes the judgment that candidates are suited for the ministry of the church.[30] Cases are to be decided on an individual basis, and in light of pastoral judgment and the opinions of diocesan personnel and other experts involved with disability issues.

32. Diocesan vocations offices and offices for ministry with persons with disabilities should provide counseling and informational resources for men with disabilities who are discerning a vocation to serve the Church through one of the ordained ministries.

33. In preparation for responsible leadership in ordained ministry, the diocesan bishop or major superior is to see to it that the formation of all students in the seminary provides for their service to the disabled community, and for their possible ministry to or with persons with disabilities. Formation personnel should consult with parents, psychologists, religious educators, and other experts in the adaptation of programs for ministerial formation.

MARRIAGE

34. By the sacrament of marriage, Christians signify and share in the mystery of the unity and fruitful love which exists between Christ and his Church. They help each other to attain holiness in their married life and in the rearing and education of their children.[31]

35. All persons not prohibited by law can contract marriage.[32]

36. The local ordinary should make the necessary provisions to ensure the inclusion of persons with disabilities in marriage preparation programs. Through this preparation all couples may become predisposed toward holiness and to the duties of their new state. In developing diocesan policies, the local ordinary should consult with men and women of proven experience and skill in understanding the emotional, physical, spiritual, and psychological needs of persons with disabilities.[33] The inclusion of persons with disabilities in sponsoring couple programs is an especially effective way of supporting both the needs and the gifts of couples preparing for marriage.

37. For matrimonial consent to be valid, it is necessary that the contracting parties possess a sufficient use of reason; that they be free of any grave lack of discretion affecting their judgment about the rights and duties to which they are committing themselves; and that they be capable of assuming the essential obligations of the married state.[34] It is also necessary that the parties understand that marriage is a permanent union and is ordered to the good of the spouses, and the procreation and education of children.[35] Pastors and other clergy are to decide cases on an individual basis and in light of pastoral judgment based upon consultation with diocesan personnel involved with disability issues, and canonical, medical, and other experts. Medical and canonical opinions should be sought in determining the presence of any impediments to marriage. It should be noted, however, that paraplegia in itself does not always imply impotence nor the permanence of such a condition, and it is not in itself an impediment. In case of doubt with regard to impotence, marriage may not be impeded.[36]

38. Catholics who are deaf are to be offered the opportunity to express their matrimonial consent in sign language, if sign language is their primary means

of communication.[37] Marriage may also be contracted through a sign language interpreter whose trustworthiness has been certified by the pastor.[38]

39.   Pastoral care for married persons extends throughout the married couple's life. By their care and example, the entire ecclesial community bears witness to the fact that the matrimonial state may be maintained in a Christian spirit and make progress toward perfection. Special care is to be taken to include parishioners with disabilities in parish programs aimed at assisting and nourishing married couples in leading holier and fuller lives within their families.[39]

These guidelines are presented to all who are involved in pastoral ministry with persons with disabilities. They reaffirm the determination expressed by the bishops of the United States on the 10th anniversary of the pastoral statement on persons with disabilities "to promote accessibility of mind and heart, so that all persons with disabilities may be welcomed at worship and at every level of service as full members of the Body of Christ."

NOTES

1. Cf. CIC, c. 213.
2. Cf. CIC, c. 843 §1.
3. RCIA, Gen. Intro., 1.
4. CIC, c. 868 §1.2.
5. CIC, cc. 868 §1.1 and 852.
6. CIC, cc. 856 and 857.
7. Cf. RBaptC, 4, 10.
8. CIC, c. 851 §2.
9. Cf. CIC, cc. 851 §1 and 852 §1.
10. RConf, 1–2.
11. Cf. CIC, c. 890.
12. CIC, c. 885 §1.
13. CIC, c. 889.
14. Cf. CIC, c. 892.
15. CIC, c. 893 §2.
16. CIC, c. 897.
17. CIC, c. 914.
18. LG, 11.
19. CIC, c. 990.
20. CIC, cc. 983 §2 and 1388 §2.
21. CIC, cc. 978 §1; 979; and 981.
22. CIC, c. 998.
23. CIC, c. 1001.
24. Cf. CIC, c. 1004.
25. PCS, 12, 14.
26. CIC, c. 1005.
27. Cf. CIC, c. 1002.
28. CIC, c. 1008.
29. CIC, cc. 1029 and 1041 §1.
30. CIC, cc. 241 §1; 1025 §2; and 1051 §1.
31. RMarr, 1.
32. CIC, c. 1058.
33. CIC, cc. 1063 §2 and 1064.
34. CIC, c. 1095.
35. CIC, c. 1096.
36. CIC, c. 1084 §2.
37. CIC, c. 1104 §2.
38. CIC, c. 1106.
39. CIC, c. 1063 §4.

INSTRUCTION *COMME LE PRÉVOIT*

ON THE TRANSLATION
OF LITURGICAL TEXTS
FOR CELEBRATIONS WITH
A CONGREGATION

CONSILIUM
1969

OVERVIEW OF *COMME LE PRÉVOIT*: ON THE TRANSLATION OF LITURGICAL TEXTS FOR CELEBRATIONS WITH A CONGREGATION, *TO SPEAK AS A CHRISTIAN COMMUNITY* AND *CRITERIA FOR THE EVALUATION OF INCLUSIVE LANGUAGE TRANSLATIONS*

Gilbert W. Ostdiek, OFM

The three documents covered in this overview deal with the language to be used in the reformed liturgy. The first, a document issued by Rome for the entire church, concerns the translation of the Roman rites into the vernacular; the second and third, written by the Canadian and U.S. conferences of Catholic bishops respectively, address the question of inclusive language.

BACKGROUND

In December 1963 the Second Vatican Council promulgated the Constitution on the Sacred Liturgy *Sacrosanctum concilium* (SC). One of the most striking elements of the renewal of the liturgy decreed in SC was the return to a vernacular liturgy. In the late fourth century, Latin had replaced Greek as the vernacular language of the Roman liturgy. Latin was retained as the official language of the Roman liturgy after the rise of the modern European languages, even though it was no longer the living language of the people. The conciliar decision to let go of that long tradition, which seemed so startling at the time, was not taken precipitously or without struggle. Calls for a return to the vernacular had gradually increased within the liturgical movement before Vatican II, and the question was hotly debated on the Council floor.

What motivated the final conciliar decision? The goal of Vatican II was primarily pastoral. In the reform of the liturgy the "aim to be considered before all else" is "that full, conscious, and active participation" of the faithful, which is "called for by the very nature of the liturgy" and is "their right and duty by reason of their baptism" (SC, 14). As one of the chief means of accomplishing the goal of making the liturgy intelligible and spiritually fruitful, the Council provided for the use of the mother tongue of the people (#36).

How far was the use of the vernacular to extend? Though the Council sought to preserve the use of Latin (#36 §1), it allowed the mother tongue to be used in a number of places in the Mass. These included the readings, instructions, some prayers and chants, the prayers of the faithful, and the parts belonging to the people (#36 §2, 54). The vernacular could be used throughout the other sacraments (#63.a). When these provisions were brought to the Council floor, however, the presenter noted that there was no intent to exclude any part of the Mass; parts such as the eucharistic prayer would require further permission from Rome.

Requests for approval of local vernacular texts and for extensions of the use of the vernacular in the Mass were not long in coming. By March 1965 Paul VI had approved the use of the vernacular for most of the Mass. The preface to the eucharistic prayer was added to this list in April of that year, and permission for translating the eucharistic prayer into the vernacular followed in January 1967. These extensions were granted to keep the language uniform throughout the liturgy and thus to further the goal of the assembly's participation.

The decision to return to the vernacular, along with the determination that all the rites should be reformed (#21), led to another major question about language that had to be faced after the Council. The reformed rites were all issued in an official Latin version, the *editio typica*. What modern language versions of the liturgical texts were to be used? Vatican II had been content to indicate only that translations should be approved by the competent territorial authority (#36 §4). Implementation of the reform was entrusted to the oversight of a special Roman commission (known by its Latin title, Consilium) from 1964 to 1969, and thereafter to the newly-established Sacred Congregation for Divine Worship. During its tenure the Consilium gradually worked out the criteria and procedures for the translation of liturgical texts. These were issued in an ongoing series of letters and directives, even as the so-called "mixed" (international) commissions for the various modern languages were already working on translations. Preparation of texts for English-speaking countries was under the care of the International Commission on English in the Liturgy (ICEL).

Perusal of these letters and directives reveals a consistent set of concerns and priorities for shaping vernacular liturgy: the pastoral value of celebrating the liturgy in the mother tongue of the people; the need for a common text to promote within a language-family the kind of unity that Latin had once provided on a worldwide scale; and the need to develop a balanced style of liturgical language that is accessible to the people yet theologically faithful to and worthy of the holy mysteries celebrated. These values and priorities found expression early on in an address given by Paul VI at an international conference of translators of liturgical books held in Rome in November 1965; they reached full development in an instruction issued by the Consilium in 1969.

INSTRUCTION ON THE TRANSLATION OF LITURGICAL TEXTS

The English title of this document, issued by the Consilium on January 25, 1969, is "Instruction on the Translation of Liturgical Texts for Celebrations with a Congregation." Though official versions of the document were issued simultaneously in English and five other modern languages, it is often cited by the title of the French version, *Comme le prévoit* (CP).

The process by which CP came into being is instructive. In April 1967 a working group established by the Consilium took up the task of preparing a document on the translation of liturgical books. An initial working draft of the document, written in French, was sent to each of the major modern language commissions. They were asked to prepare draft translations in their own languages, with illustrations and alterations appropriate to the genius of their language. In the meantime, the working group prepared its own Latin draft, which in the end was never finalized or published. In the course of 1968, the Consilium reviewed and revised the drafts it had received from the mixed commissions, making them its own. In December of that year, Paul VI reviewed the Italian version, amending it and noting in the margin that "it can be issued." The changes made by the Pope were incorporated into the other modern language versions of the document, and CP was issued in January 1969. The collaborative process used in preparing the document gives striking witness to the Consilium's conviction that the common texts of the church, whether an instruction like this or the prayers of the liturgy, should be expressed in the idiom of each language. That same conviction runs throughout CP.

In its introductory paragraphs, CP notes that it intends to lay down, in common and non-technical terms, some of the more important theoretical and practical principles that are to guide the work of preparing, approving and confirming translations (#4). Three sections follow.

Section I, entitled "General Principles," states three foundational principles: "a liturgical text, inasmuch as it is a ritual sign, is a medium of spoken communication" (#5); "the purpose of liturgical translations is to proclaim the message of salvation and to express the prayer of the Church to the Lord" (#6); and translations "must be faithful to the art of communication in all its various aspects" (#7). That fidelity must especially be shown to the message itself, to the audience for which it is intended, and to the manner of expression. The interim Latin draft of CP labels these three aspects "[A], [B] and [C]" and makes them the topical subdivisions for the remainder of this section.

Fidelity to the message [A] is taken up in articles 8–13. Two basic guidelines are given: translators should give first consideration to translating the meaning (#8) and keep in mind that the "unit of meaning" is not the individual word but the whole passage (#12). This approach to translation is known as "dynamic equivalence," as contrasted to a literal, word-for-word approach.

Fidelity to the intended audience [B] is the focus of articles 14–24. The opening theme of this section is that the accuracy and value of a translation can be assessed only in terms of the goal of communicating to a particular congregation (#14). Accordingly, the language chosen should be in "common usage," accessible to all in the community, yet "worthy of expressing the highest realities" (#15). The thrust of this section is summed up best when it notes,

> [t]he prayer of the Church is always the prayer of some actual community, assembled here and now. It is not sufficient that a formula handed down from some other time or region be translated verbatim, even if accurately, for liturgical use. The formula translated must become the genuine prayer of the congregation and in it each member should be able to find and express himself or herself. (#20)

Fidelity to the manner of expression [C] is treated briefly in articles 25–29. CP directs that attention be paid to the spoken or rhetorical style of the language (#25) and to the literary genre of the texts (#26). Although effective proclamation of liturgical texts is a high priority for CP, it offers only general directions here rather than detailed maps on how translators are to forge such a style. This is appropriate, for translation is, in the end, an art.

Section II takes up "Some Particular Considerations" (#30–37), distinguishing different kinds of texts and how they are to be translated. What might be called a "sliding scale" seems to be envisioned: The more central a text is in expressing the assembly's faith (for example, the readings from scripture), the more careful the translator must be not to paraphrase; conversely, the more unique the proper ritual performance of an oral text is (such as liturgical hymns), the more free the translation may need to be if the text is to be effective for a contemporary assembly.

Section III focuses on "Committees for Translating" (#40–43). This section defines the structures and procedures involved in preparing, approving and confirming translations. In the final paragraph, CP concludes with what Annibale Bugnini has called an "extraordinary expression of openness." The opening paragraph of the document had described two steps in the preparation of the vernacular liturgy: translating the Latin texts, and then revising them in light of pastoral experience (#1). The concluding paragraph adds a third step:

> Texts translated from another language are clearly not sufficient for the celebration of a fully renewed liturgy. The creation of new texts will be necessary. But translation of texts transmitted through the tradition of the Church is the best school and discipline for the creation of new texts. (#43)

TO SPEAK AS A CHRISTIAN COMMUNITY:
PASTORAL MESSAGE ON INCLUSIVE LANGUAGE

The values and priorities embodied in CP were shaped by the immediate and demanding task of translating massive amounts of new liturgical material generated by Rome. Little attention was paid on the Roman level to contemporary social-cultural issues inevitably embedded in a living language. The issue of inclusivity, for example, was just beginning to be raised in the 1960s and received no attention in CP. Public awareness of that issue was increasingly heightened in the 1970s by various liberation movements, especially those of African Americans and women. By the mid-1980s, major publishing houses and various associations such as the Modern Language Association of America (MLA) and the National Council of Teachers of English (NCTE) had issued guidelines on nondiscriminatory language. Church circles also began to feel the impact of the issue. The commissions charged with translating liturgical texts into the vernacular had to wrestle with it as they entered the second phase of their work, that of revising the vernacular prayer texts that had been in use for a decade or more. It became a pastoral concern for the national conferences of bishops of North America during the 1980s, and they addressed it in documents such as those that follow.

On August 16, 1989, the Pastoral Team of the Canadian Conference of Catholic Bishops (CCCB) issued a pastoral message entitled *To Speak as a Christian Community*. In that document, inclusive language is defined broadly to mean "using words which affirm the equality and dignity of each person regardless of race, gender, creed, age or ability." Focusing on non-sexist language, this message reminds us that Christians are to read the "signs of the times." Reflection on those signs yields significant theological reasons for using and promoting inclusive language. Such language expresses our belief that men and women are fundamentally equal, as originally created by God, as new creations in Christ, and as baptized members of the church.

The document notes that long-term implementation of inclusive language in the life of the church will be slow. The work of specialists in translating biblical and liturgical texts will be required, and open and respectful discussion will be needed to bridge the different levels of awareness within the church. In the short term, we can already act to introduce inclusive language at home, at social gatherings, on the job. Parishes can commit themselves to using inclusive language in the prayers of the faithful, in the choice of hymns, in parish bulletins and written materials, in homilies and pulpit announcements. Presentations, discussion groups and reading are further options. Using inclusive language, the message concludes, is one way to exercise the church's responsibility to stand against one of the widespread forms of discrimination in our society.

CRITERIA FOR THE EVALUATION OF INCLUSIVE LANGUAGE TRANSLATIONS OF SCRIPTURAL TEXTS PROPOSED FOR LITURGICAL USE

On November 15, 1990, the U.S. National Conference of Catholic Bishops (NCCB) approved its *Criteria for the Evaluation of Inclusive Language Translations of Scriptural Texts Proposed for Liturgical Use*. As the title indicates, this document focuses more narrowly on biblical texts translated for liturgical use. It also confines itself to the question of how the NCCB can "distinguish a legitimate translation from one that is imprecise" (#2) when exercising its canonical responsibility to approve such translations.

In part one (#7–13), two general principles are laid out. The primary principle is fidelity to the Word of God, which is to be proclaimed integrally. The second principle, following from the nature of the liturgical assembly, calls for texts that facilitate the full, conscious and active participation of all in the assembly. Part two (#14–20) enunciates principles for inclusive language in lectionary translations. Translations must reflect the original cultural context of the passage (#16). At the same time, inclusive language is one of the principles of public communication of biblical meaning (#15), and language that denies the common dignity of all the baptized ought not be used (#17). Words no longer considered inclusive (for example, "men") should not be used when the reference is generic (#18). Part three (#21–24) deals with the preparation of texts for use in the lectionary, allowing in individual cases for changing the third person from singular to plural (#23) and for adaptation of the psalms in ways appropriate to cultural and liturgical contexts (#24). Part four (#25–31) takes up four special questions: naming God, naming Christ, naming the Trinity, and naming the church in biblical translations. The conclusion (#32–35) notes that inclusive language should not distract hearers (#32) and that authority to adapt the biblical text for use in the liturgy remains with the conference of bishops (#35).

CONCLUSION

In the mere four decades since Vatican II restored vernacular to the liturgy, much has been done to shape vernacular translations truly appropriate to the liturgy. *Comme le prévoit*, which has guided that work, shows a remarkably balanced concern for language faithful at once to the message received, the assembled people of God, and the uniqueness of their mother tongue.

Adopting the language of a people inevitably introduces contemporary cultural issues, such as that of inclusivity. Translators working with the texts, along with the pastors of the local churches, are the first to face such issues. Rome is reportedly working on a second instruction on translation; its actions regarding the *Catechism of the Catholic Church* and the biblical translations used in lectionaries in North America would suggest that the new instruction will stress a more literal approach and what some call a more "sacral" language. Nonetheless, Rome now acknowledges that formerly generic words may no longer be such, and that is an important first step. The experience of the local church, if attended to, will be an important factor in furthering the development of the language of our prayer.

In the meantime, the CCCB and NCCB statements offer advice worth heeding. As CP foresaw (see #43), we live in a time of schooling when we together learn to care for inclusivity in the prayers, homilies and all the words we speak and write for and about the liturgy. In this process, we are learning to shape our language to be beautiful, dignified and inclusive without calling attention to itself. Above all, we are learning to give voice to the prayer of the church in our mother tongue.

OUTLINE

INSTRUCTION *COMME LE PRÉVOIT*

ON THE TRANSLATION OF LITURGICAL TEXTS FOR CELEBRATIONS WITH A CONGREGATION

1.   The Constitution on the Sacred Liturgy foresees that many Latin texts of the Roman liturgy must be translated into different languages (art. 36). Although many of them have already been translated, the work of translation is not drawing to a close. New texts have been edited or prepared for the renewal of the liturgy. Above all, after sufficient experiment and passage of time, all translations will need review.

2.   In accordance with art. 36 of the Constitution *Sacrosanctum Concilium* and no. 40 of the Instruction of the Congregation of Rites Inter *Oecumenici*, the work of translation of liturgical texts is thus laid down: It is the duty of the episcopal conferences to decide which texts are to be translated, to prepare or review the translations, to approve them, and "after approval, that is, confirmation, by the Holy See" to promulgate them.

When a common language is spoken in several different countries, international commissions should be appointed by the conferences of bishops who speak the same language to make one text for all (letter of Cardinal Lercaro to the presidents of episcopal conferences, dated 16 October 1964).

3.   Although these translations are the responsibility of the competent territorial authority of each country, it seems desirable to observe common principles of procedure, especially for texts of major importance, in order to make confirmation by the Apostolic See easier and to achieve greater unity of practice.

4.   The Consilium has therefore thought fit in this declaration to lay down, in common and nontechnical terms, some of the more important theoretical and practical principles for the guidance of all who are called upon to prepare, to approve, or to confirm liturgical translations.

I. GENERAL PRINCIPLES

5.   A liturgical text, inasmuch as it is a ritual sign, is a medium of spoken communication. It is, first of all, a sign perceived by the senses and used by men to communicate with each other. But to believers who celebrate the sacred rites a word is itself a "mystery." By spoken words Christ himself speaks to his people and the people, through the Spirit in the Church, answer their Lord.

6.   The purpose of liturgical translations is to proclaim the message of salvation to believers and to express the prayer of the Church to the Lord: "Liturgical translations have become . . . the voice of the Church" (address of Paul VI to participants in the congress on translations of liturgical texts, 10 November 1965). To achieve this end, it is not sufficient that a liturgical translation merely reproduce the expressions and ideas of the original text. Rather it must faithfully communicate to a given people, and in their own language, that which the Church by means of this given text originally intended to communicate to another people in another time. A faithful translation, therefore, cannot be judged on the basis of individual words: the total context of this specific act of communication must be kept in mind, as well as the literary form proper to the respective language.

7.   Thus, in the case of liturgical communication, it is necessary to take into account not only the message to be conveyed, but also the speaker, the audience, and the style. Translations, therefore, must be faithful to the art of communication in all its various aspects, but especially in regard to the message itself, in regard to the audience for which it is intended, and in regard to the manner of expression.

8.   Even if in spoken communication the message cannot be separated from the manner of speaking, the translator should give first consideration to the meaning of the communication.

9.   To discover the true meaning of a text, the translator must follow the scientific methods of textual study as used by experts. This part of the translator's task is obvious. A few points may be added with reference to liturgical texts:

10.   a. If need be, a critical text of the passage must first be established so that the translation can be done from the original or at least from the best available text.

11.   b. Latin terms must be considered in the light of their uses—historical or cultural, Christian or liturgical. For example, the early Christian use of *devotio* differs from its use in classical or more modern times. The Latin *oratio* means in English not an oration (one of its senses in classical Latin) but a *prayer*—and in this English word bears different meanings, such as prayer of praise or prayer in general or prayer of petition. *Pius* and *pietas* are very inadequately rendered in English as *pious* and *piety*. In one case the Latin *salus* may mean *salvation* in the theological sense; elsewhere it may mean *safety, health* (physical health or total health), or *well-being*. *Sarx-caro* is inadequately rendered in English as *flesh*. *Doulos-servus* and *famula* are inadequately rendered in English by *slave, servant, handmaid*. The force of an image or metaphor must also be considered, whether it is rare or common, living or worn out.

12.   c. The translator must always keep in mind that the "unit of meaning" is not the individual word but the whole passage. The translator must there be careful that the translation is not so analytical that it exaggerates the importance of particular phrases while it obscures or weakens the meaning of the whole. Thus, in Latin, the piling up of *ratam, rationabilem, acceptabilem* may increase the sense of invocation. In other tongues, a succession of adjectives may actually

weaken the force of the prayer. The same is true of *beatissima Virgo* or *beata et glorisa* or the routine addition of *sanctus* or *beatus* to a saint's name, or the too casual use of superlatives. Understatement in English is sometimes the more effective means of emphasis.

13.   d. To keep the correct signification, words and expressions must be used in their proper historical, social, and ritual meanings. Thus, in prayers for Lent, *ieiunium* now has the sense of lenten observance, both liturgical and ascetic; the meaning is not confined to abstinence from food. *Tapeinos-humilis* originally had "class" overtones not present in the English *humble* or even *lowly*. Many of the phrases of approach to the Almighty were originally adapted from forms of address to the sovereign in the courts of Byzantium and Rome. It is necessary to study how far an attempt should be made to offer equivalents in modern English for such words as *quaesumus, dignare, clementissime, maiestas,* and the like.

14.   The accuracy and value of a translation can only be assessed in terms of the purpose of the communication. To serve the particular congregations who will use it, the following points should be observed in translating.

15.   a. The language chosen should be that in "common" usage, that is, suited to the greater number of the faithful who speak it in everyday use, even "children and persons of small education" (Paul VI in the allocution cited). However, the language should not be "common" in the bad sense, but "worthy of expressing the highest realities" *(ibid.)*. Moreover, the correct biblical or Christian meaning of certain words and ideas will always need explanation and instruction. Nevertheless no special literary training should be required of the people; liturgical texts should normally be intelligible to all, even to the less educated. For example, *temptation* as a translation of *tentatio* in the Lord's Prayer is inaccurate and can only be misleading to people who are not biblical scholars. Similarly, *scandal* in the ordinary English sense of gossip is a misleading translation of the scriptural *scandalum*. Besides, liturgical texts must sometimes possess a truly poetic quality, but this does not imply the use of specifically "poetic diction."

16.   b. Certain other principles should be observed so that a translation will be understood by the hearers in the same sense as the revealed truths expressed in the liturgy.

17.   1. When words are taken from the so-called sacral vocabulary now in use, the translator should consider whether the everyday common meaning of these words and phrases bears or can bear a Christian meaning. These phrases may carry a pre-Christian, quasi-Christian, Christian, or even anti-Christian meaning. The translator should also consider whether such words can convey the exact Christian liturgical action and manifestation of faith. Thus in the Greek Bible, the word *hieros (sacer)* was often avoided because of its connection was the pagan cults and instead the rarer word *hagios (sanctus)* was substituted. Another example. The proper meaning of the biblical *hesed-eleos-misericordia,* is not accurately expressed in English by *mercy* or *pity*. Again, the word *mereri* in classical Latin often signifies *to be worthy of something*, but in the language

of the liturgy it carries a meaning very different from the ancient meaning: "I do something because of which I am worthy of a prize or a reward." In English the word *to deserve* when used by itself retains the stricter sense. A translation would lead to error if it did not consider this fact, for example, in translating *Quia quem meruisti portare* in the hymn *Regina caeli* as *Because you deserved to bear . . . .*

18.   2. It often happens that there is no word in common use that exactly corresponds to the biblical or liturgical sense of the term to be translated, as in the use of the biblical *iustitia*. The nearest suitable word must then be chosen which, through habitual use in various catechetical texts and in prayer, lends itself to take on the biblical and Christian sense intended by the liturgy. Such has been the evolution of the Greek word *doxa* and the Latin *gloria* when used to translate the Hebrew *kabod*. The expression *hominibus bonae voluntatis* literally translated as *to men of good will* (or *good will to men* in order to stress divine favor) will be misleading; no single English word or phrase will completely reflect the original Latin or the Greek which the Latin translates. Similarly in English there is no exact equivalent for *mysterium*. In English, *mystery* means something which cannot be readily explained or else a type of drama or fiction. Nor can the word *venerabilis* (as in *sanctas et venerabiles manus*) be translated as *venerable*, which nowadays means *elderly*.

19.   3. In many modern languages a biblical or liturgical language must be created by use. This will be achieved rather by infusing a Christian meaning into common words than by importing uncommon or technical terms.

20.   c. The prayer of the Church is always the prayer of some actual community, assembled here and now. It is not sufficient that a formula handed down from some other time or region be translated verbatim, even if accurately, for liturgical use. The formula translated must become the genuine prayer of the congregation and in it each of its members should be able to find and express himself or herself.

21.   A translation of the liturgy therefore often requires cautious adaptation. But cases differ:

22.   a. Sometimes a text can be translated word for word and keep the same meaning as the original, for example, *pleni sunt caeli et terra gloria tua*.

23.   b. Sometimes the metaphors must be changed to keep the true sense, as in *locum refrigerii* in northern regions.

24.   c. Sometimes the meaning of a text can no longer be understood, either because it is contrary to modern Christian ideas (as in *terrena despicere* or *ut inimicos sanctae Ecclesiae humiliare digneris*) or because it has less relevance today (as in some phrases intended to combat Arianism) or because it no longer expresses the true original meaning "as in certain obsolete forms of lenten penance." In these cases, so long as the teaching of the Gospel remains intact, not only must inappropriate expressions be avoided, but others found which

express a corresponding meaning in modern words. The greatest care must be taken that all translations are not only beautiful and suited to the contemporary mind, but express true doctrine and authentic Christian spirituality.

25.   A particular form of expression and speech is required for spoken communication. In rendering any liturgical text, the translator must keep in mind the major importance of the spoken or rhetorical style or what might, by extension of the term, be called the literary genre. On this matter several things should be noted:

26.   1. The literary genre of every liturgical text depends first of all on the nature of the ritual act signified in the words—acclamation or supplication, proclamation or praying, reading or singing. Each action requires its proper form of expression. Moreover a prayer differs as it is to be spoken by one person alone or by many in unison; whether it is in prose or in verse; spoken or sung. All these considerations affect not only the manner of delivery, but also the choice of words.

27.   2. A liturgical text is a "linguistic fact" designed for celebration. When it is in written form (as is usually the case), it offers a stylistic problem for translators. Each text must therefore be examined to discover the significant elements proper to the genre, for example, in Roman prayers the formal structure, cursus, dignity, brevity, etc.

28.   Among the separate elements are those which are essential and others which are secondary and subsidiary. The essential elements, so far as is possible, should be preserved in translation, sometimes intact, sometimes in equivalent terms. The general structure of the Roman prayers can be retained unchanged: the divine title, the motive of the petition, the petition itself, the conclusion. Other cannot be retained: the oratorical cursus, rhetorical-prose cadence.

29.   It is to be noted that if any particular kind of quality is regarded as essential to a literary genre (for example, intelligibility of prayers when said aloud), this may take precedence over another quality less significant for communication (for example, verbal fidelity).

II. SOME PARTICULAR CONSIDERATIONS

30.   Among liturgical texts, sacred Scripture has always held a special place because the Church recognizes in the sacred books the written voice of God (DV, 9). The divine word has been transmitted to us under different historical forms or literary genres and the revelation communicated by the documents cannot be entirely divorced from these forms or genres. In the case of biblical translations intended for liturgical readings, the characteristics of speech or writing are proper to different modes of communication in the sacred books and should be preserved with special accuracy. This is particularly important in the translations of psalms and canticles.

31. Biblical translations in the Roman liturgy ought to conform "with the Latin liturgical text" (instruction *Inter Oecumenici*, 26 September 1964, no. 40 a). In no way should there be a paraphrasing of the biblical text, even if it is difficult to understand. Nor should words or explanatory phrases be inserted. All this is the task of catechesis and the homily.

32. In some cases it will be necessary that "suitable and accurate translations be made into the different languages from the original texts of the sacred books. And if, given the opportunity and the approval of church authority, these translations are produced in cooperation with the separated brethren as well, all Christians will be able to use them" (DV, 22). Translations approved for liturgical used should closely approximate the best versions in a particular language.

33. Some euchological and sacramental formularies like the consecratory prayers, the anaphoras, prefaces, exorcisms, and those prayers which accompany an action, such as the imposition of hands, the anointing, the signs of the cross, etc., should be translated integrally and faithfully, without variations, omissions, or insertions. These texts, whether ancient or modern, have a precise and studied theological elaboration. If the text is ancient, certain Latin terms present difficulties of interpretation because of their use and meaning, which are much different from their corresponding terms in modern language. The translation will therefore demand an astute handling and sometimes a paraphrasing, in order to render accurately the original pregnant meaning. If the text is a more recent one, the difficulty will be reduced considerably, given the use of terms and a style of language which are closer to modern concepts.

34. The prayers (opening prayer, prayer over the gifts, prayer after communion, and prayer over the people) from the ancient Roman tradition are succinct and abstract. In translation they may need to be rendered somewhat more freely while conserving the original ideas. This can be done by moderately amplifying them or, if necessary, paraphrasing expressions in order to concretize them for the celebration and the needs of today. In every case pompous and superfluous language should be avoided.

35. All texts which are intended to be said aloud follow the laws proper to their delivery and, in the case of written texts, their literary genre. This applies especially to the acclamations where the act of acclaiming by voice is an essential element. It will be insufficient to translate only the exact meaning of an idea unless the text can also be expressed by sound and rhythm.

36. Particular care is necessary for texts which are to be sung.

a. The form of singing which is proper to every liturgical action and to each of its parts should be retained (antiphon alternated with the psalm, responsory, etc. See Instruction *Musicam sacram*, 5 March 1967, nos. 6 and 9).

b. Regarding the psalms, in addition to the division into versicles as given in Latin, a division into stanzas may be particularly desirable if a text is used which is well known by the people or common to other Churches.

c. The responses (versicles, responsories) and antiphons, even though they come from Scripture, become part of the liturgy and enter into a new literary form. In translating them it is possible to give them a verbal form which, while preserving their full meaning, is more suitable for singing and harmonizes them with the liturgical season or a special feast. Examples of such adaptations which include minor adaptations of the original text are numerous in ancient antiphonaries.

d. When the content of an antiphon or psalm creates a special difficulty, the episcopal conferences may authorize the choice of another text which meets the same needs of the liturgical celebration and the particular season or feast.

e. If these same texts are likewise intended for recitation without singing, the translation should be suitable for that purpose.

37. Liturgical hymns lose their proper function unless they are rendered in an appropriate verse rhythm, suitable for singing by the people. A literal translation of such texts is therefore generally out of the question. It follows that hymns very often need a new rendering made according to the musical and choral laws of the popular poetry in each language.

III. COMMITTEES FOR TRANSLATING

38. To make the translations, committees should be formed of experts in the various disciplines, namely, liturgy, Scripture, theology, pastoral study, and especially languages and literature, and according to circumstances, music. If several committees are concerned with the different parts of liturgical texts, their work should be coordinated.

39. Before a text is promulgated, sufficient opportunity should be allowed for experiment by selected congregations in different places. An *ad interim* translation should be properly approved by the liturgical commission of the conference of bishops.

40. Close collaboration should be established between the committee of experts and the authorities who must approve the translations (such as a conference of bishops), so that:

a. the same people, for the most part, share in the work from beginning to end;

b. when the authority asks for emendations, these should be made by the experts themselves and a new text then submitted for the judgment of the authority. Otherwise, it should give the task to a new committee which is more suitable, but also composed of qualified people.

41. Those countries which have a common language should employ a "mixed commission" to prepare a single text. There are many advantages to such a procedure: in the preparation of a text the most competent experts are able to cooperate;

a unique possibility for communication is created among these people; participation of the people is made easier. In this joint venture between countries speaking the same language it is important to distinguish between the texts which are said by one person and heard by the congregation and those intended to be recited or sung by all. Uniformity is obviously more important for the latter category than for the former.

42.   In those cases where a single text is prepared for a large number of countries, the text should satisfy the "different needs and mentalities of each region" (letter of Cardinal Lercaro to the presidents of episcopal conferences, 16 October 1964). Therefore:

1. Each episcopal conference sharing the same language should examine the translation program or the first draft of a text.

2. Meanwhile, to avoid anxiety and unnecessary delay for priests and people, the coordinating secretariat should provide a provisional text which, with the consent of the proper authority (see no. 39), can be published and printed as an ad interim text in each country. It is preferable that the same provisional text be used everywhere since the result will contribute to a better final text for all the countries.

3. Each of the countries will receive the definitive text at the same time. If a particular episcopal conference requires a change or substitution for specific local needs, it should propose the change to the "mixed commission," which must first agree. This is necessary in order to have a single text which remains substantially unchanged and under the supervision of the "mixed commission."

4. Each country can publish texts which are provisional as well as texts which are officially approved by the Holy See, but ought to contribute, on a prorated basis according to the extent it publishes, to the expenses of the "mixed commission," which must pay the periti and bishops of the commission. National liturgical commissions should make prior arrangements with the secretariat regarding these publications.

5. In the publications of works from the "mixed commissions," the appropriate notice should appear on the first page: "A provisional text prepared by the 'mixed commission' . . ." or "Text approved by the 'mixed commission' . . . and confirmed by the Consilium for the Implementation of the Constitution on the Sacred Liturgy." If a change or substitution is desirable in an individual country, as indicated in no. 42, 3, a further notice is necessary, namely: "with adaptations authorized by the episcopal conference of . . . and the 'mixed commission'."

43.   Texts translated from another language are clearly not sufficient for the celebration of a fully renewed liturgy. The creation of new text will be necessary. But translation of texts transmitted through the tradition of the Church is the best school and discipline for the creation of new text so "that any new forms adopted should in some way grow organically from forms already in existence" (SC, 23).

TO SPEAK AS
A CHRISTIAN COMMUNITY
PASTORAL MESSAGE ON
INCLUSIVE LANGUAGE

BISHOPS' PASTORAL TEAM
CANADIAN CONFERENCE OF CATHOLIC BISHOPS
1989

OUTLINE

TO SPEAK AS A CHRISTIAN COMMUNITY

[1.] As Christians, we are called to witness to the fundamental equality and dignity of all people. This involves diverse actions for social justice which protect and promote human life and dignity. One relatively simple but effective action is the use of inclusive language.

INCLUSIVE LANGUAGE DEFINED

[2.] Inclusive language, in the broadest sense, means using words which affirm the equality and dignity of each person regardless of race, gender, creed, age or ability. Most people associate it, however, with language which includes women and men in contexts where the message is directed to, refers to and affects both and which avoids stereotypes when speaking about either sex. This understanding of inclusive language is the subject of these reflections.

SIGNS OF THE TIMES

[3.] Inclusive language was introduced into society by the contemporary women's movement. As a result, some people feel it may be only a cultural question. Vatican II, however, reminded us that the church exists in the world and the Christians have a responsibility to read the "signs of the times" and interpret them in light of the Gospel. One of the signs of the times identified by Vatican II and recent popes is the changing role of women in society. There is, therefore, a special duty to listen to what women are saying about the need for inclusive language. Through listening and reflecting, it becomes apparent that there are significant theological reasons for using and promoting inclusive language.

LANGUAGE EXPRESSES OUR BELIEFS

[4.] Language is an important matter for the whole church because it is through language that we express our belief of God and proclaim the good news of salvation to the world. Throughout our history, great care has been taken in choosing words to reflect our beliefs. For example, at the Council of Nicea in 325 new language was introduced to better express our understanding of Jesus. Today the use of inclusive language indicates care is being taken to ensure that words reflect our belief in the equality of men and women, our understanding of the Gospel and our affirmation of the church as a communion.

FUNDAMENTAL EQUALITY OF MEN AND WOMEN

[5.] For Christians, language which is inclusive recalls the original harmony of creation as seen in the Book of Genesis. It also gives visible expression to the good news that through the life, death and resurrection of Jesus we are reconciled with God and a new creation is initiated where we are all one in Christ. At its most profound level, inclusive language is a sign of our respect for the fundamental equality of men and women, and a means of proclaiming the Gospel message of inclusiveness.

THE CHURCH AS A COMMUNION

[6.] Concern about inclusive language is also rooted in a theological understanding of the church as a communion. This understanding of the church was a central insight of the Second Vatican Council and was reaffirmed by the extraordinary synod of 1985. When the church is described as a communion, it means that Christians are in union with God and with one another, through Jesus Christ, in the power of the Holy Spirit. In this sense, the church is a sacrament or sign of the unity to which the whole of humanity is called. "Hence, there is in Christ and in the church no inequality on the basis of race or nationality, social condition or sex" (LG, 32). This passage from Vatican II also recalls the fundamental equality and partnership of all the baptized who are united in Christ.

IMPLEMENTATION—LONG TERM

[7.] The theological reasons for using inclusive language are powerful. Yet implementation of inclusive language in the daily life of the church will take time. More work is required on the part of specialists, and there are different levels of awareness among members of the church community.

BIBLICAL AND LITURGICAL TEXTS

[8.] All translations of the Bible and all texts contained in the Sacramentary and other liturgical texts are protected by copyright. Biblical translations and liturgical texts are revised periodically, and efforts are being made to be attentive to inclusive language. It is a long process, however, because the biblical translator must communicate the message in a way that is both faithful to its original meaning and understandable today's reader. The translator must also work with other specialists such as theologians, historians and archeologists in order to produce good translations of ancient texts. The revision of liturgical texts involves a lengthy approval process culminating in confirmation by the Vatican. Other specialists, such as composers of hymns and linguists, also have a role to play in the smooth transition from exclusive to inclusive language.

EVOLUTION OF LANGUAGE

[9.] The rules of grammar also affect the use of inclusive language. There is sometimes tension between the desire to respect the rules which protect the beauty and clarity of a language and the reality of a living language which is evolving to effectively recognize the equality of men and women.

LEVELS OF AWARENESS

[10.] Another reason for slow implementation of inclusive language is the different levels of awareness among members of the church. Some believe that a word such as man is already inclusive of women and therefore reflects the theological principles which have been outlined. Others believe that over the years the meaning of man has narrowed to the point that it no longer includes women and therefore no longer expresses these theological principles. And still others may not appreciate the linkage between language and theology or the important role that language plays in reflecting our beliefs. The diversity of views sometimes makes for lively debate, but if discussion continues in a spirit of openness and respect, it will contribute to increased awareness and understanding.

IMPLEMENTATION—SHORT TERM

[11.] Action can be taken while awaiting the completion of the work of specialists. Initiatives can be taken to introduce inclusive language at home, at social gatherings and on the job. Parishes can commit themselves to using inclusive language in the prayers of the faithful, in their choice of hymns, in written material such as parish bulletins, in announcements from the pulpit, at parish gatherings, etc. They might consider forming discussion groups or inviting experts (e.g., theologians, linguists, historians, liturgists) to assist them in deepening their awareness of the need for inclusive language. All those who preach should also be attentive to inclusive language. And everyone can read more on the subject, listen more sensitively and be more responsive to women who do not see themselves included in our language. As the presidents of six national episcopal commissions, we undertake to pay special attention to inclusive language in all of our communications.

CONCLUSION

[12.] Using inclusive language is one way of emphasizing the church's responsibility to take a stand against one of the widespread forms of discrimination found in our society. As sensitivity to the inclusion of women grows, there should be a corresponding increase in awareness of the need to include all regardless of race, gender, creed, age or ability. By seeking to overcome discrimination wherever it is encountered, we live more fully as a communion, respond more fully to the Gospel and speak as a Christian community.

CRITERIA FOR THE EVALUATION
OF INCLUSIVE LANGUAGE TRANSLATIONS
OF SCRIPTURAL TEXTS
PROPOSED FOR LITURGICAL USE

NATIONAL CONFERENCE OF CATHOLIC BISHOPS
1990

OUTLINE

CRITERIA FOR THE EVALUATION OF INCLUSIVE LANGUAGE TRANSLATIONS OF SCRIPTURAL TEXTS PROPOSED FOR LITURGICAL USE

INTRODUCTION: ORIGINS AND NATURE OF THE PROBLEM

1.   Five historical developments have converged to present the Church in the United States today with an important and challenging pastoral concern. First, the introduction of the vernacular into the Church's worship has necessitated English translations of the liturgical books and of Sacred Scripture for use in the liturgy. Second, some segments of American culture have become increasingly sensitive to "exclusive language," i.e., language which seems to exclude the equality and dignity of each person regardless of race, gender, creed, age or ability.[1] Third, there has been a noticeable loss of the sense of grammatical gender in American usage of the English language. Fourth, English vocabulary itself has changed so that words which once referred to all to all human beings are increasingly taken as gender specific and, consequently, exclusive. Fifth, impromptu efforts at inclusive language, while pleasing to some, have often offended others who expect a degree of theological precision and linguistic or aesthetic refinement in the public discourse of the liturgy. Some impromptu efforts may also have unwittingly undermined essentials of Catholic doctrine.

These current issues confront a fundamental conviction of the Church, namely, that the Word of God stands at the core of our faith as a basic theological reality to which all human efforts respond and by which they are judged.

2.   The bishops of the United States wish to respond to this complex and sensitive issue of language in the English translation of the liturgical books of the Church in general and of Sacred Scripture in particular. New translations of scriptural passages used in the liturgy are being proposed periodically for their approval. Since the promulgation of the 1983 *Code of Canon Law*, these translations must be approved by a conference of bishops or by the Apostolic See.[2] The question confronts the bishops: With regard to a concern for inclusive language, how do we distinguish a legitimate translation from one that is imprecise?

3.   The recognition of this problem prompted the submission of a *varium* to the National Conference of Catholic Bishops requesting that the Bishops' Committee on the Liturgy and the Committee on Doctrine be directed jointly to

formulate guidelines that would assist the bishops in making appropriate judgments on the inclusive language translations of biblical texts for liturgical use. These two committees established a Joint Committee on Inclusive Language, which prepared this text.

4.   This document, while providing an answer to the question concerning translations of biblical texts for liturgical use, does not attempt to elaborate a complete set of criteria for inclusive language in the liturgy in general, that is, for prayers, hymns and preaching. These cognate areas will be treated only insofar as they overlap the particular issues being addressed here.

5.   This document presents practical principles for the members of the National Conference of Catholic Bishops to exercise their canonical responsibility for approving translations of Scripture proposed for liturgical use. However, just as this document does not deal with all cases of inclusive language in the liturgy, neither is it intended as a theology of translation. The teaching of *Dei Verbum* and the instructions of the Pontifical Biblical Commission prevail in matters of inspiration, inerrancy, and hermeneutics and their relationship with meaning, language, and the mind of the author. While there would be a value in producing a study summarizing these issues, it would distract from the immediate purpose of this document.

6.   This document treats the problem indicated above in four parts: General Principles; Principles for Inclusive Language Lectionary Translations; Preparation of Texts for Use in the Lectionary; Special Question, viz., naming God, the Trinity, Christ and the Church.

PART 1: GENERAL PRINCIPLES

7.   There are two general principles for judging translations for liturgical use: the principle of fidelity to the Word of God and the principle of respect for the nature of the liturgical assembly. Individual questions, then, must be judged in light of the textual, grammatical, literary, artistic and dogmatic requirements of the particular scriptural passage, and in light of the needs of the liturgical assembly. In cases of conflict or ambiguity, the principle of fidelity to the Word of God retains its primacy.

I. FIDELITY TO THE WORD OF GOD

The following considerations derive from the principle of fidelity to the Word of God.

8.   The People of God have the right to hear the Word of God integrally proclaimed[3] in fidelity to the meaning of the inspired authors of the sacred text.

9.   Biblical translations must always be faithful to the original language and internal truth of the inspired text. It is expected, therefore, that every concept in the original text will be translated within its context.

10. All biblical translations must respect doctrinal principles of revelation, inspiration, and biblical interpretation (hermeneutics) as well as the formal rhetoric intended by the author (e.g., Hebrews 2:5–18). They must be faithful to Catholic teaching regarding God and divine activity in the world and in human history as it unfolds. "[D]ue attention must be paid both to the customary and characteristic patterns of perception, speech, and narrative which prevailed at the age of the sacred writer and to the conventions which the people of his time followed. . . ."[4]

II. THE NATURE OF THE LITURGICAL ASSEMBLY

The following considerations derive from the nature of the liturgical assembly.

11. Each and every Christian is called to and indeed has a right to full and active participation in worship. This was stated succinctly by the Second Vatican Council: "The Church earnestly desires that all the faithful be led to that full, conscious, and active participation in liturgical celebrations called for by the very nature of the liturgy. Such participation by the Christian people as 'a chosen race, a royal priesthood, a holy nation, God's own people' (1 Peter 2:9, see 2:4–5) is their right and duty by reason of their baptism."[5] An integral part of liturgical participation is hearing the word of Christ, ". . . who speaks when the holy Scriptures are read in the church."[6] Full and active participation in the liturgy demands that the liturgical assembly recognize and accept the transcendent power of God's word.

12. According to the Church's tradition, biblical texts have many liturgical uses. Because their immediate purposes are somewhat different, texts translated for public proclamation in the liturgy may differ in some respects (cf. Part 2) from those translations which are meant solely for academic study, private reading or *lectio divina*.

13. The language of biblical texts for liturgical use should be suitably and faithfully adapted for proclamation and should facilitate the full, conscious and active participation of all members of the Church, women and men, in worship.

PART 2: PRINCIPLES FOR INCLUSIVE LANGUAGE LECTIONARY TRANSLATIONS

14. The Word of God proclaimed to all nations is by nature inclusive, that is, addressed to all peoples, men and women. Consequently, every effort should be made to render the language of biblical translations as inclusively as a faithful translation of the text permits, especially when this concerns the People of God, Israel and the Christian community.

15. When a biblical translation is meant for liturgical proclamation, it must also take into account those principles that apply to the public communication of the biblical meaning. Inclusive language is one of those principles, since the text is proclaimed in the Christian assembly to women and men who possess

equal baptismal dignity and reflects the universal scope of the Church's call to evangelize.

16.   The books of the Bible are the product of particular cultures, with their limitations as well as their strengths. Consequently not everything in Scripture will be in harmony with contemporary cultural concerns. The fundamental mystery of incarnational revelation requires the retention of those characteristics that reflect the cultural context within which the Word was first received.

17.   Language which addresses and refers to the worshiping community ought not use words or phrases which deny the common dignity of all the baptized.

18.   Words such as *men, sons, brothers, brethren, forefathers, fraternity,* and *brotherhood,* which were once understood as inclusive generic terms, today are often understood as referring only to males. In addition, although certain uses of *he, his* and *him* once were generic and included both women and men, in contemporary American usage these terms are often perceived to refer only to males. Their use has become ambiguous and is increasingly seen to exclude women. Therefore, these terms should not be used when the reference is meant to be generic, observing the requirements of No.7 and No. 10.

19.   Words such as *adam, anthropos,* and *homo* have often been translated in many English biblical and liturgical texts by the collective terms *man* and *family of man.* Since in the original languages these words actually denote human beings rather than only males, English terms which are not gender specific, such as *person, people, human family* and *humans,* should be used in translating these words.

20.   In narratives and parables the sex of individual persons should be retained. Sometimes, in the synoptic tradition, the gospel writers select examples or metaphors from a specific gender. Persons of the other sex should not be added merely in a desire for balance. The original references of the narrative or images of the parable should be retained.

PART 3: THE PREPARATION OF TEXTS
FOR USE IN THE LECTIONARY

21.   The liturgical adaptation of readings for use in the lectionary should be made in light of the norms of the Introduction to the *Ordo Lectionum Missae* (1981). Incipits should present the context of the various pericopes. At times, transitions may need to be added when verses have been omitted from pericopes. Nouns may replace pronouns or be added to participial constructions for clarity in proclamation and aural comprehension. Translation should not expand upon the text, but the Church recognizes that in certain circumstances a particular text may be expanded to reflect adequately the intended meaning of the pericope.[7] In all cases, these adaptations must remain faithful to the intent of the original text.[8]

22.   Inclusive language adaptations of lectionary texts must be made in light of exegetical and linguistic attention to the individual text within its proper context. Blanket substitutions are inappropriate.

23.   Many biblical passages are inconsistent in grammatical person, that is, alternating between second person singular or plural *(you)* and third person singular *(he)*. In order to give such passages a more intelligible consistency, some biblical readings may be translated so as to use either the second person plural *(you)* throughout or the third person plural *(they)* throughout. Changes from the third person singular to the third person plural are allowed in individual cases where the sense of the original text is universal. It should be noted that, at times, either the sense or the poetic structure of a passage may require that the alternation be preserved in the translation.

24.   Psalms and canticles have habitually been appropriated by the Church for use in the liturgy, not as readings for proclamation, but as the responsive prayer of the liturgical assembly. Accordingly, adaptations have justifiably been made, principally by the omission of verses which were judged to be inappropriate in a given culture or liturgical context. Thus, the liturgical books allow the adaptation of psalm texts to encourage the full participation of the liturgical assembly.

PART 4: SPECIAL QUESTIONS

25.   Several specific issues must be addressed in regard to the naming of God, the persons of the Trinity, and the Church, since changes in language can have important doctrinal and theological implications.

I. NAMING GOD IN BIBLICAL TRANSLATIONS

26.   Great care should be taken in translations of the names of God and in the use of pronouns referring to God. While it would be inappropriate to attribute gender to God as such, the revealed Word of God consistently uses a masculine reference for God. It may sometimes be useful, however, to repeat the name of God as used earlier in the text rather than to use the masculine pronoun in every case. But care must be taken that the repetition not become tiresome.

27.   The classic translation of the Tetragrammaton (YHWH) as LORD and the translation of *Kyrios* as *Lord* should be used in lectionaries.

28.   Feminine imagery in the original language of the biblical texts should not be obscured or replaced by the use of masculine imagery in English translations, e.g., Wisdom literature.

II. NAMING CHRIST IN BIBLICAL TRANSLATIONS

29.   Christ is the center and focus of all Scripture.[9] The New Testament has interpreted certain texts of the Old Testament in an explicitly Christological fashion. Special care should be observed in the translation of these texts so that

the Christological meaning is not lost. Some examples include the Servant Songs of Isaiah 42 and 53, Psalms 2 and 110, and the Son of Man passage in Daniel 7.

III. NAMING THE TRINITY IN BIBLICAL TRANSLATIONS

30. In fidelity to the inspired Word of God, the traditional biblical usage for naming the persons of the Trinity as *Father, Son,* and *Holy Spirit* is to be retained. Similarly, in keeping with New Testament usage and the Church's tradition, the feminine pronoun is not to be used to refer to the person of the Holy Spirit.

IV. NAMING THE CHURCH IN BIBLICAL TRANSLATIONS

31. Normally, the neuter third person singular or the third person plural pronoun is used when referring to the People of God, Israel, the Church, the Body of Christ, etc., unless their antecedents clearly are a masculine or feminine metaphor, for instance, the reference to the church as the *Bride of Christ* or *Mother* (cf. Revelation 12).

CONCLUSION

32. These criteria for judging the appropriateness of inclusive language translations of Sacred Scripture are presented while acknowledging that the English language is continually changing. Contemporary translations must reflect developments in American English grammar, syntax, usage, vocabulary, and style. The perceived need for a more inclusive language is part of this development. Such language must not distract hearers from prayer and God's revelation. It must manifest a sense of linguistic refinement. It should not draw attention to itself.

33. While English translations of the Bible have influenced the liturgical and devotional language of Christians, such translations have also shaped and formed the English language itself. This should be true today as it was in the age of the King James and Douay-Rheims translations. Thus, the Church expects for its translations not only accuracy but facility and beauty of expression.

34. Principles of translation when applied to lectionary readings and psalm texts differ in certain respects from those applied to translations of the Bible destined for study or reading (see Nos. 22–25 above). Thus, when submitting a new or revised translation of the Bible, and edition of the lectionary, or a liturgical psalter for approval by the National Conference of Catholic Bishops, editors must supply a complete statement of the principles used in the preparation of the submitted text.

35. The authority to adapt the biblical text for use in the lectionary remains with the conference of bishops. These *Criteria for the Evaluation of Inclusive Language Translations of Scriptural Texts Proposed for Liturgical Use* have been developed to assist the members of the National Conference of Catholic Bishops to exercise their responsibility so that all the People of God may be assisted in hearing God's Word and keeping it.

NOTES

1. Cf. SCC, p. 2.

2. CIC, c. 825 §1.

3. CIC, c. 213.

4. DV, 12.

5. SC, 14. English translation is from DOL, 1, 14.

6. SC, 7.

7. Secretariat for Christian Unity (Commission for Religious Relations With Judaism), *Guidelines and Suggestions for the Application of No. 14 of the Conciliar Declaration "Nostra Aetate,"* Oct. 28, 1975 (AAS 67 [1975] 73–79).

8. CP, 30–32.

9. Cf. DV, 16.

GENERAL INSTRUCTION
OF THE
LITURGY OF THE HOURS

CONGREGATION FOR DIVINE WORSHIP
1971

OVERVIEW OF *GENERAL INSTRUCTION OF THE LITURGY OF THE HOURS*

Joyce Ann Zimmerman, CPPS

Some 25 years after the promulgation of the revised Liturgy of the Hours, ask the average parishioner what it is and whether he or she prays it, and there tends to be a blank stare in response. The *General Instruction of the Liturgy of the Hours* (GILOH) is still little known, even by the "professionals." Paradoxically enough, this document clearly embodies the tensions that have kept the Liturgy of the Hours from assuming its role as the usual daily prayer of the whole church, while at the same time suggesting (even recommending) adaptations that would result in a greater popular celebration of the Hours.

The promulgation of the *editio typica* of each of the revised rites was accompanied by a General Instruction that presents the liturgical, pastoral and doctrinal theology of the rite, along with its overall purpose, structure, ways of celebration and fruits. GILOH is unique among them. From its promulgation to its implementation, everything about this document alerts us to something new and unusual. Unlike any other General Instruction, this one did not accompany the revised Liturgy of the Hours, but preceded the rite by over two months. (GILOH was released on February 2, 1971, but the Latin *editio typica* of the revised Liturgy of the Hours was not available until April 11; the English translation was not available until 1976.) This unusual occurrence had a two-fold explanation: 1) the rite was not ready yet; but, 2) Pope Paul VI had authorized the release of GILOH by itself, in order that those who would use the revised Liturgy of the Hours would have the opportunity to study the rite and prepare themselves for its implementation. This action ought to have alerted us to the fact that the revisions were extensive—requiring some preparation and getting used to—and that there were some problems in the process of revision. Both facts proved to be true when the rite became available. The revised Liturgy of the Hours is, indeed, something new and quite different from the breviary of Pius V. It also incorporates many compromises, which themselves create a tension within the rite.

SUMMARY

GILOH has five chapters and a total of 284 articles. The first three chapters are the longest, taking up almost three-fourths of the document, and deal with the nature and structure of the Hours. The last two chapters address how the Hours are celebrated during the liturgical year and with communities.

Chapter one, "Importance of the Liturgy of the Hours or Divine Office in the Life of the Church," sets the tone for the whole document and for the prayer itself. Because it is more a presentation of theology than a guide to specific issues of implementation, there may be a tendency to skip over this chapter. In fact, the first chapter deserves the most attention because a rich theology of the Hours is contained therein, one that deserves ongoing meditative study. This chapter opens up the new perspective that makes the revised rite of the Liturgy of the Hours so potentially exciting for the whole church, not just for the clergy, monastics and some religious. It also sets up some of the tensions that are addressed below.

The very first words of GILOH insist categorically that the Liturgy of the Hours is the "[p]ublic and common prayer by the people of God" and one of "the primary duties of the Church" (GILOH, 1). This startling statement goes far beyond the Constitution on the Sacred Liturgy's limited attention to the Hours being the prayer of the *whole* church (see #100) and immediately raises our expectations that something is unfolding that is quite different from the earlier tradition of the Hours (in which the number of those who prayed it was extremely limited). It is the prayer of the church, the Body of Christ, because it is the prayer of Christ, which the church continues in the Holy Spirit (GILOH, 3–8). The shift from perceiving the Hours as the prayer of part of the Body to the Hours as the prayer of the whole Body is perhaps the most significant innovation of the whole document. Related to this question of who celebrates the Hours are two more issues: 1) this prayer is essentially a communal activity (#9, 20–27); and 2) the clergy have a mandate to pray it (#28–32). We will see below how the issue of who prays the Hours is the source of one of the major tensions within the document.

Two articles address the essential elements of the structure of the Liturgy of the Hours. GILOH asserts, on the one hand, that it is largely a prayer of praise and supplication (#2). On the other hand, it outlines its main structure as hymnody, psalmody, scripture reading and prayers (#33). The scripture reading fits into the stated purpose of praise and supplication only by a stretch of the basic purpose of the proclamation of scripture at liturgy. We will see below how the relative importance of structural elements that affect the very purpose of the rite is a second major tension within the document.

Beyond the "who" and "what" of the prayer, chapter one briefly mentions a number of other points that open up a rich theology of the prayer: the Hours consecrate time (#10–11), are an extension of and preparation for the celebration of the eucharist (#12), are an exercise of the priesthood of Christ (#13), are a means of sanctification (#14), unite our praise with the heavenly praise (#15–16), and express petition and intercession for all God's people. Thus, the Liturgy of the Hours is related to pastoral action (#17–18).

Chapter two, "Sanctification of the Day: The Different Liturgical Hours," introduces some of the "how-to" of the Hours, but some gems of theology punctuate its articles as well. To begin, three articles (#34–36) explain the use of the invitatory at the first prayer of the day; it "invites the faithful each day to sing God's praise and to listen to his voice and draws them to hope . . ." Morning and Evening Prayer are the two "hinge prayers," as the Constitution on the Sacred Liturgy told us (#89). Morning Prayer recalls the resurrection (#38) and Evening Prayer gives thanks, recalls redemption and reminds us of the parousia (#39). In the revised rite, Morning Prayer and Evening Prayer have a similar structure: opening versicle, hymn, psalmody (that is, two psalms and an Old Testament canticle in the morning and a New Testament canticle in the evening), scripture (a brief homily may be preached at communal celebrations, a responsorial is provided, and there is provision for silence), gospel canticles (Canticle of Zechariah in the morning and Canticle of Mary in the evening), intercessions, Lord's Prayer, concluding prayer, and blessing and dismissal (#37–54). Unfortunately, GILOH makes no provision for using a *lucernarium* (light service) at the beginning of evening prayer. This would have been a welcome addition, especially since several articles encourage communal celebration.

Since Morning and Evening Prayer are the two "hinge" prayers, and the two Hours that the average lay person would tend to pray, it is unfortunate that their theology was not plumbed a bit more (for example, bringing out the point that these two Hours frame our day with the paschal mystery). It is also unfortunate that greater encouragement for pastoral implementation was not given. However, at the time of the revision of the rite and the writing of GILOH, any widespread parochial use of the Liturgy of the Hours was simply not taking place. As such, it is amazing in itself that as much spark is given for something so startlingly new and unusual.

The office of readings (#55–69), vigils (#70–73), daytime hours (#74–83), and Night Prayer (#84–92) are discussed in terms of their structure and options. A final section of chapter two outlines the methods for combining one of the Hours with the eucharist or with each other (#93–99); this may be done for serious pastoral reasons, but this practice is not greatly encouraged, since there is a chance that combining liturgies might compromise the unique nature of each.

Chapter three, "Different Elements in the Liturgy of the Hours," treats more fully the specific structural elements that were only outlined in chapter two. The psalms and the scripture reading receive the most attention, which once again points to an intrinsic tension with respect to purpose of the Hours.

The first part of the discussion of the psalms includes some very helpful pastoral comments on their use in the Hours. The psalms are poems of praise (#103) with an inherent musical quality that suggests they are preferably sung; even when recited they can retain their musical quality. GILOH makes another important point by reminding us that praying the Hours is praying with the whole church (#108); consequently, our own personal feelings and moods do not have to match up with the psalm we may be praying. It also considers the christological sense of the psalms (#109), taken up in the next major section of the chapter.

Consistent with the Fathers of the church, who read the psalms in the light of Christ and his messianic mission, the Latin tradition has included three elements in the Liturgy of the Hours that aid a christological interpretation: captions (or titles), psalm-prayers and antiphons (#110–120). It might be noted that recent scholarship, although acknowledging the long tradition of christological interpretation of the psalms, has underscored their value as prayers coming to us from the Hebrew Scriptures, with value in their own right. This opens up for us a wider dimension to praying the Hours and perhaps encourages us to learn more about this essential element of our daily prayer. Ways of singing the psalms are mentioned (#121–125) and an explanation of how the psalms are distributed in the Hours is given (#126–135).

What the explanation of the distribution of the psalms in the Hours does *not* say is perhaps more revealing than what it does. Almost the entire psalter is included in the revised rite; only three psalms were omitted entirely (Psalms 58, 83 and 109) because of their offensive content (the curses); some verses of other psalms were omitted for the same reason. In principle, this fits with the monastic tradition of praying the entire psalter over a given period of time (the revised rite distributes the psalms over a four-week cycle; see #126) and is one of two elements that heavily colors this prayer as essentially monastic (the other element being the cycle of readings). Nonetheless, these few omissions—limited though they are—do at least minimally challenge the monastic use of the psalter and open the door for a more parochial approach that uses fewer, well-chosen psalms, which might encourage the celebration of at least Morning and Evening Prayer in parishes and homes.

A brief section (only four articles, #136–139) discusses the Old and New Testament canticles, then several major sections address the use of sacred scripture (#140–172). Two cycles of scripture readings are provided: A one-year cycle is incorporated into the Liturgy of the Hours; a two-year cycle is offered in a supplement for optional use. The inclusion of so much scripture is a second element that heavily colors the rite as essentially monastic. The inclusion of scripture also contests the purpose of the prayer as praise and petition, since the scripture reading is intended as a meditative element, especially in the Office of Readings. Interestingly enough, GILOH opens its discussion of scripture readings from an arresting perspective, in which the readings are seen as a *liturgical* requirement: "The reading of sacred scripture, which, following an ancient tradition, takes place publicly in the liturgy, is to have special importance for all Christians, not only in the celebration of the eucharist but also in the divine office" (#140). GILOH takes great pains to provide a variety of possibilities for readings (#141–142 and other articles throughout this section); this is a pastorally sensitive move to recognize the different needs of different praying groups.

But this has its down side. It is true that the post-conciliar revisions restored a liturgy of the word to all of the church's rites so that God's word can inform their celebration. But this raises two troublesome points with respect to the Liturgy of the Hours. First, what is the status, then, of the psalms as God's word? And second, what does such an emphasis on the readings do to the basic thrust of the Hours as praise and petition (a question raised above)?

Three smaller sections round off chapter three: hymns and nonbiblical songs (#173–178); the intercessions, Lord's Prayer and concluding prayer (#179–200); and sacred silence (#201–203).

Chapter four, "Various Celebrations throughout the Year," deals with the way the Hours are prayed during the different liturgical seasons and for the varying degrees of festivities on certain days (#204–252). For the average reader of this document, this section has a fair amount of technical material, and any questions on this particular material can be answered more simply by consulting an ordo (a small booklet that correlates prayer texts with calendar dates for the celebration of liturgy). Nonetheless, consulting this section of GILOH teaches us the hierarchy of importance of various celebrations (Sunday standing first) and advises us of the many options for celebration that are open to us.

Chapter 5, "Rites for Celebration in Common," underscores the communal nature of liturgy as the prayer of the whole Body of Christ. Singing is highly encouraged (#267–284). One article in particular stands out in this section. Article 273 explains the principle of "progressive solemnity"; that is, the principle that not all liturgical celebrations have the same degree of festivity, so that elements of celebration necessarily vary from liturgy to liturgy. For example, some liturgies will have more singing, others less.

Our overview of GILOH has already uncovered a number of internal tensions; these are embedded in the revised rite as well.

The first tension arises in connection with the issue of *who* really is to celebrate the Hours. For a great part of its history, this daily prayer of the church was limited to clerics and monks. Clearly, GILOH underscores the Liturgy of the Hours as the prayer of the whole church. It does so not only by a lucid statement in its first article, but continually throughout. The most forceful statement comes almost at the end of the document: ". . . nor is the church's praise to be considered either by origin or by nature the exclusive possession of clerics and monks but the property of the whole Christian community" (#270).

This being said, the revised rite nonetheless obstructs this understanding in several ways. For example, the clergy are mandated to pray the Liturgy of the Hours (#28–32), but there is no equally strong mandate for all the members of the Body of Christ to pray it as an essential part of their baptismal privilege and responsibility. Various structural elements also militate against widespread popular implementation of the Hours: namely, its magnitude, complexity and especially those elements that come from a monastic tradition, such as the inclusion of scripture readings and (almost) the entire psalter. Elements that by their structure belong to a choral form (for example, psalm antiphons so the psalms can be sung responsorially) are also mandated for private recitation. In addition, the exclusion of some popular elements (for example, a *lucernarium* at Evening Prayer, the use of processions and incense, or the use of a variety of ministers) also limits the Hours as the prayer of a parish community. As noted below, GILOH provides options that give some latitude for adapting the rite for parochial use, but there are problems with adaptation, too.

A second tension involves the question of *why* we have the Liturgy of the Hours to begin with. GILOH plainly states the purpose of praying the Hours: "The primary aim must be to inspire hearts with a desire for genuine prayer and to show that the celebration of God's praise is a thing of joy (see Psalm 147)" (#279). This fits nicely with a structure that primarily underscores the intent of the prayer as praise (#15–16) and petition (#17–18): "They should offer praise and petition" (#19). Yet, GILOH gives a four-fold structure for the Hours—hymn, psalmody, reading, prayers (#33)—that tends to give equal weight to unequal elements, thereby compromising the character of the prayer itself. Further, so much emphasis on the scripture reading moves us to think of the purpose of the Hours in terms of our becoming "more fervent and devout" (#140) and *listening* to God's self-revelation to us, rather than our *offering* praise and thanksgiving to God. As has been the tradition, scripture readings—especially as *lectio continua*—is part of the monastic tradition that nourishes monastic contemplation. The Hours as a prayer of praise and petition marks a more parochial tradition. This tension remains unresolved in GILOH, as well as in the revised rite itself.

OPTIONS AND ADAPTATIONS

Perhaps no other of our revised rites has an accompanying General Instruction that permits so many options and adaptations. Of the 284 articles in the document, no fewer than 60 of them *explicitly* permit options and adaptations. A number of other articles *imply* adaptations that would be permissible. These accommodations are intended to promote the *single* revised rite in a number of circumstances: prayed alone or in community; prayed by monastics or by priests, apostolic religious or laity. In fact, "it is possible for the public praise of the church . . . to be adapted in a variety of ways to different circumstances" (#273). The crafters of the revised rite and of GILOH understood clearly the challenge of what they were promulgating, and even cautioned that the "main consideration is to ensure that the celebration is not too inflexible or elaborate nor concerned merely with formal observance of rules, but that it matches the reality of what is celebrated" (#279).

After careful study of GILOH and consideration of all the possible options and adaptations, the revised Liturgy of the Hours can be a fruitful daily prayer for the whole Body of Christ. At least the two hinge hours—Morning and Evening Prayer—ought to be prayed by all the baptized. When this becomes a regular part of Christian practice, the assertion of GILOH that Liturgy of the Hours is the prayer of all the baptized will be realized. However, the number of options and adaptations suggested by the document leads us to conclude that the rite is probably not very helpful for most who would pick it up in its present form and try to develop a regular pattern of praying. Adaptation is required. Indeed, the *editio typica* requires at least some minimum choices to be made before praying it at all. This raises at least two critical questions: 1) What is "minimally" required for this prayer to be *liturgy?* 2) Who is competent to make the appropriate choices for adapting this prayer to various circumstances?

Judging from the four-fold structure of the Hours, we might initially answer the first question by saying that what is minimally required is hymn, psalmody, reading and prayers. Judging from its character as a prayer of praise and petition, we might answer this question by saying that what is minimally required is psalmody and prayers. The point here is not to *minimalize* the prayer; the point is to show that what at first appears to be an incredibly complex and perhaps burdensome prayer can rather easily—by competent, informed choices—be made "prayable." This leads to the second question.

In some circumstances—for example, a parish celebration—someone with some reasonable degree of knowledge and competency regarding the liturgy would be the one to adapt the rite. Such practical issues as the skill levels of the parish members, cantors and musicians would need to be assessed and would help inform decisions. In other circumstances—for example, when the Hours are prayed privately—at least some knowledge of this prayer as the church's prayer would figure into choices about what and how to pray. There are a number of adaptations of the Hours already available from various publishers to help people get started in praying this vital daily liturgical prayer.

Ultimately, what is at stake—and there are hints throughout GILOH to this effect—is that Liturgy of the Hours is the *daily prayer of the whole church* and leads us into Christ's paschal mystery. So, finally, the criteria for whether a choice is suitable or not is whether it enhances our daily efforts to live Christ's dying and rising. If this is so, then not only have GILOH's desires been fulfilled but, more importantly, God is praised everywhere and always.

OUTLINE

GENERAL INSTRUCTION OF
THE LITURGY OF THE HOURS

CHAPTER 1
IMPORTANCE OF THE LITURGY OF THE HOURS
OR DIVINE OFFICE IN THE LIFE OF THE CHURCH

1.   Public and common prayer by the people of God is rightly considered to be among the primary duties of the Church. From the very beginning those who were baptized "devoted themselves to the teaching of the apostles and to the community, to the breaking of the bread, and to prayer" (Acts 2:42). The Acts of the Apostles give frequent testimony to the fact that the Christian community prayed with one accord.[1]

The witness of the early Church teaches us that individual Christians devoted themselves to prayer at fixed times. Then, in different places, it soon became the established practice to assign special times for common prayer, for example, the last hour of the day when evening draws on and the lamp is lighted, or the first hour when night draws to a close with the rising of the sun.

In the course of time other hours came to be sanctified by prayer in common. These were seen by the Fathers as foreshadowed in the Acts of the Apostles. There we read of the disciples gathered together at the third hour.[2] The prince of the apostles "went up on the housetop to pray, about the sixth hour" (10:9); "Peter and John were going up to the temple at the hour of prayer, the ninth hour" (3:1); "about midnight Paul and Silas were praying and singing hymns to God" (16:25).

2.   Such prayer in common gradually took the form of a set cycle of hours. This liturgy of the hours or divine office, enriched by readings, is principally a prayer of praise and petition. Indeed, it is the prayer of the Church with Christ and to Christ.

I. PRAYER OF CHRIST

CHRIST THE INTERCESSOR WITH THE FATHER

3.   When the Word, proceeding from the Father as the splendor of his glory, came to give us all a share in God's life, "Christ Jesus, High Priest of the new

and eternal covenant, taking human nature, introduced into this earthly exile the hymn of praise that is sung throughout all ages in the halls of heaven."[3] From then on in Christ's heart the praise of God assumes a human sound in words of adoration, expiation, and intercession, presented to the Father by the Head of the new humanity, the Mediator between God and his people, in the name of all and for the good of all.

4.   In his goodness the Son of God, who is one with his Father (see John 10:30) and who on entering the world said: "Here I am! I come, God, to do your will" (Hebrews 10:9; see John 6:38), has left us the lesson of his own prayer. The Gospels many times show us Christ at prayer: when his mission is revealed by the Father;[4] before he calls the apostles;[5] when he blesses God at the multiplication of the loaves;[6] when he is transfigured on the mountain;[7] when he heals the deaf-mute;[8] when he raises Lazarus;[9] before he asks for Peter's confession of faith;[10] when he teaches the disciples how to pray;[11] when the disciples return from their mission;[12] when he blesses the little children;[13] when he prays for Peter.[14]

The work of each day was closely bound up with his prayer, indeed flowed out from it: he would retire into the desert or into the hills to pray,[15] rise very early[16] or spend the night up to the fourth watch[17] in prayer to God.[18]

We are right in thinking that he took part both in public prayers: in the synagogues, which he entered on the Sabbath "as his custom was;"[19] in the temple, which he called a house of prayer;[20] and in the private prayers that for devout Israelites were a daily practice. He used the traditional blessings of God at meals, as is expressly mentioned in connection with the multiplication of the loaves,[21] the last supper,[22] and the meal at Emmaus.[23] He also joined with disciples in a hymn of praise.[24]

To the very end of his life, as his passion was approaching,[25] at the last supper,[26] in the agony in the garden,[27] and on the cross,[28] the divine teacher showed that prayer was the soul of his Messianic ministry and paschal death. "In the days of his life on earth he offered up prayers and entreaties with loud cries and tears to the one who would deliver him from death and because of his reverence his prayer was heard" (Hebrews 5:7). By a single offering on the altar of the cross "he has made perfect forever those who are being sanctified" (Hebrews 10–14). Raised from the dead, he lives for ever, making intercessions for us.[29]

II. PRAYER OF THE CHURCH

COMMANDMENT TO PRAY

5.   Jesus has commanded us to do as he did. On many occasions he said: "Pray," "ask," "seek"[30] "in my name."[31] He taught us how to pray in what is known as the Lord's Prayer.[32] He taught us that prayer is necessary,[33] that it should be humble,[34] watchful,[35] persevering, confident in the Father's goodness,[36] single-minded, and in conformity with God's nature.[37]

Here and there in their letters the apostles have handed on to us many prayers, particularly of praise and thanks. They instruct us on prayer in the Holy

Spirit,[38] through Christ,[39] offered to God,[40] as to its persistence and constancy,[41] its power to sanctify,[42] and on prayer of praise,[43] thanks,[44] petition[45] and intercession for all.[46]

CHRIST'S PRAYER CONTINUED BY THE CHURCH

6.   Since we are entirely dependent on God, we must acknowledge and express this sovereignty of the Creator, as the devout people of every age have done by means of prayer.

Prayer directed to God must be linked with Christ, the Lord of all, the one Mediator[47] through whom alone we have access to God.[48] He unites himself to the whole human community[49] in such a way that there is an intimate bond between the prayer of Christ and the prayer of all humanity. In Christ and in Christ alone human worship of God receives its redemptive value and attains its goal.

7.   There is a special and very close bond between Christ and those whom he makes members of his Body, the Church, through the sacrament of rebirth. Thus, from the Head all the riches belonging to the Son flow throughout the whole Body: the communication of the Spirit, the truth, the life, and the participation in the divine sonship that Christ manifested in all his prayer when he dwelt among us.

Christ's priesthood is also shared by the whole Body of the Church, so that the baptized are consecrated as a spiritual temple and holy priesthood through the rebirth of baptism and the anointing by the Holy Spirit[50] and are empowered to offer the worship of the New Covenant, a worship that derives not from our own powers but from Christ's merit and gift.

"God could give us no better gift than to establish as our Head the Word through whom he created all things and to unite us to that Head as members. The results are many. The Head is Son of God and Son of Man, one as God with the Father and one as man with us. When we speak in prayer to the Father, we do not separate the Son from him and when the Son's Body prays it does not separate itself from its Head. It is the one Savior of his Body, the Lord Christ Jesus, who prays for us and in us and who is prayed to by us. He prays for us as our priest, in us as our Head; he is prayed to by us as our God. Recognize therefore our own voice in him and his voice in us."[51]

The excellence of Christian prayer lies in its sharing in the reverent love of the only-begotten Son for the Father and in the prayer that the Son put into words in his earthly life and that still continues without ceasing in the name of the whole human race and for its salvation, throughout the universal Church and in all its members.

ACTION OF THE HOLY SPIRIT

8.   The unity of the Church at prayer is brought about by the Holy Spirit, who is the same in Christ,[52] in the whole Church, and in every baptized person. It is this Spirit who "helps us in our weakness" and "intercedes for us with longings too deep for words" (Romans 8:26). As the Spirit of the Son, he gives us "the

spirit of adopted children, by which we cry out: Abba, Father" (Romans 8:15; see Galatians 4:6; 1 Corinthians 12:3, Ephesians 5:18; Jude 20). There can be therefore no Christian prayer without the action of the Holy Spirit, who unites the whole Church and leads it through the Son to the Father.

COMMUNITY CHARACTER OF PRAYER

9.   It follows that the example and precept of our Lord and the apostles in regard to constant and persevering prayer are not to be seen as a purely legal regulation. They belong to the very essence of the Church itself, which is a community and which in prayer must express its nature as a community. Hence, when the community of believers is first mentioned in the Acts of the Apostles, it is seen as a community gathered together at prayer "with the women and Mary, the mother of Jesus, and his brothers" (Acts 1:14). "There was one heart and soul in the company of those who believed" (Acts 4:32). Their oneness in spirit was founded on the word of God, on the communion of charity, on prayer, and on the eucharist.[53]

Though prayer in private and in seclusion[54] is always necessary and to be encouraged[55] and is practiced by the members of the Church through Christ in the Holy Spirit, there is a special excellence in the prayer of the community. Christ himself has said: "Where two or three are gathered together in my name, I am there in their midst" (Matthew 18:20).

III. LITURGY OF THE HOURS

CONSECRATION OF TIME

10.   Christ taught us: "You must pray at all times and not lose heart" (Luke 18:1). The Church has been faithful in obeying this instruction; it never ceases to offer prayer and makes this exhortation its own: "Through him (Jesus) let us offer to God an unceasing sacrifice of praise" (Hebrews 15:15). The Church fulfills this precept not only by celebrating the eucharist but in other ways also especially through the liturgy of the hours from other liturgical services is that it consecrates to God the whole cycle of the day and the night.[56]

11.   The purpose of the liturgy of the hours is to sanctify the day and the whole range of human activity. Therefore its structure has been revised in such a way as to make each hour once more correspond as nearly as possible to natural time and to take account of the circumstances of life today.[57]

Hence, "that the day may be truly sanctified and the hours themselves recited with spiritual advantage, it is best that each of them be prayed at a time most closely corresponding to the true time of each canonical hour."[58]

LITURGY OF THE HOURS AND THE EUCHARIST

12.   To the different hours of the day the liturgy of the hours extends[59] the praise and thanksgiving, the memorial of the mysteries of salvation, the petitions and the foretaste of heavenly glory that are present in the eucharistic mystery, "the center and high point in the whole life of the Christian community."[60]

The liturgy of the hours is in turn an excellent preparation for the celebration of the eucharist itself, for it inspires and deepens in a fitting way the dispositions necessary for the fruitful celebration of the eucharist: faith, hope, love, devotion, and the spirit of self-denial.

PRIESTHOOD OF CHRIST IN THE LITURGY OF THE HOURS

13. In the Holy Spirit Christ carries out through the Church "the task of redeeming humanity and giving perfect glory to God,"[61] not only when the eucharist is celebrated and the sacraments administered but also in other ways and especially when the liturgy of the hours is celebrated.[62] There Christ himself is present— in the gathered community, in the proclamation of God's word, "in the prayer and song of the Church."[63]

SANCTIFICATION OF GOD'S PEOPLE

14. Our sanctification is accomplished[64] and worship is offered to God in the liturgy of the hours in such a way that an exchange or dialogue is set up between God and us, in which "God is speaking to his people . . . and his people are responding to him by both song and prayer."[65]

Those taking part in the liturgy of the hours have access to holiness of the richest kind through the life-giving word of God, which in this liturgy receives great emphasis. Thus its readings are drawn from sacred Scripture, God's words in the psalms are sung in his presence, and the intercessions, prayers, and hymns are inspired by Scripture and steeped in its spirit.[66]

Hence, not only when those things are read "that are written for our instruction" (Romans 15:4), but also when the Church prays or sings, faith is deepened for those who take part and their minds are lifted up to God, in order to offer him their worship as intelligent beings and to receive his grace more plentifully.[67]

PRAISING GOD WITH THE CHURCH IN HEAVEN

15. In the liturgy of the hours the Church exercises the priestly office of its Head and offers to God "without ceasing"[68] a sacrifice of praise, that is, a tribute of lips acknowledging his name.[69] This prayer is "the voice of a bride addressing her bridegroom; it is the very prayer that Christ himself, together with his Body, addresses to the Father."[70] "All who render this service are not only fulfilling a duty of the Church, but also are sharing in the greatest honor of Christ's Bride for by offering these praises to God they are standing before God's throne in the name of the Church, their Mother."[71]

16. When the Church offers praise to God in the liturgy of the hours, it unites itself with that hymn of praise sung throughout all ages in the halls of heaven;[72] it also receives a foretaste of the song of praise in heaven, described by John in the Book of Revelation, the song sung continually before the throne of God and of the Lamb. Our close union with the Church in heaven is given effective voice "when we all, from every tribe and tongue and people and nation redeemed by Christ's blood (see Revelation 5:9) and gathered together into the one Church, glorify the triune God with one hymn of praise."[73]

The prophets came almost to a vision of this liturgy of heaven as the victory of a day without night, of a light without darkness: "The sun will no more be your light by day, and the brightness of the moon will not shine upon you, but the Lord will be your everlasting light" (Isaiah 60:19; see Revelation 21:23 and 25). "There will be a single day known to the Lord, not day and night, and at evening there will be light" (Zechariah 14:7). Already "the end of the ages has come upon us (see 1 Corinthians 10:11) and the renewal of the world has been irrevocably established and in a true sense is being anticipated in this world."[74] By faith we too are taught the meaning of our temporal life, so that we look forward with all creation to the revealing of God's children.[75] In the liturgy of the hours we proclaim this faith, we express and nourish this hope, we share in some degree the joy of everlasting praise and of that day knows no setting.

PETITION AND INTERCESSION

17.   But besides the praise of God, the Church in the liturgy of the hours expresses the prayers and desires of all the faithful; indeed, it prays to Christ, and through him to the Father, for the salvation of the whole world.[76] The Church's voice is not just its own; it is also Christ's voice, since its prayers are offered in Christ's name, that is, "through our Lord Jesus Christ," and so the Church continues to offer the prayer an petition that Christ poured out in the days of his earthly life[77] and that have therefore a unique effectiveness. The ecclesial community thus exercises a truly maternal function in bringing souls to Christ, not only by charity, good example, and works of penance but also by prayer.[78]

The concern with prayer involves those especially who have been called by a special mandate to carry out the liturgy of the hours: bishops and priests as they pray in virtue of their office for their own people and for the whole people of God;[79] other sacred ministers, and also religious.[80]

18.   Those then who take part in the liturgy of the hours bring growth to God's people in a hidden but fruitful apostolate,[81] for the work of the apostolate is directed to this end, "that all who are made children of God by faith and baptism should come together to praise God in the midst of this Church, to take part in the sacrifice, and to eat the Lord's Supper."[82]

Thus by their lives the faithful show forth and reveal to others "the mystery of Christ and the real nature of the true Church. It is of the essence of the Church to be visible yet endowed with invisible resources, eager to act yet intent on contemplation, present in this world yet not at home in it."[83]

In their turn the readings and prayer of the liturgy of the hours form a wellspring of the Christian life: the table of sacred Scripture and the writings of the saints nurture its life and prayers strengthen it. Only the Lord, without whom we can do nothing,[84] can, in response to our request, give power and increase to what we do,[85] so that we may be built up each day in the Spirit into the temple of God,[86] to the measure of Christ's fullness,[87] and receive greater strength also to bring the good news of Christ to those outside.[88]

19.   Mind and voice must be in harmony in a celebration that is worthy, attentive, and devout, if this prayer is to be made their own by those taking part and to be a source of devotion, a means of gaining God's manifold grace, a deepening of personal prayer, and an incentive to the work of the apostolate.[89] All should be intent on cooperating with God's grace, so as not to receive it in vain. Seeking Christ, penetrating ever more deeply into his mystery through prayer[90] they should offer praise and petition to God with the same mind and heart as the divine Redeemer when he prayed.

IV. PARTICIPANTS IN THE LITURGY OF THE HOURS

A. Celebration in Common

20.   The liturgy of the hours, like other liturgical services, is not a private matter but belongs to the whole Body of the Church, whose life it both expresses and affects.[91] This liturgy stands out most strikingly as an ecclesial celebration when, through the bishop surrounded by his priests and ministers,[92] the local Church celebrates it. For "in the local Church the one, holy, catholic, and apostolic Church is truly present and at work."[93] Such a celebration is therefore most earnestly recommended. When, in the absence of the bishop, a chapter of canons or other priests celebrate the liturgy of the hours, they should always respect the true time of day and, as far as possible, the people should take their part. The same is to be said of collegiate chapters.

21.   Wherever possible, other groups of the faithful should celebrate the liturgy of the hours communally in church. This especially applies to parishes—the cells of the diocese, established under their pastors, taking the place of the bishop; they "represent in some degree the visible Church established throughout the world."[94]

22.   Hence, when the people are invited to the liturgy of the hours and come together in unity of heart and voice, they show forth the Church in its celebration of the mystery of Christ.[95]

23.   Those in holy orders or with a special canonical mission[96] have the responsibility of initiating and directing the prayer of the community; "they should expend every effort so that those entrusted to their care may become of one mind in prayer."[97] They must therefore see to it that the people are invited, and prepared by suitable instruction, to celebrate the principal hours in common, especially on Sundays and holydays.[98] They should teach the people how to make this participation a source of genuine prayer;[99] they should therefore give the people suitable guidance in the Christian understanding of the psalms, in order to progress by degrees to a greater appreciation and more frequent use of the prayer of the Church.[100]

24.   Communities of canons, monks, nuns, and other religious who celebrate the liturgy of the hours by rule or according to their constitutions, whether

with the general rite or a particular rite, in whole or in part, represent in a special way the Church at prayer. They are a fuller sign of the Church as it continuously praises God with one voice and they fulfill the duty of "working," above all by prayer, "to build up and increase the whole Mystical Body of Christ, and for the good of the local Churches."[101] This is especially true of those living the contemplative life.

25.   Even when having no obligation to communal celebration, all sacred ministers and all clerics living in a community or meeting together should arrange to say at least some part of the liturgy of the hours in common, particularly morning prayer and evening prayer.[102]

26.   Men and women religious not bound to a common celebration, as well as members of any institute or perfection, are strongly urged to gather together, by themselves or with the people, to celebrate the liturgy of the hours or part of it.

27.   Lay groups gathering for prayer, apostolic work, or any other reason are encouraged to fulfill the Church's duty[103] by celebrating part of the liturgy of the hours. The laity must learn above all how in the liturgy they are adoring God the Father in spirit and in truth;[104] they should bear in mind that through public worship and prayer they reach all humanity and can contribute significantly to the salvation of the whole world.[105]

Finally, it is of great advantage for the family, the domestic sanctuary of the Church, not only to pray together to God but also to celebrate some parts of the liturgy of the hours as occasion offers, in order to enter more deeply into the life of the Church.[106]

B. Mandate to Celebrate the Liturgy of the Hours

28.   Sacred ministers have the liturgy of the hours entrusted to them in such a particular way that even when the faithful are not present they are to pray at themselves with the adaptations necessary under these circumstances. The Church commissions them to celebrate the liturgy of the hours so as to ensure at least in their persons the regular carrying out of the duty of the whole community and the unceasing continuance of Christ's prayer in the Church.[107]

The bishop represents Christ in an eminent and conspicuous way and is the high priest of his flock; the life in Christ of his faithful people may be said in a sense to derive from him and depend on him.[108] He should, then, be the first of all the members of his Church in offering prayer. His prayer in the recitation of the liturgy of the hours is always made in the name of the Church and on behalf of the Church entrusted to him.[109]

United as they are with the bishop and the whole presbyterium, priests are themselves representative in a special way of Christ the Priest[110] and so share the same responsibility of praying to God for the people entrusted to them and indeed for the whole world.[111]

All these ministers fulfill the ministry of the Good Shepherd who prays for his sheep that they may have life and so be brought into perfect unity.[112] In the liturgy of the hours that the Church sets before them they are not only to find a source of devotion and a strengthening of personal prayer,[113] but must also nourish and foster pastoral missionary activity as the fruit of their contemplation to gladden the whole Church of God.[114]

29.   Hence bishops, priests, and other sacred ministers, who have received from the Church the mandate to celebrate the liturgy of the hours (see no. 17), should recite the full sequence of hours each day, observing as far as possible the true time of day.

They should first and foremost, attach due importance to those hours that are, so to speak, the two hinges of the liturgy of the hours, that is, morning prayer and evening prayer," which should not be omitted except for a serious reason.

They should faithfully pray the office of readings, which is above all a liturgical celebration of the word of God. In this way they fulfill daily a duty that is peculiarly their own, that is, of receiving the word of God into their lives, so that they may become more perfect as disciples of the Lord and experience more deeply the unfathomable riches of Christ.[115]

In order to sanctify the whole day more completely, they will also treasure the recitation of daytime prayer and night prayer, to round off the whole *Opus Dei* and to commend themselves to God before retiring.

30.   It is most fitting that permanent deacons recite daily at least some part of the liturgy of the hours, to be determined by the conference of bishops.[116]

31.   a. Cathedral and collegiate chapters should celebrate in choir those parts of the liturgy of the hours that are prescribed for them by the general law or by particular law.

In private recitation individual members of these chapters should include those hours that are recited in their chapter, in addition to the hours prescribed for all sacred ministers.[117]

b. Religious communities bound to the recitation of the liturgy of the hours and their individual members should celebrate the hours in keeping with their own particular law; but the prescription of no. 29 in regard to those in holy orders is to be respected.

Communities bound to choir should celebrate the whole sequence of the hours daily in choir;[118] when absent from choir their members should recite the hours in keeping with their own particular law; but the prescriptions in no. 29 are always to be respected.

32.   Other religious communities and their individual members are advised to celebrate some parts of the liturgy of the hours, in accordance with their own situation, for it is the prayer of the Church and makes the whole Church, scattered throughout the world, one in heart and mind.[119]

This recommendation applies also to laypersons.[120]

33.   The structure of the liturgy of the hours follows laws of its own and incorporates in its own way elements found in other Christian celebrations. Thus it is so constructed that, after a hymn, there is always psalmody, then a long or short reading of sacred Scripture, and finally prayer of petition.

In a celebration in common and in private recitation the essential structure of this liturgy remains the same, that is, it is a conversation between God and his people. Celebration in common, however, expresses more clearly the ecclesial nature of the liturgy of the hours; it makes for active participation by all, in a way suited to each one's condition, through the acclamations, dialogue, alternating psalmody, and similar elements. It also better provides for the different literary genres that make up the liturgy of the hours.[121] Hence, whenever it is possible to have a celebration in common, with the people present and actively taking part, this kind of celebration is to be preferred to one that is individual and, as it were, private.[122] It is also advantageous to sing the office in choir and in community as opportunity offers, in accordance with the nature and function of the individual parts.

In this way the Apostle's exhortation is obeyed: "Let the word of the Christ dwell in you in all its fullness, as you teach and counsel each other in all wisdom by psalms, hymns, and spiritual canticles, singing thankfully to God in your hearts" (Colossians 3:16; see Ephesians 5:19–20).

CHAPTER II
SANCTIFICATION OF THE DAY:
THE DIFFERENT LITURGICAL HOURS

I. INTRODUCTION TO THE WHOLE OFFICE

34.   The whole office begins as a rule with an invitatory. This consists in the verse, *Lord, open my lips. And my mouth will proclaim your praise,* and Psalm 95. This psalm invites the faithful each day to sing God's praise and to listen to his voice and draw them to hope for "the Lord's rest."[1]

In place of Psalm 95, Psalm 100, Psalm 67, or Psalm 24 may be used as circumstances may suggest:

It is preferable to recite the invitatory psalm responsorially as it is set out in the text, that is, with the antiphon recited at the beginning, then repeated, and repeated after each strophe.

35.   The invitatory is placed at the beginning of the whole sequence of the day's prayer, that is, it precedes either morning prayer or the office of readings, whichever of these liturgical rites begins the day. The invitatory is the prelude to morning prayer.

36.   The variation of the invitatory antiphon, to suit the different liturgical days, is indicated at its place of occurrence.

II. MORNING PRAYER AND EVENING PRAYER

37. "By the venerable tradition of the universal Church, lauds as morning prayer and vespers as evening prayer are the two hinges on which the daily office turns; hence they are to be considered as the chief hours and celebrated as such."[2]

38. As is clear from many of the elements that make it up, morning prayer is intended and arranged to sanctify the morning. St. Basil the Great gives an excellent description of this character in these words: "It is said in the morning in order that the first stirrings of our mind and will may be consecrated to God and that we may take nothing in hand until we have been gladdened by the thought of God and it is written: 'I was mindful of God and was glad' (Psalm 77:4 [Jerome's translations from Hebrew]), or set our bodies to any task before we do what has been said: 'I will pray to you, Lord, you will hear my voice in the morning; I will stand before you in the morning and gaze on you' (Psalm 5:4–5)."[3]

Celebrated as it is as the light of a new day is dawning, this hour also recalls the resurrection of the Lord Jesus, the true light enlightening all people (see John 1:9) and "the sun of justice" (Malachi 4:2), "rising from on high" (Luke 1:78). Hence, we can well understand the advice of St. Cyprian: "There should be prayer in the morning so that the resurrection of the Lord may thus be celebrated."[4]

39. When evening approaches and the day is already far spent, evening prayer is celebrated in order that "we may give thanks for what has been given us, or what we have done well, during the day."[5] We also recall the redemption through the prayer we send up "like incense in the Lord's sight," and in which "the raising up of our hands" becomes "an evening sacrifice."[6] This sacrifice "may also be interpreted more spiritually as the true evening sacrifice that our Savior the Lord entrusted to the apostles at supper on the evening when he instituted the sacred mysteries of the Church or of the evening sacrifice of the next day, the sacrifice, that is, which raising his hands, he offered to the Father at the end of the ages for the salvation of the whole world."[7] Again, in order to fix our hope on the light that knows no setting, "we pray and make petition for the light to come down on us anew; we implore the coming of Christ who will bring the grace of eternal light."[8] Finally, at this hour we join with the Churches of the East in calling upon the "joy-giving light of that holy glory, born of the immortal, heavenly Father, the holy and blessed Jesus Christ; now that we have come to the setting of the sun and have seen the evening star, we sing in praise of God, Father, Son, and Holy Spirit . . . ."

40. Morning prayer and evening prayer are therefore to be accorded the highest importance as the prayer of the Christian community. Their public or communal celebration should be encouraged, especially in the case of those who live in community. Indeed, the recitation of these hours should be recommended also to individual members of the faithful unable to take part in a celebration in common.

41. Morning prayer and evening prayer begin with the introductory verse, *God, come to my assistance. Lord, make haste to help me.* There follows the *Glory*

to the Father, with *As it was in the beginning* and *Alleluia* (omitted in Lent). This introduction is omitted at morning prayer when the invitatory immediately precedes it.

42.   Then an appropriate hymn is sung immediately. The purpose of the hymn is to set the tone for the hour or the feast and, especially in celebrations with a congregation, to form a simple and pleasant introduction to prayer.

43.   After the hymn the psalmody follows, in accordance with the rules laid down in nos. 121–125. The psalmody of morning prayer consists of one morning psalm, then a canticle from the Old Testament and, finally, a second psalm of praise, following the tradition of the Church.

The psalmody of evening prayer consists of two psalms (or two parts of a longer psalm) suited to the hour and to celebration with a congregation and a canticle from the letters of the apostles or from the Book of Revelation.

44.   After the psalmody there is either a short reading or a longer one.

45.   The short reading is provided to fit the day, the season, and the feast. It is to be read and received as a true proclamation of God's word that emphasizes some holy thought or highlights some shorter passages that may be overlooked in the continuous cycle of Scripture readings.

The short readings are different for each day of the psalter cycle.

46.   Especially in a celebration with a congregation, a longer Scripture reading may be chosen either from the office of readings or the Lectionary for Mass, particularly texts that for some reason have not been used. From time to time some other more suitable reading may be used, in accordance with the rules in nos. 248–249 and 251.

47.   In a celebration with a congregation a short homily may follow the reading to explain its meaning, as circumstances suggest.

48.   After the reading or homily a period of silence may be observed.

49.   As a response to the word of God, a responsorial chant or short responsory is provided; this may be omitted. Other chants with the same purpose and character may also be substituted in its place, provided these have been duly approved by the conference of bishops.

50.   Next is the solemn recitation of the gospel canticle with its antiphon, that is, the Canticle of Zechariah at morning prayer and the Canticle of Mary at evening prayer. Sanctioned by age-old popular usage in the Roman Church, these canticles are expressions of praise and thanksgiving for our redemption. The antiphon for each canticle is indicated, according to the character of the day, the season, or the feast.

51.   After the canticle, at morning prayer come the petitions for the consecration of the day and its work to God and at evening prayer, the intercessions (see nos. 179–193).

52.   After the petitions or intercessions the Lord's Prayer is said by all.

53.   Immediately after the Lord's Prayer there follows the concluding prayer, which for weekdays in Ordinary Time is found in the psalter and for other days in the proper.

54.   Then, if a priest or deacon is presiding, he dismisses the congregation with the greeting, *The Lord be with you,* and the blessing as at Mass. He adds the invitation, *Go in peace.* R. *Thanks be to God.* In the absence of a priest or deacon the celebration concludes with *May the Lord bless us,* etc.

III. OFFICE OF READINGS

55.   The office of readings seeks to provide God's people, and in particular those consecrated to God in a special way, with a wider selection of passages from sacred Scripture for meditation, together with the finest excerpts from spiritual writers. Even though the cycle of scriptural readings at daily Mass is now richer, the treasures of revelation and tradition to be found in the office of readings will also contribute greatly to the spiritual life. Bishops and priests in particular should prize these treasures, so that they may hand on to others the word of God they have themselves received and make their teaching "the true nourishment for the people of God."[9]

56.   But prayer should accompany "the reading of sacred Scripture so that there may be a conversation between God and his people: 'we talk with God when we pray, we listen to him when he read God's words.'"[10] For this reason the office of readings consists also of psalms, a hymn, a prayer, and other texts, giving it the character of true prayer.

57.   The Constitution on the Liturgy directs that the office of readings, "though it should retain its character as a night office of praise when celebrated in choir, shall be adapted so that it may be recited at any hour of the day; it shall be made up of fewer psalms and longer readings."[11]

58.   Those who are obliged by their own particular law and others who commendably wish to retain the character of this office as a night office of praise (either by saying it at night or very early in the morning and before morning prayer), during Ordinary Time choose the hymn from the selection given for this purpose. Moreover, for Sundays, solemnities, and certain feasts what is said in nos. 70–73 about vigils must be kept in mind.

59.   Without prejudice to the regulations just given, the office of readings may be recited at any hour of the day, even during the night hours of the previous day, after evening prayer has been said.

60.   If the office of readings is said before morning prayer, the invitatory precedes it, as noted (nos. 34–36). Otherwise it begins with the verse, *God, come to my assistance* with the *Glory to the Father, As it was in the beginning*, and the *Alleluia* (omitted in Lent).

61.   Then the hymn is sung. In Ordinary Time this is taken either from the night selections, as already indicated (nos. 34–36), or from the morning selections, depending on what the true time of day requires.

62.   The psalmody follows and consists of three psalms (or parts in the case of longer psalms. During the Easter triduum, on days within the octaves of Easter and Christmas, on solemnities and feasts, the psalms are proper, with their proper antiphons.

On Sundays and weekdays, however, the psalms and their antiphons are taken from the current week and day of the psalter. On memorials of the saints they are similarly taken from the current week and day of the psalter, unless there are proper psalms or antiphons (see nos. 218ff.).

63.   Between the psalmody and the readings there is, as a rule, a verse, marking a transition in the prayer from psalmody to listening.

64.   There are two readings: the first is from the Scriptures, the second is from the writings of the Fathers or church writers, or else is a reading connected with the saints.

65.   After each reading there is a responsory (see nos. 169–172).

66.   The scriptural reading is normally to be taken from the Proper of Seasons, in accordance with the rules to be given later (nos. 140–155). On solemnities and feasts, however, it is taken from the proper or the common.

67.   On solemnities and feasts of saints a proper second reading is used; if there is none, the second reading is taken from the respective Common of Saints. On memorials of saints when the celebration is not impeded, the reading in connection with the saint replaces the current second reading (see nos. 166–235).

68.   On Sundays outside Lent, on days within the octaves of Easter and Christmas, and on solemnities and feasts the *Te Deum* is said after the second reading with its responsory but is omitted on memorials and weekdays. The last part of this hymn, that is, from the verse, *Save your people, Lord* to the end, may be omitted.

69.   The office of readings normally concludes with the prayer proper to the day and, at least in recitation in common, with the acclamation, *Let us praise the Lord*. R. *And give him thanks*.

IV. VIGILS

70. The Easter Vigil is celebrated by the whole Church, in the rites given in the relevant liturgical books. "The vigil of this night," as St. Augustine said, "is of such importance that it could claim exclusively for itself the name 'vigil,' common though this is to all others."[12] "We keep vigil on that night when the Lord rose again and inaugurated for us in his humanity that life . . . in which there is neither death nor sleep. . . . Hence, the one whose resurrection we celebrate by keeping watch a little longer will see to it that we reign with him by living a life without end."[13]

71. As with the Easter Vigil, it was customary to begin certain solemnities (different in different Churches) with a vigil. Among these solemnities Christmas and Pentecost are preeminent. This custom should be maintained and fostered, according to the particular usage of each Church. Whenever it seems good to add a vigil for other solemnities or pilgrimages, the general norms for celebrations of the word should be followed.

72. The Fathers and spiritual writers have frequently encouraged Christians, especially those who lead the contemplative life, to pray during the night. Such prayer expresses and awakens our expectation of the Lord's Second Coming: "At midnight the cry went up: 'See, the bridegroom is coming, go out to meet him'" (Matthew 25:6). "Keep watch, then, for you do not know when the master of the house is coming, whether late or at midnight or at cockcrow or in the morning, so that if he comes unexpectedly he may not find you sleeping" (Mark 13:35–36). All who maintain the character of the office of readings as a night office, therefore, are to be commended.

73. Further, since in the Roman Rite the office of readings is always of a uniform brevity, especially for the sake of those engaged in apostolic work, those who desire, in accordance with tradition, to extend the celebration of the vigils of Sundays, solemnities, and feasts should do so as follows.

First, the office of readings is to be celebrated as in *The Liturgy of the Hours* up to the end of the readings. After the two readings and before the *Te Deum* canticles should be added from the special appendix of *The Liturgy of the Hours*. Then the gospel should be read; a homily on the gospel may be added. After this the *Te Deum* is sung and the prayer said.

On solemnities and feasts the gospel is to be taken from the Lectionary for Mass; on Sundays, from the series on the paschal mystery in the appendix of *The Liturgy of the Hours.*

V. DAYTIME HOURS

74. Following a very ancient tradition Christians have made a practice of praying out of private devotion at various times of the day, even in the course of their work, in imitation of the Church in apostolic times. In different ways with the passage of time this tradition has taken the form of a liturgical celebration.

75.   Liturgical custom in both East and West has retained midmorning, midday, and midafternoon prayer, mainly because these hours were linked to a commemoration of the events of the Lord's passion and of the first preaching of the Gospel.

76.   Vatican Council II decreed that these lesser hours are to be retained in choir.[14]

   The liturgical practice of saying these three hours is to be retained, without prejudice to particular law, by those who live the contemplative life. It is recommended also for all, especially those who take part in retreats or pastoral meetings.

77.   Outside choir, without prejudice to particular law, it is permitted to choose from the three hours the one most appropriate to the time of day, so that the tradition of prayer in the course of the day's work may be maintained.

78.   Daytime prayer is so arranged as to take into account both those who recite only one hour and those who are obliged, or desire, to say all three hours.

79.   The daytime hours begin with the introductory verse, *God come to my assistance* with the *Glory to the Father, As it was in the beginning,* and the *Alleluia* (omitted in Lent). Then a hymn appropriate to the hour is sung. The psalmody is next, then the reading, followed by the verse. The hour concludes with the prayer and, at least in recitation in common, with the acclamation, *Let us praise the Lord.* R. *And give him thanks.*

80.   Different hymns and prayers are given for each of the hours so that, in keeping with tradition, they may correspond to the true time of day and thus sanctify it in a more pointed way. Those who recite only one hour should therefore choose the texts that correspond to the true time of day.

   In addition, the readings and prayers vary in keeping with the character of the day, the season, or the feast.

81.   Two psalmodies are provided: the current psalmody and the complementary psalmody. Those who pray one hour should use the current psalmody. Those who pray more than one hour should use the current psalmody at one hour and the complementary psalmody at the others.

82.   The current psalmody consists of three psalms (or parts in the case of longer psalms) form the psalter, with their antiphons, unless directions are given to the contrary.

   On solemnities, the Easter triduum, and days within the octave of Easter, proper antiphons are said with three psalms chosen from the complementary psalmody, unless special psalms are to be used or the celebration falls on a Sunday, when the psalms are those from the Sunday of Week I of the psalter.

83.   The complementary psalter consists of three sets of three psalms, chosen as a rule form the Gradual Psalms.

VI. NIGHT PRAYER

84. Night prayer is the last prayer of the day, said before retiring, even if that is after midnight.

85. Night prayer begins like the other hours, with the verse, *God, come to my assistance,* the *Glory to the Father, As it was in the beginning,* and the *Alleluia* (omitted in Lent).

86. It is a laudable practice to have next an examination of conscience; in a celebration in common this takes place in silence or as part of a penitential rite based on the formularies in the Roman Missal.

87. The appropriate hymn follows.

88. After evening prayer I of Sunday the psalmody consists of Psalm 4 and Psalm 134; after evening prayer II of Sunday it consists of Psalm 91.

On the other days psalms are chosen that are full of confidence in the Lord; it is permissible to use the Sunday psalms instead, especially for the convenience of those who may wish to pray night prayer from memory.

89. After the psalmody there is a reading, followed by the responsory, *Into your hands.* Then, as a climax to the whole hour, the Canticle of Simeon, *Lord, now you let your servant go in peace* follows, with its antiphon.

90. The concluding prayer then follows, as it appears in the psalter.

91. After the prayer the blessing, *May the all-powerful Lord* is used, even in private recitation.

92. Finally, one of the antiphons in honor of the Blessed Virgin Mary is said. In the Easter season this is always to be the *Regina caeli.* In addition to the antiphons given in the *Liturgy of the Hours,* others may be approved by the conferences of bishops.[15]

VII. COMBINING THE HOURS WITH MASS OR WITH EACH OTHER

93. In particular cases, if circumstances require, it is possible to link an hour more closely with Mass when there is a celebration of the liturgy of the hours in public or in common, according to the norms that follow, provided the Mass and the hour belong to one and the same office. Care must be taken, however, that this does not result in harm to pastoral work, especially on Sundays.

94. When morning prayer, celebrated in choir or in common, comes immediately before Mass, the whole celebration may begin either with the introductory verse and hymn of morning prayer, especially on weekdays, or with the entrance song, procession, and celebrant's greeting, especially on Sundays and holydays; one of the introductory rites is thus omitted.

The psalmody of morning prayer follows as usual, up to, but excluding, the reading. After the psalmody the penitential rite is omitted and, as circumstances suggest, the *Kyrie;* the *Gloria* then follows, if required by the rubrics, and the celebrant says the opening prayer of the Mass. The liturgy of the word follows as usual.

The general intercessions are made in the place and form customary at Mass. But on weekdays, at Mass in the morning, the intercessions of morning and evening prayer may replace the daily form of the general intercessions at Mass.

After the communion with its communion song the Canticle of Zechariah, *Blessed be the Lord,* with its antiphon from morning prayer, is sung. Then follow the prayer after communion and the rest as usual.

95.   If public celebration of a daytime hour, whichever corresponds to the time of day, is immediately followed by Mass, the whole celebration may begin in the same way, either with the introductory verse and hymn for the hour, especially on weekdays, or with the entrance song, procession, and celebrant's greeting, especially on Sundays and holydays; one of the introductory rites is thus omitted.

The psalmody of the hour follows as usual up to, but excluding, the reading. After the psalmody the penitential rite is omitted and, as circumstances suggest, the *Kyrie;* the *Gloria* then follows, if required by the rubrics, and the celebrant says the opening prayer of the Mass.

96.   Evening prayer, celebrated immediately before Mass, is joined to it in the same way as morning prayer. Evening prayer I of solemnities, Sundays, or feasts of the Lord falling on Sundays may not be celebrated until after Mass of the preceding day or Saturday.

97.   When a daytime hour or evening prayer follows Mass, the Mass is celebrated in the usual way up to and including the prayer after communion.

When the prayer after communion has been said, the psalmody of the hour begins without introduction. At the daytime hour, after the psalmody the short reading is omitted and the prayer is said at once and the dismissal takes place as at Mass. At evening prayer, after the psalmody the short reading is omitted and the Canticle of Mary with its antiphon follows at once; the intercessions and the Lord's Prayer are omitted; the concluding prayer follows, then the blessing of the congregation.

98.   Apart from Christmas eve, the combining of Mass with the office of readings is normally excluded, since the Mass already has its own cycle of readings, to be kept distinct from any other. But if by way of exception, it should be necessary to join the two, then immediately after the second reading from the office, with its responsory, the rest is omitted and the Mass begins with the *Gloria,* if it is called for; otherwise the Mass begins with the opening prayer.

99.   If the office of readings comes immediately before another hour of the office, then the appropriate hymn for that hour may be sung at the beginning of

the office of readings. At the end of the office of readings the prayer and conclusion are omitted and in the hour following the introductory verse with the *Glory to the Father* is omitted.

CHAPTER III
DIFFERENT ELEMENTS IN THE LITURGY OF THE HOURS

I. PSALMS AND THEIR CONNECTION WITH CHRISTIAN PRAYER

100. In the liturgy of the hours the Church in large measure prays through the magnificent songs that the Old Testament authors composed under the inspiration of the Holy Spirit. The origin of these verses gives them great power to raise the mind to God, to inspire devotion, to evoke gratitude in times of favor, and to bring consolation and courage in times of trial.

101. The psalms, however, are only a foreshadowing of the fullness of time that came to pass in Christ the Lord and that is the source of the power of the Church's prayer. Hence, while the Christian people are all agreed on the supreme value to be placed on the psalms, they can sometimes experience difficulty in making this inspired poetry their own prayer.

102. Yet the Holy Spirit, under whose inspiration the psalms were written, is always present by his grace to those believers who use them with good will. But more is necessary: the faithful must "improve their understanding of the Bible, especially of the psalms,"[1] according to their individual capacity, so that they may understand how and by what method they can truly pray through the psalms.

103. The psalms are not readings or prose prayers, but poems of praise. They can on occasion be recited as readings, but from their literary genre they are properly called *Tehillim* ("songs of praise") in Hebrew and *psalmoi* ("songs to be sung to the lyre") in Greek. In fact, all the psalms have a musical quality that determines their correct style of delivery. Thus even when a psalm is recited and not sung or is said silently in private, its musical character should govern its use. A psalm does present a text to the minds of the people, but its aim is to move the heart of those singing it or listening to it and also of those accompanying it "on the lyre and harp."

104. To sing the psalms with understanding, then, is to meditate on them verse by verse, with the heart always ready to respond in the way the Holy Spirit desires. The one who inspired the psalmist will also be present to those who in faith and love are ready to receive his grace. For this reason the singing of psalms, though it demands the reverence owed to God's majesty, should be the expression of a joyful spirit and a loving heart, in keeping with their character as sacred poetry and divine song and above all with the freedom of the children of God.

105. Often the words of a psalm helps us to pray with greater ease and fervor, whether in thanksgiving and joyful praise of God or in prayer for help in the throes of suffering. But difficulties may arise, especially when the psalm is not

addressed directly to God. The psalmist is a poet and often addresses the people as he recalls Israel's history; sometimes he addresses others, including subrational creatures. He even represents the words as being spoken by God himself and individual people, including, as in Psalm 2, God's enemies. This shows that a psalm is a different kind of prayer from a prayer or collect composed by the Church. Moreover, it is in keeping with the poetic and musical character of the psalms that they do not necessarily address God but are sung in God's presence. Thus St. Benedict's instruction: "Let us reflect on what it means to be in the sight of God and his angels, and let us so stand in his presence that our minds are in harmony with our voices."[2]

106. In praying the psalms we should open our hearts to the different attitudes they express, varying with the literary genre to which each belongs (psalms of grief, trust, gratitude, etc.) and to which biblical scholars rightly attach great importance.

107. Staying close to the meaning of the words, the person who prays the psalms looks for the significance of the text for the human life of the believer.

It is clear that each psalm was written in its own individual circumstances, which the titles given for each psalm in the Hebrew psalter are meant to indicate. But whatever its historical origin, each psalm has its own meaning, which we cannot overlook even in our own day. Though the psalms originated very many centuries ago among an Eastern people, they express accurately the pain and hope, the unhappiness and trust of people of every age and country, and sing above all of faith in God, of revelation, and of redemption.

108. Those who pray the psalms in the liturgy of the hours do so not so much in their own name as in the name of the entire Body of Christ. This consideration does away with the problem of a possible discrepancy between personal feelings and the sentiments a psalm is expressing: for example, when a person feels sad and the psalm is one of joy or when a person feels happy and the psalm is one of mourning. Such a problem is readily solved in private prayer, which allows for the choice of a psalm suited to personal feelings. The divine office, however, is not private; the cycle of psalms is public, in the name of the Church, even for those who may be reciting an hour alone. Those who pray the psalms in the name of the Church nevertheless can always find a reason for joy or sadness, for the saying of the Apostle applies in this case also: "Rejoice with the joyful and weep with those who weep" (Romans 12:15). In this way human frailty, wounded by self-love, is healed in proportion to the love that makes the heart match the voice that prays the psalms.[3]

109. Those who pray the psalms in the name of the Church should be aware of their full sense (sensus plenus), especially their Messianic sense, which was the reason for the Church's introduction of the psalter into its prayer. This Messianic sense was fully revealed in the New Testament and indeed was affirmed publicly by Christ the Lord in person when he said to the apostles: "All that is written about me in the law of Moses and the prophets and the psalms must be fulfilled" (Luke 24:44). The best-known example of this Messianic sense is the

dialogue in Matthew's Gospel on the messiah as Son of David and David's Lord,[4] where Psalm 110 is interpreted as Messianic.

Following this line of thought, the Fathers of the Church saw the whole psalter as a prophecy of Christ and the Church and explained it in this sense; for the same reason the psalms have been chosen for use in the liturgy. Though somewhat contrived interpretations were at times proposed, in general the Fathers and the liturgy itself had the right to hear in the singing of the psalms the voice of Christ crying out to the Father or of the Father conversing with the Son; indeed, they also recognized in the psalms the voice of the Church, the apostles, and the martyrs. This method of interpretation also flourished in the Middle Ages; in many manuscripts of the period the Christological meaning of each psalm was set before those praying by means of the caption prefixed. A Christological meaning is by no means confined to the recognized Messianic psalms but is given also to many others. Some of these interpretations are doubtless Christological only in an accommodated sense, but they have the support of the Church's tradition.

On the great feasts especially, the choice of psalms is often based on their Christological meaning and antiphons taken from these psalms are frequently used to throw light on this meaning.

II. ANTIPHONS AND OTHER AIDS TO PRAYING THE PSALMS

110. In the Latin tradition of psalmody three elements have greatly contributed to an understanding of the psalms and their use as Christian prayer: the captions, the psalm-prayers, and in particular the antiphons.

111. In the psalter of *The Liturgy of the Hours* a caption is given for each psalm to explain its meaning and its import for the personal life of the believer. These captions are intended only as an aid to prayer. A quotation from the New Testament or the Fathers of the Church is added to foster prayer in their Christological meaning.

112. Psalm-prayers for each psalm are given in the supplement to *The Liturgy of the Hours* as an aid to understanding them in a predominantly Christian way. An ancient tradition provides a model for their use: after the psalm a period of silence is observed, then the prayer gives a resume and resolution of the thoughts and aspirations of those praying the psalms.

113. Even when the liturgy of the hours is recited, not sung, each psalm retains its own antiphon, which is also to be said in private recitation. The antiphons help to bring out the literary genre of the psalm; they highlight some theme that may otherwise not attract the attention it deserves; they suggest an individual tone in a psalm, varying with different contexts: indeed, as long as farfetched accommodated senses are avoided, antiphons, are of great value in helping toward an understanding of the typological meaning or the meaning appropriate to the feast; they can also add pleasure and variety to the recitation of the psalms.

114. The antiphons in the psalter have been designed to lend themselves to vernacular translation and to repetition after each strophe, in accordance with no. 125. When the office of Ordinary Time is recited, not sung, the quotations printed with the psalms may be used in place of these antiphons (see no. 111).

115. When a psalm may be divided because of its length into several sections within one and the same hour, an antiphon is given for each section. This is to provide variety, especially when the hour is sung, and also to help toward a better understanding of the riches of the psalm. Still, it is permissible to say or sing the complete psalm without interruption, using only the first antiphon.

116. Proper antiphons are given for each of the psalms of morning prayer and evening prayer during the Easter triduum, on the days within the octaves of Easter and Christmas, on the Sundays of the seasons of Advent, Christmas, Lent, and Easter, on the weekdays of Holy Week and the Easter season, and from the 17th to the 24th of December.

117. On solemnities proper antiphons are given for the office of readings, morning prayer, the daytime hours, and evening prayer; if not, the antiphons are taken from the common. On feasts the same applies to the office of readings and to morning prayer and evening prayer.

118. Any memorials of the saints that have proper antiphons retain them (see no. 235).

119. The antiphons for the Canticles of Zechariah and of Mary are taken, during Ordinary Time, from the Proper of Seasons, if they are given there; if not, they are taken from the current week and day of the psalter. On solemnities and feasts they are taken from the proper if they are given there; if not, they are taken from the common. On memorials without proper antiphons the antiphon may be taken at will either from the common or from the current week.

120. During the Easter season *Alleluia* is added to all antiphons, unless it would clash with the meaning of a particular antiphon.

III. WAYS OF SINGING THE PSALMS

121. Different psalms may be sung in different ways for a fuller grasp of their spiritual meaning and beauty. The choice of ways is dictated by the literary genre or length of each psalm, by the language used, whether Latin or the vernacular, and especially by the kind of celebration, whether individual, with a group, or with a congregation. The reason for using psalms is not the establishment of a fixed amount of prayer but their own variety and the character proper to each.

122. The psalms are sung or said in one of three ways, according to the different usages established in tradition or experience: directly *(in directum)*, that is, all sing the entire psalm, or antiphonally, that is, two choirs or sections of the congregation sing alternate verses or strophes, or responsorially.

123. At the beginning of each psalm its own antiphon is always to be recited, as noted in nos. 113–120. At the end of the psalm the practice of concluding with the *Glory to the Father* and *As it was in the beginning* is retained. This is the fitting conclusion endorsed by tradition and it gives to Old Testament prayer a note of praise and a Christological and Trinitarian sense. The antiphon may be repeated at the end of the psalm.

124. When longer psalms occur, sections are marked in the psalter that divide the parts in such a way as to keep the threefold structure of the hour; but great care has been taken not to distort the meaning of the psalm.

It is useful to observe this division, especially in a choral celebration in Latin; the *Glory to the Father* is added at the end of each section.

It is permissible, however, either to keep this traditional way or to pause between the dfferent sections of the same psalm or to recite the whole psalm and its antiphon as a single unit without a break.

125. In addition, when the literary genre of a psalm suggests it, the divisions into strophes are marked in order that, especially when the psalm is sung in the vernacular, the antiphons may be repeated after each strophe; in this case the *Glory to the Father* need to be said only at the end of the psalm.

IV. PLAN FOR THE DISTRIBUTION OF THE PSALMS IN THE OFFICE

126. The psalms are distributed over a four-week cycle in such a way that very few psalms are omitted, while some, traditionally more important, occur more frequently than others; morning prayer and evening prayer as well as night prayer have been assigned psalms appropriate to these hours.[5]

127. Since morning prayer and evening prayer are particularly designed for celebration with a congregation, the psalms chosen for them are those more suited to this purpose.

128. For night prayer the norm given in no. 88 has been followed.

129. For Sunday, including its office of readings and daytime prayer, the psalms chosen are those that tradition has particularly singled out as expressions of the paschal mystery. Certain psalms of a penitential character or connected with the passion are assigned to Friday.

130. Three psalms (78, 105, and 106) are reserved for the seasons of Advent, Christmas, Lent, and Easter, because they throw a special light on the Old Testament history of salvation as the forerunner of its fulfillment in the New.

131. Three psalms (58, 83, and 109) have been omitted from the psalter cycle because of their curses; in the same way, some verses have been omitted from certain psalms, as noted at the head of each. The reason for the omission is a certain psychological difficulty, even though the psalms of imprecation are in

fact used as prayer in the New Testament, for example, Revelation 6:10, and in no sense to encourage the use of curses.

132. Psalms too long to be included in one hour of the office are assigned to the same hour on different days so that they may be recited in full by those who do not usually say other hours. Thus Psalm 119 is divided in keeping with its own internal structure and is spread over twenty-two days during daytime prayer, because tradition has assigned it to the day hours.

133. The four-week cycle of the psalter is coordinated with the liturgical year in such a way that on the First Sunday Advent, the First Sunday in Ordinary Time, the First Sunday of Lent, and Easter Sunday they cycle is always begun again with Week I (others being omitted when necessary).

After Pentecost, when the psalter cycle follows the series of weeks in Ordinary Time, it begins with the week indicated in the Proper of Seasons at the beginning of the appropriate week in Ordinary Time.

134. On solemnities and feasts, during the Easter triduum, and on the days within the octaves of Easter and Christmas, proper psalms are assigned to the office of readings from those with a tradition of use at these times and their relevance is generally highlighted by the choice of antiphon. This is also the case at daytime prayer on certain solemnities of the Lord and during the octave of Easter. At morning prayer the psalms and canticle are taken form the Sunday of the Week I of the psalter. On solemnities the psalms at evening prayer I are taken from the *Laudate* Psalms, following an ancient custom. At evening prayer II on solemnities and at evening prayer on feasts the psalms and canticle are proper. At daytime prayer on solemnities (except those already mentioned and those falling on Sunday) the psalms are taken from the Gradual Psalms; at daytime prayer on feasts the psalms are those of the current week and day of the psalter.

135. In all other cases the psalms are taken from the current week and day of the psalter, unless there are proper antiphons or proper psalms.

V. CANTICLES FROM THE OLD AND NEW TESTAMENTS

136. At morning prayer between the first and the second psalm a canticle from the Old Testament is inserted, in accordance with custom. In addition to the series handed down from the ancient Roman tradition and the other series introduced into the breviary by St. Pius X, several other canticles have been added to the psalter from different books of the Old Testament, in order that each weekday of the four-week cycle may have its own proper canticle and on Sunday the two sections of the Canticle of the Three Children may be alternated.

137. At evening prayer, after the two psalms, a canticle of the New Testament is inserted, from the letters of the apostles or the Book of Revelation. Seven canticles are given for each week of the four-week cycle, one for each day. On the Sundays of Lent, however, in place of the *Alleluia* Canticle from the Book of Revelation, the canticle is from the First Letter of Peter. In addition, on the

solemnity of the Epiphany and the feast of the Transfiguration the canticle is from the First Letter to Timothy; this is indicated in those offices.

138. The gospel Canticles of Zechariah, of Mary, and of Simeon are to be treated with the same solemnity and dignity as are customary at the proclamation of the gospel itself.

139. Both psalmody and readings are arranged in keeping with the received rule of tradition that the Old Testament is read first, then the writings of the apostles, and finally the gospel.

VI. READINGS FROM SACRED SCRIPTURE

A. Reading of Sacred Scripture in General

140. The reading of sacred Scripture, which, following an ancient tradition, takes place publicly in the liturgy, is to have special importance for all Christians, not only in the celebration of the eucharist but also in the divine office. The reason is that this reading is not the result of individual choice or devotion but is the planned decision of the Church itself, in order that in the course of the year the Bride of Christ may unfold the mystery of Christ "from his incarnation and birth until his ascension, the day of Pentecost, and the expectation of blessed hope and of the Lord's return."[6] In addition, the reading of sacred Scripture in the liturgical celebration is always accompanied by prayer in order that the reading may have greater effect and that, in turn, prayer—especially the praying of the psalms—may gain fuller understanding and become more fervent and devout because of the reading.

141. In the liturgy of the hours there is a longer reading of sacred Scripture and a shorter reading.

142. The longer reading, optional at morning prayer and evening prayer, is described in no. 46.

B. Cycle of Scripture Readings in the Office of Readings

143. The cycle of readings from sacred Scripture in the office of readings takes into account both those special seasons during which by an ancient tradition particular books are to be read and the cycle of readings at Mass. The liturgy of the hours is thus coordinated with the Mass in such a way that the scriptural readings in the office complement the readings at Mass and so provide a complete view of the history of salvation.

144. Without prejudice to the exception noted in no. 73, there are no readings from the Gospel in the liturgy of the hours, since in the Mass each year the Gospel is read in its entirety.

145. There are two cycles of biblical readings. The first is a one-year cycle and is incorporated into *The Liturgy of the Hours;* the second, given in the supplement

for optional use, is a two-year cycle, like the cycle of readings at weekday Masses in Ordinary Time.

146. The two-year cycle of readings for the liturgy of the hours is so arranged that each year there are readings from nearly all the books of sacred Scripture as well as longer and more difficult texts that are not suitable for inclusion in the Mass. The New Testament as a whole is read each year, partly in the Mass, partly in the liturgy of the hours; bur for the Old Testament books a selection has been made of those parts that are of greater importance for the understanding of the history of salvation and for deepening devotion.

The complementarity between the readings in the liturgy of the hours and in the Mass in no way assigns the same texts to the same days or spreads the same books over the same seasons. This would leave the liturgy of the hours with the less important passages and upset the sequence of texts. Rather this complementarity necessarily demands that the same book be used in the Mass and in the liturgy of the hours in alternate years or that, if it is read in the same year, there be some interval between them.

147. During Advent, following an ancient tradition, passages are read from Isaiah in a semicontinuous sequence, alternating in a two-year cycle. In addition, the Book of Ruth and certain prophecies from Micah are read. Since there are special readings from 17 to 24 December (both dates included), readings for the Third Week of Advent which fall on these dates are omitted.

148. From 29 December until 5 January the readings for Year I are taken from the Letter to the Colossians (which considers the incarnation of the Lord within the context of the whole history of salvation) and the readings for Year II are taken from the Song of Songs (which foreshadows the union of God and humanity in Christ): "God the Father prepared a wedding feast for God his Son when he united him with human nature in the womb of the Virgin, when he who is God before all ages willed that his Son should become man at the end of the ages."[7]

149. From 7 January until the Saturday after the Epiphany the readings are eschatological texts from Isaiah 60–66 and Baruch. Readings remaining unused are omitted for that year.

150. During Lent the readings for the first year are passages from Deuteronomy and the Letter to the Hebrews. Those for the second year review the history of salvation from Exodus, Leviticus, and Numbers. The Letter to the Hebrews interprets the Old Covenant in the light of the paschal mystery of Christ. A passage from the same letter, on Christ's sacrifice (Hebrews 9:11–28), is read on Good Friday; another, on the Lord's rest (Hebrews 4:1–6), is read on Holy Saturday. On the other days of Holy Week the readings in Year I are the third and fourth Songs of the Servant of the Lord and extracts from Lamentations; in Year II the prophet Jeremiah is read, as a type of Christ in his passion.

151. During the Easter season, apart from the First and Second Sundays of Easter and the solemnities of the Ascension and Pentecost, there are the traditional

readings from the First Letter of Peter, the Book of Revelation, and the Letters of John (for Year I), and from the Acts of the Apostles (for Year II).

152. From the Monday after the feast of the Baptism of the Lord until Lent and from the Monday after Pentecost until Advent there is a continuous series of thirty-four weeks in Ordinary Time.

This series is interrupted from Ash Wednesday until Pentecost. On the Monday after Pentecost Sunday the cycle of readings in Ordinary Time is resumed, beginning with the week after the one interrupted because of Lent; the reading assigned to the Sunday is omitted.

In years with only thirty-three weeks in Ordinary Time, the week immediately following Pentecost is dropped, in order to retain the readings of the last weeks, which are eschatological readings.

The books of the Old Testament are arranged so as to follow the history of salvation: God reveals himself in the history of his people as he leads and enlightens them in progressive stages. This is why prophetic books are read along with the historical books, but with due consideration of the period in which the prophets lived and taught. Hence, the cycle of readings from the Old Testament contains, in Year I, the historical books and prophetic utterances from the Book of Joshua as far as, and including, the time of the exile. In Year II, after the readings from Genesis (read before Lent), the history of salvation is resumed after the exile up to the time of the Maccabees. Year II includes the later prophets, the wisdom literature, and the narratives in Esther, Tobit, and Judith.

The letters of the apostles not read at special times are distributed through the year in a way that takes into account the readings at Mass and the chronological order in which these letters were written.

153. The one-year cycle is shortened in such a way that each year special passages from sacred Scripture are read, but in correlation with the two-year cycle of readings at Mass, to which it is intended to be complementary.

154. Proper readings are assigned for solemnities and feasts; otherwise the readings are taken from the respective Common of Saints.

155. As far as possible, each passage read keeps to a certain unity. In order therefore to strike a balance in length (otherwise difficult to achieve in view of the different literary genres of the books), some verses are occasionally omitted, though omissions are always noted. But it is permissible and commendable to read the complete passage from an approved text.

C. Short Readings

156. The short readings or "chapters" (capitula) are referred to in no. 45, which describes their importance in the liturgy of the hours. They have been chosen to give clear and concise expression to a theme or an exhortation. Care has also been taken to ensure variety.

157. Accordingly, four weekly series of short readings have been composed for Ordinary Time. They are incorporated into the psalter in such a way that the reading changes during the four weeks. There are also weekly series for the seasons of Advent, Christmas, Lent, and Easter. In addition there are proper short readings for solemnities, feasts, and some memorials, as well as one-week series for night prayer.

158. The following determined the choice of short readings:

  a. in accordance with tradition, exclusion of the Gospels;
  b. respect for the special character of Sunday, or even of Friday, and of the individual hours;
  c. use only of the New Testament or the readings at evening prayer, following as they do a New Testament canticle.

VII. READINGS FROM THE FATHERS AND CHURCH WRITERS

159. In keeping with the tradition of the Roman Church the office of readings has, after the biblical reading, a reading from the Fathers or church writers, with a responsory, unless there is to be a reading relating to a saint (see nos. 228–239).

160. Texts for this reading are given from the writings of the Fathers and doctors of the Church, and from other ecclesiastical writers of the Easter and Western Church. Pride of place is given to the Fathers because of their distinctive authority in the Church.

161. In addition to the readings that *The Liturgy of the Hours* assigns to each day, the optional lectionary supplies a larger collection, in order that the treasures of the Church's tradition may be more widely available to those who pray the liturgy of the hours. Everyone is free to take the second reading either from *The Liturgy of the Hours* or from the optional lectionary.

162. Further, the conferences of bishops may prepare additional texts, adapted to the traditions and cultures of their own region,[8] for inclusion in the optional lectionary as a supplement. These texts are to be taken from the works of Catholic writers, outstanding for their teaching and holiness of life.

163. The purpose of the second reading is principally to provide for meditation on the word of God as received by the Church in its tradition. The Church has always been convinced of the need to teach the word of God authentically to believers, so that "the line of interpretation regarding the prophets and apostles may be guided by an ecclesial and catholic understanding."[9]

164. By constant use of the writings handed down by the universal tradition of the Church, those who read them are led to a deeper reflection on sacred Scripture and to a relish and love for it. The writings of the Fathers are an outstanding witness to the contemplation of the word of God over the centuries by the Bride of the incarnate Word: the Church, "possessing the counsel and spirit of

its Bridegroom and God,"[10] is always seeking to attain a more profound understanding of the sacred Scriptures.

165. The reading of the Fathers leads Christians to an understanding also of the liturgical seasons and feasts. In addition, it gives them access to the priceless spiritual treasures that form the unique patrimony of the Church and provide a firm foundation for the spiritual life and a rich source for increasing devotion. Preachers of God's word also have at hand each day superb examples of sacred preaching.

VIII. READINGS IN HONOR OF SAINTS

166. The "hagiograhical" readings or readings in honor of saints are either texts from a Father of the Church or another ecclesiastical writer, referring specifically or rightly applicable to the saint being commemorated, or the readings are texts from the saint's own writings, or are biographical.

167. Those who compose particular propers for saints must ensure historical accuracy[11] as well as genuine spiritual benefit for those who will read or hear the readings about the saints. Anything that merely excites amazement should be carefully avoided. Emphasis should be given to the individual spiritual characteristics of the saints, in a way suited to modern conditions; stress should also be laid on their contribution to the life and spirituality of the Church.

168. A short biographical note, simply giving historical facts and a brief sketch of the saint's life, is provided at the head of the reading. This is for information only and is not for reading aloud.

IX. RESPONSORIES

169. Its responsory follows the biblical reading in the office of readings. The text of this responsory has been drawn from traditional sources or freshly composed, in order to throw new light on the passage just read, put it in the context of the history of salvation, lead from the Old Testament to the New, turn what has been read into prayer and contemplation, or provide pleasant variety by its poetic beauty.

170. A pertinent responsory also follows the second reading. It is less closely liked with the text of the reading, however, and thus makes for a greater freedom in meditation.

171. The responsories and the portions to be repeated even in private recitation therefore retain their value. The customary reprise of the whole responsory may be omitted when the office is not being sung, unless the sense requires this repetition.

172. In a similar but simpler way, the responsory at morning prayer, evening prayer, and night prayer (see nos. 49 and 89), and the verse at daytime prayer,

are linked to the short reading as a kind of acclamation, enabling God's word to enter more deeply into the mind and heart of the one listening or reading.

X. HYMNS AND OTHER NONBIBLICAL SONGS

173. A very ancient tradition gives hymns the place in the office that they still retain.[12] By their mystical and poetic character they are specifically designed for God's praise. But they also are an element for the people; in fact more often than the other parts of the office the hymns bring out the proper theme of individual hours or feasts and incline and draw the spirit to a devout celebration. The beauty of their language often adds to this power. Furthermore, in the office hymns are the main poetic element created by the Church.

174. A hymn follows the traditional rule of ending with a doxology, usually addressed to the same divine person as the hymn itself.

175. In the office for Ordinary Time, to ensure variety, a twofold cycle of hymns is given for each hour, for use in alternate weeks.

176. In addition, a twofold cycle of hymns has been introduced into the office of readings for Ordinary Time, one for use at night and the other for use during the day.

177. New hymns can be set to traditional melodies of the same rhythm and meter.

178. For vernacular celebration, the conferences of bishops may adapt the Latin hymns to suit the character of their own language and introduce fresh compositions,[13] provided these are in complete harmony with the spirit of the hour, season, or feast. Great care must be taken not to allow popular songs that have no artistic merit and are not in keeping with the dignity of the liturgy.

XI. INTERCESSIONS, LORD'S PRAYER, AND CONCLUDING PRAYER

A. The Prayers or Intercessions at Morning Prayer and Evening Prayer

179. The liturgy of the hours is a celebration in praise of God. Yet Jewish and Christian tradition does not separate prayer of petition from praise of God; often enough, praise turns somehow to petition. The Apostle Paul exhorts us to offer "prayers, petitions, intercessions, and thanksgiving for all: for kings and all in authority, so that we may be able to live quiet and peaceful lives in all reverence and decency, for this is good and acceptable before God our Savior, who wishes all to be saved and to come to the knowledge of the truth" (1 Timothy 2:1–4). The Fathers of the Church frequently explained this as an exhortation to offer prayer in the morning and in the evening.[14]

180. The general intercessions, restored in the Mass of the Roman Rite, have their place also at evening prayer, though in a different fashion, as will be explained later.

181. Since traditionally morning prayer puts the whole day in God's hands, there are invocations at morning prayer for the purpose of commending or consecrating the day to God.

182. The word *preces* covers both the intercessions at evening prayer and the invocations for dedicating the day to God at morning prayer.

183. In the interest of variety and especially of giving fuller expression to the many needs of the Church and of all people in relation to different states of life, groups, persons, circumstances, and seasons, different intercessory formularies are given for each day of the four-week psalter in Ordinary Time and for the special seasons of the liturgical year, as well as for certain feasts.

184. In addition, the conferences of bishops have the right to adapt the formularies given in the book of the liturgy of the hours and also to approve new ones,[15] in accordance with the norms that follow.

185. As in the Lord's Prayer, petitions should be linked with praise of God and acknowledgment of his glory or with a reference to the history of salvation.

186. In the intercessions at evening prayer the last intention is always for the dead.

187. Since the liturgy of the hours is above all the prayer of the whole Church for the whole Church, indeed for the salvation of the whole world,[16] universal intentions should take precedence over all others, namely, for: the Church and its ministers; secular authorities; the poor, the sick, and the sorrowful; the needs of the whole world, that is, peace and other intentions of this kind.

188. It is permissible, however, to include particular intentions at both morning and evening prayer.

189. The intercessions in the office are so arranged that they can be adapted for celebration with a congregation or in a small community or for private recitation.

190. The intercessions in a celebration with a congregation or in common are thus introduced by a brief invitation, given by the priest or minister and designating the single response that the congregation is to repeat after each petition.

191. Further, the intentions are phrased as direct addresses to God and thus are suitable for both common celebration and private recitation.

192. Each intention consists of two parts; the second may be used as an alternative response.

193. Different methods can therefore be used for the intercessions. The priest or minister may say both parts of the intention and the congregation respond with a uniform response or a silent pause, or the priest or minister may say only the first part of the intention and the congregation respond with the second part.

B. Lord's Prayer

194. In accord with ancient tradition, the Lord's prayer has a place suited to its dignity, namely, after the intercessions at morning prayer and evening prayer, the hours most often celebrated with the people.

195. Henceforth, therefore, the Lord's prayer will be said with the solemnity on three occasions during the day: at Mass, at morning prayer, and at evening prayer.

196. The Lord's Prayer is said by all after a brief introduction, if this seems opportune.

C. Concluding Prayer

197. The concluding prayer at the end marks the completion of an entire hour. In a celebration in public and with a congregation, it belongs by tradition to a priest or deacon to say this prayer.[17]

198. In the office of readings, this prayer is as a rule the prayer proper to the day. At night prayer, the prayer is always the prayer given in the psalter for that hour.

199. The concluding prayer at morning prayer and evening prayer is taken from the proper on Sundays, on the weekdays of the seasons of Advent, Christmas, Lent, and Easter, and on solemnities, feasts, and memorials. On weekdays in Ordinary Time the prayer is the one given in the four-week psalter to express the character of these two hours.

200. The concluding prayer at daytime prayer is taken from the proper on Sundays, on the weekdays of the seasons of Advent, Christmas, Lent, and Easter, and on solemnities and feasts. On other days the prayers are those that express the character of the particular hour. These are given in the four-week psalter.

XII. SACRED SILENCE

201. It is a general principle that care should be taken in liturgical services to see that "at the proper times all observe a reverent silence."[18] An opportunity for silence should therefore be provided in the celebration of the liturgy of the hours.

202. In order to receive in our hearts the full sound of the voice of the Holy Spirit and to unite our personal prayer more closely with the word of God and the public voice of the Church, it is permissible, as occasion offers and prudence suggests, to have an interval of silence. It may come either after the repetition of the antiphon at the end of the psalm, in the traditional way, especially if the psalm-prayer is to be said after the pause (see no. 112), or after the shortest or longest readings, either before or after the responsory.

Care must be taken to avoid the kind of silence that would disturb the structure of the office or annoy and weary those taking part.

203. In individual recitation there is even greater freedom to pause in meditation on some text that moves the spirit; the office does not on this account lose its public character.

CHAPTER IV
VARIOUS CELEBRATIONS THROUGHOUT THE YEAR

I. MYSTERIES OF THE LORD

A. Sunday

204. The office of Sunday begins with evening prayer I, which is taken entirely from the four-week psalter, except those parts that are marked as proper.

205. When a feast of the Lord is celebrated on Sunday, it has a proper evening prayer I.

206. The way to celebrate Sunday vigils, as circumstances suggest, has been discussed in no. 73.

207. It is of great advantage to celebrate, when possible, at least evening prayer with the people, in keeping with a very ancient tradition.[1]

B. Easter Triduum

208. For the Easter triduum in the office is celebrated in the way set forth in the Proper of Seasons.

209. Those who take part in the evening Mass of the Lord's Supper or the celebration of the Lord's passion on Good Friday do not say evening prayer on either day.

210. On Good Friday and Holy Saturday the office of readings should be celebrated publicly with the people before morning prayer, as far as this is possible.

211. Night prayer for Holy Saturday is said only by those who are not present at the Easter Vigil.

212. The Easter Vigil takes the place of the office of readings. Those not present at the solemn celebration of the Vigil should therefore read at least four of its readings with the chants and prayers. It is desirable that these be the readings from Exodus, Ezekiel, St. Paul, and from the Gospel. The *Te Deum* follows, then the prayer of the day.

213. Morning prayer for Easter Sunday is said by all. It is fitting that evening prayer be celebrated in a more solemn way to mark the ending of so holy a day and to commemorate the occasions when the Lord showed himself to his disciples. Great care should be taken to maintain, where it exists, the particular tradition of celebrating evening prayer on Easter Sunday in honor of baptism. During this there is a procession to the font as the psalms are being sung.

214. The liturgy of the hours takes on a paschal character from the acclamation, Alleluia that concludes most antiphons (see no. 120), from the hymns, antiphons, and special intercessions, and from the proper readings assigned to each hour.

D. Christmas Season

215. On Christmas eve it is fitting that by means of the office of readings, a solemn vigil be celebrated before Mass. Night prayer is not said by those present at the vigil.

216. Morning prayer on Christmas Day is said as a rule before the Mass at Dawn.

E. Other Solemnities and Feasts of the Lord

217. In arranging the office for solemnities and feasts of the Lord, what is said in nos. 225–233 should be observed, with any necessary changes.

II. THE SAINTS

218. The celebrations of the saints are arranged so that they do not take precedence over those feast days and special seasons that commemorate the mysteries of salvation.[2] Nor are they allowed to break up the sequence of psalms and biblical readings or to give rise to undue repetitions. At the same time, the plan makes proper provision for the rightful honoring of the individual saints. These principles form the basis for the reform of the calendar, carried out by order of Vatican Council II, and for the plan for celebrating the saints in the liturgy of the hours that is described in the following paragraphs.

219. Celebrations in honor of the saints are either solemnities, feasts, or memorials.

220. Memorials are either obligatory memorials or, when not so classified, optional memorials. In deciding on the merits of celebrating an optional memorial in an office to be celebrated with the people or in common, account should be taken of the general good or of the genuine devotion of the congregation, not simply that of the person presiding.

221. When more than one optional memorial falls on the same day, only one may be celebrated; the rest are omitted.

222. Only solemnities are transferred, in accordance with the rubrics.

223. The norms that follow apply to the saints entered in the General Roman Calendar and to those with a place in particular calendars.

224. Where proper parts are not given, they are supplied from the respective Common of Saints.

1. Arrangement of the Office for Solemnities

225. Solemnities have an evening prayer I on the preceding day.

226. At evening prayer I and II, the hymn, the antiphons, the short reading with its responsory, and the concluding prayer are proper. Where anything proper is missing, it is supplied from the common.

In keeping with an ancient tradition, at evening prayer I both psalms are as a rule taken form the *Laudate* Psalms (Psalm 113, 117, 135, 146, 147 A, 147 B). The New Testament canticle is noted in its appropriate place. At evening prayer II the psalms and canticles are proper; the intercessions are either proper or from the common.

227. At morning prayer, the hymn, the antiphons, the short reading with its responsory, and the concluding prayer are proper. Where anything proper is missing, it is supplied from the common. The psalms are to be taken from the Sunday of Week I of the four-week psalter; the intercessions are either proper or from the common.

228. In the office of readings, everything is proper: the hymn, the antiphons and psalms, the readings and the responsories. The first reading is from Scripture; the second is about the saint. In the case of a saint with a purely local cult and without special texts even in the local proper, everything is taken from the common.

At the end of the office of readings the *Te Deum* and the proper prayer are said.

229. At daytime prayer, the hymn of the weekday is used, unless other directions are given. The psalms are from the Gradual Psalms with a proper antiphon. On Sundays the psalms are taken from the Sunday of Week I of the four-week psalter and the short reading and concluding prayer are proper. But on certain solemnities of the Lord there are special psalms.

230. At night prayer, everything is said as on Sundays, after evening prayer I and II respectively.

2. Arrangement of the Office for Feasts

231. Feasts have no evening prayer I, except those feasts of the Lord that fall on a Sunday. At the office of readings, at morning prayer, and at evening prayer, all is done as on solemnities.

232. At daytime prayer, the hymn of the weekday is used. The weekday psalms with their antiphons are said, unless a special reason or tradition requires a proper antiphon; this will be indicated as the case occurs. The reading and concluding prayer are proper.

233. Night prayer is said as on ordinary days.

3. Arrangement of the Office for Memorials

234. In the arrangement of the office there is no difference between obligatory and optional memorials, except in the case of optional memorials falling during privileged seasons.

A. MEMORIALS DURING ORDINARY TIME

235. In the office of readings, at morning prayer, and at evening prayer:

   a. the psalms and their antiphons are taken from the current week and day, unless there are proper antiphons or proper psalms, which is indicated as the case occurs;

   b. the antiphon at the invitatory, the hymn, the short reading, the antiphons at the Canticles of Zechariah and of Mary, and the intercessions must be those of the saint if these are given in the proper; otherwise, they are taken either from the common or from the current week and day;

   c. the concluding prayer from the office of the saint is to be said;

   d. in the office of readings, the Scripture reading with its responsory is from the current cycle. The second reading is about the saint, with a proper responsory or one taken from the common; if there is no proper reading, the patristic reading for the day is used. The *Te Deum* is not said.

236. At daytime prayer and night prayer, all is from the weekday and nothing is from the office of the saint.

B. MEMORIALS DURING PRIVILEGED SEASONS

237. On Sundays, solemnities, and feasts, on Ash Wednesday, during Holy Week, and during the octave of Easter, memorials that happen to fall on these days are disregarded.

238. On the weekdays from 17 to 24 December, during the Octave of Christmas, and on the weekdays of Lent, no obligatory memorials are celebrated, even to particular calendars. When any happen to fall during Lent in a given year, they are treated as optional memorials.

239. During privileged seasons, if it is desired to celebrate the office of a saint on a day assigned to his or her memorial:

   a. in the office of readings, after the patristic reading (with its responsory) from the Proper of Seasons, a proper reading about the saint (with its responsory) may follow, with the concluding prayer of the saint;

   b. at morning prayer and evening prayer, the ending of the concluding prayer may be omitted and the saint's antiphon (from the proper or common) and prayer may be added.

C. MEMORIAL OF THE BLESSED VIRGIN MARY ON SATURDAY

240. On Saturdays in Ordinary Time, when optional memorials are permitted, an optional memorial of the Blessed Virgin Mary may be celebrated in the same way as other memorials, with its own proper reading.

III. CALENDAR AND OPTION TO CHOOSE AN OFFICE OR PART OF AN OFFICE

A. Calendar to Be Followed

241. The office in choir and in common is to be celebrated according to the proper calendar of the diocese, of the religious family, or of the individual churches.[3] Members of religious institutes join with the community of the local Church in celebrating the dedication of the cathedral and the feasts of the principal patrons of the place and of the wider geographical region in which they live.[4]

242. When clerics or religious who are obliged under any title to pray the divine office join in an office celebrated in common according to a calendar or rite different from their own, they fulfill their obligation in respect to the part of the office at which they are present.

243. In private celebration, the calendar of the place or the person's own calendar may be followed, except on proper solemnities and on proper feasts.[5]

B. Option to Choose an Office

244. On weekdays when an optional memorial is permitted, for a good reason the office of a saint listed on that day in the Roman Martyrology, or in an approved appendix to it, may be celebrated in the same way as other memorials (see nos. 234–239).

245. For a public cause or out of devotion, except on solemnities, the Sundays of the seasons of Advent, Lent, and Easter, Ash Wednesday, Holy Week, the octave of Easter, and 2 November, a votive office may be celebrated, in whole or in part: for example, on the occasion of a pilgrimage, a local feast, or the external solemnity of a saint.

C. Option to Choose Texts

246. In certain particular cases there is an option choose texts different from those given for the day, provided there is no distortion of the general arrangement of each hour and the rules that follow are respected.

247. In the office for Sundays, solemnities, feasts of the Lord listed in the General Calendar, the weekdays of Lent and Holy Week, the days within the octaves of Easter and Christmas, and the weekdays from 17 to 24 December inclusive, it is never permissible to change the formularies that are proper or adapted to the celebration, such as antiphons, hymns, readings, responsories, prayers, and very often also the psalms.

In place of the Sunday psalms of the current week, there is an option to substitute the Sunday psalms of a different week, and, in the case of an office celebrated with a congregation, even other psalms especially chosen to lead the people step by step to an understanding of the psalms.

248. In the office of readings, the current cycle of sacred Scripture must always be respected. The Church's intent that "a more representative portion of the holy Scriptures will be read to the people in the course of a prescribed number of years"[6] applies also to the divine office.

Therefore the cycle of readings from Scripture that is provided in the office of readings must not be set aside during the seasons of Advent, Christmas, Lent, and Easter. During Ordinary Time, however, on a particular day or for a few days in succession, it is permissible, for a good reason, to choose readings from those provided on other days or even other biblical readings: for example, on the occasion of retreats, pastoral gatherings, prayers for Christian unity, or other such events.

249. When the continuous reading is interrupted because of a solemnity or feast or special celebration, it is allowed during the same week, taking into account the readings for the whole week, either to combine the parts omitted with others or to decide which of the texts are to be preferred.

250. The office of readings also offers the option to choose, with a good reason, another reading from the same season, taken from *The Liturgy of the Hours* or the optional lectionary (no. 161), in preference to the second reading appointed for the day. On weekdays in Ordinary Time and, if it seems opportune, even in the seasons of Advent, Christmas, Lent, and Easter, the choice is open for a semi-continuous reading of the work of a Father of the Church, in harmony with the biblical and liturgical context.

251. The readings, prayers, songs, and intercessions appointed for the weekdays of a particular season may be used on other weekdays of the same season.

252. Everyone should be concerned to respect the complete cycle of the four-week psalter.[7] Still, for spiritual or pastoral advantage, the psalms appointed for a particular day may be replaced with others from the same hour of a different day. There are also circumstances occasionally arising when it is permissible to choose suitable psalms and other texts in the way done for a votive office.

CHAPTER V
RITES FOR CELEBRATION IN COMMON

I. OFFICES TO BE CARRIED OUT

253. In the celebration of the liturgy of the hours, as in all other liturgical services, "each one, minister or layperson, who has an office to perform, should do all of, but only, those parts which pertain to that office by the nature of the rite and the principles of liturgy."[1]

254. When a bishop presides, especially in the cathedral, he should be attended by his college of priests and by ministers and the people should take a full and active part. A priest or deacon should normally preside at every celebration with a congregation and ministers should also be present.

255. The priest or deacon who presides at a celebration may wear a stole over the alb or surplice; a priest may also wear a cope. On greater solemnities the wearing of the cope by many priests or of the dalmatic by many deacons is permitted.

256. It belongs to the presiding priest or deacon, at the chair, to open the celebration with the introductory verse, begin the Lord's Prayer, say the concluding prayer, greet the people, bless them, and dismiss them.

257. Either the priest or a minister may lead the intercessions.

258. In the absence of a priest or deacon, the one who presides at the office is only one among equals and does not enter the sanctuary or greet and bless the people.

259. Those who act as readers, standing in a convenient place, read either the long readings or the short readings.

260. A cantor or cantors should intone the antiphons, psalms, and other chants. With regard to the psalmody, the directions of nos. 121–125 should be followed.

261. During the gospel canticle at morning prayer and evening prayer there may be an incensation of the altar, then of the priest and congregation.

262. The choral obligation tot he community, not to the place of celebration which need not be a church, especially in the case of those hours that are celebrated without solemnity.

263. All taking part stand during:
   a. the introduction to the office and the introductory verses of each hour;
   b. the hymn;
   c. the gospel canticle;
   d. the intercessions, the Lord's Prayer, and the concluding prayer.

264. All sit to listen to the readings, except the gospel.

265. The assembly either sits or stands, depending on custom, while the psalms and other canticles (with their antiphons) are being said.

266. All make the sign of the cross, from the forehead to breast and from left shoulder to right, at:
   a. the beginning of the hours, when *God, come to my assistance* is being said;
   b. the beginning of the gospel, the Canticles of Zechariah, of Mary, and of Simeon.

The sign of the cross is made on the mouth at the beginning of the invitatory, at *Lord, open my lips.*

II. SINGING IN THE OFFICE

267. In the rubrics and norms of this Instruction, the words "say," "recite," etc., are to be understood to refer to either singing or recitation, in the light of the principles that follow.

268. "The sung celebration of the divine office is more in keeping with the nature of this prayer and a mark of both higher solemnity and closer union of hearts in offering praise to God. . . . Therefore the signing of the office is earnestly recommended to those who carry out the office in choir or in common."[2]

269. The declarations of Vatican Council II on liturgical singing apply to all liturgical services but in a special way to the liturgy of the hours.[3] Though every part of it has been revised in such a way that all may be fruitfully recited even by individuals, many of these parts are lyrical in form and do not yield their fuller meaning unless they are sung, especially the psalms, canticles, hymns, and responsories.

270. Hence, in celebrating the liturgy singing is not to be regarded as an embellishment superimposed on prayer; rather, it wells up from the depths of a soul intent on prayer and the praise of God and reveals in a full and complete way the community nature of Christian worship.

Christian communities of all kinds seeking to use this form of prayer as frequently as possible are to be commended. Clerics and religious, as well as all the people of God, must be trained by suitable catechesis and practice to join together in singing the hours in a spirit of joy, especially on Sundays and holydays. But it is no easy task to sing the entire office; nor is the Church's praise to be considered either by origin or by nature the exclusive possession of clerics and monks but the property of the whole Christian community. Therefore several principles must be kept simultaneously in mind if the sung celebration of the liturgy of the hours is to be performed correctly and to stand out in its true nature and splendor.

271. It is particularly appropriate that there be singing at least on Sundays and holydays, so that the different degrees of solemnity will thus come to be recognized.

272. It is the same with the hours: all are not equal importance; thus it is desirable that those that are the true hinges of the office, that is, morning prayer and evening prayer, should receive greater prominence through the use of singing.

273. A celebration with singing throughout is commendable, provided it has artistic and spiritual excellence; but it may be useful on occasion to apply the principle of "progressive solemnity." There are practical reasons for this, as well as the fact that in this way the various elements of liturgical celebration are not

treated indiscriminately, but each can again be given its connatural meaning and genuine function. The liturgy of the hours is then not seen as a beautiful memorial of the past demanding intact preservation as an object of admiration; rather it is seen as open to constantly new forms of life and growth and to being the unmistakable sign of a community's vibrant vitality.

The principle of "progressive solemnity" therefore is one that recognizes several intermediate stages between singing the office in full and just reciting all the parts. Its application offers the possibility of a rich and pleasing variety. The criteria are the particular day or hour being celebrated, the character of the individual elements comprising the office, the size and composition of the community, as well as the number of singers available in the circumstances.

With this increased range of variation, it is possible for the public praise of the Church to be sung more frequently than formerly and to be adapted in a variety of ways to different circumstances. There is also great hope that new ways and expressions of public worship may be found for our own age, as has clearly always happened in the life of the Church.

274. For liturgical celebrations sung in Latin, Gregorian chant, as the music proper to the Roman liturgy, should have pride of place, all other things being equal.[4] Nevertheless, "the Church does not exclude any type of sacred music from liturgical services as long as the music matches the spirit of the service itself and the character of individual parts and is not a hindrance to the required active participation of the people."[5] At a sung office, if a melody is not available for the given antiphon, another antiphon should be taken from those in the repertoire, provided it is suitable in terms of nos. 113 and 121–125.

275. Since the liturgy of the hours may be celebrated in the vernacular, "appropriate measures are to be taken to prepare melodies for use in the vernacular singing of the divine office."[6]

276. But it is permissible to sing the various parts in different languages at one and the same celebration.[7]

277. The decision on which parts to choose for singing follows from the authentic structure of a liturgical celebration. This demands that the significance and function of each part and of singing should be fully respected. Some parts by their nature call for singing:[8] in particular, acclamations, responses to the greetings of priest and ministers, responses in litanies, also antiphons and psalms, the verses and reprises in responsories, hymns and canticles.[9]

278. Clearly the psalms are closely bound up with music (see nos. 103–120), as both Jewish and Christian tradition confirm. In fact a complete understanding of many of the psalms is greatly assisted by singing them or at least not losing sight of their poetic and musical character. Accordingly, whenever possible singing the psalms should have preference, at least for the major days and hours and in view of the character of the psalms themselves.

279. The different ways of reciting the psalms have been described in nos. 121–123. Varying these ways should depend not so much on external circumstances as on the different genres of the psalms to be recited in the same celebration. Thus the wisdom psalms and the narrative psalms are perhaps better listened to, whereas psalms of praise and thanksgiving are of their nature designed for singing in common. The main consideration is to ensure that the celebration is not too inflexible or elaborate nor concerned merely with formal observance of rules, but that it matches the reality of what is celebrated. The primary aim must be to inspire the hearts with a desire for genuine prayer and to show that the celebration of God's praise is a thing of joy (see Psalm 147).

280. Even when the hours are recited, hymns can nourish prayer, provided they have doctrinal and literary excellence; but of their nature they are designed for singing and so, as far as possible, at a celebration in common they should be sung.

281. The short responsory after the reading at morning prayer and evening prayer (see no. 49) is of its nature designed for singing and indeed for congregational singing.

282. The responsories following the readings in the office of readings by their very nature and function also call for their being sung. In the plan of the office, however, they are composed in such a way that they retain their power even in individual and private recitation. Responsories set to simpler melodies can be sung more frequently than those responsories drawn from the traditional liturgical books.

283. The longer readings and the short readings are not of themselves designed for singing. When they are proclaimed, great care should be taken that the readings is dignified, clear, and distinct and that it is really audible and fully intelligible for all. The only acceptable melody for a reading is therefore one that best ensures the hearing of the words and the understanding of the text.

284. Texts that are said only by the person presiding, such as the concluding prayer, can be sung gracefully and appropriately, especially in Latin. This, however, will be more difficult in some languages, unless singing makes the texts more clearly audible for all.

NOTES

CHAPTER I

1. See Acts 1:14, 4:24, 12:5 and 12. See also Ephesians 5:19–21.

2. See Acts 2:1–15.

3. SC, 83.

4. See Luke 3:21–22.

5. See Luke 6:12.

6. See Matthew 14:19, 15:36; Mark 6:41, 8:7; Luke 9:16; John 6:11.

7. See Luke 9:28–29.

8. See Mark 7:34.

9. See John 11:41f.

10. See Luke 9:18.

11. See Luke 11:1.

12. See Matthew 11:25ff; Luke 10:21ff.

13. See Matthew 19:13.

14. See Luke 22:32.

15. See Mark 1:35, 6:46; Luke 5:16. See also Matthew 4:1 and par.; Matthew 14:23.

16. See Mark 1:35.

17. See Matthew 14:23 and 25; Mark 6:46 and 48.

18. See Luke 6:12.

19. See Luke 4:16.

20. See Matthew 21:13.

21. See Matthew 14:19 and par.; Matthew 15:36 and par.

22. See Matthew 26:26 and par.

23. See Luke 24:30.

24. See Matthew 26:30 and par.

25. See John 12:27ff.

26. See John 17:1–26.

27. See Matthew 26:36–44 and par.

28. See Luke 23:34 and 46; Matthew 27:46; Mark 15:34.

29. See Hebrews 7:25.

30. Matthew 5:44, 7:7, 26:41; Mark 13:33, 14:38; Luke 6:28, 10:2, 11:9, 22:40 and 46.

31. John 14:13ff., 15:16, 16:23ff. And 26.

32. See Matthew 6:9–13; Luke 11:2–4

33. See Luke 18:1.

34. See Luke 18:9–14.

35. See Luke 21:36; Mark 13:33.

36. See Luke 11:5–13, 18:1–8; John 14:13, 16:23.

37. See Matthew 6:5–8, 23:14; Luke 20:47; John 4:23.

38. See Romans 8:15 and 26:1; 1 Corinthians 12:3; Galatians 4:6; Jude 20.

39. See 2 Corinthians 1:20; Colossians 3:17.

40. See Hebrews 13:15.

41. See Romans 12:12; 1 Corinthians 7:5; Ephesians 6:18; Colossians 4:2; 1 Thessalonians 5:17; 1 Timothy 5:5; 1 Peter 4:7.

42. See 1 Timothy 4:5; James 5:1ff.; 1 John 3:22, 5:14ff.

43. See Ephesians 5:19ff.; Hebrews 13:15; Revelation 19:5.

44. See Colossians 3:17; Philippians 4:6; 1 Thessalonians 5:17; 1 Timothy 2:1.

45. See Romans 8:26; Philippians 4:6.

46. See Romans 15:30; 1 Timothy 2:1ff.; Ephesians 6:18; 1 Thessalonians 5:25; James 5:14 and 16.

47. See 1 Timothy 2:5; Hebrews 8:6, 9:15, 12:24.

48. See Romans 5:2; Ephesians 2:18, 3:12.

49. See SC, 83.

50. See LG, 10.

51. Augustine, *Enarrat. In Ps. 85,* 1: CCL 39, 1176.

52. See Luke 10:21, the occasion when Jesus "rejoiced in the Holy Spirit and said: 'I thank you, Father . . . .'"

53. See Acts 2:42 Gr.

54. See Matthew 6:6.

55. See SC, 12.

56. See SC, 83–84.

57. See SC, 88.

58. SC, 94.

59. See PO, 5.

60. CD, 30.

61. SC, 5.

62. See SC, 83 and 98.

63. SC, 7.

64. See SC, 10.

65. SC, 33.

66. See SC, 24.

67. See SC, 33.

68. 1 Thessalonians 5:17.

69. See Hebrews 13:15.

70. SC, 84.

71. SC, 85.

72. See SC, 83.

73. LG, 50; SC, 8 and 104.

74. LG, 48.

75. See Romans 8:19.

76. See SC, 83.

77. See Hebrews 5:7.

78. See PO, 6.

79. See LG, 41.

80. See n. 24 of this Instruction.

81. See PC, 7.

82. See, 10.

83. See, 2.

84. See John 15:5.

85. See SC, 86.

86. See Ephesians 2:21–22.

87. See Ephesians 4:13.

88. See SC, 2.

89. See SC, 90 and *Rule of St. Benedict*, ch. 19.

90. See PO, 14; OT, 8.

91. See SC, 26.

92. See SC, 41.

93. CD, 11.

94. See, 42. See also AA, 10.

95. See SC, 26 and 84.

96. See AG, 17.

97. CD, 15.

98. See SC, 100.

99. See PO, 5.

100. See nn. 100–109 of this Instruction.

101. CD, 33; see also PC, 6, 7, 15; AG, 15.

102. See SC, 99.

103. See SC, 100.

104. See John 4:23.

105. See GE, 2; AA, 16.

106. See AA, 11.

107. See PO, 13.

108. See SC, 41; LG, 21.

109. See LG, 26; CD, 15.

110. See PO, 13.

111. See PO, 5.

112. See John 10:11, 17:20 and 23.

113. See SC, 90.

114. See LG, 41.

115. See DV, 25; PO, 13.

116. See Paul VI, Motu Proprio *Sacrum Diacornatus Ordinem*, 18 June 1967, n. 27.

117. See SCR, Instr. *Inter oecumenici*, 78b.

118. See SC, 95.

119. See Acts 4:32.

120. See SC, 100.

121. See SC, 26, 28–30.

122. See SC, 27.

CHAPTER II

1. See Hebrews 3:7–4:17

2. SC, 89a; see also n. 100.

3. Basil the Great, *Regulae fusius tractatae resp.* 37, 3: PG 31, 1014.

4. Cyprian, *De oratione dominica* 35: PL 4, 561.

5. Basil the Great, *Regulae fusius tractatae resp.* 37, 3: PG 31, 1015.

6. See Psalm 141:2.

7. John Cassian, *De institutione coenob.* 3,3: PL 49, 124, 125.

8. Cyprian, *De oratione dominica* 35: PL 4, 560.

9. *The Roman Pontifical*, Ordination of Priests, n. 14.

10. Ambrose, *De officiis ministrorum* 1, 20, 88: PL 16, 50. See also DV, 25.

11. SC, 89 c.

12. Augustine, *Sermo Guelferbytanus* 5; PL Suppl 2, 550.

13. Ibid.: PL Suppl 2, 552.

14. See SC, 89.

15. See SC, 38.

CHAPTER III

1. SC, 90.

2. *Rule of St. Benedict*, ch. 19.

3. See *Rule of St. Benedict*, ch. 19.

4. See Matthew 22:44ff.

5. See SC, 91.

6. SC, 102.

7. Gregory the Great, *Homila 34 in Evangelia:* PL 76: 1282.

8. See SC, 38.

9. Vincent of Lerins, *Commonitorium* 2: PL 50, 640.

10. Bernard of Clairvaux, *Sermo 3 in vigilia Nativitatis* 1: PL 183 (ed. 1879) 94.

11. See SC, 92 c.

12. See SC, 93.

13. See SC, 38.

14. Thus, for example, John Chrysostom, *In Epist. Ad Tim 1*, Homilia 6: PG 62, 530.

15. See SC, 38.

16. See SC, 83 and 89.

17. See n. 256 of this Instruction.

18. SC, 30.

CHAPTER IV

1. See SC, 100.

2. See SC, 111.

3. See GNLY, 52.

4. See *ibid.*, 52 c.

5. See *ibid.* Table of Liturgical Days, nos. 4 and 8.

6. SC, 51.

7. See nn. 100–109 of this Instruction.

CHAPTER V

1. SC, 28.

2. SCR, Instr. *Musicam sacram*, 5 March 1967, 37. See also SC, 99.

3. See SC, 113.

4. See SC, 116.

5. *Musicam sacram*, 9; see also SC, 116.

6. *Musicam sacram*, 41; see also nn. 54–61.

7. See *ibid.*, n. 51.

8. See *ibid.*, n. 6.

9. See *ibid.*, nn. 16 a and 38.

DEDICATION OF
A CHURCH AND AN ALTAR

EXCERPTS
CONGREGATION FOR THE SACRAMENTS AND DIVINE WORSHIP
1989

OVERVIEW OF *DEDICATION OF A CHURCH AND AN ALTAR*

Thomas G. Simons

The rites for the dedication of a church and an altar *(Ordo dedicationis ecclesiae et altaris)* were published by the Congregation for the Sacraments and Divine Worship on the solemnity of Pentecost, May 29, 1977, and are part of *The Roman Pontifical.* The English translation of the rites was prepared by the International Commission on English in the Liturgy and approved in 1978 for interim use by the Executive Committee of the U.S. National Conference of Catholic Bishops. A revised text was approved on August 15, 1989, and currently remains in use.

The 1977 rites were actually the product of two developments. They were in part the result of a reform of the pontifical, which appeared in a revised edition in 1961, on the eve of the Second Vatican Council. They were also the result of the conciliar reform of all of the liturgical books of the Roman church. A detailed review of the various steps and stages in the evolution of these rites can be found in Annibale Bugnini's work, *The Reform of the Liturgy (1948–1975)* (Collegeville, Minnesota: The Liturgical Press, 1990).

Vatican II's Constitution on the Sacred Liturgy *Sacrosanctum concilium* (SC), in its chapter on sacred art and furnishings, states that "[w]hen churches are to be built, let great care be taken that they are well suited to celebrating liturgical services and to bringing about the active participation of the faithful" (#124). The rites for dedicating a church and an altar express this goal and bring the connection between ecclesiology and liturgy to the forefront. The rites also mark and celebrate the preparation, prayer and process that lead to the construction of the church building.

OVERVIEW OF THE RITES

Dedication of a Church and an Altar is divided into eight chapters. Introductory notes precede each chapter and offer directives and other material to aid in the celebration of the rites. The introduction to chapter two serves as a pastoral introduction to all of the rites.

Chapter one presents the "Rite of Laying of a Foundation Stone or Beginning Work on the Building of a Church." The rite is a blessing of the human work that is beginning and a dedication of that work to God. This is in accord with all of the revised dedication rituals. The rite signifies the beginning of the dedication of the people, which will be completed when the eucharist is celebrated in the new church. This rite reminds the members of the community that "unless the *Lord* builds the house, those who build it labor in vain" (Psalm 127:1).

Chapter two, "Dedication of a Church," constitutes the largest part of the text. The first three paragraphs of the pastoral introduction to this chapter discuss the nature and dignity of church buildings and offer a theological framework for the Rite of Dedication. The norms of the *General Instruction of the*

Roman Missal are recalled, as is the understanding that the nature of the liturgical assembly and the celebration of the sacraments should guide the plan and shape of the church.

The introduction to chapter two also discusses the "title" or name of the church; the role of the bishop as the presider at the rite; other ministers of the liturgy; the day chosen for the celebration of the dedication; the appropriate texts from the lectionary, sacramentary and the Liturgy of the Hours; adaptation of the rite; pastoral preparation for the celebration of the rite; requisites (such as furnishings and appointments) needed for the celebration of the rite; and the celebration of the anniversary of the dedication of the cathedral church or any other particular church.

Chapter three concerns the "Dedication of a Church in Which Mass Is Already Being Celebrated Regularly." While the introduction to this chapter states clearly that "as far as possible, Mass is not celebrated in a new church before it is dedicated," this chapter sets out the rite to be used when the sacred mysteries are already being regularly celebrated in a new church building. This rite differs from that described in chapter two in that ritual actions and texts that are clearly extraneous to the situation or irrelevant to the condition of the church being dedicated are either adapted or omitted.

Chapter four, "Rite of Dedication of an Altar," addresses the rich, symbolic character of the altar in Christian tradition. The Rite of Dedication of an Altar makes the symbolism of the altar explicit: The Christian altar is a sign of Christ, the anointed one, and is likewise anointed as a visible sign of the mystery of Christ present. There may be occasions when only the altar (and not the church) is to be dedicated; for example, when a permanent altar is replacing a temporary one, or when a new altar has been fashioned or restored from a previous altar, or when a totally new altar has been acquired.

The placement of relics beneath the altar, a time-honored practice, needs to be properly understood and carefully considered. This issue is given some attention in this chapter, but is more thoroughly discussed in chapter two.

Chapters five and six deal with the "Rite of Blessing a Church" and the "Rite of Blessing an Altar," respectively. The difference between "dedication" and "blessing," according to the *General Instruction of the Roman Missal* (see #265) and the texts of the rites themselves, is one of the degree of solemnity. "Dedication" implies permanence while "blessing" assumes that the building is to be used for worship only for a time, or, as noted in chapter five, the building, "because of special conditions, [is] destined for divine worship only for a time" (Rite of Blessing of a Church, 1). The rites of blessing reflect this understanding in their relative simplicity. If only the altar (and not the building) is to be blessed, the blessing of the altar takes place during the Mass of the day.

Chapter seven contains rites for the blessing (within and outside Mass) of a chalice and paten. While these blessings are already provided in the *Book of Blessings,* they are also presented here, no doubt because they are related to the blessing of an altar.

An appendix contains the litany of the saints. The names of other saints, such as the church's titular, local saints, or the martyrs or saints whose relics are being deposited beneath the altar, may also be added to the litany, along with "petitions suitable for the occasion." A number of musical versions of the litany are available from music publishers.

SOME PASTORAL CONSIDERATIONS

1. Read the rites provided in *Dedication of a Church and an Altar* many times, slowly and thoughtfully, and absorb their theological flavor and liturgical character. The rites are rich and full; they are banquets of signs and symbols. Their celebration takes time and should not be rushed. A well-organized and well-prepared liturgy will help participants appreciate the various parts not as a series of disjointed segments but as a symphony with movements that need to be savored.

2. Let the signs and symbols speak. Avoid minimalism and businesslike efficiency when preparing for and celebrating the rites. Let anointings and incensing be full signs and gestures. Allow processions and ritual movements to be ample and gracious. Let the ritual prayer and song be primary, and leave other commentaries for bulletin inserts and the dedication booklet. Be conscious of how things are handled and what is communicated by the symbols of the building, the vessel of water to sprinkle people and walls, the lectionary, the chrism and incense, the altar coverings and communion vessels, the candles and lights, the vesture. There are many elements that need to be attended to carefully so that they can be experienced fully.

3. Help people become familiar with the rich prayer texts of the Rite of Dedication before the celebration of the liturgy, perhaps by providing parishioners with the booklet, *Prayers for the Dedication of a Church* (Chicago: Liturgy Training Publications, 1997). Use these prayers in all kinds of gatherings prior to the dedication; share them with the homebound; help children to understand and pray about what is happening. Most of all, use these rites and prayers as tools to help the members of the parish understand who and what we are as a church.

4. Extend the occasion of the dedication of the church building into the community through picnics, an open house, concerts, ecumenical celebrations, even fireworks. Find ways to connect with other segments of the community, perhaps by volunteering in local soup kitchens or homeless shelters, working with Habitat for Humanity, or twinning with a Third World faith community. The just word that is proclaimed in this house for the church needs to resonate throughout the community and find its natural connection in works of justice.

5. Along with the commissioning of art and furnishings for the new church, commission a musician to compose a hymn or other musical work that the community can come to know and that will have a part in the dedication liturgy. Be attentive and sensitive to the cultural heritage and ethnic identity of the community so that local customs and practices are integrated into the celebration of the Rite of Dedication.

TOWARD THE FUTURE

The dedication of a church is a very special event in the life of a community and an occasion of great joy and local pride. The shared faith and stewardship of the members of the church have made the building possible. People are often deeply moved by the Rite of Dedication, a rite in which some might participate only once in a lifetime. The ability to preserve the memory of the day through photographs and videos extends this joyfulness even further.

This rite has yet to undergo any adaptation based on the specific needs experienced through its use. Such adaptations and additions might include celebrations for a church that has been renovated or restored, liturgies for the closure of a church building or the consolidation of churches, blessings for particular church furnishings and appointments, and public prayers for the reconciliation of a vandalized church.

The subject of dedicating or setting aside spaces exclusively for worship will continue to raise all sorts of questions in the years ahead. Questions continue to be raised about the expense of maintaining spaces that may be used for only a few hours each week. What about multi-purpose spaces? What about leasing space in a mall, where people are to be found? These and many similar questions will continue to challenge our thinking.

Our church buildings, through their many shapes, sizes and expressions, are a part of the landscape of our cities and towns, and share their fortunes for better or worse. Often, churches are vibrant places that serve the total person, reaching out in charitable service with programs that foster education, health and welfare. In the midst of all manner of change and development, sacred spaces remain places of "eschatological significance" (*Catechism of the Catholic Church*, 1186). They are epiphanies of the active presence of Christ and of the people of God, and as such cannot help but proclaim God-with-us as well as God-yet-to-come. It is right and proper that we dedicate our new churches and celebrate the following rites with vigor and great joy.

OUTLINE

DEDICATION OF A CHURCH AND AN ALTAR
CHAPTERS 1–5, EXCERPTS

CHAPTER ONE
RITE OF LAYING OF A FOUNDATION STONE OR BEGINNING WORK ON THE BUILDING OF A CHURCH

INTRODUCTION

1.   When the building of a new church begins, it is desirable to celebrate a rite to ask God's blessing for the success of the work and to remind the people that the structure built of stone will be a visible sign of the living Church, God's building that is formed of the people themselves.[1]

In accordance with liturgical tradition, this rite consists of the blessing of the site of a new church and the blessing and laying of the foundation stone. When there is to be no foundation stone because of the particular architecture of the building, the rite of the blessing of the site of the new church should still be celebrated in order to dedicate the beginning of the work of God.

2.   The rite for the laying of a foundation stone or for beginning a new church may be celebrated on any day except during the Easter triduum. But the preference should be for a day when the people can be present in large numbers.

3.   The bishop of the diocese is rightly the one to celebrate the rite. If he cannot do so himself, he shall entrust the function to another bishop or priest, especially to one who is his associate and assistant in the pastoral care of the diocese or of the community for which the new church is to be built.

4.   Notice of the date and hour of the celebration should be given to the people in good time. The pastor or others concerned should instruct them in the meaning of the rite and the reverence to be shown toward the church that is to be built for them.

It is also desirable that the people be asked to give their generous and willing support in the building of the church.

5.   Insofar as possible, the area for the erection of the church should be marked out clearly. It should be possible to walk about without difficulty.

6.   In the place where the altar will be located, a wooden cross of suitable height is fixed in the ground.

7.   For the celebration of the rite the following should be prepared:

—The Roman Pontifical and Lectionary;

—chair for the bishop;

—depending on the circumstances, the foundation stone, which by tradition is a rectangular cornerstone, together with cement and the tools for setting the stone in the foundation;

—container of holy water with sprinkler;

—censer, incense boat and spoon;

—processional cross and torches for the servers.

Sound equipment should be set up so that the assembly can clearly hear the readings, prayers, and instructions.

8.   For the celebration of the rites the vestments are white or of some festive color. The following should be prepared:

—for the bishop: alb, stole, cope, miter and pastoral staff;

—for the priest, when one presides over the celebration: alb, stole and cope;

—for the deacons: albs, stoles, and if opportune, dalmatics;

—for other ministers: albs or other lawfully approved dress.

CHAPTER TWO
DEDICATION OF A CHURCH

INTRODUCTION

I. Nature and Dignity of Churches

1.   Through his death and resurrection, Christ became the true and perfect temple[1] of the New Covenant and gathered together a people to be his own.

This holy people, made one as the Father, Son and Holy Spirit are one, is the Church,[2] that is, the temple of God built of living stones, where the Father is worshiped in spirit and in truth.[3]

Rightly then, from early times "church" has also been the name given to the building in which the Christian community gathers to hear the word of God, to pray together, to receive the sacraments, and to celebrate the eucharist.

2.   Because the church is a visible building, it stands as a special sign of the pilgrim Church on earth and reflects the Church dwelling in heaven.

When a church is erected as a building destined solely and permanently for assembling the people of God and for carrying out sacred functions, it is fitting that it be dedicated to God with a solemn rite, in accordance with the ancient custom of the Church.

3.   The very nature of a church demands that it be suited to sacred celebrations, dignified, evincing a noble beauty, not mere costly display, and it should stand as a sign and symbol of heavenly realities. "The general plan of the sacred edifice should be such that in some way it conveys the image of the gathered assembly. It should also allow the participants to take the place most appropriate to them and assist all to carry out their individual functions properly." Moreover, in what concerns the sanctuary, the altar, the chair, the lectern, and the place for the reservation of the blessed sacrament, the Norms of the General Instruction of the Roman Missal are to be followed.[4]

Also, the norms must be observed that concern things and places destined for the celebration of other sacraments, especially baptism and penance.[5]

II. Titular of a Church and the Relics of the Saints to Be Placed in It

4.   Every church to be dedicated must have a titular. This may be: the Blessed Trinity; our Lord Jesus Christ invoked according to a mystery of his life or a title already accepted in the liturgy; the Holy Spirit; the Blessed Virgin Mary, likewise invoked according to some appellation already accepted in the liturgy; one of the angels; or, finally, a saint inscribed in the Roman Martyrology or in a duly approved Appendix. A blessed may not be the titular without an indult of the Apostolic See. A church should have one titular only, unless it is a question of saints who are listed together in the Calendar.

5.   The tradition in the Roman liturgy of placing relics of martyrs or other saints beneath the altar should be preserved, if possible.[6] But the following should be noted:

a) Such relics should be of a size sufficient for them to be recognized as parts of human bodies. Hence excessively small relics of one or more saints must not be placed beneath the altar.

b) The greatest care must be taken to determine whether the relics in question are authentic. It is better for an altar to be dedicated without relics than to have relics of doubtful authenticity placed beneath it.

c) A reliquary must not be placed upon the altar or set into the table of the altar; it must be placed beneath the table of the altar, as the design of the altar permits.

III. Celebration of the Dedication

MINISTER OF THE RITE

6.   Since the bishop has been entrusted with the care of the particular Church, it is his responsibility to dedicate to God the new churches built in his diocese.

If he cannot himself preside at the rite, he shall entrust his function to another bishop, especially to one who is his associate and assistant in the pastoral care of the community for which the church has been built or, in altogether special circumstances, to a priest, to whom he shall give a special mandate.

7.   A day should be chosen for the dedication of the new church when the people can be present in large numbers, especially a Sunday. Since the theme of the dedication pervades this entire rite, the dedication of a new church may not take place on days on which it is altogether improper to disregard the mystery then being commemorated: the Easter triduum, Christmas, Epiphany, Ascension, Pentecost, Ash Wednesday, the weekdays of Holy Week, and All Souls.

MASS OF THE DEDICATION

8.   The celebration of the eucharist is inseparably bound up with the rite of the dedication of a church; when a church is dedicated therefore the liturgical texts of the day are omitted and texts proper to the rite are used for both the liturgy of the word and the liturgy of the eucharist.

9.   It is fitting that the bishop concelebrate the Mass with the priests who take part with him in the rite of dedication and those who have been given charge over the parish or the community for which the church has been built.

OFFICE OF THE DEDICATION

10.   The day on which a church is dedicated is kept as a solemnity in that church.

The office of the dedication of a church is celebrated, beginning with Evening Prayer I. When the rite of depositing relics takes place, it is highly recommended to keep a vigil at the relics of the martyr or saint that are to be placed beneath the altar; the best way of doing this is to have the office of readings, taken from the respective common or proper. This vigil should be properly adapted to encourage the people's participation, but the requirements of the law are respected.[7]

PARTS OF THE RITE

A. Entrance into the Church

11.   The rite of the dedication begins with the entrance into the church; this may take place in one of the three following ways; the one best suited to the circumstances of time and place is to be used.

—Procession to the church to be dedicated: all assemble in a nearby church or other suitable place, from which the bishop, the ministers, and the congregation proceed to the church to be dedicated, praying and singing.

—Solemn entrance: if the procession cannot take place or seems inopportune, the community gathers at the entrance of the church.

—Simple entrance: the congregation assembles in the church itself; the bishop, the concelebrants, and the ministers enter from the sacristy in the usual way.

Two rituals are most significant in the entrance into a new church:

a) the handing over of the church: representatives of those who have been involved in the building of the church hand it over to the bishop.

b) the sprinkling of the church: the bishop blesses water and with it sprinkles the people, who are the spiritual temple, then the walls of the church, and finally, the altar.

B. Liturgy of the Word

12. Three readings are used in the liturgy of the word. The texts are chosen from those in the Lectionary (nos. 704 and 706) for the rite of the dedication of a church.

The first reading is always, even during the Easter season, the passage of Nehemiah that tells of the people of Jerusalem gathered in the presence of the scribe Ezra to hear the proclamation of the law of God (Nehemiah 8:1–4a, 5–6, 8–10).

13. After the readings the bishop gives the homily, in which he explains the biblical readings and the meaning of the dedication of a church.

The profession of faith is always said. The general intercessions are omitted, since the Litany of the Saints is sung in their place.

C. Prayer of Dedication and the Anointing of the Church and the Altar

Depositing the Relics of the Saints

14. If it is to take place, the relics of a martyr are deposited after the singing of the Litany of the Saints, to signify that the sacrifice of the members has its source in the sacrifice of the Head.[8] When relics of a martyr are not available, relics of another saint may be deposited in the altar.

Prayer of Dedication

15. The celebration of the eucharist is the most important and the one necessary rite for the dedication of a church.

Nevertheless, in accordance with the tradition in both East and West, a special prayer of dedication is also said. This prayer is a sign of the intention to dedicate the church to the Lord for all times and a petition for his blessing.

Rites of Anointing, Incensing, Covering, and Lighting the Altar

16. The rites of anointing, incensing, covering and lighting the altar express in visible signs several aspects of the invisible work that the Lord accomplishes through the Church in its celebration of the divine mysteries, especially the eucharist.

a) *Anointing* of the altar and the walls of the church:

—The anointing with chrism makes the altar a symbol of Christ, who, before all others, is and is called "The Anointed One"; for the Father anointed him with the Holy Spirit and constituted him the High Priest so that on the altar of his body he might offer the sacrifice of his life for the salvation of all.

—The anointing of the church signifies that it is given over entirely and perpetually to Christian worship. In keeping with liturgical tradition, there are twelve anointings, or, where it is more convenient, four, as a symbol that the church is an image of the holy city of Jerusalem.

b) *Incense* is burned on the altar to signify that Christ's sacrifice, there perpetuated in mystery, ascends to God as an odor of sweetness and also to signify that the people's prayers rise up pleasing and acceptable, reaching the throne of God.[9]

The incensation of the nave of the church indicates that the dedication makes it a house of prayer, but the people of God are incensed first, because they are the living temple in which each faithful member is a spiritual altar.[10]

c) *The covering of the altar* indicates that the Christian altar is the altar of the eucharistic sacrifice and the table of the Lord; around it priests and people, by one and the same rite but with a difference of function, celebrate the memorial of Christ's death and resurrection and partake of his supper. For this reason the altar is prepared as the table of the sacrificial banquet and adorned as for a feast. Thus the dressing of the altar clearly signifies that it is the Lord's table at which all God's people joyously meet to be refreshed with divine food, namely, the body and blood of Christ sacrificed.

d) *The lighting of the altar*, which is followed by the lighting of the church, reminds us that Christ is "a light to enlighten the nations";[11] his brightness shines out in the Church and through it in the whole human family.

D. Celebration of the Eucharist

17.   After the altar has been prepared, the bishop celebrates the eucharist, the principal and the most ancient part of the whole rite,[12] because the celebration of the eucharist is in the closest harmony with the rite of the dedication of a church:

—For the celebration of the eucharistic sacrifice achieves the end for which the church was built and the altar erected and expresses this end by particularly clear signs.

—Furthermore, the eucharist, which sanctifies the hearts of those who receive it, in a sense consecrates the altar and the place of celebration, as the ancient Fathers of the Church often assert: "This altar should be an object of awe: by nature it is stone, but it is made holy when it receives the body of Christ."[13]

—Finally, the bond closely connecting the dedication of a church with the celebration of the eucharist is likewise evident from the fact that the Mass for the dedication has its own preface, which is a central part of the rite itself.

IV. Adaptation of the Rite

ADAPTATIONS WITHIN THE COMPETENCE OF THE CONFERENCES OF BISHOPS

18.   The conferences of bishops may adapt this rite, as required, to the character of each region, but in such a way that nothing of its dignity and solemnity is lost.

However, the following are to be respected:

a) The celebration of Mass with the proper preface and prayer for a dedication must never be omitted.

b) Rites that have a special meaning and force from liturgical tradition (see no. 16) must be retained, unless weighty reasons stand in the way, but the wording may be suitably adapted if necessary.

With regard to adaptations, the competent ecclesiastical authority is to consult the Holy See and introduce adaptations with its consent.[14]

ADAPTATIONS WITHIN THE COMPETENCE OF THE MINISTERS

19.   It is for the bishop and for those in charge of the celebration of the rite:

—to decide the manner of entrance into the church (see no. 11);

—to determine the manner of handing over the new church to the bishop (no. 11);

—to decide whether to have the depositing of relics of saints. The decisive consideration is the spiritual good of the community; the prescriptions in no. 5 must be followed.

It is for the rector of the church to be dedicated, helped by those who assist him in the pastoral work, to decide and prepare everything concerning the readings, singing, and other pastoral aids to foster the fruitful participation of the people and to ensure a dignified celebration.

V. Pastoral Preparation

20.   In order that the people may take part fully in the rite of dedication, the rector of the church to be dedicated and others experienced in the pastoral ministry are to instruct them on the import of the celebration and its spiritual, ecclesial, and evangelizing power.

Accordingly, the people are to be instructed about the various parts of the church and their use, the rite of dedication, and the chief liturgical symbols employed in it. Thus led by suitable pastoral resources to a full understanding of the meaning of the dedication of a church through its rites and prayers, they will take an active, intelligent, and devout part in the sacred service.

VI. Requisites for the Dedication of a Church

21.   For the celebration of the rite the following should be prepared:

a) *In the place of assembly:*

—The Roman Pontifical;

—processional cross;

—if relics of the saints are to be carried in procession, the items in no. 24a.

b) *In the sacristy or in the sanctuary or in the body of the church to be dedicated,* as each situation requires:

—The Roman Missal;

—The Lectionary;

—container of water to be blessed and sprinkler;

—container with the chrism;

—towels for wiping the table of the altar;

—if needed, a waxed linen cloth or waterproof covering of the same size as the altar;

—basin and jug of water, towels, and all that is needed for washing the bishop's hands and those of the priests after they have anointed the walls of the church;

—linen gremial;

—brazier for burning incense or aromatic spices; or grains of incense and small candles to burn on the altar;

—censer, incense boat and spoon;

—chalice, corporal, purificators, and hand towel;

—bread, wine, and water for the celebration of Mass;

—altar cross, unless there is already a cross in the sanctuary or the cross that is carried in the entrance procession is to be placed near the altar;

—altar cloth, candles, and candlesticks;

—flowers, if opportune.

22.   It is praiseworthy to keep the ancient custom of hanging on the walls of the church crosses made of stone, brass, or other suitable material or of having the crosses carved on the walls. Thus twelve or four crosses should be provided, depending on the number of anointings (see no. 16), and fixed here and there at a suitable height on the walls of the church. Beneath each cross a small bracket should be fitted and in it a small candlestick is placed, with a candle to be lighted.

23.   For the Mass of the dedication the vestments are white or of some festive color. The following should be prepared:

—for the bishop: alb, stole, chasuble, miter, pastoral staff, and pallium, if the bishop has the right to wear one;

—for the concelebrating priests: the vestments for concelebrating Mass;

—for the deacons: albs, stoles, and dalmatics;

—for other ministers: albs or other lawfully approved dress.

24. If relics of the saints are to be placed beneath the altar, the following should be prepared:

a) *In the place of assembly:*

—reliquary containing the relics, placed between flowers and lights. When the simple entrance is used, the reliquary must be placed in a suitable part of the sanctuary before the rite begins;

—for the deacons who will carry the relics to be deposited: albs, red stoles, if the relics are those of a martyr, or white in other cases, and, if available, dalmatics. If the relics are carried by priests, then in place of dalmatics chasubles should be prepared.

The relics may also be carried by other ministers, vested in albs or other lawfully approved dress.

b) *In the sanctuary:*

—a small table on which the reliquary is placed during the first part of the dedication rite.

c) *In the sacristy:*

—a sealant or cement to close the cover of the aperture. In addition, a stone-mason should be on hand to close the depository of the relics at the proper time.

25. The record of a dedication of a church should be drawn up in duplicate, signed by the bishop, the rector of the church, and representatives of the local community; one copy is to be kept in the diocesan archives, the other in the archives of the church. Where the depositing of relics takes place, a third copy of the record should be made, to be placed at the proper time in the reliquary.

In this record mention should be made of the day, month, and year of the church's dedication, the name of the bishop who celebrated the rite, also the titular of the church and, where applicable, the names of the martyrs or saints whose relics have been deposited beneath the altar.

Moreover, in a suitable place in the church, an inscription should be placed stating the day, month, and year when the dedication took place, the titular of the church, and the name of the bishop who celebrated the rite.

VII. Anniversary of the Dedication

A. ANNIVERSARY OF THE DEDICATION OF THE CATHEDRAL CHURCH

26. In order that the importance and dignity of the local Church may stand out with greater clarity, the anniversary of the dedication of its cathedral is to be celebrated, with the rank of a solemnity in the cathedral itself, with the rank of a feast in the other churches of the diocese, on the date on which the dedication of the church recurs.[15] If this date is always impeded, the celebration is assigned to the nearest date open. It is desirable that in the cathedral church on the anniversary the bishop concelebrate the eucharist with the chapter of canons or the priests' senate and with the participation of as many of the people as possible.

27.   The anniversary of a church's dedication is celebrated with the rank of a solemnity.[16]

CHAPTER THREE
DEDICATION OF A CHURCH IN WHICH MASS IS ALREADY BEING CELEBRATED REGULARLY

INTRODUCTION

1.   In order to bring out fully the symbolism and the significance of the rite, the opening of a new church and its dedication should take place at one and the same time. For this reason, as was said before, care should be taken that, as far as possible, Mass is not celebrated in a new church before it is dedicated (see chapter two, nos. 8, 15, 17).

Nevertheless in the case of the rite of the dedication of a church where the sacred mysteries are already being celebrated regularly, the rite set out in this chapter must be used.

Moreover, a clear distinction exists in regard to these churches. In the case of those just built the reason for a dedication is obvious. In the case of those standing for some time the following requirements must be met for them to be dedicated:

—that the altar has not already been dedicated, since it is rightly forbidden both by custom and by liturgical law to dedicate a church without dedicating the altar, for the dedication of the altar is the principal part of the whole rite;

—that there be something new or notably altered about the edifice, relative either to its structure (for example, a total restoration) or its status in law (for example, the church's being ranked as a parish church).

2.   All the directions given in the Introduction to chapter two apply to this rite, unless they are clearly extraneous to the situation which this rite envisages or other directions are given.

This rite differs chiefly from that described in chapter two on these points:

a) The rite of opening the doors of the church (see chapter two, no. 34 or no. 41) is omitted, since the church is already open to the community; consequently, the entrance rite takes the form of the simple entrance (see chapter two, nos. 43–47). However, in the case of dedicating a church closed for a long time and now being opened again for sacred celebrations, the rite of opening the doors may be carried out, since in this case it retains its point and significance.

b) The rite of handing over the church to the bishop (see chapter two, no. 33 or no. 40 or no. 47), depending on the situation, is either to be followed, omitted, or adapted in a way relevant to the condition of the church being dedicated (for example, it will be right to retain it in dedicating a church built recently; to omit it in dedicating an older church where nothing has been changed in the structure; to adapt it in dedicating an older church completely restored).

c) The rite of sprinkling the church walls with holy water (see chapter two, nos. 48–50), purificatory by its very nature, is omitted.

d) All the rites belonging to the first proclamation of the word of God in a church (see chapter two, no. 53) are omitted; thus the liturgy of the word takes place in the usual way. A different, pertinent reading is chosen in place of Nehemiah 8:1–4a and its responsorial psalm, Psalm 19b:8–9, 10, 15 (see chapter two, no. 54a).

CHAPTER FOUR
RITE OF DEDICATION OF AN ALTAR

INTRODUCTION

I. Nature and Dignity of the Altar

1.   From meditating on God's word, the ancient Fathers of the Church did not hesitate to assert that Christ was the victim, priest, and altar of his own sacrifice.[1] For in the Letter to the Hebrews Christ is presented as the High Priest who is also the living altar of the heavenly temple,[2] and in the Book of Revelation our Redeemer appears as the Lamb who has been sacrificed[3] and whose offering is taken by the holy angel to the altar in heaven.[4]

THE CHRISTIAN IS ALSO A SPIRITUAL ALTAR

2.   Since Christ, Head and Teacher, is the true altar, his members and disciples are also spiritual altars on which the sacrifice of a holy life is offered to God. The Fathers seem to have this in mind. St. Ignatius of Antioch asks the Romans quite plainly: "Grant me only this favor: let my blood be spilled in sacrifice to God, while there is still an altar ready."[5] St. Polycarp exhorts widows to lead a life of holiness, for "they are God's altar."[6] Among others, St. Gregory the Great echoes these words when he says: "What is God's altar if not the souls of those who lead good lives? . . . Rightly, then, the heart of the just is said to be the altar of God."[7]

In another image frequently used by the writers of the Church, Christians who give themselves to prayer, offer petitions to God, and present sacrifices of supplication, are the living stones out of which the Lord Jesus builds the Church's altar.[8]

THE ALTAR, TABLE OF THE SACRIFICE AND THE PASCHAL MEAL

3.   By instituting in the form of a sacrificial meal the memorial of the sacrifice he was about to offer the Father on the altar of the cross, Christ made holy the table where the community would come to celebrate their Passover. Therefore the altar is the table for a sacrifice and for a banquet. At this table the priest, representing Christ the Lord, accomplishes what the Lord himself did and what he

handed on to his disciples to do in his memory. The Apostle clearly intimates this: "The blessing cup that we bless is a communion with the blood of Christ and the bread that we break is a communion with the body of Christ. The fact that there is only one loaf means that though there are many of us, we form a single Body because we all have a share in this one loaf."[9]

THE ALTAR, SIGN OF CHRIST

4.   The Church's children have the power to celebrate the memorial of Christ and take their place at the Lord's table anywhere that circumstances might require. But it is in keeping with the eucharistic mystery that the Christian people erect a permanent altar for the celebration of the Lord's Supper and they have done so from the earliest times.

The Christian altar is by its very nature properly the table of sacrifice and of the paschal banquet. It is:

—a unique altar on which the sacrifice of the cross is perpetuated in mystery throughout the ages until Christ comes;

—a table at which the church's children gather to give thanks to God and receive the body and blood of Christ.

In every church, then, the altar "is the center of the thanksgiving that the eucharist accomplishes"[10] and around which the Church's other rites are, in a certain manner, arrayed.[11]

At the altar the memorial of the Lord is celebrated and his body and blood given to the people. Therefore the Church's writers have seen in the altar a sign of Christ himself. This is the basis for the saying: "The altar is Christ."

THE ALTAR AS HONORING MARTYRS

5.   All the dignity of the altar rests on its being the Lord's table. Thus the martyr's body does not bring honor to the altar; rather the altar does honor to the martyr's tomb. For it is altogether proper to erect altars over the burial place of martyrs and other saints or to deposit their relics beneath altars as a mark of respect and as a symbol of the truth that the sacrifice of the members has its source in the sacrifice of the Head.[12] Thus "the triumphant victims come to their rest in the place where Christ is victim: he, however, who suffered for all is on the altar; they who have been redeemed by his sufferings are beneath the altar."[13] This arrangement would seem to recall in a certain manner the spiritual vision of the Apostle John in the Book of Revelation: "I saw underneath the altar the souls of all the people who have been killed on account of the word of God, for witnessing to it."[14] His meaning is that although all the saints are rightly called Christ's witnesses, the witness of blood has a special significance that only the relics of the martyrs beneath the altar express in its entirety.

II. Erecting an Altar

6.   It is desirable that in every church there be a fixed altar and that in other places set apart for sacred celebrations there be either a fixed or a movable altar.

A fixed altar is one so constructed that it is attached to the floor so that it cannot be moved; a movable altar can be transferred from place to place.[15]

7.   In new churches it is better to erect only one altar so that in the one assembly of the people of God the single altar signifies the one Savior Jesus Christ and the one eucharist of the Church.

But an altar may also be erected in a chapel (somewhat separated, if possible, from the body of the church) where the tabernacle for the reservation of the blessed sacrament is situated. On weekdays when there is a small gathering of people Mass may be celebrated at this altar.

The merely decorative erection of several altars in a church must be entirely avoided.

8.   The altar should be freestanding so that the priest can easily walk around it and celebrate Mass facing the people. "It should be so placed as to be a focal point on which the attention of the whole congregation centers naturally."[16]

9.   In accordance with received custom in the Church and the biblical symbolism connected with an altar, the table of a fixed altar should be of stone, indeed of natural stone. But, at the discretion of the conference of bishops, any becoming, solid, and finely wrought material may be used in erecting an altar.

The pedestal or base of the table may be of any sort of material, provided it is becoming and solid.[17]

10.   The altar is of its very nature dedicated to the one God, for the eucharistic sacrifice is offered to the one God. This is the sense in which the Church's practice of dedicating altars to God in honor of the saints must be understood. St. Augustine expresses it well: "It is not to any of the martyrs, but to the God of the martyrs, though in memory of the martyrs, that we raise our altars."[18]

This should be made clear to the people. In new churches statues and pictures of saints may not be placed above the altar.

Likewise, when relics of saints are exposed for veneration, they should not be placed on the table of the altar.

11.   It is fitting to continue the tradition in the Roman liturgy of placing relics of martyrs or other saints beneath the altar.[19] But the following should be noted.

a) Such relics should be of a size sufficient for them to be recognizable as parts of human bodies. Hence excessively small relics of one or more saints must not be placed beneath an altar.

b) The greatest care must be taken to determine whether the relics in question are authentic. It is better for an altar to be dedicated without relics than to have relics of doubtful authenticity placed beneath it.

c) A reliquary must not be placed on the altar or set into the table of the altar, but placed beneath the table of the altar, as the design of the altar permits.

When the rite of depositing relics takes place, it is highly recommended to keep a vigil at the relics of the martyr or saint, in accordance with the provisions of chapter two, no. 10.

III. Celebration of the Dedication

MINISTER OF THE RITE

12.   Since the bishop has been entrusted with the care of the particular Church, it is his responsibility to dedicate to God new altars built in his diocese.

If he cannot himself preside at the rite, he shall entrust the function to another bishop, especially to one who is his associate and assistant in the pastoral care of the community for which the new altar has been erected or, in altogether special circumstances, to a priest, to whom he shall give a special mandate.

CHOICE OF DAY

13.   Since an altar becomes sacred principally by the celebration of the eucharist, in fidelity to this truth the celebration of Mass on a new altar before it has been dedicated is to be carefully avoided, so that the Mass of dedication may also be the first eucharist celebrated on the altar.

14.   A day should be chosen for the dedication of a new altar when the people can be present in large numbers, especially a Sunday, unless pastoral considerations suggest otherwise. However, the rite of the dedication of an altar may not be celebrated during the Easter triduum, on Ash Wednesday, the weekdays of Holy Week, and All Souls.

MASS OF THE DEDICATION

15.   The celebration of the eucharist is inseparably bound up with the rite of the dedication of an altar. The Mass is the Mass for the dedication of an altar. On Christmas, Epiphany, Ascension, Pentecost, and on the Sundays of Advent, Lent, and the Easter season, the Mass is the Mass of the day, with the exception of the prayer over the gifts and the preface, which are closely interwoven with the rite itself.

16.   It is fitting that the bishop concelebrate the Mass with the priests present, especially with those who have been given charge over the parish or the community for which the altar has been erected.

PARTS OF THE RITE

A. Introductory Rites

17.   The introductory rites of the Mass of the dedication of an altar take place in the usual way except that in place of the penitential rite the bishop blesses water and with it sprinkles the people and the new altar.

B. Liturgy of the Word

18.   It is commendable to have three readings in the liturgy of the word, chosen, according to the rubrical norm, either from the liturgy of the day (see no. 15) or from those in the Lectionary for the rite of the dedication of an altar (nos. 704 and 706).

19.   After the readings, the bishop gives the homily, in which he explains the biblical readings and the meaning of the dedication of an altar.

After the homily, the profession of faith is said. The general intercessions are omitted, since the Litany of the Saints is sung in their place.

C. Prayer of Dedication and the Anointing of the Altar

Depositing of the Relics of the Saints

20.   If it is to take place, the relics of martyrs or other saints are placed beneath the altar after the Litany of the Saints. The rite is meant to signify that all who have been baptized in the death of Christ, especially those who have shed their blood for the Lord, share in Christ's passion (see no. 5).

Prayer of Dedication

21.   The celebration of the eucharist is the most important and the one necessary rite for the dedication of an altar. Nevertheless, in accordance with the universal tradition of the Church in both East and West, a special prayer of dedication is also said. This prayer is a sign of the intention to dedicate the altar to the Lord for all times and a petition for his blessing.

Rites of Anointing, Incensing, Covering, and Lighting the Altar

22.   The rites of anointing, incensing, covering, and lighting the altar express in visible signs several aspects of the invisible work that the Lord accomplishes through the Church in its celebration of the divine mysteries, especially the eucharist.

a) *Anointing* of the altar: The anointing with chrism makes the altar a symbol of Christ, who, before all others, is and is called "The Anointed One"; for the Father anointed him with the Holy Spirit and constituted him the High Priest so that on the altar of his body he might offer the sacrifice of his life for the salvation of all.

b) *Incense* is burned on the altar to signify that Christ's sacrifice, there perpetuated in mystery, ascends to God as an odor of sweetness, and also to signify that the people's prayers rise up pleasing and acceptable, reaching the throne of God.[20]

c) *The covering of the altar* indicates that the Christian altar is the altar of the eucharistic sacrifice and the table of the Lord; around it priests and people, by one and the same rite but with a difference of function, celebrate the memorial of Christ's death and resurrection and partake of his supper. For this reason the altar is prepared as the table of the sacrificial banquet and adorned as for a feast. Thus the dressing of the altar clearly signifies that it is the Lord's table at which all God's people joyously meet to be refreshed with divine food, namely, the body and blood of Christ sacrificed.

d) *The lighting of the altar* teaches us that Christ is "a light to enlighten the nations";[21] his brightness shines out in the Church and through it in the whole human family.

D. Celebration of the Eucharist

23.   After the altar has been prepared, the bishop celebrates the eucharist, the principal and the most ancient part of the whole rite,[22] because the celebration of the eucharist is in the closest harmony with the rite of the dedication of an altar:

—For the celebration of the eucharistic sacrifice achieves the end for which the altar was erected and expresses this end by particularly clear signs.

—Furthermore, the eucharist, which sanctifies the hearts of those who receive it, in a sense consecrates the altar, as the ancient Fathers of the Church often assert: "This altar should be an object of awe: by nature it is stone, but it is made holy when it receives the body of Christ."[23]

—Finally, the bond closely connecting the dedication of an altar with the celebration of the eucharist is likewise evident from the fact that the Mass for the dedication has its own preface, which is a central part of the rite itself.

IV. Adaptation of the Rite

ADAPTATIONS WITHIN THE COMPETENCE OF THE CONFERENCES OF BISHOPS

24.   The conferences of bishops may adapt this rite, as required, to the character of each region, but in such a way that nothing of its dignity and solemnity is lost.

However, the following are to be respected:

a) The celebration of Mass with the proper preface and prayer for a dedication must never be omitted.

b) Rites that have a special meaning and force from liturgical tradition (see no. 22) must be retained, unless weighty reasons stand in the way, but the wording may be suitably adapted if necessary.

With regard to adaptations, the competent ecclesiastical authority is to consult the Holy See and introduce adaptations with its consent.[24]

ADAPTATIONS WITHIN THE COMPETENCE OF THE MINISTERS

25.   It is for the bishop and for those in charge of the celebration of the rite to decide whether to have the depositing of relics of the saints; in so doing, they are to follow what is laid down in no. 11 and they are to take as the decisive consideration the spiritual good of the community and a proper sense of liturgy.

It is for the rector of the church in which the altar is to be dedicated, helped by those who assist him in the pastoral work, to decide and prepare everything concerning the readings, singing, and other pastoral aids to foster the fruitful participation of the people and to ensure a dignified celebration.

V. Pastoral Preparation

26.   The people are to be informed in good time about the dedication of a new altar and they are to be properly prepared to take an active part in the rite. Accordingly, they should be taught what each rite means and how it is carried out. For the purpose of giving this instruction, use may be made of what has been said earlier about the nature and dignity of an altar and the meaning and import of the rites. In this way the people will be imbued with the rightful love that is owed to the altar.

VI. Requisites for the Dedication of an Altar

27.   For the celebration of the rite the following should be prepared:

—The Roman Missal;

—The Lectionary;

—The Roman Pontifical;

—the cross and the Book of the Gospels to be carried in the procession;

—container of water to be blessed and sprinkler;

—container with the holy chrism;

—towels for wiping the table of the altar;

—if needed, a waxen linen cloth or waterproof covering of the same size as the altar;

—basin and jug of water, towels, and all that is needed for washing the bishop's hands;

—linen gremial;

—brazier for burning incense or aromatic spices; or grains of incense and small candles to burn on the altar;

—censer, incense boat and spoon;

—chalice, corporal, purificators, and hand towel;

—bread, wine, and water for the celebration of Mass;

—altar cross, unless there is already a cross in the sanctuary, or the cross that is carried in the entrance procession is to be placed near the altar;

—altar cloth, candles, and candlesticks;

—flowers, if opportune.

28.   For the Mass of the dedication the vestments are white or of some festive color. The following should be prepared:

—for the bishop: alb, stole, chasuble, miter, pastoral staff, and pallium, if the bishop has the right to wear one;

—for the concelebrating priests: the vestments for concelebrating Mass;

—for the deacons: albs, stoles, and dalmatics;

—for other ministers: albs or other lawfully approved dress.

29.   If relics of the saints are to be placed beneath the altar, the following should be prepared:

a) *In the place from which the procession begins:*

—a reliquary containing the relics, placed between flowers and lights. But as circumstances dictate, the reliquary may be placed in a suitable part of the sanctuary before the rite begins;

—for the deacons who will carry the relics to be deposited: albs, red stoles, if the relics are those of a martyr, or white in other cases, and, if available, dalmatics. If the relics are carried by priests, then, in place of dalmatics, chasubles should be prepared. Relics may also be carried by other ministers, vested in albs or other lawfully approved dress.

b) *In the sanctuary:*

—a small table on which the reliquary is placed during the first part of the dedication rite.

c) *In the sacristy:*

—a sealant or cement to close the cover of the aperture. In addition, a stone-mason should be on hand to close the depository of the relics at the proper time.

30.   It is fitting to observe the custom of enclosing in the reliquary a parchment on which is recorded the day, month, and year of the dedication of the altar, the name of the bishop who celebrated the rite, the titular of the church, and the names of the martyrs or saints whose relics are deposited beneath the altar.

A record of the dedication of the church is to be drawn up in duplicate and signed by the bishop, the rector of the church, and representatives of the local community; one copy is to be kept in the diocesan archives, the other in the archives of the church.

CHAPTER FIVE
RITE OF BLESSING A CHURCH

INTRODUCTION

1.   Since sacred edifices, that is, churches, are permanently set aside for the celebration of the divine mysteries, it is right for them to receive a dedication to God. This is done according to the rite in chapters two and three for dedicating a church, a rite impressive for its striking ceremonies and symbols.

Oratories, chapels, or other sacred edifices set aside only temporarily for divine worship because of special conditions, more properly receive a blessing, according to the rite described below.

2. As to the structure of the liturgy, the choice of a titular, and the pastoral preparation of the people, what is said in the Introduction to chapter two, nos. 4–5, 7, 20, is to be followed, with the necessary modifications.

A church or an oratory is blessed by the bishop of the diocese or by a priest delegated by him.

3. A church or an oratory may be blessed on any day, apart from the Easter triduum. As far as possible a day should be chosen when the people can be present in large numbers, especially a Sunday, unless pastoral considerations suggest otherwise.

4. On days mentioned in the Table of Liturgical Days, nos. 1–4, the Mass is the Mass of the day; but on other days the Mass is either the Mass of the day or the Mass of the titular of the church or oratory.

5. For the rite of the blessing of a church or an oratory all things needed for the celebration of Mass are prepared. But even though it may have already been blessed or dedicated, the altar should be left bare until the beginning of the liturgy of the eucharist. In a suitable place in the sanctuary the following also should be prepared:

—container of water to be blessed and sprinkler;

—censer, incense boat and spoon;

—The Roman Pontifical;

—altar cross, unless there is already a cross in the sanctuary, or the cross that is carried in the entrance procession is to be placed near the altar;

—altar cloth, candles, candlesticks, and flowers, if opportune.

6. When at the same time as the church is blessed the altar is to be consecrated, all those things should be prepared that are listed in chapter four, no. 27 and no. 29, if relics of the saints are to be deposited beneath the altar.

7. For the Mass of the blessing of a church the vestments are white or some festive color. The following should be prepared:

—for the bishop: alb, stole, chasuble, miter, pastoral staff;

—for a priest: the vestments for celebrating Mass;

—for the concelebrating priests: the vestments for concelebrating Mass;

—for the deacons: albs, stoles, and dalmatics;

—for other ministers: albs or other lawfully approved dress

NOTES

CHAPTER 1

1. See 1 Corinthians 3:9; LG, 6

CHAPTER 2

1. See John 2:21.

2. See Cyprian, *The Lord's Prayer*, 23: PL, 4, 553; LG, 4.

3. See John 4:23

4. See GIRM, 253, 257, 258, 259–267, 271, 272, 276–277. See also Roman Ritual, *Holy Communion and Worship of the Eucharist outside Mass*, 6 and 9–11.

5. See RBaptC, 25; RPen, 12.

6. See GIRM, 266.

7. See GILOH, 70–73.

8. See RomM, Common of Martyrs, 8, prayer over gifts. Ambrose, *Epistula* 22:13: PL 16, 1023: "Let the triumphant victims rest in the place where Christ is victim: he however, who suffered for all, upon the altar; they, who have been redeemed by his sufferings, beneath the altar." See Ps. Maximus of Turin, *Sermo* 78: PL 57, 689–690. Revelation 6:9, "I saw underneath the altar the souls of all people who had been killed on account of the word of God, for witnessing to it."

9. See Revelation 8:3–4.

10. See Romans 12:1.

11. Luke 2:32.

12. See Pope Vigilius, *Epistula ad Profuturum episcopum*, 4: PL 84, 832.

13. John Chrysostom, *Homilia 20 in Cor 3:* PG 61, 540.

14. See SC, 40.

15. See GNLY, Table of Liturgical Days, I, 4b and II,8b.

16. See GNLY, Table of Liturgical Days, I, 4b.

CHAPTER 4

1. See Epiphanius, *Panarium* 2, 1, *Haeresis* 55: PG 41, 979. Cyril of Alexandria, *De adoratione in spiritu et veritate* 9: PG 68, 647.

2. See Hebrews 4:14; 3:10.

3. See Revelation 5:6.

4. See RomM, Order of Mass, 96.

5. Ignatius of Antioch, *Ad Romanos* 2:2: F. X. Funk 1:255.

6. Polycarp, *Ad Philippenses* 4:3: F. X. Funk 1:301.

7. Gregory the Great, *Homilarium in Ezechielem* 10, 19: PL 76, 1069.

8. See Origen, *In librum Iesu Nave*, Homilia 9, 1; SC 71, 244 and 246.

9. See 1 Corinthians 10:16–17.

10. GIRM, 259.

11. See Pius XII, encylical letter *Mediator Dei:* AAS 39 (1947) 529.

12. See RomM, Common of Martyrs, 8, prayer over the gifts.

13. Ambrose, *Epistula* 22, 13: PL 16, 1023. See Ps. Maximus of Turin, *Sermo* 78: PL 57, 689–690.

14. Revelation 6:9.

15. See GIRM, 265, 261.

16. GIRM, 262.

17. See GIRM, 263.

18. Augustine, *Contra Faustum*, 20, 21: PL 42, 384.

19. See GIRM, 266.

20. See Revelation 8:3–4: An angel "who had a golden censer, came and stood at the altar. A large quantity of incense was given to him to offer with the prayers of all the saints on the golden altar that stood in front of the throne; and so from the angel's hand the smoke of the incense went up in the presence of God and with it the prayers of the saints."

21. Luke 2:32.

22. See Pope Vigilius, *Epistula ad Profuturum episcopum* 4: PL 84, 832.

23. John Chrysostom, *Homilia 20 in 2 Cor 3:* PG 61, 540.

24. See SC, 40.

BOOK OF BLESSINGS:
GENERAL INTRODUCTION

CONGREGATION FOR DIVINE WORSHIP
1989

OVERVIEW OF *BOOK OF BLESSINGS:* GENERAL INTRODUCTION

Paul F. Ford

In a very special way the *Book of Blessings* (BB) is the fruit not only of the Constitution on the Sacred Liturgy *Sacrosanctum concilium* (SC) but also of the Dogmatic Constitution on Divine Revelation *Dei verbum* and the Dogmatic Constitution on the Church *Lumen gentium*. BB underscores three interrelated realities: blessings are liturgies; they flow from the proclamation of the inspired word of God; they are celebrated by and for those who share in the one priesthood of Jesus Christ on behalf of the world, for which Christ died and rose. This overview will concentrate on the first reality but will also reflect the other two, especially in the following summary.

Blessings are liturgies. Blessings are public praise of and prayer to God, especially in the form of *epiclesis,* the gesture that asks for the gift of the Holy Spirit. As liturgies they presume an assembly, as well as song, proclamation, psalmody, intercession, gesture and ritual activity.

Blessings flow from the proclamation of the inspired word of God. The "bottom line" of this proclamation is always the renewal of the promise contained in the Name of God: "I shall be there as who I am shall I be there" (John Courtney Murray, *The Problem of God* [New Haven: Yale, 1960], page 10); the deepest meaning of the ritual *delivers* on this promise. Blessings make available to the senses the fact that the Father, Son and Spirit desire to communicate themselves to every human being. Indeed, as the General Introduction to BB points out, Christ, the Incarnate Word of God, is God's "supreme blessing" (#3).

Blessings presume faith, a faith inspired by God's word and awakened in the hearts of the assembly, particularly in those members who will benefit most directly from the blessing being celebrated. To aid in the awakening of this faith, the ordained minister may preach a homily, or the lay minister may offer an instruction. Unlike the sacraments, whose fruitfulness depends only in part on the faith of those who receive them, blessings are sacramentals and do not "work" without this lively faith. As we shall see, all magic and superstition have been ruled out in the revised BB.

Blessings are celebrated by and for those who share in the one priesthood of Jesus Christ on behalf of the world, for which Christ died and rose. In the teaching of the Second Vatican Council, and as it has been reinforced by Paul VI and John Paul II, the whole assembled body of the new covenant is established as "a spiritual house," "a holy priesthood" (1 Peter 2:5). This new priestly people that is the church not only has its authentic image in Christ, but also receives from Christ a real ontological share in Christ's one eternal priesthood, bestowed in the sacraments of initiation—baptism, confirmation, eucharist—through which the one initiated takes her or his unique place in the body of the worshiping Christ. All members of the body of Christ thus exercise Christ's priesthood in their use of BB.

As its foreword indicates, the 1989 BB is an interim collection that contains the entire Roman volume *De benedictionibus* (1985), as well as 42 other orders and prayers of blessing prepared by the U.S. Bishops' Committee on the Liturgy and approved both by the U.S. bishops and by the Congregation for Divine Worship. Some time in the future BB will be revised based on the comments sent to the U.S. Bishops' Committee on the Liturgy. All of us who use or experience the blessings should not hesitate to submit reflections to the committee.

Obviously there are many blessings that are not in BB. Apart from those that are connected to the celebration of the eucharist and the other sacraments, the rites of consecrating chrism and of dedicating churches and altars, and the blessing of persons (abbots and abbesses, consecration of virgins, and the like), the most significant collection of blessings outside BB is *Catholic Household Blessings and Prayers* (Washington, D.C.: United States Catholic Conference, 1985). If this treasury were used in every home, the goal of the liturgical renewal would be close to being achieved. In the less-familiar words of the paragraph that follows the justly famous "summit and source" description of the liturgy:

> [t]he liturgy in its turn moves the faithful, filled with "the paschal sacra-ments," to be "one in holiness"; it prays that "they may hold fast in their lives to what they have grasped by their faith"; the renewal in the eucharist of the covenant between the Lord and his people *draws the faithful into the compelling love of Christ and sets them on fire.* From the liturgy, therefore, particularly the eucharist, grace is poured forth upon us as from a fountain; the liturgy is the source for achieving in the most effective way possible human sanctification and God's glorification, the end to which all the Church's other activities are directed. (SC, 10; emphasis added)

Like the 1981 Introduction to the *Lectionary for Mass*, the 1984 General Introduction to BB is one of the most mature and passionate of our liturgical docu-ments. It must be noted, however, that there are many more introductions to orders and prayers of blessing than just the General Introduction. In fact, one-fifth of the book is introductory in character, perhaps a greater percentage than in any other liturgical book. To understand and use this collection properly, one must also read the 100 particular introductions to the various sections and sub-sections throughout the volume. Although it is vital to master the 39 articles of the General Introduction, one must also be cognizant of the 392 articles in these particular introductions. The first paragraphs in each of these 100 sections con-tain the theological and liturgical rationale for the blessings that follow them.

THE PLAN OF THE GENERAL INTRODUCTION

The General Introduction has five parts. The first, "Blessings in the History of Salvation," presents a trinitarian theology of blessing. The second and third parts, "Blessings in the Life of the Church" and "Offices and Ministries," focus on concerns of ecclesiology and sacramental theology. The fourth part, "Cele-bration of a Blessing," is concerned with some practical needs (such as gestures, preparation and vestments); and the last part, "Adaptations Belonging to the Conferences of Bishops," presents some considerations based on canon law. (The prerogative of making such adaptations was used in the U.S. edition.)

The seven articles in "Blessings in the History of Salvation" are a masterpiece of concision, and their message is succinct. In every blessing there is a confession of the goodness of God, a "blessing" of God, Father, Son and Spirit. In the Incarnation, the goodness of all that God has made is underscored.

> Blessings therefore refer first and foremost to God, whose majesty and goodness they extol, and, since they indicate the communication of God's favor, they also involve human beings, whom he governs and in his providence protects. Further, blessings apply to other created things through which, in their abundance and variety, God blesses human beings. (General Introduction, 7)

The reflections on ecclesiology and sacramental theology in the next twelve articles remind us of the fundamentally eucharistic nature and mission of the church. The following section from the General Introduction uses the language and terms of modern sacramental theology:

> Blessings are signs that have God's word as their *basis* and that are celebrated from motives of *faith*. They are therefore meant to *declare* and to *manifest* the newness of life in Christ that has its origin and growth in the sacraments of the New Covenant established by the Lord. In addition, since they have been established as *a kind of imitation of the sacraments*, blessings are signs above all of spiritual effects that are achieved through the Church's *intercession*. (#10; emphasis added)

One can hear in this definition echoes of the *General Instruction of the Roman Missal* and the Introduction to the *Lectionary for Mass*. Two statements from the latter come to mind:

> . . . the liturgical celebration, based primarily on the word of God and sustained by it, becomes a new event and enriches the word itself with new meaning and power . . .
>
> [T]he word of God unceasingly calls to mind and extends the plan of salvation, which achieves its fullest expression in the liturgy. The liturgical celebration becomes therefore the continuing, complete, and effective presentation of God's word." (#3–4)

Since blessings are liturgical celebrations, this ecclesiology and sacramental understanding of the word of God applies to them, too.

Articles 12 and 13 of the General Introduction to BB stress that blessings are for people in the events of their lives, in the objects they use, and in the places where they work and live. (Later, article 31 explains that "people" in the foregoing sentence includes catechumens and non-Catholics.) Here the General Introduction makes two cautions. First, with respect to blessing objects and places, it states that "such blessings are invoked always with a view to the people who use the object to be blessed and frequent the places to be blessed" (#12). Hence, throughout BB, ministers are instructed not to bless any thing or place without the presence of the persons who use or live in them. Here we can anticipate the point made in article 17: "The celebration of the blessing of things or places according to custom should not take place without the participation of at least some of the faithful."

The second caution—"every celebration of a blessing must be weighed beforehand with pastoral prudence"—is perhaps more clearly expressed in the particular introduction to the last blessing in the book. This blessing, "Order for a Blessing to Be Used in Various Circumstances," is meant to be an exemplar for situations not already provided for. Article 1985 of BB states,

> The present order is in no sense meant to violate principles concerning blessings; it is not fitting to turn every object or situation into an occasion for celebrating a blessing (for example, every monument erected no matter what its theme, the installation of military weapons, frivolous events). Rather, every celebration must be considered with balanced pastoral judgment, particularly when there is any foreseeable danger of shocking the faithful or other people.

The last two articles in "Blessings in the Life of the Church" so admirably summarize the theology of blessings that no overview can substitute for a prayerful pondering of the texts themselves, along with the full texts of the biblical references in notes 20–24.

Part three, "Offices and Ministries," underscores the fact that blessings, as liturgies, presume an assembly that is hierarchically integrated. Article 16 describes the ideal and article 17 prescribes the minimum. Because SC instructs that "provision be made that some sacramentals . . . may be administered by qualified laypersons" (#79), article 18 of BB describes the exercise of the ministry of blessing by the ordained and by lay men and women. Finally, article 19 reminds the one presiding at a celebration of a blessing that "[d]uring the celebration of a blessing and in preaching and catechesis beforehand, [they] should therefore explain to the faithful the meaning and power of blessings."

THE TYPICAL STRUCTURE OF A BLESSING

Blessings have two central parts—a liturgy of the word, and a praise/petition of God with its accompanying proper outward sign. A blessing also has an introduction and a conclusion (#20–22). So important are the central parts that article 23 lays down the rule that they "may never be omitted even when the shorter form of a rite is used," and article 27 states that "it is ordinarily not permissible to impart the blessing of any article or place merely through a sign of blessing and without either the word of God or any sort of prayer being spoken."

Articles 24 and 28–38 presume that the celebration of a blessing does not happen without preparation and planning. (Articles 28–38 cover pastoral planning, the vesture of ministers, and the manner in which the celebration of a blessing may be joined with Mass or other rites.) Article 26 lists the signs to be used in blessings, emphasizing "the outstretching, raising, or joining of the hands, the laying on of hands, the sign of the cross, sprinkling with holy water, and incensation," and gives a brief explanation of each sign.

Apart from the material contained in articles 25 and 26, a close inspection of the approximately 100 orders of blessing in BB reveals that clear (perhaps too clear) distinctions are made between the ways in which a lay minister uses some of these signs and the ways an ordained person does:

- A lay minister does not make any greeting that would normally elicit the response, "And also with you."
- A lay minister does not stretch out his or her hands in the *orans* gesture but keeps them folded.
- A lay minister does not stretch out his or her hands in blessing nor trace the sign of the cross in the air; rather, the lay minister signs himself or herself with the sign of the cross and thus leads the assembly in doing likewise.

While these distinctions are made clear in the rubrics of each blessing, BB does not offer an explanation for them.

The General Introduction concludes with article 39, which treats the rights and responsibilities of national conferences of bishops to prepare adaptations of BB for use in their respective regions. The bishops of the United States have made such adaptations, preparing and including (among others) 12 new orders of blessing related to feasts and seasons, 10 new orders of blessing for various pastoral needs and occasions, and, as an appendix, a new order for the installation of a pastor.

OUTLINE

BOOK OF BLESSINGS: GENERAL INTRODUCTION

I. BLESSINGS IN THE HISTORY OF SALVATION

1.   The source from whom every good gift comes[1] is God, who is above all, blessed for ever.[2] He who is all good has made all things good, so that he might fill his creatures with blessings[3] and even after the Fall he has continued his blessings as a sign of his merciful love.

2.   But when the fullness of time arrived, the Father sent his own Son and through him, who took our flesh, gave us a new gift in every spiritual blessing.[4] The ancient curse upon us was thus changed into a blessing: when "the glorious Sun of Justice, Christ our God, appeared, he freed us from the age-old curse and filled us with holiness.[5]

3.   Christ, the Father's supreme blessing upon us, is portrayed in the gospel as blessing those he encountered, especially the children,[6] and as offering to his Father prayers of blessing.[7] Glorified by the Father, after his ascension Christ sent the gift of his Spirit upon the brothers and sisters he had gained at the cost of his blood. The power of the Spirit would enable them to offer the Father always and everywhere praise, adoration, and thanksgiving and, through the works of charity, to be numbered among the blessed in the Father's kingdom.[8]

4.   In Christ the blessing of God upon Abraham[9] reached its complete fulfillment. Through the Spirit sent by Christ, those who are called to a new life, "showered with every blessing,"[10] become children by adoption and so as members of Christ's Body spread the fruits of the same Spirit in order to bring God's healing blessings to the world.

5.   In anticipation of Christ's coming as Savior, the Father had reaffirmed his original covenant of love toward us by the outpouring of many gifts. Thus he prepared a chosen people to welcome the Redeemer and he intervened to make them ever more worthy of the covenant. By walking in the path of righteousness, they had the power to honor God with their lips and with their hearts and thus to become before the world a sign and sacrament of divine blessings.

6.   The God from who all blessings flow favored many persons—particularly the patriarchs, kings, priests, Levites, and parents[11]—by allowing them to offer blessings in praise of his name and to invoke his name, so that other persons or the works of creation would be showered with divine blessings.

   Whether God blessed the people himself or through the ministry of those who acted in his name, his blessing was always a promise of divine help, a proclamation of his favor, a reassurance of his faithfulness to the covenant he had made with his people. When, in turn, others uttered blessings, they were offering praise to the one whose goodness and mercy they were proclaiming.

In a word, God bestows his blessing by communicating or declaring his own goodness; his ministers bless God by praising him and thanking him and by offering him their reverent worship and service. Whoever blesses others in God's name invokes the divine help upon individuals or upon an assembled people.

7.   Scripture attests that all the beings God has created and keeps in existence[12] by his gracious goodness declare themselves to be blessings from him and should move us to bless him in return. This is above all true after the Word made flesh came to make all thing holy by the mystery of his incarnation.

Blessings therefore refer first and foremost to God, whose majesty and goodness they extol, and, since they indicate the communication of God's favor, they also involve human beings, whom he governs and in his providence protects. Further, blessings apply to other created things through which, in their abundance and variety, God blesses human beings.[13]

II. BLESSINGS IN THE LIFE OF THE CHURCH

8.   Taught by the Savior's own command, the Church shares the cup of blessing,[14] as it gives thanks for the inexpressible gift received first in Christ's paschal mystery and then brought to us in the eucharist. From the grace and power received in the eucharist the Church itself becomes a blessing existing in the world. The Church as the universal sacrament of salvation[15] continues the work of sanctifying and in the Holy Spirit joins Christ its Head in giving glory to the Father.

9.   As the Church, through the working of the Holy Spirit, fulfills its many-sided ministry of sanctifying, it has accordingly established many forms of blessing. Through them it calls us to praise God, encourages us to implore his protection, exhorts us to seek his mercy by our holiness of life, and provides us with ways of praying that God will grant the favors we ask.

The blessings instituted by the Church are included among those signs perceptible to the senses by which human sanctification in Christ and the glorification of God are "signified and brought about in ways proper to each of these signs."[16] Human sanctification and God's glorification are the ends toward which all the Church's other activities are directed.[17]

10.   Blessings are signs that have God's word as their basis and that are celebrated from motives of faith. They are therefore meant to declare and to manifest the newness of life in Christ that has its origin and growth in the sacraments of the New Covenant established by the Lord. In addition, since they have been established as a kind of imitation of the sacraments, blessings are signs above all of spiritual effects that are achieved through the Church's intercession.[18]

11.   Because of these considerations, the Church has a profound concern that the celebration of blessings should truly contribute to God's praise and glory and should serve to better God's people. In order that this intent of the Church might stand out more clearly, blessing formularies have, from age-old tradition, centered above all on glorifying God for his gifts, on imploring favors from him, and on restraining the power of evil in this world.

12.   The Church gives glory to God in all things and is particularly intent on showing forth his glory to those who have been or will be reborn through his grace. For them and with them therefore the Church in celebrating its blessings praises the Lord and implores divine grace at important moments in the life of its members. At times the Church also invokes blessings on objects and places connected with human occupations or activities and those related to the liturgy or to piety and popular devotions. But such blessings are invoked always with a view to the people who use the objects to be blessed and frequent the places to be blessed. God has given into our use and care the good things he has created, and we are also the recipients of his own wisdom. Thus the celebration of blessings becomes the means for us to profess that as we make use of what God has created we wish to find him and to love and serve him with all fidelity.

13.   Through the guidance of faith, the assurance of hope, and the inspiration of charity the faithful receive the wisdom to discern the reflections of God's goodness not only in the elements of creation but also in the events of human life. They see all of these as signs of that fatherly providence by which God guides and governs all things. At all times and in every situation, then, the faithful have an occasion for praising God through Christ in the Holy Spirit, for calling on divine help, and for giving thanks in all things, provided there is nothing that conflicts with the letter and spirit of the Gospel. Therefore every celebration of a blessing must be weighed beforehand with pastoral prudence, particularly if there is any danger of shocking the faithful or other persons.

14.   This pastoral evaluation of the blessings of creation is in keeping with another text of Vatican Council II: "Thus, for well-disposed members of the faithful, the effect of the liturgy of the sacraments and the sacramentals is that almost every event in their lives is made holy by divine grace that flows from the paschal mystery of Christ's passion, death, and resurrection, the fount from which all the sacraments and sacramentals draw their power. The liturgy means also that there is hardly any proper use of material things that cannot thus be directed toward human sanctification and the praise of God."[19]

The celebration of a blessing, then, prepares us to receive the chief effect of the sacraments and makes holy the various situations of human life.

15.   "But in order that the liturgy may possess its full effectiveness, it is necessary that the faithful come to it with proper dispositions."[20] When through the Church we ask for God's blessing, we should intensify our personal dispositions through faith, for which all things are possible;[21] we should place our assurance in the hope that does not disappoint;[22] above all we should be inspired by the

love that impels us to keep God's commandments.[23] Then, seeking what is pleasing to God,[24] we will fully appreciate his blessing and will surely receive it.

III. OFFICES AND MINISTRIES

16.   Blessings are a part of the liturgy of the Church. Therefore their communal celebration is in some cases obligatory but in all cases more in accord with the character of liturgical prayer; as the Church's prayer places truth before the minds of the faithful, those who are present are led to join themselves with heart and voice to the voice of the Church.

For the more important blessings that concern the local Church, it is fitting that the diocesan or parish community assemble, with the bishop or pastor (parish priest) presiding, to celebrate the blessing.

Even in the case of other blessings, the presence of an assembly of the faithful is preferable, since what is done on behalf of any group within in community redounds in some way to the good of the entire community.

17.   Whenever there is no assembly of the faithful for the celebration, the person who wishes to bless God's name or to ask God's favor and the minister who presides should still keep in mind that they represent the Church in celebration. In this way from their shared prayer and petition a blessing results that "although a human being pronounces it, does not have a merely human source,[25] a blessing that is "the longed-for bestowal of sanctification and divine favor."[26]

The celebration of the blessing of things or places according to custom should not take place without the participation of at least some of the faithful.

18.   The ministry of blessing involves a particular exercise of the priesthood of Christ and, in keeping with the place and office within the people of God belonging to each person, the exercise of this ministry is determined in the following manner:

a. It belongs to the ministry of the *bishop* to preside at celebrations that involve the entire diocesan community and that are carried out with special solemnity and with a large attendance of the faithful. The bishop, accordingly, may reserve certain celebrations to himself, particularly those celebrated with special solemnity.[27]

b. It belongs to the ministry of a *presbyter or priest*, in keeping with the nature of his service to the people of God, to preside at those blessings especially that involve the community he is appointed to serve. Priests therefore may preside at the celebration of all the blessings in this book, unless a bishop is present as presider.

c. It belongs to the ministry of a *deacon* to preside at those blessings that are so indicated in place in this book, because, as the minister of the altar, of the word, and of charity, the deacon is the assistant of the bishop and the college of presbyters.

But whenever a priest is present, it is more fitting that the office of presiding be assigned to him and that the deacon assist by carrying out those functions proper to the diaconate.

d. An *acolyte* or a *reader* who by formal institution has this special office in the Church is rightly preferred over another layperson as the minister designated at the discretion of the local Ordinary to impart certain blessings.

Other *laymen* and *laywomen*, in virtue of the universal priesthood, a dignity they possess because of their baptism and confirmation, may celebrate certain blessings, as indicated in the respective orders of blessings, by use of the rites and formularies designated for a lay minister. Such laypersons exercise this ministry in virtue of their office (for example, parents on behalf of their children) or by reason of some special liturgical ministry or in fulfillment of a particular charge in the Church, as is the case in many places with religious or catechists appointed by decision of the local Ordinary.[28] after ascertaining their proper pastoral formation and prudence in the apostolate.

But whenever a priest or a deacon is present, the office of presiding should be left to him.

19.   The participation of the faithful will be the more active in proportion to the effectiveness of their instruction on the importance of blessings. During the celebration of a blessing and in preaching and catechesis beforehand, priests and ministers should therefore explain to the faithful the meaning and power of blessings. There is a further advantage in teaching the people of God the proper meaning of the rites and prayers employed by the Church in imparting blessings: this will forestall the intrusion into the celebration of anything that might replace genuine faith with superstition and/or a shallow credulity.

IV. CELEBRATION OF A BLESSING

TYPICAL STRUCTURE

20.   The typical celebration of a blessing consists of two parts: first, the proclamation of the word of God, and second, the praise of God's goodness and the petition for his help.

In addition there are usually rites for the beginning and conclusion that are proper to each celebration.

21.   The purpose of the first part of the celebration is to ensure that the blessing is a genuine sacred sign, deriving its meaning and effectiveness from God's word that is proclaimed.[29]

Thus the proclamation of God's word is the central point of the first part and the word proclaimed should provide a basis for the introductory comments and the brief instruction on the readings, as well as for any exhortation or homily that may be given, as occasion suggests.

Particularly when there are several readings, an intervening psalm or song or an interval of prayerful silence may be included, in order to intensify the faith of those taking part in the celebration.

22.   The purpose of the second part of the celebration is that through its rites and prayers the community will praise God and, through Christ in the Holy Spirit, implore divine help. The central point of this part, then, is the blessing formulary itself, that is, the prayer of the Church, along with the accompanying proper outward sign.

But intercessions may also be added as way of fostering the prayerful petition of those present; the intercessions usually precede, but also may follow the prayer of blessing.

23.   In the adaptation of celebrations a careful distinction must be made between matters of less importance and those principal elements of the celebrations that are here provided, namely, the proclamation of the word of God and the Church's prayer of blessing. These may never be omitted even when the shorter form of a rite is used.

24.   For the planning of celebration these are the foremost considerations:

a. in most cases a communal celebration is to be preferred,[30] and in such a way that a deacon, reader, cantor or psalmist, and choir all fulfill their proper functions;

b. a primary criterion is that the faithful are able to participate actively, consciously, and easily;[31]

c. provision should be made for the particular circumstances and persons involved,[32] but with due regard for the principles of the liturgical reform and the norms laid down by the responsible authority.

SIGNS TO BE USED

25.   The purpose of the outward signs frequently accompanying prayer is above all to bring to mind God's saving acts, to express a relationship between the present celebration and the Church's sacraments, and in this way to nurture the faith of those present and move them to take part in the rite attentively.[33]

26.   The outward signs or gestures that are especially employed are: the outstretching, raising, or joining of the hands, the laying on of hands, the sign of the cross, sprinkling with holy water, and incensation.

a. Because the blessing formulary is before all else an *oratio*, the minister stretches out his hands, joins them, or raises them during it, according to the rubrics in each order of blessing.

b. The laying on of hands holds a special place among gestures of blessing. Christ often used this sign of blessing, spoke of it to his disciples, saying: "They will lay hands on the sick and these will recover" (Mark 16:18), and continues to use it in and through the Church.

c. In keeping with an ancient tradition, the tracing of the sign of the cross also often accompanies a blessing.

d. Some of the orders of blessing provide for sprinkling with holy water, and in these cases ministers should urge the faithful to recall the paschal mystery and renew their baptismal faith.

e. Some orders of blessing provide for incensation, which is a sign of veneration and honor and, in some uses, a symbol of the Church's prayer.

27. The outward signs of blessing, and particularly the sign of the cross, are in themselves forms of preaching the Gospel and of expressing faith. But to ensure active participation in the celebration and to guard against any danger of superstition, it is ordinarily not permissible to impart the blessing of any article or place merely through a sign of blessing and without either the word of God or any sort of prayer being spoken.

MANNER OF JOINING THE CELEBRATION OF A BLESSING
WITH OTHER CELEBRATIONS OR WITH OTHER BLESSINGS

28. Because some blessings have a special relationship to the sacraments, they may sometimes be joined with the celebration of Mass.

This book specifies what such blessings are and the part or rite with which they are to be joined; it also provides ritual norms that may not be disregarded. No blessings except those so specified may be joined with the eucharistic celebration.

29. As indicated in the individual orders of blessing, some blessings may be joined with other liturgical celebrations.

30. At times it may suit the occasion to have several blessings in a single celebration. The principle of arrangement for such a celebration is that the rite belonging to the more important blessing is to be used, and in the introductory comments and in the intercessions suitable words and signs are added that indicate the intention also of bestowing the other blessings.

RESPONSIBILITIES OF THE MINISTER IN PREPARING AND PLANNING A BLESSING

31. The minister should keep in mind that blessings are intended, first of all, for the faithful. But they may also be celebrated for catechumens and, in view of the provision of can. 1170, for non-Catholics, unless there is a contrary prohibition of the Church.

Whenever the celebration of a blessing is shared with Christians with whom we do not have full communion, the provisions laid down by the local Ordinary are to be respected.

32. With a view to the particular circumstances and taking into account the wishes of the faithful, the celebrant or minister is to make full use of the options authorized in the various rites, but also is to maintain the structure of the celebration and is not to mix up the order of the principal parts.

33.   In planning a communal celebration care must be taken to ensure that all, both ministers and faithful, exercise their proper functions and carry them out devoutly and with proper decorum and order.

34.   Due attention must also be paid to the character proper to the liturgical season, in order that the minister's introductory comments and the people's prayers and intercessions will be linked with the annual cycle of the mysteries of Christ.

VESTMENTS

35.   A bishop when presiding at major celebrations wears the vestments prescribed in the *Ceremonial of Bishops*.

36.   A priest or deacon when presiding at blessings celebrated communally, especially those that are celebrated in a church or with special solemnity, is to wear an alb with stole. A surplice may replace the alb when a cassock is worn; a cope may be worn for more solemn celebrations.

37.   Vestments are to be either white or of a color corresponding to the liturgical season or feast.

38.   A formally instituted minister when presiding at blessings celebrated communally is to wear the vesture prescribed for liturgical celebrations by the conference of bishops or by the local Ordinary.

V. ADAPTATIONS BELONGING
TO THE CONFERENCES OF BISHOPS

39.   In virtue of the Constitution of the Liturgy,[34] each conference of bishops has the right to prepare a particular ritual, corresponding to the present title of the Roman Ritual, adapted to the needs of the respective region. Once the decisions of the conference have been reviewed by the Apostolic See,[35] the ritual prepared by the conference is to be used in the region concerned.

     In this matter the conference of bishops has the following responsibilities:

     a. to decide on adaptations, in keeping with the principles established in the present book, and preserving the proper structure of the rites;

     b. to weigh carefully and prudently what elements from the traditions and culture of individual peoples may be appropriately admitted into divine worship, then to propose further adaptations that the conference considers to be necessary or helpful;[36]

     c. to retain or to adapt blessings belonging to particular rituals or those of the former Roman Ritual that are still in use, as long as such blessings are compatible with the tenor of the Constitution on the Liturgy, with the principles set out in this General Introduction, and with contemporary needs;

d. to add different texts of the same kind to the various orders of blessing whenever the present book gives a choice between several alternative texts;

e. not only to translate in the entirety but also, where necessary, to expand the Introductions in this book, so that the ministers will fully understand the meaning of the rites and carry them out effectively and the faithful will take part more consciously and actively;

f. to supply elements missing from this book, for example, to provide other readings that may be useful and to indicate what songs are suited to the celebrations;

g. to prepare translations of the texts that are adapted to the idiom of the different languages and to the genius of the diverse cultures;

h. to arrange the contents of editions of a book of blessings in a format that will be as convenient as possible for pastoral use; to publish sections of the book separately, but with the major introductions always included.

NOTES

1. See RomM, Solemn Blessing no. 3, Beginning of the New Year.

2. See Romans 9:5.

3. See RomM, Eucharistic Prayer IV, Preface.

4. See Galatians 4:4; Ephesians 1:3.

5. See The Liturgy of the Hours, Birthday of Mary, 8 September, antiphon for the Canticle of Zechariah.

6. See Acts 3:26; Mark 10:16, 6:14; Luke 24:50, etc.

7. See Matthew 9:31, 14:19, 26:26; Mark 6:41, 8:7 and 9, 14:22; Luke 9:16, 24:30; John 6:11.

8. See RomM, Common of Holy Men and Women, 9: For those who work for the underprivileged, Opening Prayer.

9. See Genesis 12:3.

10. Basil the Great, *De Spiritu Sancto*, cap. 15, 36: PG 32, 131. See Ambrose, *De Spiritu Sancto*, 1, 7, 89: PL 16, 755; CSEL, 79, 53.

11. See Genesis 14:19–20; Hebrews 7:1; Genesis 27:27–29, 38, 40; Hebrews 11:20; Genesis 49:1–28; Hebrews 11:21; Deuteronomy 21:5; Deuteronomy 33; Joshua 14:13, 22:6; 2 Chronicles 30:27; Leviticus 9:22–23; Nehemiah 8:6; Sirach 3:9–11.

12. See, for example, Daniel 3:57–88; Psalm 66:8; Psalm 103; Psalm 135; 1 Timothy 4:4–5.

13. See Genesis 27:27; Exodus 23:25; Deuteronomy 7:13, 28:12; Job 1:10; Psalm 65:11; Jeremiah 31:23.

14. See 1 Corinthians 10:16.

15. See LG, 48.

16. SC, 7.

17. SC, 7 and 10.

18. See SC, 60.

19. SC, 61.

20. SC, 11.

21. See Mark 9:23.

22. See Romans 5:5.

23. See John 14:21.

24. See Romans 12:2; Ephesians 5:17; Matthew 12:50; Mark 3:35.

25. Caesarius of Arles, *Serm.* 77, 5: CCL 103, 321.

26. Ambrose, *De benedictionibus patriarcharum*, 2, 7: PL 14, 709; CSEL, *De Patriarchis*, 32, 2, 18.

27. See SC, 79.

28. See SC, 79.

29. See LMIntro, 3–9.

30. See SC, 27.

31. See SC, 79.

32. See SC, 38.

33. See SC, 59–60.

34. See SC, 63b.

35. See CIC, c. 838 §2 and §3; see also CIC, c. 1167 §1.

AUTHORS

John F. Baldovin, SJ, is professor of historical and liturgical theology at Weston Jesuit School of Theology, Cambridge, Massachusetts. He is currently president of the international *Societas Liturgica* and a member of the Advisory Committee of the International Commission on English in the Liturgy.

Paul F. Ford is professor of systematic theology and liturgy at St. John's Seminary in Camarillo, California.

Mark R. Francis, CSV, a priest of the Congregation of the Clerics of Saint Viator, holds a doctorate in sacred liturgy from Sant' Anselmo in Rome and is associate professor of liturgy at Catholic Theological Union in Chicago.

Barry Glendinning is an instructor at the Summer Institute in Pastoral Liturgy at Saint Paul University, Ottawa. He has worked in liturgical formation at the parish and diocesan levels.

Mary Therese Harrington, SH, works as a staff member of Special Religious Development (SPRED) for the archdiocese of Chicago, where there are 100 SPRED centers. SPRED provides resources for 28 other dioceses in the United States and other English-speaking countries.

Frederick R. McManus is professor emeritus in the department of canon law at the Catholic University of America, Washington, D.C.

J-Glenn Murray, SJ, is the director for the Office for Pastoral Liturgy in the diocese of Cleveland and the final drafter of *Plenty Good Room*.

Gilbert W. Ostkiek, OFM, is professor of liturgy at Catholic Theological Union in Chicago. He has served as a member of the Advisory Committee of the International Commission on English in the Liturgy since 1986. In 1998, he was the recipient of the Michael Mathis Award from the Notre Dame Center for Pastoral Liturgy. His writings include *Catechesis for Liturgy: A Program for Parish Involvement*.

Thomas G. Simons is a priest of the diocese of Grand Rapids, Michigan, where he serves as pastor of St. Francis de Sales Parish in Muskegon. He also serves as chairperson for the Diocesan Liturgical Art and Environment Commission.

Gerard S. Sloyan is a priest of the diocese of Trenton and is distinguished lecturer in the department of religion and religious education at the Catholic University of America, Washington, D.C.

Paul Turner is pastor of St. John Francis Regis Parish in Kansas City, Missouri. A priest of the diocese of Kansas City–St. Joseph, he holds a doctorate in sacred theology from Sant' Anselmo in Rome.

Joyce Ann Zimmerman, CPPS, holds a doctorate in sacred theology from St. Paul's University, Ottawa, Canada, and a doctorate from the University of Ottawa. She is the director of the Institute for Liturgical Ministry and editor of the journal *Liturgical Ministry*.

INDEX, VOLUMES ONE AND TWO

References are to paragraph or section numbers of individual documents. For a list of abbreviations of document names, see pages vii–viii.

regulations governing, SC 52; GIRM 42, 97, 165; LM 25–26

sources for, SC 35, 55; GIRM 41; LM 24; FYH 50–55

see also LITURGY OF THE WORD; SCRIPTURE

IGNATIUS OF ANTIOCH, SAINT
DD 23; DedCh 4.2

INCENSATION
GIRM 85, 105, 235–36; CB 84–98; EACW 12

INCULTURATION
adaptation of liturgical texts and practices, IRL 35–45, 53–70; PGR 105–24; CP 1–43; CEILT 1–35

among African Americans, PGR 77–124

general principles of, SC 37–40, 65, 68, 119; EACW 16, 35, 85–87; IRL 1–8, 21–37, 46–51; PGR 3–10, 24–29

historical precedents for, IRL 9–20; PGR 13–23, 34–70

value of diversity, EACW 18, 101; PS 106; IRL 1–2, 30–32; PGR 40–42

INNOCENT I, POPE
DD 19

IN SPIRIT AND TRUTH
PGR 105–24

INSTITUTE OF PASTORAL LITURGY
SC 44

JEROME, SAINT
DD 2

JOHN CHRYSOSTOM, SAINT
DD 71; PGR 17

JOHN PAUL II, POPE
IRL 2; GMEF 6, 27, 29; PGR 32, 123

JUDAISM
and anti-Semitism, GMEF 7, 9, 21–26

concept of *Shabbat*, DD 11–18, 23–26, 59–63

and the Holocaust, GMEF 27, 29

and the origins of Christianity, IRL 9–10, 14–15, 19; GMEF 1–10; PGR 14–15

presentation of in Catholic homilies, GMEF 11–32

JUSTIN, SAINT
DD 27, 46; PGR 16

KING, MARTIN LUTHER, JR.
PGR 10, 32

LANGUAGE
within African American worship, PGR 95–100

inclusive, CP intro; SCC 1–12; CEILT 1–35

and inculturation, GIRM, 19; IRL 13, 28–30, 33, 35–39, 50

use of vernacular, SC 36, 54, 63, 101; LM 111, 117; DMC 31

see also SCRIPTURE; TEXTS, LITURGICAL

LENT
character of, SC 109–10; GNLY 27–31; CB 249

liturgies of, GIRM 308; LM 97–98; CB 260; PS 6–26; GILOH 130, 133, 150

presentation of Jews during, GMEF 16–20

and sacrament of reconciliation, CB 253

see also ASH WEDNESDAY

LEO THE GREAT, POPE
PGR 18

LEO XIII, POPE
DD 66

LITURGICAL YEAR
adaptation and revision of, SC 107–11; IRL 60

nature of, SC 102; GNLY 1–2, 17–44; LMT 46–48; PS 2; GMEF 2, 9

see also individual days and seasons by name

LITURGIES
see individual liturgical components by name

LITURGY COMMITTEES
GIRM 69, 73, 313; CB 34; DMC 29; MCW 10–14, 42; EACW 44, 66

LITURGY OF THE EUCHARIST
elements of, GIRM 23, 48–56; MCW 72

during Ordinary Time, DD 31–54; GILOH 12

preparation of the gifts, GIRM 16, 49–53, 100–107, 221–23; GIapp 50; MCW 71; LMT 19

relationship to Liturgy of the Word, SC 56; FYH 60–62

and reservation of the eucharist, GIRM 276–77; CB 49; EACW 78–80

variations of for special Masses, GIRM 100–122, 166–206, 221–30, 339; DMC 52–54; EACW 96; GSPD 19–21; DedCh 2.17, 4.23

see also COMMUNION UNDER BOTH FORMS; EUCHARIST, SACRAMENT OF

ORDINARY TIME
GNLY 43–44; CB 377–80
role of Sunday in, SC 106; GNLY 4–7, 16;
DD 76–80
seasons of, SC 107–10; GNLY 18–42
solemnities, feasts, and memorials,
GNLY 8–15, 59

ORIGEN
DD 83; PGR 48

PARISHES
see COMMUNITY OF THE CHURCH

PASSION (PALM) SUNDAY
GNLY 30–31; CB 263; PS 28–34;
GMEF 21–25

PAUL, SAINT
DD 23; IRL 14

PAUL VI, POPE
DD 3, 39, 58; PGR 30

PEACE, SIGN OF
GIRM 56, 112, 194, 225; GIapp 56;
CB 99–103

PENANCE
see RECONCILIATION, SACRAMENT OF

PENTECOST
GNLY 22, 26; DD 20, 28, 76; PS 103, 107;
IRL 13; GMEF 2

PIUS V, POPE
PGR 20

PIUS X, POPE
GILOH 136

PIUS XII, POPE
PS 1; PGR 23

POSTURES AND GESTURES,
LITURGICAL
among African Americans, PGR 92–94, 120
bowing and genuflecting, GIRM 84,
232–34; CB 68–71
with children, DMC 33–34
during concelebration, GIRM 169–91
dancing, EACW 59
and inculturation, IRL 41–42, 48
kissing of altar, GIRM 85, 125, 232;
CB 72–74
kneeling, GIRM 21; GIapp 21; EACW 57
significance of, SC 30; GIRM 20–22, 62;
GIapp 21; CB 68–83; EACW 56–58
sitting, GIRM 21; EACW 57
standing, GIRM 21; EACW 52

PRAYER
among African Americans, PGR 71, 93,
95–96, 114
with children, DMC 10, 22, 27, 29, 50–52
after communion, GIRM 56, 122, 230
ecumenical, DE 108–15, 187; GMEF 4, 29
eucharistic, GIRM 53–55, 107–9, 168–91,
223; DMC 52
general intercessions, SC 53–54;
GIRM 16, 45–47, 99, 220; GIapp 45;
LM 30–31; DMC 22, 29; MCW 74
importance of, SC 12; GIRM 10–13;
GILOH 1–33
Lord's Prayer, GIRM 16, 56, 110, 192, 224;
MCW 59, 67
and music, MCW 47, 53, 56–58;
LMT 15, 17
opening, GIRM 32, 88, 216
see also LITURGY OF THE HOURS

PRIESTS
as pastors, SC 11, 14, 19, 42, 56, 100, 114;
GIRM 341
as preachers, FYH 1–12, 18–39, 77
as presiders, GIRM 10–13, 48, 54, 60;
LM 38–43; DMC 23; MCW 21–22;
LMT 67; EACW 60
shortage of, DD 5, 49, 53; PS 43
training of, SC 14–18, 115, 129

PROCESSIONS, LITURGICAL
communion, GIRM 119, 137, 206, 210
entrance, GIRM 82, 127–28, 142–43, 148,
162, 235; CB 54; DMC 34
gospel, GIRM 94
and music, MCW 60–62
offertory, GIRM 49, 101, 133, 147

PROFESSION OF FAITH
GIRM 16, 43, 98, 219; DMC 39, 49;
MCW 69

PROTESTANT CHURCHES
appeal of to African Americans, PGR 49,
77, 107
and ecumenism, DE 101, 129–36, 159

PSALMS
SC 90–91; CB 33; DMC 48; MCW 72;
LMT 34–43, 69; CP 36; GILOH 100–135
see also MUSIC, LITURGICAL

READERS
SC 29; GIRM 34, 66, 89, 91, 148–52;
LM 14, 49–55; CB 30–32

TEXTS, LITURGICAL

adaptation and translation of, SC 25, 31,
38; DE 187; IRL 34–39, 53–70; CP 1–43;
CEILT 1–35

character of, EACW 91; CB 115–18

inclusive language in, SCC 1–12;
1–35

see also LITURGY OF THE WORD; SCRIPTURE

TIME

and historical changes, DD 3–5, 48, 64–68,
80, 82; PS 3–4; SCC 3; CEILT 1

significance of the resurrection in,
DD 2–3, 18, 74–80; PGR 12

see also CALENDAR, CHURCH; LITURGICAL
YEAR

UNITED BIBLE SOCIETIES

DE 185

USHERS

GIRM 49, 68

VATICAN II

see SECOND VATICAN COUNCIL

VESSELS, LITURGICAL

blessing and consecration of, GIRM 289,
296

materials used in, GIRM 290–92, 294;
HLS 40–41; EACW 97

number and design of, GIRM 293, 295;
HLS 40–42; EACW 96

types of, GIRM 80, 100, 103, 292, 293;
EACW 96–97

VESTMENTS

design of, SC 128; GIRM 304–7; CB 37–38;
EACW 93–94

liturgical colors of, GIRM 307–10;
GIapp 308

meaning of, GIRM 297; EACW 93

various types of, GIRM 161, 298–303;
CB 65–67

WOMEN, ROLE OF IN LITURGIES

GIRM 66, 70; GIapp 66

Also AVAILABLE
FROM LTP

THE
LITURGY DOCUMENTS
VOLUME ONE
A PARISH RESOURCE

Includes the most important and useful documents of the liturgical reform, collected under one cover for reference and study by clergy, parish staffs, liturgists, musicians, liturgy committees and students. Each is preceded by an overview that notes the origins, importance, strengths and weaknesses of the document. Third edition.

Includes the following documents:

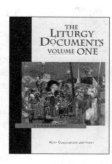

- Constitution on the Sacred Liturgy
- General Instruction of the Roman Missal
- Appendix to the General Instruction for the Dioceses of the United States
- Lectionary for Mass: Introduction
- General Norms for the Liturgical Year and Calendar
- Directory for Masses with Children
- Environment and Art in Catholic Worship
- Music in Catholic Worship
- Liturgical Music Today
- Fulfilled in Your Hearing
- This Holy and Living Sacrifice
- Ceremonial of Bishops (excerpts)

DOCUMENTS FOR THE PARISH: LITURGICAL, CATECHETICAL, BIBLICAL

A convenient CD-ROM containing over 50 major documents on liturgy, scripture and catechesis with outlines, overviews and a comprehensive index. You'll find all of the overviews and documents contained in *The Liturgy Documents Volume One: A Parish Resource*, *The Liturgy Documents Volume Two: A Parish Resource*, *Bible Documents*, and *The Catechetical Documents: A Parish Resource* as well as the current *Introduction to the Lectionary* and the *General Catechetical Directory*. Also contains five Spanish documents from U.S. and Latin American sources. For use with Windows.

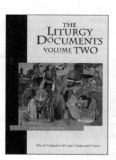

THE
LITURGY DOCUMENTS
VOLUME TWO
A PARISH RESOURCE

A second volume containing many more important and useful documents of the liturgical reform for reference and study.

PLEASE SUPPORT YOUR LOCAL BOOKSTORE OR CONTACT:

 LITURGY TRAINING PUBLICATIONS
1800 North Hermitage Avenue
Chicago IL 60622-1101

Phone	1-800-933-1800
Fax	1-800-933-7094
E-Mail	orders@ltp.org

ALSO AVAILABLE FROM LTP

LOS DOCUMENTOS LITÚRGICOS
UN RECURSO PASTORAL

This is a Spanish-language version of *The Liturgy Documents: A Parish Resource*, containing the complete texts of 14 major church documents with introductions.

Includes the following documents:

- Constitución sobre la Sagrada Liturgia
- Instrucción General para el Uso del Misal Romano
- Ordenación de las Lecturas de la Misa
- Normas Universales sobre el Año Litúrgico y sobre el Calendario
- Directorio de Misas para Niños
- La Música en el Culto Catolico
- La Música Litúrgica Hoy
- La Ambientación y el Arte el el Culto Católico
- La Liturgia Romana y la Inculturación
- Mendellín
- Puebla
- Santo Domingo
- La Presencia Hispana
- Plan Pastoral Nacional para el Ministerio Hispano

THE CATECHETICAL DOCUMENTS
A PARISH RESOURCE

A collection of documents on the major teachings about catechesis from the Second Vatican Council until the present, gathered in one convenient book. Each document is preceded by an overview that notes its strengths, weaknesses and impact over time.

Includes the following documents:

- General Catechetical Directory
- To Teach as Jesus Did
- Basic Teachings for Catholic Religious Education
- On Evangelization in the Modern World
- Sharing the Light of Faith
- On Catechesis in Our Time
- Rite of Christian Initiation of Adults
- The Religious Dimension of Education in a Catholic School
- The Challenge of Adolescent Catechesis
- Adult Catechesis in the Christian Community
- Guidelines for Doctrinally Sound Catechetical Materials
- Guide for Catechists
- The Catechism of the Catholic Church

THE BIBLE DOCUMENTS

A collection of key church documents on the Bible, presented by leading scholars in the field. Ideal for scripture students, seminarians, and catechists.

Included are documents such as:

- Pius XII's Divino Afflante Spiritu
- Vatican II's Dogmatic Constitution on Divine Revelation
- The NCCB's Pastoral Statement for Catholics on Biblical Fundamentalism
- The Pontifical Biblical Commission's Instructions on the Historicity of the Gospels and the Interpretation of the Bible in the in the Church
- Selections from the Catechism of the Catholic Church

PLEASE SUPPORT
YOUR LOCAL BOOKSTORE OR CONTACT:

Phone	1-800-933-1800
Fax	1-800-933-7094
E-Mail	orders@ltp.org

LITURGY TRAINING PUBLICATIONS
1800 North Hermitage Avenue
Chicago IL 60622-1101